Reforming
or Conforming?

Reforming or Conforming?

Post-Conservative Evangelicals and the Emerging Church

Edited by Gary L. W. Johnson
and Ronald N. Gleason

Foreword by David F. Wells

CROSSWAY BOOKS

WHEATON, ILLINOIS

For our two respective helpmates, Suzanne and Sally.
Their value cannot be measured in this brief space.

Reforming or Conforming? Post-Conservative Evangelicals and the Emerging Church
Copyright © 2008 by Gary L. W. Johnson and Ronald N. Gleason

Published by Crossway Books
      a publishing ministry of Good News Publishers
      1300 Crescent Street
      Wheaton, Illinois 60187

Design and typesetting: Lakeside Design Plus
Cover design: Amy Bristow
Cover Photo: Getty Images; Veer Images
First printing 2008
Printed in the United States of America

Unless otherwise indicated, Scripture quotations are from *The Holy Bible, English Standard Version*®, copyright © 2001 by Crossway Bibles, a publishing ministry of Good News Publishers. Used by permission. All rights reserved.

Scripture quotations marked NASB are from *The New American Standard Bible*®. Copyright © The Lockman Foundation 1960, 1962, 1963, 1968, 1971, 1972, 1973, 1975, 1977, 1995. Used by permission.

All emphases in Scripture quotations have been added.

Trade Paperback ISBN: 978-1-4335-0118-0
PDF ISBN: 978-1-4335-0472-3
Mobipocket ISBN: 978-1-4335-0473-0

Library of Congress Cataloging-in-Publication Data
    Reforming or conforming? : post-conservative evangelicals and the emerging church / edited by
Gary L. W. Johnson and Ronald N. Gleason ; foreword by David F. Wells.
        p. cm.
    Includes bibliographical references (p.) and index.
    ISBN 978-1-4335-0118-0 (tpb)
      1. Evangelicalism. 2. Theology, Doctrinal. 3. Postmodernism—Religious aspects—
Christianity. I. Johnson, Gary L. W., 1950– II. Gleason, Ronald N., 1945– III. Title.

BR1640.R43 2008
270.8'3—dc22
                          2008020096

VP   16 15 14 13 12 11 10 09 08
            9   8   7   6   5   4   3   2   1

Contents

Contributors   7

Foreword by David F. Wells   9

Introduction   15
   Gary L. W. Johnson

1. The Doctrine of Scripture: Only a Human Problem   27
   Paul Wells

2. *Sola Scriptura* as an Evangelical Theological Method?   62
   John Bolt

3. No Easy Task: John R. Franke and the Character of Theology   93
   Paul Helm

4. Whosoever Will Be Saved: Emerging Church, Meet Christian Dogma   112
   R. Scott Clark

5. "Right Reason" and Theological Aesthetics at Old Princeton
   Seminary: The "Mythical Evangelical Magisterium" Reconsidered   129
   Paul Kjoss Helseth

6. Cornelius Van Til: "Principled" Theologian or Foundationalist?   154
   Jeffrey C. Waddington

7. Church and Community or Community and Church?   166
   Ronald N. Gleason

8. It's "Wright," but Is It Right? An Assessment and Engagement
   of an "Emerging" Rereading of the Ministry of Jesus   188
   Guy Prentiss Waters

9. Joyriding on the Downgrade at Breakneck Speed: The Dark Side
   of Diversity   211
   Phil Johnson

10. Entrapment: The Emerging Church Conversation and the Cultural
    Captivity of the Gospel   224
    Martin Downes

11. Saved from the Wrath of God: An Examination of Brian McLaren's
    Approach to the Doctrine of Hell   245
    Greg D. Gilbert

12. The Emergent Church   269
    Gary Gilley

    Index   292

Contributors

John Bolt (PhD, St. Michael's College) is professor of systematic theology at Calvin Theological Seminary.

R. Scott Clark (PhD, Oxford) is professor of church history and historical theology at Westminster Seminary California.

Greg D. Gilbert (MDiv, Southern Baptist Theological Seminary) is special assistant to Al Mohler.

Gary Gilley (ThD, Cambridge Graduate School) has pastored Southern View Chapel, Springfield, Illinois, since 1975.

Ronald N. Gleason (PhD, Westminster Theological Seminary) is senior pastor of Grace Presbyterian Church (PCA) in Yorba Linda, California.

Paul Helm (MA, Oxford) taught for many years at the University of Liverpool and later was Professor of History and Philosophy of Religion at King's College, London (1994–2000), and a teaching fellow at Regent College, Vancouver.

Paul Kjoss Helseth (PhD, Marquette University) is associate professor of Christian thought at Northwestern College, St. Paul.

G. L. W. Johnson (ThM, Westminster Theological Seminary) is senior pastor of Church of the Redeemer, Mesa, Arizona.

Jeffrey C. Waddington (PhD cand., Westminster Theological Seminary) is a minister in the Orthodox Presbyterian Church.

Guy Prentiss Waters (PhD, Duke University) is associate professor of Bible at Belhaven College.

David F. Wells (PhD, Manchester) is Andrew Mutch Professor of Historical and Systematic Theology at Gordon-Conwell Theological Seminary.

Paul Wells (PhD, Vrije Universiteit, Amsterdam) is professor of systematic theology at Faulté Libre de Théologic Réformée in Aix-en-Provence.

Foreword

~~~~~~~~

This is a remarkable moment in which we are living. Here in the West, in the very moment in which our affluence is growing, Christian organizations are multiplying, and Christian presses are in high production, Christian faith itself is departing. At least, that is the story the statistics tell us.

The flight of Christian faith out of the West is less true in the United States than it is in Europe. In the United States, though, Christian faith is only just holding its nose above the water line. The situation is far worse outside the U.S. In Europe, Canada, Australia, and New Zealand, it is drowning. It is disappearing. It has vanished from much public life, has left behind many empty churches, and lives on in only small, often isolated pockets of belief. It is not in the West that Christian faith is flourishing but, as Philip Jenkins's *The Coming Christendom* makes clear, in Africa, parts of Asia, and Latin America. In these parts of the world, it is growing almost exponentially.

This paradox of a Christian faith in the West that has everything and yet is being diminished by the day is just one of several paradoxes that we encounter today. In the last forty years in America, for example, the average American's income measured in terms of buying power has actually doubled. Over the last century, life expectancy has almost doubled, thanks to incredible medical breakthroughs, and the average American now inhabits a world completely transformed by technology and affluence. But, at the same time, as David Myers has noted in his *The American Paradox,* research is showing that we are less happy, more depressed; our relationships are more private, self-focused, and fragile; our children are more demoralized; and we have less vocational security. These are, of course, generalizations, and the picture is undoubtedly more complex.

It is obviously the case, for example, that amidst American affluence, there is also poverty. It is also the case that despite the fact that modernization is undoubtedly trailed by psychological shadows, there are many who have indeed found a compass in life and have a measure of internal stability. And yet, growing research does raise this interesting question: how can Americans as a whole have so much and yet be so empty? Why are we so unsatisfied, as study after study shows that we are, when we live in such a paradise? This is surely another Dickensian moment: the best of times and the worst of times, the spring of hope and the winter of despair. We are so much better off and yet we are also so much emptier. We have more but we believe less.

This paradox we see in the church, too. We have everything. We have pastors, church buildings, church programs, educational institutions, presses, radio programs, television programs, educational materials, and Bibles. We have in abundance what, in many other parts of the world, is significantly lacking. And yet, there Christianity is growing, at least numerically, and here it is struggling.

The irony of this flight from the Western to the non-Western world is especially striking when looked at from the cultural perspective. In the United States, Christianity is floundering in the very moment when it is finding widespread cultural acceptance. This is not to say that America has become a Christian country, because it surely has not. Nor is it to say that America is being "taken back," as some had hoped, because it has not. In fact, in its origins America was, theologically speaking, quite a mixed bag. There is not a whole lot today that can, in fact, be taken back. Let us not forget that at the time of the Revolution, only 17 percent even belonged to a church, which is, proportionally speaking, a third of the number today. What, then, does this cultural acceptance mean?

Today, the idea of belonging to a church seems quite normal and natural, and a Christian profession of belief, say in the workplace, no longer automatically places a person outside of the cultural norm. If Barna is to be believed, 45 percent of Americans claim to be born-again, which is, after all, a religious idea, specifically a Christian idea. This is a very sizable number of people who significantly affect what is culturally acceptable and what is not. And it does not even include those from other Christian traditions for whom being born-again has not been a matter of great familiarity or acceptability but who, nevertheless, also attend various churches. America, when one thinks about this total picture, is a very religious country. Being religious, or specifically Christian, is not at all a bizarre thing anymore. There is a place under the sun where Christians can now stand, but that has not always been the case.

During the long period of Enlightenment dominance of American culture, all religion was seen to be a sorry case of a maladjustment to reality. It was irrational. It was retrograde superstition. In religion, especially of a supernatural sort, we encounter a throwback to pre-modern days, it was said. Here is something that no modern could possibly believe. Enlightenment ideologues who, in time, morphed into garden-variety secular humanists, really were deeply wedded to their idea of inevitable social progress. They actually did think, and often said, that the time was coming when all religion would disappear as a matter of necessity.

It has not turned out that way. These Enlightenment attitudes, it is true, have remained ensconced in pockets of the culture. Since the 1960s, however, the Enlightenment ideology has steadily collapsed. It has been replaced by our postmodern ethos with its openness to all religions and spiritualities, to all belief systems and worldviews, to all lifestyles and cultural habits. It is much more reflective of the globalized culture of which we are also now a part. Indeed, Asians sometimes say that they have been postmodern for centuries, and in these ways they have been. Under the Enlightenment rationalism, Christianity—especially of a biblical kind— had no place at the conversation table; under the postmodern sun, Christianity is welcome, as is every other viewpoint. Why, then, is it now floundering in its very moment of welcome?

The answer, quite simply, is that Christians have not understood the difficulties of living in a modernized culture. That there is something amiss is widely recognized. Exactly what this is and how to remedy it are matters of great uncertainty.

The Reformed have always been uneasy about the post–World War II evangelical alliance that brought together so many ministries and viewpoints into a working relationship around a small core of commonly held beliefs. For the Reformed, that core was too skinny to begin with and, besides, it was not rooted in a confessional tradition or in the life of the church. With the passage of time, these misgivings have been shown to be correct. However, the Reformed were not the only ones to have misgivings.

Beginning in the 1970s, and led by Bill Hybels, a huge swath of the evangelical world in America began to realize that Christian faith was losing ground, that the evangelical movement was not replicating itself well enough to be able to sustain itself. And so, Hybels and his many followers did what pragmatic Americans often do: he rested his confidence on our know-how, our worldly-wise, humanly-driven, business savvy. *We* will rescue Christian belief! Inspired by the corporate world, modeled after some of its successes like Disneyworld, and directed by Barna's polling numbers, the church set about selling itself and its gospel. What has happened is that the consumer model on which it was based reduced Christianity to just another product and its buyer to another sovereign consumer. In no time at all, Christianity was dancing to the tune of consumer desire, and the major casualty was biblical truth. Given the direction all of this has taken, is it any surprise that while 45 percent claim to be born-again, only about 7 percent show even the most modest knowledge of the core essentials of a biblical faith? That being the case, the numerical success of the market-created megachurches is hollow and misleading. What does it matter that some have attracted two, five, ten, or twenty thousand to their "worship"? It is no more significant, culturally speaking, than that there are twenty, thirty, or fifty thousand present at a ballgame.

It is the emptiness of marketed faith, its superficiality—a superficiality that is necessary if it is to be marketed as widely as Coca-Cola—that has alienated many of those in the emergent conversation. The interesting thing to note here, however, is that they might be appalled at the emptiness of marketed faith, its loss of mystery, its flatness, but they themselves are also marketers. The difference is that the Hybels faction marketed to Boomers, who were much more a part of modernity, whereas the emergents are marketing to Gen Xers who are much more attuned to postmodernity. These postmoderns are at home in a world where truth is what is true to any individual, where there are no all-encompassing narratives to life, where there are no absolutes, where moral judgments, especially on sexual matters, are not acceptable, and where each is free to find his own sense of mystery in his own way.

These attitudes have both popular and sophisticated expressions. They may simply be part of the new spirituality, one that is spiritual but not religious, or they may attack historic Christian faith in the name of what is now emerging, despising foundationalism, attacking the idea of objective truth as arrogant, rejecting the idea of penal substitution, which is tied into an objective moral world as barbaric and a case of child abuse, and celebrating the belief that salvation is found in other places and other religions. This, too, no less than the Hybels debacle, is a case of cultural capitulation, and the outcome will be no less disastrous.

Clearly, there is a story here that we are largely missing. It is that Christian faith is not sustaining itself very well in the midst of Western culture. The affluence and safety that have allowed for so much institution-building, from churches to colleges, and so much servicing of those institutions, from presses to parachurch organizations, are not themselves sustaining Christianity. All of these things, desirable as they are, are about the fabric of Christianity, about its body, as it were. They are not necessarily about its soul. Its soul is now being corrupted by the culture despite the many churches, many books, and many ministries.

That is what those in the global South often notice about American Christianity, and it is probably the most important thing the West has to teach them: do not do as we have done! They, therefore, need to prepare themselves for the day when they, too, are drawn into a fully modernized world, are able to enjoy all of its stunning benefits—but must also be prepared for its terrible dangers.

When the stock market goes into a slump, or the housing market declines, experts ponder when it has "bottomed out." Markets are cyclical, and so it is quite reasonable to think that once internal corrections have been made, the market in question will recover. Christian faith is a little like that, too. It has its cycles. It has its declines, and before it enjoys a recovery, it must undergo an internal correction. The book of Judges is a good illustration of this.

That Christianity in the West is in decline is beyond dispute, at least statistically speaking. The question is whether or not it is "bottoming out" and whether it has made the necessary internal corrections. My view is that it could still have a long way to fall. There is nothing in our self-generated organizational wizardry that will prevent this. There is nothing in our marketing genius, regardless of the particular generational niche to which we are pitching, that is going to prevent this. The correction that is needed is not in how we "do church," not in our organizations, but it is an internal one.

Christianity is about truth, the truth that stands outside of us and over against us because the God of that truth does. Historic Christianity, rooted in and determined by what we have in Scripture, has always declared this. Truth-affirmations like these are where we must start. That, after all, is the Protestant principle. But by themselves they are not enough.

Christianity will continue to decline until we become people of the truth, people of integrity who are awed by the God of that truth. Only that is powerful enough to wrench around lives in a different direction from that in which they are now being pulled by all of the powerful currents of modernization and of our postmodern world. It is far less important to say what a church of such people would "look like" in its internal organization and life than it is to say that no church deserves the name of *church* unless it is the home of people like this. It is not our garments that we need to keep rending, but our hearts. That is the key to our engaging our postmodern culture effectively. Engagement will happen. The only question we need to consider is really quite simply: will Christianity engage the culture or will it be engaged by the culture?

This seemingly innocent question has many facets to it. No book can address them all. However, this particular book is helpful because it is beginning at the beginning. Given the interactions with the academic end of postmodern culture, what does historic Christian faith look like in its engagement with this culture? That, after all, is where we need to start.

David F. Wells

Introduction

GARY L. W. JOHNSON

〜〜〜〜〜

Evangelicalism, in the assessment of Carl Raschle, is in a state of crisis because it is being confronted with "an intellectual challenge of a magnitude it has never before confronted."[1] And just what is this foreboding thing? Simply put (but difficult to define precisely) it is "postmodernity." Raschle, as the title of his book makes clear, contends that the church at large must embrace this state of affairs. But this kind of "Chicken Little" response to the changing tides engulfing our culture is nothing new. A similar alarm was sounded at the turn of the eighteenth century by Friedrich Schleiermacher. Sinclair Ferguson recently observed along these lines that, "in his own way, Schleiermacher had patented and branded a 'seeker sensitive' theology that (he certainly believed) made the gospel relevant to his contemporaries—'the cultured despisers of religion' who, under the spell of the Enlightenment had given up on the possibility that Christian doctrine could be true. For them the knowledge of God was no longer attainable. Kant's critique of reason had limited it to the knowledge of the phenomenal realm; access to the noumenal was barred. Schleiermacher, refusing to believe that all was lost, turned things on their head, stressing that the essence of true Christian faith was the feeling or sense of absolute dependence upon God."[2] Despite the rasping protests of some post-conservatives, the parallels between what Schleiermacher was attempting to do in the early decades of the nineteenth century and the proposals of this group of evangelicals that fondly

---

1. Carl Raschle, *The Next Reformation: Why Evangelicals Must Embrace Postmodernity* (Grand Rapids: Zondervan, 2004), 1. Perhaps more difficult to define than "postmodern" is the equally confusing term "evangelical." I discuss this in my chapter, "The Reformation, Today's Evangelicals, and Mormons" in G. L. W. Johnson and Guy P. Waters, ed., *By Faith Alone: Answering the Challenges to the Doctrine of Justification* (Wheaton, IL.: Crossway, 2006).
2. Sinclair Ferguson in *Justified in Christ,* ed. K. Scott Oliphint (Ross-shire, Scotland: Christian Focus, 2007), 1X.

refers to themselves as "emergents" or "post-conservatives," are striking.[3] In a provocative essay that attempts to sanitize Schleiermacher for contemporary evangelicals, Nicola Hoggard Creegan rightly observes that Schleiermacher is the one voice from the past that speaks directly to our postmodern situation.[4] How so? B. A. Gerrish pinpoints with this observation the similarities between the late Stanley Grenz and Schleiermacher:

> Grenz does not seem to recognize, or perhaps he prefers not to say, that his theological program for the twenty-first century is pretty much the program that the supposed arch-liberal Friedrich Schleiermacher proposed for the nineteenth century. Differences there may be. But the threefold emphasis on experience, community, and context was precisely Schleiermacher's contribution to evangelical dogmatics. Successive waves of neoorthodox and postmodernist attacks on him have submerged his contribution beneath an ocean of misunderstandings. He never renounced his evangelical-pietistic experience: rather, his theology at its center was reflection upon this experience from within the believing community in its new situation. He was certain that his experience must point to something constant since the time of the apostles, yet always to be conveyed in language that is historically conditioned. No less a critic of his doctrines than Karl Barth correctly perceived in Schleiermacher's faith "a personal relationship with Jesus that may well be called 'love.'"[5]

In both cases the attempt to contextualize the Christian faith in terms of the contemporary culture produces a syncretic grid that, in our times, in turn gives ultimate priority to our postmodern matrix.

Gerrish's mentioning of Karl Barth is also significant, because there are those in the postmodern camp who claim Barth as their own. But, despite our own reservations about Barth, we think he would be flabbergasted by the attempt to enlist him as a spokesman for this crowd.

Perhaps nowhere is this more obvious than in his famous debate with his neoorthodox ally and onetime close friend Emil Brunner over the question of natural theology. Brunner came out in defense of it, and Barth responded with his thunderous *Nein*!

His opening remarks would make most postmoderns shudder:

> I should like nothing better than to walk together with him [Brunner] in concord, but in the Church we are concerned with *truth,* and today with an urgency such as

---

3. Cf. Roger Olson, *Reformed and Always Reforming: The Postconservative Approach to Evangelical Theology* (Grand Rapids: Baker Academic, 2007). Olson repeatedly denies that there is any valid correlation, but does reluctantly concede that a formal similarity exists, but it is purely coincidental (62)!
4. Nicola Hoggard Creegan, "Schleiermacher as Apologist: Reclaiming the Father of Modern Theology" in *Christian Apologetics in the Postmodern World,* ed. T. R. Phillips and D. L. Okholm (Downers Grove, IL: InterVarsity Press, 1995), 59–74.
5. B. A. Gerrish, "The New Evangelical Theology and the Old: An Opportunity for the Next Century?" as cited in *Reclaiming the Center: Confronting Evangelical Accommodation in Postmodern Times,* ed. M. J. Erickson, P. K. Helseth, and J. Taylor (Wheaton, IL: Crossway, 2004), 240n101.

probably has not been the case for centuries. And *truth* is not to be trifled with. If it divides the spirits, they *are* divided. To oppose this commandment for the sake of a general idea of "peace" and "unity" would be a greater disaster for all concerned than such division.[6]

Oh, my, Barth is concerned with this thing called "truth." Postmoderns will squirm at the thought. But this should come as no big surprise to those familiar with Barth, who viewed Schleiermacher and his enterprise with what borders on contempt.

Mark Patterson, in a perceptive article on how relevant Barth's *Nein!* is today says:

As much as Barth was adverse to controversy and disputes, he nevertheless believed that there were times when they were necessary. When the truth of the Gospel was at risk, when the church was in danger of losing the reason for her existence, it becomes not only important but necessary to boldly enter the fray and stand for the Gospel. As Barth wrote his response to Brunner, the church in Germany had almost completely succumbed to the populist theology of its day, a belief that was built not upon the unique revelation of God in Christ but a theology built upon human feelings, presuppositions, aspirations, and prejudices. In other words, a natural theology of the very type Brunner espoused. That is not to say it did not use the right words—Jesus, faith, grace, and all the others—or to say that they had flagrantly or openly rejected the church's theology and historic perspectives. What they had done was turn to a new revelatory center, and from this center redefine classic words and reinterpret traditional perspectives. Barth watched in horror and grief as the church rejected its astonishingly unique message of God's mercy, love, and grace in Christ, and replaced it instead with an all too common message that simply affirmed the biases and opinions of the culture. The populist ideas and values were given a theological vocabulary, dressed up as divine, priceless, and authoritative and presented to a people who had little interest or ability to discern the true and drastic changes that had occurred. Barth was astonished to find his friend and theological partner furthering it by defining grace as more a part of the natural order than a specific act of God uniquely tied to the person and work of Christ.[7]

This stands in sharp contrast to the proposals we are now hearing from those self-identified postmoderns who are part of the emergent conversation. One of the reasons Barth so disliked Schleiermacher and natural theology is that Schleiermacher collapsed natural revelation and special revelation, and then gave priority to the former over the latter. In particular, the cultural paradigm served as the grid through

---

6. German for "no." As cited by Mark R. Patterson, "Nein! A Response to Progressives," *Theology Matters* 13, no. 2 (2007): 2 (emphasis added). Originally published as *Nein! Antwort an Emil Brunner* (Zurich: Theologischer Verlag, 1935). An English translation of Brunner's work and Barth's response may be found in *Emil Brunner and Karl Barth,* trans. Peter Fraenkel, with introduction by John Baillie, "Natural Theology: Comprising 'Nature and Grace' by Professor Dr. Emil Brunner and the Reply 'No!' by Dr. Karl Barth" (Eugene, OR: Wipf & Stock, 2002).
7. Patterson, "Nein! A Response to Progressives," 2.

which theology was constructed. This was Schleiermacher's approach and is now being duplicated by those wearing the post-conservative badge.

In a recent commentary commending a new book by two prominent voices in emergent circles (Doug Pagitt and Tony Jones), Fuller Seminary professor Barry Taylor gives us this Schleiermachian panegyric:

> What it means exactly when a person declares himself or herself to be "spiritual but not religious" is a matter of some debate. Some people find spiritual an irritating term that means nothing of any real substance, a marker for a sort of "wishy-washy" sentimentalism that passes itself off as real faith. Others have embraced it wholeheartedly, and the rise of spiritual language in sermons and discussions, as well as a growing interest in spiritual directors in many churches, point to an embrace of the term on some levels even amongst the "religious."
>
> I don't think there is one definition for the term or for its usage. Spirituality is an umbrella word, a catchall concept used to characterize a commitment to the sacred elements of life. It defies a singular definition, hence the fluidity of the usage of the word; it is also an evolving term rather than one of fixed determination.
>
> One thing that it does signify, almost universally, is the rejection of traditional faiths as a primary source of connection to the divine. I would argue that traditional faiths are no longer the first resource that people go to in order to develop and nurture their spiritual lives, but instead function more as secondary archives with which new spiritual permutations are created. Those who do choose to explore their spiritual quests within traditional faith environments do so with very different eyes and intentions than previous generations of seekers have. For me spirituality is the religion of the twenty-first century.
>
> This is a dramatic shift, and one that some might contest, but the momentum seems to be toward this perspective; it should come as no surprise to us that our understanding of religion is undergoing a transformation. In times of significant cultural change, all the ways in which we order ourselves socially are usually affected. For instance, religion as it was experienced in the post-Reformation period was quite unlike its pre-Reformation incarnation. That faith in the postmodern world is showing itself to be markedly different from faith in modernity only serves to underscore the significance of the cultural changes we are presently experiencing.
>
> If then we truly find ourselves in a new situation, one in which the old ways simply no longer suffice, what then of the future for Christian faith? I have already raised the notion that there may not be a future for "Christianity," the religion of Christian faith. I mean no disrespect to historic Christianity when I make this comment, nor do I seek to simply dismiss centuries of faithful service, worship, and theology.
>
> I think that the Christian faith has been held captive to a "pseudoorthodoxy" for much of the late twentieth century. Christianity's love affair with modernity and its universalizing tendencies created a climate in which the general assumption is a singular understanding of the faith. The easiest way to undermine different perspectives on issues like faith and practice during my lifetime has been to call someone's commit-

ment to orthodoxy into question. But Christian faith is open to discussion. Historically it always has been. It can be questioned and reinterpreted. In fact, I would argue that it is meant to be questioned and reinterpreted.

Religion is always a cultural production, and sociocultural issues cannot be discounted from the ways in which we envision and understand faith. Issues and questions raised by our particular cultural situation not only inform but shape the various ways in which we interpret the gospel. If there ever was a time to question the status quo, it is now.[8]

Barth would have been appalled and rightly so. Taylor, however, is right about one thing. We cannot escape the powerful undercurrents of postmodernity that course through the times we live in. The question that confronts us all is, how do we respond to such things? Since the apostle Paul tells in a very direct way—we are not to be conformed to the pattern of this world (Rom. 12:1–2)—exactly what do we do when we find ourselves being molded and shaped by the culture around us? Well, one thing is clear—we should not accommodate our theology to the cultural despisers of our times. But this has happened (in the case of Schleiermacher), and it is happening at an alarming rate today with those enamored with postmodernity. How did this come about?

The term "post-conservative" was first coined by erstwhile evangelical Arminian Roger Olson in the pages of *The Christian Century*.[9] Critics like Millard Erickson described this as the new "Evangelical Left" and have taken umbrage with how Olson has responded to his critics.[10] Olson, in mirroring the postliberal Yale School theologians like the late Hans Frei and George Lindbeck, wants very much for evangeli-

---

8. Barry Taylor, "Goodbye Religion, Hello Spirituality: Is there a place for the Christian 'religion' in the 21st Century?" http://blog.christianitytoday.com/ourofur/archives/2007/03/goodbye_religio_1.html.

9. Roger Olson, "Post-conservatives Greet the Postmodern Age," *The Christian Century* 112 (May 3, 1995). Cf. Olson's *Reformed and Always Reforming*, 84. Olson proudly flies his post-conservative colors in this book, as the title makes clear. Prior to this, however, Olson claimed otherwise. In his exchange with Mike Horton, Olson declared that he never claimed that he was a "post-conservative" evangelical, saying, "I did not 'spearhead' postconservative evangelicalism, nor did I announce it as a 'program.' In my descriptive article in *Christian Century* where I coined that term ('postconservative evangelicalism') I merely set out to describe a new mood among certain evangelicals. I said that it is not a movement (let alone a 'program'). And nowhere did I identify myself as postconservative; in fact I included some cautionary notes at the end of the article. I gladly admit that I have some sympathies with this new mood of evangelical theology that is dissatisfied with maintenance of the status quo as evangelicalism theology's main task. But I have not promoted any 'postconservative evangelical program.' I have simply sought to bring this new mood to public attention and gain some understanding for it. When I wrote that postconservative evangelicals are not necessarily committed to the Chalcedonian formula of Christology I did not mean that they have anything less than a high Christology of Christ as human and divine; I only meant that they are not necessarily committed to the technical language and concepts of the doctrine of the hypostatic union. There are other ways to express a high Christology and some postconservative theologians have attempted to do it without in any way denying Christ's full and true deity and humanity." See "The Nature and Future of Evangelicalism: A Dialogue; between Michael Horton & Roger Olson," *Modern Reformation* 12, no. 2 (2003), http://www.modernreformation.org/mhro03dial.htm.

10. M. Erickson, *The Evangelical Left* (Grand Rapids: Baker, 2000), and his chapter "On Flying in Theological Fog" in Erickson, Helseth, and Taylor, *Reclaiming the Center*.

calism to escape what he calls the Old Princeton hegemony with its stifling scholastic methodology. In particular, Olson complains that the Old Princeton placed way too much emphasis on such doctrines as penal substitutionary atonement and biblical inerrancy. These supposedly distinctive trademarks of genuine evangelicalism need to be abandoned.[11] As we shall see, this has struck a very responsive cord in what goes by the name "the emergent conversation."

The late Robert Webber, one of the individuals who openly celebrated the developments identified with the "evangelical megashift" (that formally introduced us in the pages of *Christianity Today* to Open-view Theism[12]), sees the rise of the postmodern evangelicals as the next step in this megashift, calling it "a new evangelical awakening."[13] Another highly influential figure (also with direct links to the evangelical megashift) was the late Stanley Grenz. Grenz was, in many ways, the most prominent figure in the group, and his writings continue to provide the theological and philosophical identity for the movement. Grenz argued that the break between the modern and postmodern worlds may rival in historical significance the shift from the Middle Ages to modernity. "Fundamentally," he argues, "post-modernism is an intellectual orientation that is critical and seeks to move beyond the philosophical tenets of the Enlightenment, which lie at the foundation of the now dying modern mindset." As such, the new intellectual era calls for "nothing less than a rebirth of theological reflection among evangelicals."[14] Embedded in this quest for a rebirth of theological reflection is a disturbing tendency to discard core evangelical beliefs. The plot thickens as the pace picks up.

Amongst the leading advocates of this new breed of professing evangelicals is the group associated with the emergent church—a group that proudly identifies itself

---

11. Olson has displayed an intense dislike for Reformed theology in general and Old Princeton in particular. In one of his most recent books, *Arminian Theology: Myths and Realities* (Downers Grove, IL: InterVarsity Press, 2006), Olson takes umbrage with Warfield's review of his contemporary, the noted Methodist theologian John Miley, which appears in the *Selected Shorter Writings of Benjamin B. Warfield II*, ed. J. Meeter (Phillipsburg, NJ: Presbyterian and Reformed, 1973), 308–20. Olson calls this "a lengthy attack" (26) and elsewhere a "caustic attack" (278), declaring that Warfield's criticisms "were stated in such an extreme way as to raise questions about Warfield's own generosity of interpretation and treatment of fellow Christians. Many twentieth-century Calvinists know little about Arminianism except what they read in nineteenth-century Calvinist theologians Charles Hodge and B. B. Warfield. Both were vitriolic critics who could not bring themselves to see any good in Arminianism. And they blamed it for every possible evil consequence they could see it possibly having" (26). He continues this same diatribe in his recent *Reformed and Always Reforming*, 44. Cf. my review of Olson, "Calvinists in the Hands of an Angry Arminian," http://teampyro.blogspot.com/2006/11/calvinists-in-hands-of-angry-arminian.html.

12. Cf. Robert Brow, "Evangelical Megashift: Why You May Not Have Heard about Wrath, Sin and Hell Recently," *Christianity Today,* February 19, 1990.

13. Robert Webber, *The Younger Evangelicals* (Grand Rapids: Baker, 2002), 5. His earlier work *Ancient-Future Faith: Rethinking Evangelicalism for a Postmodern World* (Grand Rapids: Baker, 1999), serves as a primer for many postmodern evangelicals.

14. As cited in *The Challenge of Postmodernism: An Evangelical Engagement,* ed. D. S. Dockery (Grand Rapids: Baker, 1995), 78.

as *postmodern*.[15] "For almost everyone within the movement," observes Carson, "this works out in an emphasis on feelings and affections over against linear thought and rationality; on experience over against truth; on inclusion over against exclusion; on participation over against individualism and the heroic loner. For some, this means a move from the absolute to the authentic. It means taking into account contemporary emphasis on tolerance; it means not telling others they are wrong."[16] Although the emergent church folk like to consider themselves culturally sophisticated and theologically on the cutting edge of all things new and up-to-date, they are just as culturally conditioned as they claim their evangelical forebears were! In the case of the emergent evangelicals they want desperately to be perceived as "relevant" to our postmodern society. I cannot help but notice that whenever evangelicals become consumed with being culturally relevant they almost always end up adopting a very pragmatic approach in the process, with historic evangelical theology being the first thing that gets compromised. Os Guinness, a very perceptive observer of evangelicalism writes, "Christians are always more culturally short-sighted than they realize. They are often unable to tell, for instance, where their Christian principles leave off and their cultural perspectives begin. What many of them fail to ask themselves is 'where are we coming from and what is our own context?'"[17]

Regrettably, in the hands of these emergent evangelicals it is *not* postmodernism that is poured through the sifter of historic orthodox Christianity—but just the opposite. As a result, what comes out bears hardly any resemblance to the faith once and for all delivered to the saints. As I alluded to earlier, Robert Webber celebrated the evangelical megashift and its association with Open-view Theism. Following Olson in his disdain for the Old Princeton hegemony, Brian McLaren, who is considered the leading voice in emergent circles, throws disdain on the doctrines of biblical inerrancy and penal substitutionary atonement. McLaren, in Fuller seminary's

15. F. W. Bave has wilily pointed out, "Consider it axiomatic that when church leaders finally catch on to a trend, it's over. The Counterculture movement of the Sixties ended at Kent State, yet trendy campus pastors were still doing bad folk masses with out-of-tune guitars way into the Seventies and Eighties. So it is today with Postmodernism. The buzzword is on everyone's lips in church circles, while in university English departments where the whole Pomo (Postmodern) thing began, other theories like New Historicism have taken over. I contend that Postmodernism is now fading away and is rapidly being supplanted by other cultural forces" (F. W. Bave, *The Spiritual Society: What Lurks Beyond Postmodernism?* [Wheaton, IL: Crossway, 2001], 15). More recently, James Parker III made these pertinent observations: "Postmodernism is highly overrated. While one theologian after another is rushing to turn out books and articles about some aspect or implication concerning the end of modernism or about the implications of postmodernism, it can be plausibly argued that postmodernism is overrated and that it will come to a certain (and perhaps soon) demise—or at least will be relegated to the realm of the curious but passé.... Most simply stated, postmodernism is guilty of being self-referentially absurd. When postmodernists give up the idea of objective truth, there is no reason whatsoever to take what they say as true—particularly since they have conceded up front that nothing is genuinely true." Cf. Parker's "A Requiem for Postmodernism—Whither Now?" in Erickson, Helseth, and Taylor, *Reclaiming the Center,* 307–8. We gratefully acknowledge that we, in our book, are indebted to this important book.

16. D. A. Carson, *Becoming Conversant with the Emerging Church* (Grand Rapids: Zondervan, 2005), 29.

17. O. Guinness, *The Gravedigger File* (Downers Grove, IL: InterVarsity Press, 1983), 42.

Theology, Notes, and News, penned a piece entitled, "A Radical Rethinking of Our Evangelistic Strategy" where, in reference to Mark Baker, Joel Green,[18] and N. T. Wright, he declared,

> Bona fide evangelicals are suggesting that the gospel is not atonement-centered, or, at least, not penal-substitutionary-atonement-centered. . . . This suggestion represents a Copernican revolution for Western Christianity, in both its conservative Catholic and Protestant forms. It may be judged erroneous—and likely *will* be judged so by many readers of this paper—but even those who dismiss it would be wise to consider the possibility that there is at least some small grain of truth to these ruminations on the nature and center of the gospel. A lot is at stake either way. . . . For reasons I have detailed elsewhere, I have put my eggs in the basket that suggests we need to rethink our understanding of the gospel—both for the sake of faithfulness to Holy Scripture, and for the sake of mission in the emerging postmodern culture.[19]

The fact that McLaren's remarks appeared in a publication from Fuller Theological Seminary does not automatically imply the seminary's endorsement. Following on the heels of this came the impressive contributions from two Fuller professors, James E. Bradley, professor of church history, and Seyoon Kim, professor of New Testament. Both weighed in and argued that this doctrine is at the heart of the nature of the atonement and certainly was not the private opinion of the Old Princeton Theology.[20] Not surprisingly, and right on cue, McLaren has gone on record denying biblical inerrancy, especially as it was framed by Old Princeton.

Like the doctrine of penal substitution, the doctrine of biblical inerrancy is also the object of this group's billingsgate. Under the banner of postmodernism with its *new* and *improved* way of doing theology, a growing number of professing evangelicals now confidently proclaim that the doctrine has long since outlived its usefulness and must be discarded lest we incur the contempt of thoughtful people everywhere.[21]

18. Mark Baker and Joel Green co-authored the book *Recovering the Scandal of the Cross: Atonement in New Testament & Contemporary Contexts* (Downers Grove, IL: InterVarsity Press, 2000), which constituted a frontal assault on any concept of penal substitutionary atonement.

19. Brian McLaren, "A Radical Rethinking of Our Evangelistic Strategy," *Theology, News, & Notes* (Fall 2004), 6.

20. James E. Bradley, "Evangelical—A Most Abused Word!" and Seyoon Kim, "The Atoning Death of Christ on the Cross," *Theology, News & Notes* (Winter 2008), 4–10, 14–20. A number of books have recently appeared to defend the doctrine of penal substitution. Chief among them are Paul Wells, *Crosswords: The Biblical Doctrine of the Atonement* (Ross-shire, Scotland: Christian Focus, 2006); *The Glory of the Atonement: Essays in Honor of Roger Nicole,* ed. C. E. Hill and F. A. James III (Downers Grove, IL. InterVarsity Press, 2004); and especially Steve Jeffery, Michael Ovey, and Andrew Sach, *Pierced for Our Transgressions: Recovering the Glory of Penal Substitution* (Wheaton, IL, Crossway, 2007). N. T. Wright took umbrage with this book and with the people who endorsed it. Cf. http://piercedforourtransgressions.com/content/view/107/51/.

21. Among the most vocal are Carlos R. Bovell, *Inerrancy and the Spiritual Formation of Younger Evangelicals* (Eugene, OR: Wipf & Stock, 2007); Craig D. Allert, *A High View of Scripture? The Authority of the Bible and the Formation of the New Testament Canon* (Grand Rapids: Baker Academic, 2007); Kenton L. Sparks, *God's Word in Human Words: An Evangelical Appropriation of Critical Biblical Scholarship* (Grand Rapids: Baker Academic, 2008); and A. T. B. McGowan, *The Divine Spiration of Scripture: Challenging Evangelical*

As striking as are the parallels between the post-conservatives/emergents to Schleiermacher, an even more compelling counterpart is apparent in the nineteenth-century Old Testament scholar and critic of Old Princeton, Charles A. Briggs. Like Olson, Briggs complained of the pervasive hegemony that Old Princeton exercised over conservative Presbyterianism. To begin with the most obvious, Briggs's overt rejection of the Old Princeton understanding of inerrancy has a wide following among professed evangelicals today. One might even suggest that it is the majority view.[22] But there are other areas where Briggs's perspective would find safe haven as well. The late Stanley Grenz is a prime example. Grenz specifically contrasted his view of Scripture with that of Warfield,[23] and blamed the Old Princeton theology for making propositional truth the touchstone for theology as over against pietism's (Grenz called it "classic evangelicalism") emphasis on having a relationship with God.[24] Grenz also made a very Briggs-like shift by following the lead of Schleiermacher in positing *three* sources or norms for theology: Scripture, tradition, and culture.[25] Briggs so

---

Perspectives (Great Britain: Apollos, 2007). Sparks in particular paints contemporary defenders of inerrancy in very unflattering colors. Old Testament scholars such as R. K. Harrison, Gleason Archer, and E. J. Young are accused of sticking their heads in the sand to avoid dealing with the real issues raised by critical Old Testament scholars (133ff) while New Testament scholars such as D. A. Carson and Douglas Moo are said to be guilty of deliberately dodging the issues of New Testament critics (167). Even greater disdain is heaped on Carl Henry, who had the misfortune of simply being a theologian and not a biblical scholar (138). However, the most reprehensible aspect of Sparks's work is the facile labeling of *all* defenders of inerrancy as *Cartesian* foundationalists. Sparks declares Cornelius Van Til, and his presuppositional apologetics, to be Cartesian because Van Til underscored the importance of certainty, which to Sparks's way of thinking automatically makes one a Cartesian (45). If that is the case, then we must place not only the Reformers and the church fathers in that category, but Christ and the apostles as well! Van Til was no Cartesian. His apologetical approach was rooted in classic Reformed theology, especially in the Dutch tradition of Kuyper and Bavinck, stretching back to the noted Dutch Protestant scholastic Peter Van Mastricht (1630–1706), who was an outspoken critic of all things Cartesian. As Richard Muller notes, "Mastricht's consequent stress on the necessity of revelation for Christian theology (theology defined as 'living before God in and through Christ' or as the wisdom leading to that end) led to an adamant resistance to Cartesian thought with its method of radical doubt and its insistence on the primacy of autonomy of the mind in all matters of judgment." Richard Muller, "Giving Direction to Theology: The Scholastic Dimension," *Journal of the Evangelical Theological Society* 28 (June 1985), 185.

22. Attesting to this is the work by Jack Rogers and Donald McKim, *The Authority and Interpretation of the Bible* (San Francisco: Harper & Row, 1979). Roger Olson, who has been beating this drum for some time now, openly dismisses the doctrine; see his "Why 'Inerrancy' Doesn't Matter," *The Baptist Standard* (March 26, 2006): 1–2. Dave Tomlinson, in a book that is popular in what is called "the emergent church," offers a section titled "Inerrancy? A Monumental Waste of Time." Tomlinson goes on to declare, "I have no intention of arguing against this doctrine; I simply marvel that anyone should think it plausible or necessary to believe in such a thing" (Dave Tomlinson, *The Post-Evangelical* [London: Triangle, 1995], 105). Finally, James D. G. Dunn, a leading scholar for the so-called New Perspective on Paul, echoes Briggs's assessment by declaring inerrancy "exegetically improbable, hermeneutically defective, theologically dangerous, and educationally disastrous" (James D. G. Dunn, *The Living Word* [Philadelphia: Fortress, 1988], 107).

23. See Stanley Grenz, *Renewing the Center: Evangelical Theology in a Post-Theological Era* (Grand Rapids: Baker, 2000), and the book he coauthored with John Franke, *Beyond Foundationalism: Shaping Theology in a Postmodern Context* (Louisville: Westminster John Knox, 2001). It was disappointing to see Grenz relying so heavily on the work of Rogers and McKim in assessing Warfield, and this despite the fact that Grenz alludes to the work of John Woodbridge and his devastating work *Biblical Authority: A Critique of the Rogers/McKim Proposal* (Grand Rapids: Zondervan, 1982).

24. Grenz, *Renewing the Center,* 84.

25. Stanley Grenz, *Revisioning Evangelical Theology: A Fresh Agenda for the 21st Century* (Downers Grove, IL.: InterVarsity Press, 1993), 70. D. A. Carson correctly observes, "This is, to say the least, decidedly un-

firmly endorsed this idea that he devoted a book to the subject: *The Bible, the Church, and the Reason.*[26] Elsewhere, Briggs wrote:

> Three fountains of divine authority are not and cannot be contradictory, because they are three different media for the same divine Being to make His authority known to mankind. We may compare them with the three great functions of government: the legislative, the executive and the judicial, which in the best modern governments conspire to express the authority of the nation. The Bible is the legislative principle of divine authority, for it is the only infallible *rule* of faith and practice. The Church is the executive principle of divine authority. It makes no rules save those which are executive interpretations and applications of the rules contained in apostolic teaching. The Reason is the judicial principle of divine authority to the individual man. The Reason, when it judges, must be followed at all costs. There is liability to mistake, in individuals and in ecclesiastical bodies, in interpreting the decisions that come through these three media. Two may usually be used for verification of any one of them.[27]

Briggs grew to dislike what he called "the scholastic" element in Reformed theology. He wrote:

> The scholastic spirit seeks union and communion with God by means of well-ordered forms. It searches the Bible for well-defined systems of law and doctrine by which to rule the Church and control the world. It arises from an intellectual nature, and grows into a more or less acute logical sense, and a taste for systems of order. This spirit exists in all ages and in most religions, but it was especially dominant in the middle age of the Church and in Latin Christianity. It is distinguished by an intense legality and by too exclusive attention to the works of the law, and a disproportionate consideration of the sovereignty of God, the sinfulness of man, and the satisfaction to be rendered to God for sin. In biblical studies it is distinguished by the legal, analytic method of interpretation, carried on at times with such hair-splitting distinction and subtlety of reasoning that Holy Scripture becomes, as it were, a magician's book. Through the device of the manifold sense the Bible is made as effectual to the purpose of the dogmatician for proof texts as are the sacraments to the priests in their magical operation. The doctrinal element prevails over the religious and ethical. Dogma and institution alike work *ex opera operato.*[28]

---

helpful. Quite apart from the extraordinary complexities of linking Scripture and tradition in this way, the addition of culture is astonishing. One might hazard a guess that Grenz has read enough to recognize that the interpreter cannot escape his or her own culture, and therefore has put down culture as a norm or source of theology, without recognizing the minefield he has created for himself. . . . His openness to Tillich's method of correlation is not reassuring. With the best will in the world, I cannot see how Grenz's approach to Scripture can be called 'evangelical' in any useful sense" (D. A. Carson, *The Gagging of God: Christianity Confronts Pluralism* [Grand Rapids: Zondervan, 1996], 481).

26. Charles A. Briggs, *The Bible, the Church, and the Reason* (New York: Charles Scribner's Sons, 1892).

27. Charles A. Briggs, *Church Unity* (New York: Charles Scribner's Sons, 1897), 244.

28. Charles A. Briggs, *General Introduction to the Study of Holy Scripture* (New York: Charles Scribner's Sons, 1900), 570. I have developed this in greater detail in my chapter, "Warfield and C. A. Briggs: Their

Briggs may have lost the battle with Warfield and Old Princeton, but in the space of a generation his theological distinctives gained ascendancy in the Presbyterian church when the Auburn Affirmation ratified his views in 1924, especially on the doctrine of inerrancy:

> There is no assertion in the Scriptures that their writers were kept "from error." The Confession of Faith does not make this assertion; and it is significant that this assertion is not to be found in the Apostle's Creed or the Nicene Creed or in any of the great Reformation confessions. The doctrine of inerrancy, intended to enhance the authority of the Scriptures, in fact impairs their supreme authority for faith and life, and weakens the testimony of the church to the power of God unto salvation through Jesus Christ. We hold that the General Assembly of 1923, in asserting that "the Holy Spirit did so inspire, guide and movie the writers of Holy Scripture as to keep them from error," spoke without warrant of the Scriptures or of the Confession of Faith. We hold rather to the words of the Confession of Faith, that the Scriptures "are given by inspiration of God, to be the rule of faith and life." (Conf. I, ii)

Not content to stop there, it went on to make the following assertion:

> Furthermore, this opinion of the General Assembly attempts to commit our church to certain theories concerning the inspiration of the Bible, and the Incarnation, the Atonement, the Resurrection, and the Continuing Life and Supernatural Power of our Lord Jesus Christ. We hold most earnestly to these great facts and doctrines; we all believe from our hearts that the writers of the Bible were inspired of God; that Jesus Christ was God manifest in the flesh; that God was in Christ, reconciling the world unto Himself, and through Him we have our redemption; that having died for our sins He rose from the dead and is our everliving Saviour; that in His earthly ministry He wrought many mighty works, and by His vicarious death and unfailing presence He is able to save to the uttermost. Some of us regard the particular theories contained in the deliverance of the General Assembly of 1923 as satisfactory explanations of these facts and doctrines. But we are united in believing that these are not the only theories allowed by the Scriptures and our standards as explanations of these facts and doctrines of our religion, and that all who hold to these facts and doctrines, whatever theories they may employ to explain them, are worthy of all confidence and fellowship." (conf. IV, ii)[29]

This sounds remarkably like the things that having been coming from those involved in the emergent conversation. Some seventy years ago, Gordon Clark's response sounded as if he were writing in light of the post-conservative proposals:

Polemics and Legacy" in *B. B. Warfield: Essays on His Life and Thought,* ed. G. L. W. Johnson (Phillipsburg, NJ: P&R, 2007), 195–240.
29. The entire Auburn Affirmation document is online at http://www.pcahistory.org/documents/auburn-text.html.

Now kindly note this strange fact. The Auburn Affirmation states that to believe the Bible is true impairs its authority and weakens the testimony of the Church. Or, in other words, in order for the Bible to be authoritative, it must contain error; and, no doubt, the more erroneous it is, the more authoritative it can be.

But what does the Confession say? In Chapter I, Section 4, you may read: "The authority of the Holy Scriptures, for which it ought to be believed and obeyed, dependeth—wholly upon God (who is truth itself) the author thereof; and therefore it is to be received, because it is the Word of God."

Study also Chapter XIV, Section 2. "By this (saving) faith, a Christian believeth to be true whatsoever is revealed in the Word, for the authority of God Himself speaking therein. . . ."

The Auburn Affirmation says it is wrong and harmful to believe true whatsoever is revealed. Thus the signers of the Auburn Affirmation are seen to be antagonistic to the very basis of Christian faith. In denying the truth of the Bible, they repudiate their own Confession, and so have no rightful place in the Presbyterian ministry. Do they perchance reply that they agree with the Confession that the Scriptures are the Word of God, and that they deny only that the Scriptures are inerrant? God forbid that they make that reply. For if they say that they believe the Bible is the Word of God, and at the same time claim that the Bible contains error, it follows, does it not, that they call God a liar, since He has spoken falsely? Either they have openly repudiated the Confession or else they have called God a liar. In either case they have no rightful place in the Presbyterian ministry.[30]

Under the guise of our postmodern context, post-conservatives are moving in the same direction as Schleiermacher and Briggs. Despite their protests to the contrary, they have already begun to go down this same path. There is such a thing as unintended consequences. The more things change, the more they stay the same, or to quote that great Yankee philosopher, Yogi Berra, "It's like déjà vu all over again."

---

30. This article originally appeared in the July 15, 1946, issue of *The Southern Presbyterian Journal.* It was subsequently reproduced in tract form and went through at least three printings in that form. The original *Journal* article and a collection of Dr. Clark's papers can be found at the PCA Historical Center's Web site, http://www.pcahistory.org/documents/auburnheresy.html.

1

The Doctrine of Scripture: Only a Human Problem

PAUL WELLS

~~~~~~~

"Christian theologians are engaged in a kind of war, a 'culture war' over the nature of language and textual interpretation. The doctrine of Scripture is perhaps the greatest casualty of this war as it has been waged on the postmodern front."[1]

W ho would not agree with this evaluation of the present crisis with regard to the doctrine of Scripture? Yet is seems to suppose that the evangelical doctrine of Scripture was alive and kicking before the postmodern/post-conservative front was opened, which is far from being the case. The question is as to whether postmodernism, whatever that might be, is of such a nature to require of evangelicals a new paradigm for this doctrine, different from the one called for by the results of Enlightenment rationalism. We think not, but that does not mean no adjustments can be made, particularly in the light of the mood called "post-conservative" evangelicalism.[2]

1. K. J. Vanhoozer, *First Theology: God, Scripture and Hermeneutics* (Downers Grove, IL: InterVarsity, 2002), 32.
2. M. J. Erickson, P. K. Helseth, and J. Taylor, eds., *Reclaiming the Center: Confronting Evangelical Accommodation in Postmodern Times* (Wheaton, IL: Crossway, 2004), chap. 1.

Over the last quarter of a century conservative evangelicals have expended much effort to shore up the character of Scripture as Word of God, with many publications on its inspiration and authority and the vexed question of inerrancy, against the attacks of modernism and the skepticism of the likes of James Barr. Who could gainsay the usefulness of this reaction—particularly at a time when the Christian faith is confronted "by such an array of influential theologians who profess loyalty to Scripture, who even speak emphatically in the name and on the side of what the Bible affirms, but who nonetheless range themselves against much of what Scripture actually teaches"[3]?

If the effort has been laudable, the results have not always been winning scores. Much inspiration theory in evangelicalism, as in Roman Catholicism, has not been talk directly related to the nature of the Bible, but talk about talk about the Bible.[4] In this context the temptation is to set up men of straw to win debates while sometimes missing the real problem. And where does the real problem lie, in so far as the doctrine of Scripture is concerned for evangelicals? Not primarily in its authority and inspiration, nor in its divine nature as Word of God, nor even in its inerrancy, defined by the *Chicago Statement on Biblical Inerrancy* (1978) in such a way as to satisfy even some waverers at the time, but in its humanity. It seems that each new evangelical publication added another coat of rust-preserver to the breastplate protecting the inspiration and inerrancy of the Word of God, while not even applying a Band-Aid to the Achilles' heel of the humanity of Scripture. If the major evangelical publications over the last fifty years were reviewed, relatively little would be found about the specific nature of the humanity of Scripture.[5] However, it was precisely on this point that modernist critique focused, in the belief that if the humanity of the text is taken seriously, then the nature of the divine revelatory action involved will require some reformulation. Liberals thought that because of the humanity of the Scriptures, the understanding of divine revelation needed revamping, whereas evangelicals seemed to suppose that if the divinity of the Scripture were squared away in the context of inspiration, with inerrancy following close behind, the questions about the human nature of Scripture would somehow go away.

This, it has to be admitted today, was failing to see the wood for the trees, and it is a problem that has not gone away. Some scholars who have considered themselves to be fundamentally evangelical and who have wished to be intellectually honest

---

3. C. F. H. Henry, "Modern Reductions of Biblical Authority," in *God, Revelation and Authority* (Waco: Word, 1979), 4:41, 43.

4. Cf. J. T. Burtchaell, *Catholic Theories of Biblical Inspiration since 1800* (Cambridge/New York: Cambridge University Press, 1969), 283–84.

5. C. H. Pinnock tried to do justice to the question of the humanity of Scripture in a way more consequent than most in his *The Scripture Principle* (San Francisco: Harper & Row, 1984), pt. 2. Pinnock speaks of the necessity of honoring the humanity of Scripture fully, as it is God's way, 86ff. If the recent *Evangelicals and Scripture: Tradition, Authority and Hermeneutics* (Downers Grove, IL: InterVarsity, 2004), V. Bacote, L.C. Miguélez, D. L. Okholm, eds., 7–8, purports to take the divine-human reality of Scripture seriously, once again there is no article in the collection on the humanity of Scripture as such.

have been acutely aware of the difficulties, but their questions have been, by and large, regarded with some discomfort by other evangelicals.[6] The debate's focus on the question of inerrancy has tended to have the undesirable side effect of obscuring the fact that the broader problem is one that concerns the humanity of Scripture, and this was largely forgotten. It reduced the question of humanity to that of inerrancy, which in its turn resulted in the unjustified criticisms that evangelical doctrine was static, rationalist, absolutist, or abstract.[7]

The whole question of the nature of the humanity of Scripture, far from being resolved by looking at its divinity, needs to be dusted down and aired out. There are two good reasons for thinking that this might be useful for evangelicalism today. First, there is the precedent of Benjamin B. Warfield, who, in his remarkably concise article, "The Divine and Human in the Bible" raised the question as to "how the two factors, the divine and the human, [are] to be conceived as related to each other in the act of inspiration . . . and how the two consequent elements in the Bible, the divine and human [are] to be conceived to be related to each other in the product of inspiration."[8] Warfield added that if we are more concerned with the effects of inspiration than with its nature or mode, "men will not rest in their belief in effects which are not congruous with their conception of the nature and mode of inspiration."[9]

Warfield asserted vigorously that the human aspect of Scripture claims serious attention, because the Scriptures are "human writings, written by men and bearing the traces of their human origin on their very face," and the human element is larger than supposed.[10] He also affirmed the indissoluble unity of the divine and the human elements, that one cannot be considered apart from the other, with the implication that this unity encourages us to envisage the humanity of Scripture from the broadest perspectives possible. Warfield's proposition has hardly been carried through in terms of the unity of the divine and human elements of Scripture and its implications for the human nature of the text. Perhaps this is so because the subject is mysterious and the nature of the relation is complex and difficult to explore, perhaps also because

6. One could indicate the names of G. C. Berkouwer, J. Rogers, D. K. McKim, C. Pinnock, D. Bloesch, J. Goldingay, or today the concerns that preoccupy P. Enns. See, for example, D. K. McKim, ed., *The Authoritative Word: Essays on the Nature of Scripture* (Grand Rapids: Eerdmans, 1983).
7. Cf. D. Bloesch's criticism of the packaged formulas of "evangelical rationalism" in *Holy Scripture: Revelation, Inspiration and Interpretation* (Downers Grove, IL: InterVarsity, 1994), chap. 1.
8. B. B. Warfield, *Selected Shorter Writings of Benjamin B. Warfield*, J. E. Meeter, ed. (Phillipsburg, NJ: Presbyterian and Reformed, 1973), 2:542–43. D. Bloesch's judgment that "Warfield affirmed a human side to Scripture but not an authentically human element," *Holy Scripture*, 118, seems to suppose that Bloesch knows what is authentically human and Warfield doesn't. This is precisely where the problem of speaking about the humanity of Scripture lies.
9. Warfield, *Selected Shorter Writings*, 542–43.
10. Ibid., 545. The question of the relation of Warfield's "concursus" and Bavinck's "organic inspiration" lies beyond the bounds of this study. Cf. H. Bavinck, *Reformed Dogmatics*, vol. 1 (Grand Rapids: Baker Academic, 2003), 430ff. and A. A. Hodge and B. B. Warfield, *Inspiration* (1881; repr., Grand Rapids: Baker, 1979) who use the term "superintendence" as well as "divinely related concurrence," 6, 14, 17.

it is easier to argue that the Bible is divine or that it is human rather than to develop a doctrine based on their interrelation.[11] In any case, this Achilles' heel has too often been left to fester.

Second, the debacle of the West in the twentieth century led to doubts not only about human dignity but also about human nature itself. Lack of confidence about what humanity actually is has led to a tragic view of human nature and destiny and a flight from metaphysics. In Christian theology there was a shift from handling anthropology in ontological terms to a more functional approach to human nature. Human nature has been considered in dynamic terms, as man acting in relation to God, to other human beings, with respect to oneself, and in a creational context.[12] This new accent was far from being unjustified, particularly in the light of impasses in classical theological anthropology.[13] These questions have a certain effect on considerations of humanity in relation to the human element in Scripture. When human nature is shaken to its foundations, is it possible to speak of the humanity of Scripture as if it were self-evidently a positive and given reality? Postmodern deconstruction, when it arrived, was like a little gangrene setting in on the festering heel. If the new perspectives in anthropology linked to a dynamic and functional view of man provided an incentive to reconsider the nature of the humanity of Scripture, philosophies of deconstruction make it absolutely essential in a changed context.

The aim of this chapter is to apply a little ointment to the Achilles' heel of evangelicalism, the humanity of Scripture. First, we will consider difficulties arising from the dualistic theology that separated the divine and human elements of Scripture. Second, we will refer to some classical attempts at articulating the relation between the divine and the human elements and examine their limitations. Consciousness of these limitations gives rise to some more recent propositions concerning the humanity of Scripture, which will be examined and criticized briefly. Finally some tentative remarks as to how the humanity of Scripture could be considered in another light will be mentioned.

Humanity, the Whole Humanity, and Nothing but the Humanity of Scripture

"The men whom we hear as witnesses speak as fallible erring men like ourselves." So Karl Barth.[14] Little wonder that, as Clark Pinnock comments, "classical Christians almost instinctively shy away from too close an examination of the human as-

---

11. Cf. M. Silva, *Has the Church Misread the Bible? The History of Interpretation in the Light of Current Issues* (Leicester: Apollos, 1987), 42–45. A rare effort to apply Warfield's perspective is V. S. Poythress, "What Does God Say through Human Authors?" in H. M. Conn, ed., *Inerrancy and Hermeneutic* (Grand Rapids, Baker, 1988), 81–100.

12. Cf. for example, C. Gunton, *Christ and Creation* (Carlisle: Paternoster, 1992) and also the contributions of M. J. Kline and P. E. Hughes on the subject. P. Wells, "In Search of the Image of God: Theology of a Lost Paradigm," *Themelios* 30, pt. 1 (2004): 23–38.

13. For example, concerning the broader and the narrow aspects of the image of God, the image before and after the fall, the image and corporality, etc.

14. K. Barth, *Church Dogmatics* (Edinburgh: T. & T. Clark, 1936–1969), 1.2:506–14.

pects of the Bible. They feel in their bones the danger of the human devouring the divine."[15] This may be an exaggeration, but it is an unavoidable fact that in the development of the doctrine of Scripture from the Enlightenment onward the burgeoning historical consciousness that increasingly identified humanity and autonomy was bound to drive a wedge between humanity and divinity. Where there was humanity, there could not be divinity in any direct fashion, and where there was divinity, there could not be humanity in continuous association with it. This drastically modified the sense of biblical authority.[16]

Herman Bavinck in his *Dogmatics* affirmed that a correct view of inspiration "puts the primary author and the secondary author in the right relationship to each other" and remarked that neither pantheistic nor deistic tendencies in theology could do it for either author, as the one fails to do justice to the acts of human beings and the other to the activity of God.[17] For Bavinck only a truly biblical view of the transcendence and immanence of God provided a correct basis for considering the nature of the humanity of Scripture. In matter of fact, the increasing tendency to dualism in the modernistic worldview showed a marked inclination to a deistic ethos, with an accent on the absence, silence, total otherness of God, bowing perhaps to Kantian, Kierkegaardian, and later to neoorthodox influences. Revelation was invariably considered as being an act of God distinguished from any direct material traces in Scripture.[18] Inspiration was the experience of the authors, or later of the readers, but not of the only element that provides a bridge between them—the text itself. As John Webster remarks, "The burden is the question of how we are to conceive the relation between the biblical texts as so-called 'natural' or 'historical' entities and theological claims about the self-manifesting activity of God."[19]

One tendency with regard to inspiration has been to broaden its meaning to include the whole of the religious community of the people of God,[20] or to make it a function of the way inspiration is understood in a general sense.[21] In either case, the inspiration in view will be considered a function of humanity, of individuals, or of

15. Pinnock, *The Scripture Principle*, 92. Yet for Barth, according to B. L. McCormack, "the Bible *precisely in its humanness* stands on the divine side of the great divide that distinguishes God from all things human." ("The Being of Holy Scripture Is in Becoming: Karl Barth in Conversation with American Evangelical Criticism," in Bacote, Miguélez, and Okholm, *Evangelicals and Scripture*, 69.)

16. Silva, *Has the Church Misread the Bible?* 42. Cf. P. Wells, *Dieu a parlé* (Québec: Éditions La Clairière, 1997), chap. 12.

17. Bavinck, *Reformed Dogmatics*, 1:428.

18. Cf. P. Helm, *The Divine Revelation* (London: Marshall Morgan and Scott, 1982), chap. 3.

19. J. Webster, *Holy Scripture: A Dogmatic Sketch* (Cambridge: Cambridge University Press, 2003), 18.

20. As, for example, in the theology of J. Barr, *Old and New in Interpretation* (London: SCM Press, 1966), chap. 1; *The Bible in the Modern World* (London: SCM Press, 1973), 115ff., 126ff., and later that of S. J. Grenz on the Bible as the "book of the community," *Theology for the Community of God* (Nashville: Broadman and Holman, 1994); or the tenets of the "New Yale Theology" movement. Cf. P. Wells, *James Barr and the Bible: Critique of a New Liberalism* (Phillipsburg, NJ: Presbyterian and Reformed, 1980), 207–20.

21. W. J. Abraham, *The Divine Inspiration of Holy Scripture* (Oxford: Oxford University Press), chap. 3. Inspiration, says Abraham, is a "polymorphous concept."

a group, without any specific characteristics to distinguish it from other expressions of humanity. "To be human, for believer and unbeliever, means the same thing. It means a condition of sin and fallibility. Hence error cannot be avoided. When people say we should stress more the 'human' side of Scripture they generally mean its fallibility. For them that is synonymous with being human."[22] The next stop down this road is the affirmation that "we place our trust ultimately in Jesus Christ, not in the Bible,"[23] which is true in one sense and not in another, as we can hardly trust Christ apart from the Bible. At this point a doctrine of Scripture in which humanity and fallibility are not synonymous is vital.

The panoply of humanity that modernism erected over Scripture sparkled with stars that light up the link between humanity and fallibility. Emil Brunner could say that "the Bible is the human and therefore not the infallible witness to the divine revelation . . . in the history of the incarnate Son of God." Karl Barth could top that by saying that the witnesses are not true witnesses unless they can also bear false witness through their "capacity of error." James Barr's pinch of salt was that the Bible is "verbally inspired but it remains fallible; it is not inerrant. . . ."[24]

Some other stars in the galaxy of fallibility are found nearer to home than the theologians cited above in Donald Bloesch's book *Holy Scripture*. The language of Scripture is the "earthen vessel" whereby the hidden treasure of grace is received; it is a "channel," a "medium," not revelation itself; it is "provisional" and "relative"; its true humanity involves a "vulnerability to error and a limited cultural horizon"; it is characterized by "historical inaccuracies" and "internal contradictions"; and, quoting Barth, "we recognize its human imperfection in the face of its divine perfection, and its divine perfection in spite of its human imperfection."[25] All of these attributions can of course be discussed, and we do not wish to say that it is *always* incorrect to use this kind of language in reference to the humanity of Scripture. Generalizations are a liability. When certain human traits are considered as being liabilities for divine revelation as they are for other forms of human discourse, it is obviously a very limited view of humanity that is being taken. The problem is whether or not

22. N. Weeks, *The Sufficiency of Scripture* (Edinburgh: Banner of Truth, 1988), 73.
23. Pinnock, *Scripture Principle,* 100. Cf. J. Barr, for many Christians the objective reality and authority standing over against them is in "Christ as a person and not in the Bible," *Fundamentalism* (London: SCM Press), 312.
24. E. Brunner, *Revelation and Reason* (Philadelphia: Westminster Press, 1946), 276; K. Barth, *Church Dogmatics,* 1.2, 509ff.; Barr, *Fundamentalism,* 287. Barr goes all the way, linking human and divine imperfection by saying that God does not operate "out of a static perfection" and that we can entertain the view that God's nature is imperfect and that God is vacillating and changing, 277.
25. Bloesch, *Holy Scripture,* 15, 18, 38, 39, 107ff., etc. Pinnock, *Scripture Principle,* 98ff., also speaks about "human weakness" and describes some of the "many details we can mention" in this respect; see also 89ff. and 48ff.

the humanity of Scripture is identical to all other expressions of humanity we might observe.[26]

Whatever the differences between modernism and postmodernism are thought to be in a larger sense, for the question of humanity it seems to be more of the same, although with increased lack of certainty, instability, and the absence of teleology.[27] Insofar as the doctrine of Scripture is concerned, postmodernism seems to reveal itself as the "latest representation of modernity," one that is characterized by skepticism and localizing tendencies.[28] Although this trend seems far from having reached its apex, the naturalism, subjectivism, and relativism that characterized modernity, together with its historicism and evolutionism, seem to be ever present and amenable to transposition into the postmodern view where reality is seen as a social construct. These "isms" marry felicitously with a narrative rather than a propositional approach to Scripture and one that sees meaning primarily not in the author or the text but in functions.[29]

The "mood of uncertainty" of postmodernism impinges on the doctrine of Scripture through considerations about its humanity. Is this *the* story, is it the *true* story, does the story really concern *me*?[30] Questions about Scripture nowadays might not be about its objective status, its inspiration and authority, but more about how believing Scripture would affect us. Were we to believe it, would we become arrogant and abusive fundamentalists and lose our real humanity in the process? Postmodern humanity seems to play the game of drifting, or at least of touring, and permanent anchorage is thought to restrict freedom; it is also suspicious of manipulative behavior and confuses authority with injustice; it is acquisitive of nonessentials that caress the individual ego and embellish a social image.[31]

The question of the influence of Karl Barth invariably comes up in discussions about the humanity of Scripture: was he the last of the modernists, the first of the postmodernists, or a bridge between the two because of his relational and activistic

26. Cf. P. Wells, "Covenant and the Humanity of Scripture," *Westminster Theological Journal* 48, no. 1 (1986): 17–45.
27. This question has been discussed thoroughly enough in this volume for us not to go into detail here. However, one can consult with profit D. A. Carson's works on the subject, *The Gagging of God: Christianity Confronts Pluralism* (Leicester: Apollos, 1996), chap 1; 544ff., and his *Becoming Conversant with the Emerging Church* (Grand Rapids: Zondervan, 2005), chaps. 3, 4. Also D. F. Wells, *Above All Earthly Pow'rs: Christians in the Postmodern World* (Grand Rapids: Eerdmans, 2005), chap. 2.
28. R. A. Mohler, "The Integrity of the Evangelical Tradition and the Challenge of the Postmodern Paradigm," in D. S. Dockery, ed., *The Challenge of Postmodernism* (Grand Rapids: Baker Academic, 2001), 67, 70.
29. Cf. A. B. Caneday, "Is Theological Truth Functional or Propositional? Postconservatism's Use of Language Games and Speech-Act Theory," in Erickson, Helseth, and Taylor, *Reclaiming the Center*, 137–59.
30. Categories used in chap. 2 of N. T. Wright's *Scripture and the Authority of God* (London: SPCK, 2005).
31. In a sense postmodernism bears some resemblances to the pagan values of classical Greek antiquity, its aspirations to freedom, justice, and luxury, which constitute the theme of R. L. Fox's recent book, *The Classical World: An Epic History of Greece and Rome* (London: Penguin, 2005).

dialectic view of Scripture?[32] Was he more or less evangelical?[33] However these questions are answered, and no doubt a variety of spin can be used, J. K. S. Reid's presentation of Barth's view of the authority of Scripture rings familiar to post-modern ears:

> *Theopneustos* is the act of revelation in which the prophets and apostles in all their humanness became (the witnesses) they were, and in which alone they in all their humanness can become for us (the witnesses) they are.... The Bible writers are as-sailable by reason of their characterization by the culture of their time and place, and the resulting offence cannot be evaded. Their capacity for error must be admit-ted ... of this in recent times we have become more aware because of the growing insight into the world-view which they held in common with their contemporaries ... the human word which is the Jewish word of the Bible heard as God's Word, and which comes home to us.[34]

If Reid has given a fair, if turgid account of Barth's position, and we have little reason to doubt it, the question is what happens to the human form of Scripture in the act of divine appropriation when it happens, for both the authors and the readers. Does it, as Reid says, remain a merely human word "unless as elected by the same Spirit, which created this witness as such, (it) gives to the men who are its hearers and read-ers witness of its truth"?[35]

The elements suggested by Barth, the culture-specific relativity of the human word, its historical encapsulation, and its linguistic limitations together with the importance of subjective appropriation of the truth content of Scripture all play a part in the developing matrix for Scripture in present evangelicalism.[36] Compare the activism of Barth with the following: "A doctrine of Scripture that is framed by the understanding of 'truth as an action' might focus attention on the 'performance' or 'embodiment' of the text—not as a second logical step (know first, then apply) but as inherent in the knowing."[37] This is probably as close as one can get to a clear statement

---

32. T. C. Oden, *After Modernity . . . What? Agenda for Theology* (Grand Rapids: Zondervan, 1990), 63ff., and H. Küng, *Theology for the Third Millenium* (New York: Doubleday, 1987), 271ff.

33. McCormack, "Being of Holy Scripture," 73ff.

34. J. K. S. Reid, *The Authority of Scripture* (London: Methuen, 1957), 215–16.

35. Ibid., 217.

36. Is "post-conservative" an appropriate term? In any case a good number of evangelicals favorable to postmodernism (including D. A. Williams, "Scripture, Truth and our Postmodern Context," in *Evangelicals and Scripture*, 242) seem to go beyond K. Vanhoozer's use of the term, which affirms a "plurality of normative points of view in Scripture" while seeking to maintain the cognitive dimension of theological propositions. "Lost in Interpretation: Truth, Scripture and Hermeneutics," in *Journal of the Evangelical Theological Society* 48, no. 1 (2005): 108. See the extensive critique of the thought of S. J. Grenz et al, in *Reclaiming the Center*.

37. Williams, "Scripture, Truth and our Postmodern Context," 242. For a defense of a correspondence theory of truth, cf. J. P. Moreland, "Truth, Contemporary Philosophy, and the Postmodern Turn," in *Journal of the Evangelical Theological Society* 48, no. 1 (2005): 77–88, and D. Groothuis, "Truth Defined and Defended" in *Reclaiming the Center*.

of the complexion post-conservatism puts on the function of Scripture. The difference between it and neoorthodoxy "occasionalism" is scarcely more than a hair's breadth.

If the extent of Barth's influence on late twentieth century evangelicalism is debatable, what seems evident is that its approach to questions of humanity and Scripture seemed like greener pastures for those who were alienated by the battle for the Bible on the Lindsell-Woodbridge line.[38] During the last quarter of the century it prepared the ground to be sown with the seeds of postmodernity insofar as Scripture and its interpretation are concerned. Its influence opened a way to a thoroughgoing relativism in cultural, historical, and linguistic approaches to the Bible, which was to become one of the hallmarks of the post-conservative evangelical movement at the turn of the twenty-first century.[39] It made certain questions acceptable or even fashionable because they were "dangerous"; in evangelical circles things came to be said that had not been said and had not previously been acceptable.

In terms of cultural consciousness, the evangelical involvement in missions was of considerable significance. The debate about contextualization brought to the forefront the importance of different cultural contexts for communication. The truth of Scripture was considered as being culture-related, and therefore understanding of cultural background was necessary to an appropriation of its meaning and cross-cultural communication of its message.[40] Scripture comes from a "particular time and place in history . . . [and] the writers and the text bear the limitations imposed by cultural and historical contingency."[41] Hopefully, however, the difficulty is overcome, because "the text by virtue of its inspiration and present illumination by the Holy Spirit opens to us a culturally transcendent horizon when seen in its relationship to Jesus Christ"[42]—a formula that obviously bears a Barthian imprint. The danger that Pinnock had the lucidity to grasp was that "the integration of the divine and human is lost . . . the authority of the Bible is made relative and its teachings are viewed in the context of transient human thought and time-bound cultural perspectives."[43]

Finally the way was opened to linguistic relativism by neoorthodoxy's dualism between revelation and the word of Scripture in the interest of preserving the full humanity of the Bible. As Colin Gunton put it in 1995, "We are confident we have

---

38. M. D. Thompson in *A Clear and Present Word: The Clarity of Scripture* (Leicester: Apollos, 2006) speaks about "persistent and somewhat frantic assaults on the doctrine of biblical inerrancy," referring to H. Harris, *Fundamentalism and Evangelicals* (Oxford: Clarendon, 1998), 288–89.
39. See the various articles on these themes in *Reclaiming the Center*.
40. Cf. the questions raised in H. Conn's book *Eternal Word and Changing Worlds* (1984; repr., Phillipsburg, NJ: P&R, 1992).
41. Bloesch, *Holy Scripture*, 39.
42. Ibid.
43. Pinnock, *Scripture Principle*, 91.

passed the stage when we any longer equate revelation and the actual words of Scripture."[44] If a primary victim was confidence in the clarity of Scripture, a secondary effect was to accentuate the limitations of human language and undermine its capacity to communicate truth in an objective way.[45]

Separation of the divine and human authors of Scripture leads inevitably to doubts that the Bible as such says anything to us, as James Barr one time commented,[46] an idea dressed up in somewhat different terms as follows: "There is nothing that scripture finally 'is' . . . [it] is not the texts of scripture that are to be understood and about which a theory is to be sought, but the dynamic of human involvement with them. . . ."[47] Scripture is "a subsection of the ontology of our being persons."[48] Another way of putting it would be to say that its meaning is not relative to its author or authors, but relative to us and what we make of it, and our reading is always socially located. Thus a radical version of the relativity of human language, one that implies unlimited subjectivity and pluralism in interpretation, challenges the truth and the authority of Scripture.

Just as in liberalism and neoorthodoxy the humanity of Scripture was a function of the epistemologies of modernism, so more recently the various forms of human relativity attributed to the Scripture as human text are expressions of a postmodern worldview. In both cases the conjunction of the divine and the human advocated by Warfield as a framework for considering Scripture vanishes, and it is increasingly neglected in evangelicalism too. The danger for Scripture is that of collapsing its message into an in-house community jargon, a new and zany "Holy Land–speak" without any universal references.

Models of Divine-Human Discourse

Several models have been traditionally used as a means of articulating the divine-human relationship in the case of Scripture. They will continue to be useful according to their ability to do justice to the complementary aspects of the question constituted by the divine revelation and the true humanity of the text. They are used in different ways in different contexts, and their perennity illustrates their ability to adapt to changing circumstances. We will examine four models: witness, accommodation, the analogy between Christ and the Bible, and the servant form of Scripture. We will briefly assess each according to its usefulness.[49]

44. C. Gunton, *A Brief Theology of Revelation* (Edinburgh: T. & T. Clark, 1995), 6.
45. Cf. M. D. Thompson on the clarity of Scripture as a modern and postmodern problem, and particularly his criticism of Barth in this respect, *Clear and Present Word*, 74–77.
46. Barr, *Fundamentalism*, 78. See the comments by S. Ferguson, "How Does the Bible Look at Itself," in Conn, *Inerrancy and Hermeneutic*, 49–54.
47. W. Cantwell Smith, *What Is Scripture? A Comparative Approach* (London: SCM Press, 1993), 237, quoted by J. Webster, *Holy Scripture*, 7.
48. Ibid.
49. Cf. the stimulating section on these notions in J. Webster, *Holy Scripture*, 22ff.

Witness

The notion of the human witness to divine revelation is obviously a prime candidate for expressing the involvement of both God and man in the biblical witness.[50] Its pedigree lies in that God bears witness to himself, men bear witness to God in Scripture, and the covenant involves witness to its conditions. Reformed theology has spoken of the self-attestation of Scripture, the Bible bearing witness to itself that its words are God's Word and that the humanity of the witness in no way hinders, but is the mode of the communication of divine truth.[51] The notion of witness has legal import, and the witness points to the evidence of external authority.[52] As such it is suited to both the divine and the human witness.

The difficulty with this notion lies in its annexation by neoorthodox theology in such a way as to found the quality of the witness not in its self-attestation but in the reality outside itself. As witness to revelation, it then becomes a sign, a mirror, or a lens, the usefulness of which is to look at something else. The element of divine witness in Scripture is eclipsed. John Webster lucidly comments, "The annexation of the Bible to revelation can appear almost arbitrary; the text is considered a complete and purely natural entity taken up into the self-communication of God."[53] The danger is "occasionalism" and a lack of real unity between the divine and human in witness. So Donald Bloesch: "We can even speak of a unity or identity of witness and revelation, but it is an indirect identity, not a property of the witness but a matter of divine grace."[54] When is an identity not an identity? Apparently it's when it's a witness. It seems that in such instances we fall from "two-factor" theology into a dynamic dualism that supposes the occurrence of a new event for the witness to become relational and revelational. When critical historiography takes hold, the witness of Scripture dissolves into human subjectivity, a subjectivity in which the personal vision of the author will justify the reader-response of postmodernity. However, the concept is useful insofar as its parameters are fixed by biblical exegesis, which means accepting the objectivity of the biblical witness.

Accommodation

Accommodation also has an impressive historical lineage[55] and is often closely linked with the name of Calvin.[56] Reformed orthodoxy did not make such frequent reference

50. Cf. the lengthy discussion in J. Goldingay, *Models for Scripture* (Carlisle: Paternoster, 1994), part 1.
51. W. Grudem, "Scripture's Self-attestation and the Problem of Formulating a Doctrine of Scripture," in D. A. Carson and J. D. Woodbridge, eds., *Scripture and Truth* (Leicester: InterVarsity, 1983), 19–59.
52. H. N. Ridderbos, *The Authority of the New Testament Scriptures* (Philadelphia: Presbyterian and Reformed, 1963), 62–71.
53. Webster, *Holy Scripture*, 24.
54. Bloesch, *Holy Scripture*, 57–58. Bloesch speaks of an inseparable relation but not an absolute identity between God's Word and the scriptural witness.
55. J. de Jong, *Accommodatio Dei: A Theme in K. Schilder's Theology of Revelation* (Kampen: Mondiss, 1990), 16–49.
56. Cf. the classic article by F. L. Battles, "God Was Accommodating Himself to Human Capacity," *Interpretation* 31, no. 1 (1977): 19–38. Recently, N. Wolterstorff, *Divine Discourse: Philosophical Reflections on the*

to the notion as Calvin did, but the fundamental aspects of Calvin's use were retained, that is, accommodation is an act of divine love as God condescends in his choice of men to write his Word, men with all their weaknesses, gifts, talents, and abilities. The Reformed scholastic theologian Polanus even went as far as to say that God did not choose the greatest of the earth but "ignoramuses and illiterates, who learned nothing in the schools of men which they passed on to others"![57] Accommodation is also the ground of the clarity of Scripture and its message in things necessary for salvation.

Herman Bavinck continued in this line and added the perspective that all accommodation is covenantal and leads to the final great accommodation in the incarnation.[58] Understood in this way, there is nothing in the notion of accommodation to shake our confidence that human beings can be partakers in the knowledge of God's truth.[59] On the contrary, accommodation is the very vehicle by which the truth is delivered to our doorstep, and without it nothing of divine truth could be discovered. Accommodation is not an adaptation to what men are; it is the very possibility of knowing the love of God in salvation. God did what was necessary for his truth to be known. This is very different from the Enlightenment view of accommodation put forward by Johann S. Semler and later by John Gottfried Herder, in which the accommodated character of Scripture was adapted to the unenlightened of a previous age, including the miracles that were suited to the church in its infancy.[60]

In modernism accommodation ran the risk of providing a rationale for the fact that God adapted to primitive men in such a way as to pass over human errors and incorrect knowledge. God condescended to fallibility. Postmodernism piggybacks modernism: "God did not rid his text of fallible human elements. This coheres nicely with the philosophical and theological expectations raised by our present, postmodern interpretative milieu."[61] Quite so, and of course "accommodation is not a threat to evangelical theology," at least if that is the road it is taking!

The Analogy between Christ and the Bible

The neatness of the christological analogy is both its strength and its weakness. As the divine and human are one in the incarnational revelation, so also the Scriptures

---

Claim that God Speaks (Cambridge: Cambridge University Press, 1995); J. Balserak, *Divinity Compromised: A Study of Divine Accommodation in the Thought of John Calvin* (Norwell, MA: Kluwer Academic, 2006).

57. de Jong, *Accommodatio Dei*, 47.

58. Ibid., 60.

59. J. B. Rogers and D. K. McKim, *The Authority and the Interpretation of the Bible: An Historical Approach* (San Francisco: Harper & Row, 1979), which draws a line between Calvin and scholasticism, needs some revision, particularly as it is a tool for criticizing Hodge and Warfield on inerrancy. Cf. J. Rogers, ed., *Biblical Authority* (Waco: Word, 1977), 40, who affirms that "Hodge showed no trace of the theory of accommodation."

60. de Jong, *Accommodatio Dei*, 51.

61. K. Sparks, "The Sun Also Rises: Accommodation in Inscripturation and Interpretation," in *Evangelicals and Scripture*, 130, 128. Grudem, "Scripture's Self-attestation," 53–57, gives six reasons why God does not accommodate to untrue facts. The extent to which divine accommodation relates to the mythical mentality of the Old Testament background is an issue in P. Enns's *Inspiration and Incarnation: Evangelicals and the Problem of the Old Testament* (Grand Rapids: Baker Academic, 2005), 17–18, 167–68.

are divine and human, Christ being without sin and the Scripture without error.[62] The link between christology and bibliology is not simply a theological construction, but can appeal to such passages as John 1 and Hebrews 1 and also to the obvious fact that in God's revelation the divine Word is both incarnated and inscripturated. There is no equal measure between the two; the parallel means that Scripture is subsidiary to Christ.[63] The Word becoming flesh is seen as a "general principle or characteristic of divine action in, through or under creaturely reality."[64]

Barth was even able to take this action as a model for revelation without assuming the implication of infallibility. However, as Klaas Runia commented, "To insist upon biblical fallibility along with its humanity is actually to destroy the whole parallel with the incarnation. The only thing that is left is a purely human book which can be used of God to communicate his divine message, but which as such *is* not this message."[65] Obviously, a primary intention of the analogy is not to guard against Docetism, for which it has been appropriated in recent debate, but to affirm that God works through the human authors of Scripture in such a way as to assure the truth of revelation.

The downside of the analogy is first the fact that it has been too readily pressed into the service of polemics.[66] It is probably too optimistic to claim, as Pinnock does, that "the analogy helps us to defend the true humanity of the Bible against Docetism and to defend its divine authority against the Ebionitism of liberal theology."[67] Sadly, it has been more frequently used to attack others. Evangelicalism has been accused of Docetism, liberalism of monophysitism, and neoorthodoxy has been likened to Nestorianism on the basis of the analogy, which, in this respect at least, seems to have generated more heat than light. Second, the analogy is not really an analogy at all in the formal sense of the word, since the mystery of the personal union of the two natures in Christ does not serve to shed light on the nature of the union in the divine-human word of Scripture. Christ and Scripture are not equivalent realities as there is but one hypostatic union.[68] Following along this line, it can be said that "an incarnational model may not be the best because, whereas with Christ's incarnation there is one person with two natures, with Scripture there are two persons (God

---

62. Cf. P. Wells, *James Barr and the Bible,* 9–33.

63. The analogy lies close to the notion of accommodation, particularly in Bavinck, *Reformed Dogmatics,* 2:398, 434.

64. Webster, *Holy Scripture,* 23.

65. K. Runia, *Karl Barth's Doctrine of Holy Scripture* (Grand Rapids: Eerdmans, 1962), 77; see 65–78 for a full discussion of the question.

66. Goldingay, *Models for Scripture,* 238–41.

67. Pinnock, *Scripture Principle,* 97.

68. Some other reasons why the analogy offers little help regarding the nature of Scripture and its humanity are given in P. Wells, *James Barr and the Bible,* 340–49. G. C. Berkouwer is highly critical of the analogy, *Holy Scripture* (Grand Rapids: Eerdmans, 1975), 197ff., but then Warfield and Packer also had their doubts as to its usefulness. Cf. J. I. Packer, *Fundamentalism and the Word of God* (London: InterVarsity, 1958), 82ff.

and the human prophet) and one nature (the one scriptural speech act). Thus to try to make the analogy may be like comparing apples to oranges."[69]

Recently, the question of the analogy has become an issue in relation to Peter Enns's *Inspiration and Incarnation* where it is used as a heuristic tool to secure the authentic humanity of Scripture, taking into account its diversity and even its "messiness."[70] However, a more promising recent suggestion by Kevin Vanhoozer concerns aspects of the incarnation that are useful in understanding the human dimension of Scripture when applied less stringently than in the context of a strict analogy, for instance, "as the logos indwelt the flesh of Jesus, so meaning indwells the body of the text."[71]

The Servant Form of Scripture

Finally, and closely related to the notions of accommodation and incarnational humanity, is the model of oganic inspiration, sometimes described as "the servant form of Scipture," and related to the thought of Herman Bavinck, James Orr, or Gerrit C. Berkouwer.[72]

Bavinck, perhaps the most incisive Reformed thinker of his time, fully aware as he was of new challenges to the doctrine of Scripture and the vital role of humanity in revelation, remodeled the doctrine in such a way as to be faithful to the Reformed heritage while innovatively using the biblical notions of revelation, inspiration, and covenant.[73] Bavinck eschewed the temptation of mechanical inspiration that would lift the human authors from their context, place them in a new situation, and cut them off from their old and natural context. On the contrary, revelation indicates God's coming down into human history to convey his truth by speaking through their thoughts and words. The word "organic" indicates that in inspiration God strengthens the self-activity of human beings in such a way that their words are his word. Human nature is therefore of the essence of revelation, and the words of man in their full humanity are God's words. Men were shaped and prepared by the Spirit and summoned into service of the Logos. Their writing is achieved without any coercion but constitutes through the leading of the Spirit a powerful witness to the working out of the central fact of history, that is, the incarnation of the Word himself.

69. This comment is attributed to Henri Blocher, in G. K. Beale, "Myth, History and Inspiration: A Review Article of *Inspiration and Incarnation* by Peter Enns," in *Journal of the Evangelical Theological Society* 49, no. 2 (2006): 299.
70. Enns, *Inspiration and Incarnation*, 109; cf. "Peter Enns: The 'Real' Humanity," xxx–xx.
71. K. Vanhoozer, *Is There a Meaning in This Text?* (Grand Rapids: Zondervan, 1988), 310; cf. 303–10, 460–61.
72. On James Orr and Herman Bavinck, see Andrew T. B. McGowan, *The Divine Spiration of Scripture: Challenging Evangelical Perspectives* (Nottingham, UK: Apollos, 2007).
73. Bavinck, *Reformed Dogmatics*, 1:428–46.

The divine word organically inscripturated has the "form of a servant" and partakes in the lowly and humble appearance of Christ. Like Christ, "Scripture is conceived without defect or stain; totally human in all its parts but also divine in all its parts . . . word and fact, the religious and the historical dimensions, that which was spoken by God and that which was spoken by human beings, is so tightly interwoven and intertwined that separation is impossible."[74] Inspiration includes the preparation of the authors of Scripture by the Spirit. In and through the writing process God makes "the language and the thoughts and words rise to the surface which best interpret divine ideas for all and every nation and age." In Bavinck's view of organic inspiration we find a fine expression of the unity of the divine and the human that Warfield had sought to define by the words "concurrence" and "superintendence."

G. C. Berkouwer picked up on Bavinck's fundamental insights in his study *Holy Scripture*, emphasizing particularly the servant form of Scripture and the complete identity of the divine word with the human word.[75] The human is the form of the Word, and its time-boundness is an integral part of the message of revelation. Divine accommodation espouses the views and conceptions of the period in which the biblical authors lived and out of which they were not lifted. The God-breathed character of Scripture exists in total continuity with the humanness of the authors in all its aspects. Berkouwer goes as far as to say that "when the time-relatedness of Holy Scripture is understood, it can be perceived how God's Word is the true and abiding norm."[76] The historical aspect programs the normative throughout, and only through its time-relatedness is the universal authority of Scripture disclosed.

Did Berkouwer go too far and make divine revelation so dependent on the servant form of the revelation that it has become virtually invisible? The question is complex and cannot be decided without taking into account the influence of Barth's theology on the Amsterdam theologian and the implications of his own method of correlation.[77] Berkouwer criticizes those who fall into the trap of Docetism by insisting so much on the divine that they leave nothing human in Scripture. We may well feel that Berkouwer overplayed his hand. Was he not blind to the fact that he had swung the pendulum to the other extreme? Perhaps Wayne Grudem was right when he said in criticism of Berkouwer that "the desire to depend on the divine word instead of the human word is exactly the attitude expressed by the psalmist in Ps. 12:6 and given in Scripture as an example for us to emulate."[78]

---

74. Ibid., 435, 438.
75. Berkouwer, *Holy Scripture*, chaps. 6, 7.
76. Ibid., 191.
77. Cf. the critiques of Berkouwer in: N. L. Geisler, "The Functional Theology of G. C. Berkouwer," in *Challenges to Inerrancy: A Theological Response*, G. R. Lewis, B. A. Demarest, eds. (Chicago: Moody, 1984); L. Smedes, "G. C. Berkouwer," in *Creative Minds in Contemporary Theology*, P. E. Hughes, ed. (Grand Rapids: Eerdmans, 1966), 63–98.
78. Grudem, "Scripture's Self-attestation," 362n34.

Bavinck's performance on the high wire between the divine and human in Scripture showed a fine sense of balance. Berkouwer lost it and fell heavily on the side of humanity, and even though he continued to speak of the divine God-breathing, it was thoroughly relativized by the accent on humanity. In any case, Berkouwer's radicalization of Bavinck's insights into the humanity of Scripture fashion a new theology of Scripture. It is more in harmony with the "dynamism" and mechanical inspiration Bavinck criticized when he constructed his theology of organic inspiration as a more biblical third approach.

Serious Commitments to Humanity

Meanwhile, back in the Anglo-Saxon West the debate about the doctrine of Scripture rolls on. In this specific field the influence of Brunner, Barth, Berkouwer, and more recently Barr has been considerable in encouraging an approach to the humanity of Scripture liberated from what was seen by some to be the straitjacket of Princetonian inerrancy. Barr probably hit the spot when he claimed that neoorthodoxy was a bridge that allowed uneasy fundamentalists to slip over into mainstream Christianity.[79]

In this respect it must be added that indigenous mediating figures have also played their part and perhaps none more so than Donald Bloesch. His reflections from the late 1970s onward on the essentials and the future of evangelical theology and most of all his *Holy Scripture* have made an impact on younger evangelicals. The names of Pinnock and Enns are added to that of Bloesch, as they have both contributed significantly to the developing consciousness of the importance of the human element in revelation and of the dangers of Docetism.[80] These three provide a link between the evangelical opposition to modernity in the last half century and the effort to adapt in differing ways to the developing postmodern cultural mentality. They have in common a desire to take "two-factor" theology seriously and to identify themselves as evangelicals while, in the case of at least Bloesch and Pinnock, playing the part of the "loyal opposition" through their critical attitudes. Their desire for integrity and academic honesty plus the fact that they do not avoid the knotty problems (even though some may think they glory in this overmuch) is quite admirable.

Donald Bloesch: "Biblical Evangelicalism"

Donald Bloesch's thought on Scripture is complex, nuanced, and highly personal, which makes it difficult to describe concisely without doing it injustice. He calls it "biblical evangelicalism," and contrasts it with "evangelical rationalism" on the one hand and "religioethical experimentalism" on the other. Its attractiveness lies in the

---

79. Barr, *Fundamentalism*, 213ff.
80. Cf. Berkouwer, *Holy Scripture,* 17ff.

fact that in its mediating position it can take the best of both worlds: the truth claims of classical evangelicalism and the sense of religious dependence from liberalism. It could probably best be termed a dynamic activism rooted in a sense of the presence of the Spirit, but labels don't catch the "mood." Bloesch's spirit is eclectic. He takes what is useful from many sources while refusing to carry a card for any of the parties he associates with, other than "the holy catholic faith, [which] can never be exhaustively or definitively formulated by mortal human beings."[81] He takes his distance from "postmodern orthodoxy (e.g. Oden, Pinnock)" but also from the packaged formulae coming from the "evangelical rationalist" corral. The individualistic openness of this theological lone ranger is itself highly attractive to the ethos of postmodern subjectivism.

The norm for the Christian then is not what Scripture says historically, as that which concerns the past, but what the Scripture says existentially to believers today under the influence of the Spirit. Scripture is an "earthen vessel" (an expression Berkouwer also used), and God's revealing action in sacred history is actualized by a similar present action of the Spirit. Biblical evangelicalism, affirms Bloesch, maintains the possibility of real knowledge of God as knowledge given anew by the Spirit of God in conjunction with the Scripture. Apart from faith, from redemptive transformation, no knowledge of God is possible. The truths of revelation are not empirically verifiable. The data of sacred history can be signs pointing to the truth and the opportunity for revelation, but they are not truth itself. Truth is the revelational meaning of events, and the Bible is the instrument by which the Spirit makes truth known.

The Bible is described as a mediate, not a direct, source of revelation, a position very different from that of Warfield, who made inspiration the final act of revelation. The ultimate source of truth is the living Christ who speaks by the Spirit illuminating the word of Scripture. The accent on the internal witness of the Spirit makes it sound as if the spirit of Barth lives on in Bloesch. The Holy Spirit entertains a "paradoxical relation" with the text of Scripture so that receiving its truth is a dynamic and personal affair, being both rational comprehension and a spiritual experience. God's self-communication in Christ cannot be separated from the worldly form of the scriptural witness—it is made known in this form. Without the witness there is no material for the Spirit to work with, but the word without the Spirit will remain a closed book; it cannot in itself bring the reader into a knowledge of the truth.

However, Bloesch does not throw in his hand with the "occasionalism" of neoorthodoxy; he aspires to a more consistent theology of Word and Spirit. Scripture itself is the *written* Word of God comprising a reliable witness to the truth revealed in Christ; nonetheless it must become the *living* word of God by communicating the power of the cross through the illumination of the Spirit. So the word corresponds

81. Bloesch, *Holy Scripture*, 15.

to the Word of God, but it is not identical with it—it is an "echo" or "reverberation" of what God has declared in Christ. There is correspondence but not identity, continuity but not similarity. For Bloesch the Word is living and dynamic, whereas for "rationalistic evangelicals" it is static or frozen. The Bible is not intrinsically divine revelation but becomes so by virtue of the action of the Spirit filling the words with meaning and power, an action that can be conceived of as comparable to the primary act of inspiration.

Bloesch is able to have his cake and eat it too. He can agree with Packer that Scripture is the Word of God and take distance from Barth, but he can also agree with Barth on the dynamics of the Spirit and take distance from Packer on the question of objective truth. He can appreciate Berkouwer's time-boundness of Scripture while affirming a greater continuity than Berkouwer did. However, that does not mean that Bloesch is out of the woods, as the old question that was always asked of neoorthodoxy and that Klaas Runia asked of Barth, still has to be faced: does anything happen to the words when they are filled with meaning and power, or does something just happen in the respondents? The problem of the ontological status of the text comes back to haunt us again.

Bloesch says that "the presence of the living Word in Holy Scripture is not an ontological necessity but a free decision of the God who acts and speaks . . . it is something to hope for on the basis of God's promises."[82] However, if the text has its being "by the ordering of the Spirit's sanctifying work . . . its ontology is defined out of the formative economy of the Spirit of God."[83] Surely it does not need to become anything other than it *is* to have meaning and power? Bloesch like Warfield wants to maintain a theology of the Word that confronts rationalism and illuminism. However, Bloesch moves the Princetonian's goalposts. He identifies rationalism with the fundamentalism ("evangelical rationalism" no doubt) that absolutizes the relative "merely human and temporal" words and illuminism with the morass of subjectivism that desires to have the Spirit alone.[84]

This fundamental position allows Bloesch to make a good deal of elbow room for the humanity of Scripture, unshackled from the epistemic bondage of Enlightenment rationalism, which he claims reduces truth to facticity in a strict doctrine of inerrancy. The Bible is divine in its ultimate origin and content, but human in its mode of expression and literary forms. So:

> The truthfulness of the Bible resides in the divine author of Scripture who speaks in
> and through the words of human authors, who ipso facto reflect the limitation and
> ambiguities of their cultural and historical milieu. . . . The biblical text is entirely

---

82. Ibid., 26.
83. Webster, *Holy Scripture*, 28.
84. Bloesch, *Holy Scripture*, 28. This is a move that will make Bloesch unpopular with some post-conservatives.

truthful when it is seen in relation to its divine center, God's self-revelation in Jesus Christ. When it is separated from this center, the text is not perceived in its proper context and then becomes vulnerable to error and misunderstanding.[85]

Bloesch takes seriously the fact that the true humanity of Scripture involves vulnerability to error, the limitations of cultural and historical contingency, but, "by virtue of its inspiration and present illumination by the Holy Spirit [it] opens to us a culturally transcendent horizon when seen in its relationship to Jesus Christ. This relationship constitutes the fullness of its meaning, its *sensus plenior*."[86]

Once again Bloesch seems to want to have it both ways. The unity of the human and the divine author is relational, occasional, and dynamic; and though it permits a formal union of authentic humanity and true divinity, it does so by maintaining a division and a separation between the two in the product of revelation and inspiration. This is confusing. If the biblical text is not seen in "relation to the center," is it no longer entirely truthful, just a little truthful, or not truthful at all? Bloesch's activism bears a strange likeness to the way transubstantiation is thought to happen in the Roman Mass.

Donald Bloesch's reconstruction of the doctrine of Scripture is theoretically inconsistent and self-contradictory. My apologies, but what he says about the humanity of Scripture echoes what the liberals have been saying ever since Ernst Troeltsch. However, recalling Pascal's dictum that the reasons of the heart are weightier than those of the head, it is obvious that Bloesch's remodeling of the doctrine of Scripture can be enormously seductive for a plethora of desperate evangelicals already softened up by the individualism, subjectivism, and instantaneity of the postmodern mood.

Perhaps it is surprising that the influence of Bloesch has not been more substantial in post-conservative circles. His accent on the relational and dynamic function of the Spirit in the appropriation of the "frozen" word, his critical stance toward evangelical rationalism, his concern for tradition and community, his eclecticism, and his wobbles on inerrancy would all appear to be bonuses from the post-conservative side of the tracks. Maybe it is a generational problem or even a misunderstanding caused by the off-putting "Christian Foundations" title of his systematic theology series. Whatever the case, Nancey Murphy almost commits a felony when, in one of her less aerodynamic moments, she labels Bloesch a "biblical foundationalist," so confining him to the theological limbo inhabited by such unfortunates.[87]

---

85. Ibid., 37–38; cf. 56–59. Bloesch criticizes Grudem, "Scripture's Self-attestation," for confusing the biblical understanding of truth with "a modern empiricist understanding," but also liberal scholars who reduce Scripture to disparate theologies.
86. Ibid., 39.
87. N. Murphy, *Anglo-American Postmodernity* (Boulder, CO: Westview, 1997), 92.

Clark Pinnock: From Biblical Infallibility to Open Theism

Clark Pinnock's presentation of the humanity of Scripture is another kettle of fish. His theology has moved a great deal from his *A Defense of Biblical Infallibility*, published in the late sixties. Where it will end up insofar as the doctrine of Scripture is concerned is anyone's guess.[88] His major work, *The Scripture Principle,* has many excellent features to commend it. Pinnock is chary about militant inerrancy. While maintaining that it "is deductive thinking rooted in the assumption of total divine control" and that the "theology of a Warfield or a Packer, which posits a firm divine control over everything that happens in the world, is very well suited to explain a verbally inspired Bible,"[89] he says that inerrancy is a "strong, excellent term when properly used."[90] Pinnock shows his appreciation of the positions of Barth and Berkouwer. He even affirms that "while preaching the errancy of the Bible, Barth practices its inerrancy "but even so, "neo-orthodoxy is closer to liberalism than it admits."[91] This gives the impression of wanting to run with the hare and the hounds, no doubt a charge that Pinnock would deny.

Pinnock's construction of a doctrine of Scripture is more comprehensive than that of Bloesch and shows considerable concern about Docetism and Ebionitism and a particular penchant for the place of the humanity of Scripture.[92] In their anxiety evangelicals are pushed to try and save the Bible from itself, dixit Pinnock. This is pure futility since the humanity of Scripture "is a part of God's will for the Bible and . . . has proven its effectiveness in carrying out its religious purpose in Christian experience."[93] In particular, Pinnock is concerned with the historical and cultural dynamics involved in dual-factor theology, since revelation is embedded in history. For this reason, historical criticism has a positive side because it helps see the text as it was and brackets out the readers' self-projections.

The humanity of Scripture in the light of modern consciousness implies that Scripture is part of a time-bound, transient human situation, part of a network of fallible human meanings. It strains credibility to seek to withdraw the biblical word from this context. Pinnock postulates that "the deepest problem facing biblical authority is not whether there are errors in the text but whether the text in any way can be viewed at any point as anything more than a reflection of its time and place." In other words, can the non-objectivity of God implied by historicism be avoided, and is God-talk ultimately anything other than purely finite and subjective babbling?

88. On Pinnock's evolution see, R. C. W. Roennfeldt, *Clark H. Pinnock on Biblical Authority: An Evolving Position*, Andrews University Seminary Doctoral Dissertation Series, 16 (Berrien Springs, MI: Andrews University Press, 1993), which I have not consulted.
89. Pinnock, *Scripture Principle*, 101.
90. Pinnock, "Three Views of the Bible in Contemporary Theology," in J. Rogers, ed., *Biblical Authority*, 68, a statement Pinnock defends with a multitude of qualifications, 63–69.
91. Ibid., 57, 59.
92. Pinnock, *Scripture Principle*, chaps. 4, 5.
93. Ibid., 85.

Pinnock says that Barth "was obviously close to the precipice on this" and solved the problem by the miracle of a religious encounter.[94]

Pinnock's solution is different. It is unavoidable that the recognition of humanity means accepting the cultural conditioning of Scripture, if that is what it is. However, the Bible can transcend the causal nexus of the total situation, and it can do so because the nexus is not closed but exists in a "pattern of causality created by God and fit to be the theater of his self-communication." Likewise, even if revelation comes to us in human weakness and if words do not always express their intended meaning because of the limitations of language, the message given through it overcomes its "restrictions and triumphs gloriously." God assumes the risks of his decision to speak to men in their tongue and accepts "a definite limitation on himself."[95]

These remarks set the scene for the latter-day "Open Theism" Pinnock.[96] He wishes to maintain the perspective of the interplay of the divine and human, which implies mystery when they come into contact. The danger he sees is that divine sovereignty invariably overcomes human realities and particularly freedom. Man becomes like a "piece of chalk" in the divine grasp; better a limited divine sovereignty that posits a dimension of creaturely freedom alongside the divine action. So Pinnock proposes that God's will includes all things in its scope but does not determine them. "God is not yet in full control of a world full of sin and evil ... he permits many things that displease and even anger him but is wise enough and powerful enough to weave them into the tapestry of his unfolding plan ... but he is able to overrule negative factors that come against his will and bring about a good result." This permits him to say that in revelation God avoids truth being distorted by human receptors, he oversees and directs, and humans respond. "God is present not normally in the mode of control, but in the way of stimulation and guidance."[97] Hey presto, Pinnock has managed to wriggle out of the dire constraints of "Calvinist cosmology." He can also appeal to the traditional idea of progressive revelation as a process of education in which "revelation takes human beings where it finds them and does with them what it can."[98]

Quite apart from whether Pinnock can justifiably speak about tapestries and unfolding plans in the terms of his own ideas about God and human liberty—how God can know human free choices without foreordaining them—is there not a

94. Ibid., 91–92.

95. Ibid., 95, 99. This is the context in which Pinnock speaks about accommodation and incarnation.

96. The development becomes more accentuated from the late 1980s and his *apologia pro vita sua*, "From Augustine to Arminius: A Pilgrimage in Theology," in *The Grace of God, the Will of Man: A Case for Arminianism*, C. H. Pinnock, ed. (Grand Rapids: Academie, 1989), 15–31. See also R. C. Olson, "Postconservative Evangelical Theology and the Theological Pilgrimage of Clark Pinnock," in *Semper Reformanda: Studies in Honour of Clark H. Pinnock*, S. E. Potter and A. R. Cross, eds. (Carlisle: Paternoster, 2003), not consulted by me.

97. Ibid., 103–4.

98. Ibid., 111.

contradiction between what he says on the one hand about God speaking through human authors and the inerrancy of Scripture, and his libertarian view of human freedom on the other? Can revelation on Pinnock's terms be God's *self*-revelation, and is there really a revelation of *God* in Scripture? Is it anything more than a partial communication in terms of what human conditions permit? Are the Scriptures God's Word and his truth?

John Frame states boldly that "open theists almost never formulate doctrines of biblical authority let alone inerrancy."[99] I wouldn't really know. As for Pinnock's position about the humanity of Scripture, the jury is still out. What can be said is that Open Theism *à la* Pinnock makes plenty of latitude for humanity in all its aspects, good, bad, or ugly. Can a "revelation" really be revelation of divinity when humanity is given the latitude to run amuck? Pinnock's approach will appeal to those inside the fold of Open Theism or to those who will adapt their view of the authority of Scripture because they are attracted to its general tenets. Apart from these considerations, in Pinnock's case even more so than in the case of Bloesch, the limitations of humanity remain the conditions and the cadre in which the divine must function and with which God must make do. The believer can only hope to edge toward the truth in contact with the Scripture rather than ever knowing it.

Pinnock gets the nod from Stanley J. Grenz in one of the required readings of post-conservatism, *Revisioning Evangelical Theology*:

> Clark Pinnock rejects as inflexible and undynamic the "propositional theology that sees its function as imposing systematic rationality on everything it encounters." Taking his cue from the contemporary narrative outlook, he chides academic theology for looking for truth in doctrine rather than in biblical story. Viewing revelation as primarily narrative, Pinnock sees the task of theology as expounding the story and explicating its meanings.[100]

Whether or not this does justice to Pinnock's position is immaterial; Grenz's approval is a brownie point for Pinnock in post-conservative milieux. Some years later, in *Renewing the Center,* Pinnock again got a bouquet from Grenz for being open to "the postmodern emphasis on the particular and experiential, for he saw these developments as boding well for an evangelical pietism," a factor contributing to the rebirth of centrist evangelicalism.[101]

---

99. J. Frame, *No Other God: A Response to Open Theism* (Phillipsburg, NJ: P&R, 2001), 205–7; cf. chap. 3; D. Wells, *Above All Earthly Pow'rs,* 242ff.

100. S. J. Grenz, *Revisioning Evangelical Theology: A Fresh Agenda for the Twenty-first Century* (Downers Grove, IL: InterVarsity, 1993); Grenz is referring to Pinnock's *Tracking the Maze: Finding Our Way Through Modern Theology from an Evangelical Perspective* (San Francisco: Harper & Row, 1990).

101. S. J. Grenz, *Renewing the Center: Evangelical Theology in a Post-Theological Era* (Grand Rapids: Baker, 2000), 150. Cf. D. A. Carson's "Domesticating the Gospel: A Review of Grenz's *Renewing the Center,*" in *Reclaiming the Center,* 33–55.

Peter Enns: The "Real" Humanity

Peter Enns's book *Inspiration and Incarnation* has generated a good deal of discussion. If an ocean of difference separates it from the works of Boesch and Pinnock, it does share with them a common concern for the humanity of Scripture and a critique of Docetism.[102] Its obvious pedagogical and practical intent constitutes a caveat against taking it as a definite expression of Enns's views on the doctrine of Scripture. Our concern here is not to give a review of Enns's book (space forbids), but to present some elements in his work that concern the theme of the humanity of Scripture.

A preliminary comment: the way Enns uses the incarnational parallel is rather surprising. Normally it portrays the divine entering into the arena of history and effecting the unity of the divine and human in the complementary cases of the person of Christ and the word of revelation. Enns uses it as a tool to encourage us to come to grips with the humanity of Scripture and the problems raised in the context of developing knowledge of the milieu in which revelation took place.

The way the analogy is formulated is also somewhat odd. "As Christ is both God and human, so is the Bible . . . we are to think of the Bible in the same way that Christians think about Jesus . . . Jesus is both God and human at the same time. He is not half-God and half-human. . . ."[103] It is already imprecise, to my way of thinking, to use the expression "incarnational" and not "christological" but perhaps lexical nicety is not Enns's main concern in the light of his target audience. The analogy speaks not of the movement of incarnation, the Word becoming flesh, but of the real unity of the divine and human as a result of incarnation and in inscripturation. Furthermore, the analogy is not that Christ is God and *human*, but that he is God and *man*. We can say Christ is divine and human, attributively, but not that he is God and human. The divine Logos did not assume generic human nature, but a specific human nature, that of a Jewish male, and the resultant unity was one person, Jesus Christ. A bibliological implication of "God and human" would be that God associates in some respect with human words he makes his own. The correspondence in the case of "God and man" implies a stricter unity: God speaks in specific human words that are his own word. Alternatively put, as Packer has said, this humanity exists only in the matrix of the divinity, which determines its particular human character.[104]

Had Enns approached the question from this perspective, he might not have been using the analogy as a means to the end of getting at the "real" humanity of Scripture. He would have been asking how *this* humanity is different because of its unique existence in the context of divine revelation. Would that not have altered the method-

---

102. Cf. G. K. Beale, "Myth, History and Inspiration," with Enns's reply and D. A. Carson's comments in "Three More Books on the Bible: A Critical Review," in *Trinity Journal* 27, no. 1 (2006), 1–42.

103. Enns, *Inspiration and Incarnation,* 17. Did Enns put *human* not *man* or was it a politically correct editor . . .?

104. Packer, *Fundamentalism and the Word of God,* 83–84; cf. J. Barr, *Fundamentalism,* 171–72.

ological approach of his project? Enns wishes to "allow the evidence to affect how we think about what Scripture as a whole *is*."[105] Has he not got the wrong end of the stick by starting with the phenomena and seeking to use them to hone the doctrine of Scripture? Even when he says "Christ's incarnation is analogous to Scripture's 'incarnation,'" he has got things back to front![106] The self-witness of Christ and that of Scripture have an ontological priority over the data of humanity in revelation. This in turn would have modified the *perspective* from which Enns handles the question of myth, the apparent diversities in Scripture, and the way the New Testament authors use the existing canon.

In his final chapter Enns returns belatedly to the subject of the incarnational analogy and admits its problematic nature "on at least one level": the person of Christ is not a better known factor explaining a lesser known one, because the incarnation "is itself precisely what needs explaining." Quite so, but Enns goes on to say that because of this:

> It makes more sense to speak of the incarnational *parallel* between Christ and the Bible [and that] this should lead us to a more willing recognition that the expression of our confession of the Bible as God's word has a provisional quality to it. By faith, the church confesses that the Bible is God's word. It is up to Christians of each generation, however, to work out what that means and what words work best to describe it.[107]

There may be several logical non sequiturs here, but here are two for starters. Insufficiencies in a theological construct like the christological analogy do not necessarily lead to the recognition of a "provisional quality" in the expression of belief that the Bible is God's word. Nor do they imply that any new words might be needed to express faith in the fact that the Bible is God's word. All this makes one wonder why Enns bothered with the incarnational paradigm at all and what the positive payback can be.

The answer may lie in what Enns conceives to be its usefulness, stated in the same context:

> To work with an incarnational paradigm means that our expectations of the Bible must be in conversation with the data, otherwise we run the very real risk of trying to understand the Bible in fundamental isolation from the cultures in which it was

---

105. Ibid., 15. This resembles a kind of induction, although it is obvious that Enns is not using the phenomena to test the truth claims of Scripture (as, for instance, Dewey Beegle did), which Enns doubtless presupposes to be true.

106. Ibid., 18. D. A. Carson in his review criticizes Enns for not discussing what the incarnation actually looks like, for using it in a way that focuses unilaterally on the question of humanity, and for not indicating how incarnation and inscripturation are similar and dissimilar ("Three More Books on the Bible," 30–32). This at least indicates the depth of the water Enns is in.

107. Ibid., 168.

written—which is to say, we would be working with a very nonincarnate understanding of Scripture. Whatever words Christians employ to speak of the Bible (inerrant,
infallible, authoritative, revelational, inspired), either today or in the past, must be
seen as attempts to describe what can never be fully understood . . . we can speak of
the incarnate Christ meaningfully, but never fully.

To speak "meaningfully" is to understand the Bible in the context of human culture
in which the word was written, which implies something that can "never be fully
understood," no doubt because it is "provisional." This, says Enns, is a legitimate
expectation Christians might have.

In this instance it is to be noted that Enns is not making a claim to "truthfulness"
but to "meaningfulness." One might have expected him to say that we can "speak of
the incarnate Christ truthfully" but he does not, maybe because of the spin he has
put on the incarnational analogy as a means of appreciating the full humanity of
Scripture. Of course "meaningful" humanity can also be "provisional" humanity
and something that escapes our full understanding. In other words, Enns's methodological perspective is productive of limited epistemological expectations of Scripture, ones that are lower than generally considered ideal in evangelical theology. It
is difficult to escape the impression that Enns is sailing close to the wind and that
his view of Scripture as meaningful implies a humanity that bears the marks of cultural relativity, subjectivity, temporal conditioning, and all the other limiting attributes frequently used to describe humanity. Enns's methodological misunderstanding
with regard to the christological analogy leads potentially to such epistemological
difficulties. This boomerangs on how the humanity of Scripture is construed in a
practical sense in a variety of ways, particularly its unique nature, the perspective of
its writers, and the nature of its teaching.[108]

Any presentation that accentuates the full humanity of Scripture will run up
against the problem of the way in which the Bible is the same and different from
other cultural manifestations in its milieu of origin, in a similar way to how Christ
is at once truly man and yet different from his contemporaries. Enns presents the
problem early on in his book: "It is essential to the very nature of revelation that the
Bible is not unique to its environment. The human dimension of Scripture is essential
to its being Scripture." "Situatedness" is not an embarrassment but is positive because
"the Bible, at every turn, shows how 'connected' it is to its own world [as] a necessary
consequence of God incarnating himself."[109] Obviously the human element is essential to Scripture being Scripture, because without it, there would be no revelation;
but this does not imply that the Bible must necessarily be "not unique to its environ-

---

108. Paul Helm presents these features in his review of Enns's book in terms of the provisional, the unique,
and the objective nature of the Bible on the Reformation 21 Web site, http://www.reformation21.com/
(accessed June 2008).
109. Enns, *Inspiration and Incarnation*, 20; cf. 56–59.

ment." Why should the opposite not be true if Scripture is divine revelation? Enns suffers at this point from his misconstrual of the christological analogy.

Again it is not obvious why "connectedness" should be a necessary consequence of God's self-incarnation to the exclusion of uniqueness. After all, if this is God acting to reveal *himself,* something very unique will be the outcome, not in spite of the "connectedness" but because of it. Would not many evangelical scholars say the contrary—it is essential to the very nature of revelation that the Bible *is* unique? Is this not precisely the condition of christological discourse? Enns adds a qualification later, which does nothing to limit the confusion: the Bible's "uniqueness is seen not in holding human cultures at arm's length, but in the belief that Scripture is the only book in which God speaks incarnately . . . the 'coming together' of the divine and human sets it apart from all others."[110] What makes it different is the presence of the unique God of Israel.

The "not unique and unique" ambiguity tends to color Enns's presentation of the sticky question of myth.[111] Of course, as a sincere evangelical Enns would have it that because of God's connectedness, revelation does not just parrot extrabiblical myth: "God *transformed* the ancient myths so that Israel's story would come to focus on its God, the real one."[112] Clark Pinnock seemed to do a better job when he wrote: "When we look at the Bible, it is clear that it is not radically mythical . . . the framework is no longer mythical . . . what we find are 'broken myths,' allusions to ancient myths but now translated into different terms . . . several passages in the New Testament denounce even the category of myth, so far is the message from that hazy world of discourse."[113] Some may doubt that Pinnock has gone far enough, but the point is well taken. Are the myths of the Ancient Near East anything other than idealizations of that past social and ethical world with superhuman heroes as gods, as in the Greek pantheon and its legends, and did people really believe in it? Enns could have been a little more clear in regard to the question of how the cultural milieu affects the belief of the biblical writers and the extent to which their knowledge of the God of the covenant functioned as a *de*-contextualizing factor. After all, what about Meredith J. Kline and the Old Testament polemic against pagan mythology, "a garbled, apostate version, a perversion of the pristine tradition of primordial historical realities . . ."?[114]

---

110. Ibid., 168.
111. The word "myth" itself is notorious for the misunderstandings it causes. Whether Enns has hedged his meaning around with sufficient clarity of definition is open to debate. His meaning is certainly not that of the Bultmanns of liberalism, but doubtless closer to the notion of a literary "foundational story." Enns can speak of the need to articulate the Bible's "divinity and perfection in view of the shape that the divine and perfect Author gave it." Reply to G. K. Beale's "Myth, History and Inspiration," in *JETS,* 321.
112. Ibid., 53. This bears resemblance to what Enns says about the unity of Scripture focusing on Christ.
113. Pinnock, *Scripture Principle,* 123–24.
114. M. J. Kline, *Kingdom Prologue: Genesis Foundations for a Covenantal Worldview* (Overland Park, KA: Two Age Press, 2000), 28.

The perspective of the writers, interpreted in line with their connectedness and provisionality, raises the question of the historical nature of Scripture and also its unity and diversity. Are they objective or biased? Biblical historiography is not objective; in fact Enns says at the end of his discussion on the subject, "There really is no such thing as objective historiography":

> The Bible is different. It is God's word. But what is true of all historiography is also true of biblical historiography—it is not objective. . . . What makes biblical historiography the word of God is not that it is somehow immune from such things. It is God's word because it is—this is how God did it. To be able to confess that the Bible is God's word is a gift of faith . . . our expectations should be informed by how the Bible in fact behaves and by seeing that behavior, as best we can, in the historical context in which the Bible was written."[115]

The paradoxical nature of the statement is once again puzzling. Because of the humanness of Scripture the Bible history must bear the same character as all historical reporting. Yet it is God's word because he did it this way, in conformity with the limitations of all historiography.

The difficulty in this case is similar to the one raised concerning the question of myth. To what extent does the fact that God is bearing witness to himself through human writers not require us to accept this as a guarantee that goes beyond all the biases of subjectivity? The question is, does it tell the truth or not? In reply we can but concur with D. A. Carson, who asks, "Doesn't the 'humanness' of Scripture's approach to reportage have to be tied somehow to the evidence that these words are also God's words, duly accommodated?"[116] Formally Enns can say he has done this, thank you, sir, but because of the particular way he uses the christological analogy, God remains handicapped by human bias, and objectivity is elusive. Could the writers of Scripture led by the Holy Spirit (2 Pet. 1:21) place an interpretation on the facts that would constitute a *false* bias? Or was their interpretation sufficient to satisfy human truth claims, even though such claims could never pretend to omniscience or exhaustiveness?

Likewise we think that when human diversities are recognized in the Bible, there is also a fundamental unity within Scripture per se as the Word of God, without the necessity of an appeal to the living Word, Christ himself. It is a fact, as Enns says, that "Christ is supreme and that it is in him, the embodied word that the written word ultimately finds its unity . . . and it is to him that the Bible as a whole bears witness."[117] For Enns this is the Christian's theoretical starting point. Christ is the ultimate example of how God enters the messiness of history to save his people. Of

115. Enns, *Inspiration and Incarnation*, 56.
116. Carson, "Three More Books on the Bible," 36.
117. Enns, *Inspiration and Incarnation*, 110.

course one has to agree with Enns. No evangelical will deny that Christ is the supreme unity in which the diversity of God's purposes coheres. Enns says, "God did not keep his distance, but became one of us. This is true of Christ, the embodied word. It is also true of the Bible, the written word."[118] Yes, of course, but did Christ in his resurrection appearance say, "Look at me, and then you will see it all fits together" (Luke 24:24–27)? He showed them that "all the Scriptures" fit together and spoke of things concerning himself. Christ's interpretation was not *eisegesis*, it was the interpretation of a unity that was already there.

Finally, it is only to be expected that Enns's desire to do full justice to the humanity of Scripture and avoid the pitfalls of Docetism should be reflected in his description of the nature of the biblical witness. His version of "enculturation" and his use of the word "provisional" are disquieting. He again bounces his ideas about the nature of human truths off the statement that the Bible, which "belonged in the ancient worlds that produced it . . . was not an abstract otherworldly book, dropped out of heaven." On the contrary, "it was connected to and spoke to those ancient cultures. The encultured qualities of the Bible, therefore, are not extra elements that we can discard to get to the real point, the timeless truths. . . . God's word reflects the various historical moments in which Scripture was written." Who would doubt this, and what would a timeless truth look like anyway? However, Enns goes further than this and sees enculturation both in the giving of Scripture and in its reception:

> If even the Bible is a cultural phenomenon through and through, we should not be surprised to see that our own theological thinking is wrapped in cultural clothing as well. . . . It is not that the Bible is a timeless, contextless how-to book that we are meant to apply to today's world. Rather, the Bible itself demonstrates the inevitable cultural dimension of any expression of the gospel.[119]

Enns leaves us with the unhappy impression that by being embedded in culture, both the writers and the readers of the Bible are in some way stuck in it. If that is the case, as James Barr remarked years ago, "there is no sense in which the Bible can be 'authoritative' for us."[120] Even if we are sure that Enns does not mean that, his formulation of cultural embeddedness unfortunately suggests that cultural relativity affects the biblical writers and ourselves in much the same way. In what respect can their witness be culture-transcending, and can we ever hope to cross the ugly ditch that separates us from the past to appropriate their meaning today?

This is why, says Enns, "every generation of Christians in every cultural context must seek to see how God is speaking to them in and through the Scriptures . . ." and many pages later, "this should lead us to a more willing recognition that the ex-

---

118. Ibid., 111.
119. Ibid., 17–18, 67.
120. J. Barr, *The Bible in the Modern World* (London: SCM Press, 1973), 40.

pression of our confession of the Bible as God's word has a provisional quality to it."[121] The disadvantage of something "provisional" is that it may be bettered because it was inferior, replaced because it was wrong, trashed because it's past the sell-by date, or done away with altogether because it has become superfluous. Unfortunately, the temporality implied in "provisional" means that what Christians believe is impermanent and therefore unreliable. This is a little different from affirming that God's truth forever stood and "shall from age to age endure."

Concretely speaking, let's think about the statement, "God was in Christ reconciling the world to Himself" (2 Cor. 5:19, NASB). It is a tensed proposition, not a "timeless truth," written by the apostle in a culture-specific circumstance and with a precise intention. Since the ascension, it has always and will always be true. Could it be bettered, replaced, trashed, or done away with?[122] We think not, and sincerely hope that Enns's "provisional" is only provisional.

Peter Enns is hardly in cahoots with the post-conservatives, a fact that is obvious from the major themes developed in his book. He looks more like a biblical foundationalist who wants to honor the received doctrines of the authority, inspiration, and inerrancy of Scipture.[123] As an Old Testament specialist he is profoundly aware of the questions that postmodern relativism forces upon the theologian. Enns seeks to take the humanity of Scripture seriously and reply to some of those questions in a modest, albeit flawed and unacceptable, way. His honesty is commendable, even painful at some points, as he seems to have an intuitive anticipation of the misunderstandings his proposed and, in a sense unexpected, answers might provoke.

Humanity Old, Humanity New

This presentation, like a lot of others, has fallen into the trap of being talk about talk about Scripture, and that's too bad. It was inevitable, really, in the light of the subject and because post-conservatism itself thrives on talk-talk. However, we will resist the temptation to say "goodnight and good luck" without hazarding a few personal suggestions about the humanity of Scripture.

What is depressingly uniform in our examination of the humanity of Scripture is the across-the-board negativity of the discussion. Jacques Levie, a Catholic biblical theologian of the last generation, who proposed a two-factor theandric theology from his own confessional standpoint, struggled to reconcile biblical inerrancy with the imperfections and defects of Scripture. You can sense his relief that for some matters, "the Church alone is competent to judge." Protestants have no such safety net! The second part of his book, "Inspiration and Catholic Exegesis," is a rather

121. Enns, *Inspiration and Incarnation*, 67, 168.
122. Cf. P. Helm, "Revealed Propositions and Timeless Truths," *Religious Studies* 8 (1972): 127–36.
123. His reply to Beale's "Myth, History and Inspiration," in *JETS* serves to show as much.

depressing catalogue of a struggle with the negative aspects of the humanity of Scripture exacerbated by ruthless criticism.[124]

Peter Enns is dead right when he points out that evangelicals have let modernism set the agenda for them. It is going on apace in post-conservatism too, and his efforts to find a new approach that provides a loophole through using an incarnational analogy merits our appreciation.[125] Evangelicals use exactly the same categories as liberals like Hans Küng, who puts it in a nutshell when he says the Bible "is unequivocally man's word . . . it is not without shortcomings and mistakes, concealment and confusions, limitations and errors."[126] J. K. S. Reid supplements the standard fare dished up by the modernistic thought-police by saying that men are "at fault. It is men in their finitude, and more exactly in their sinfulness, that introduce perversion into God's self-disclosure."[127] Perversion, strong word! The chains of human freedom link humanity to shortcomings, errors, finitude, and sinfulness, and postmodernity serves up a dessert of cultural, linguistic, and contextual relativities to boot. I bet not many theologians who glibly parrot Küng's words to describe Scripture would care to use them about their own books.

In other words, discussion about the humanity of Scripture has been hijacked and sequestered by the categories of a subhumanity that has become the norm. Evangelicals have ridden unawares into the ambush and then been forced to defend their position on nonbiblical grounds; Scripture's self-witness never speaks about the humanity of the writers in such a negative way; the farthest it goes is Paul's "treasure in earthen vessels." Go no further than Psalm 119 or Psalm 12: "Everyone utters lies to his neighbor; with flattering lips and a double heart they speak. . . . The words of the LORD are pure words, like silver refined in a furnace on the ground, purified seven times" (Ps. 12:2, 6). Now then, should theology follow the Küngs and the Reids of this world or the psalmist, knowing of course whom we must follow to sell books and have academia at our beck and call? Compromise will always be the devil.

How then can the humanity of Scripture be spoken about positively rather than negatively? To answer this question in a satisfying way here is impossible and would require considerable theological "imagineering," a word chosen intentionally. If the doctrine of Scripture in general benefits from many complementary models—prophecy, witness, incarnation, accommodation, regeneration, sanctification, complementarity—the humanity of Scripture does not necessarily come into its own in these constructs. The most favorable biblical model for developing a positive construction of the humanity of the Word is the *imago Dei,* created, fallen, renewed,

---

124. J. Levie, *The Bible, Word of God in the Words of Men* (London: Geoffrey Chapman, 1961), chaps. 8–10.
125. Enns, *Inspiration and Incarnation,* 46ff.
126. H. Kung, *On Being a Christian* (London: Collins, 1978), 463.
127. J. K. S. Reid, *The Authority of Scripture,* 184.

glorified, human nature in its fourfold state, to use Thomas Boston's classic categories.[128]

The advantage of this approach would be to open up an appreciation of the humanity of Scripture as wide as the functions of the image itself and its mandates. It would necessarily be eschatological in a biblico-redemptive perspective providing a context for discussion of questions of culture, history, and language. A vertical *koinonial* accent would also embrace questions of sin and grace, ethics, progressive revelation, and most centrally, christology. In addition, it would be possible to speak about the humanity of Scripture using human attributes that are related to the communicable divine attributes, a procedure that would naturally lend itself to a two-factor classical theology following Bavinck and Warfield. Attributes descriptive of the humanity of Scripture would be, following the restoration of the image in Christ (Eph. 4:24; Col. 3:10):

> *Ethical*: justice, righteousness, love, faithfulness, purity, holiness
> *Epistemological*: truth, knowledge, wisdom, discernment
> *Ontological*: inscripturation, creativity, lordship and, why not? beauty and melody[129]

In fact, the whole of the theology of the humanity of Scripture would become a theology of *beauty*, as the Lord himself, the true image, is supremely beautiful in all he was, is, did, and does, and all he will be eternally. It would be a theology of our humanity taking pleasure in and being uplifted by the humanity of Scripture, quite different from the spirit of much of the stuff I've had to plough through!

The doctrine of the humanity of Scripture cries out for a fresh approach that will liberate it from the self-destructiveness of modernism and postmodernism. Their negativity is either corrosive to confidence in and love of the Word, or simply makes it an academics' playground and preaching the Bible pastors' playtime.

Let us propose four perspectives to serve as axes for "reimagineering."

First, the fundamental matrix of the humanity of Scripture is that of *a new humanity in the old*. The primary aspect of linguistic communication is not that it is fallen but that it is creational. The postlapsarian revelation is redemptive and restorative and does not simply align itself with the conditions of fallen existence. On this point we feel obliged to part company with Bavinck and *a fortiori* with Berkouwer. Bavinck's fundamental accent is healthy in that the divine word comes into *this* fallen creation and becomes organically one with humanity and that man is not lifted from his situation by the presence of divinity. It is, however, true that the divine

---

128. Some hints of this are found in my book *James Barr and the Bible*, 349–79, and in my article "Covenant and the Humanity of Scripture."
129. W. Edgar, *Truth in All Its Glory* (Phillipsburg, NJ: P&R, 2004), 134–40. Cf. John Frame's "triadic" theology, *The Doctrine of God* (Phillipsburg, NJ: P&R, 2002), Appendix A.

presence does not accommodate itself to fallenness and leave it intact; rather it redeems and renews it. When Christ assumed human nature, it was in postlapsarian conditions, and yet in assuming a human nature the Spirit fashioned a sinless humanity.

This does not mean the specter of Docetism rears its ugly head yet again; it simply means that the God-breathed Scripture participates in the old creation as the divine sign and presence of the new creation. If fulfillment is not yet, the presence of the new creation is already certified in the resurrection of language to serve the gracious intention of God for humanity. Scripture does bear a servant form in its human aspects but it is also redemptive and provides the attestation of divine lordship in the area of communication. In the faithful and true promises of Scripture the future is already present. The new creation is present in the person of the resurrected Christ, and new humanity in Christ is already a new creation present in the old (2 Cor. 5:17; 4:6). Likewise, Scripture is tied to God's purpose in Christ, to bring the new from the old from the very start of redemptive history. It is correct to speak at one and the same time of the "oldness" of Scripture, but also of its "newness" and its uniqueness insofar as its natural home is the redemption of creation. In these three analogical instances the agent of newness is the Holy Spirit of Christ whose spiration creates Holy Scripture. This perspective can do justice, it seems to me, to the requirement of the divine and the human presented in the two-factor theologies of the Bavincks and Warfields.

Second, the humanity of Scripture has a particular *political* function, a function as broad as the creation, linked to the fashioning of the new humanity of the kingdom. In contrast with the construction of the megapoles, built by this world's megalomaniacs, Scripture partakes in the edification of *metapolis,* the metamorphosed city, the city of God.[130] The body of Christ, clothed with new-creational humanity, finds its fullness in the New Jerusalem, the focal point of which is the Lord Jesus himself:

> When revelation speaks of God and the Lamb receiving all power, glory and honor, it is because through the Lamb's victory the whole of creation is being brought back into its intended harmony, rescued from evil and death. God's authority, if we are to locate it at this point, is his sovereign power accomplishing this renewal of all creation . . . in Scripture itself God's purpose is not just to save human beings, but to renew the whole world.[131]

N. T. Wright is right to indicate that Scripture is the authority of God for establishing his eschatological kingdom, the *metapolis*. Scripture as the renewal word of the Spirit contributes to the true cultural project of mankind, a project that has as its

---

130. Kline, *Kingdom Prologue,* 269ff.
131. Wright, *Scripture and the Authority of God,* 21.

goal justice and the knowledge of the Lord that will fill the earth "as the waters cover the sea" (Isa. 11:9).[132]

Humanity is defined in relation to God before human culture begins and language with it (Gen. 1:26). Communication is a function of the divine image, not simply the social play of a group of self-interested consumers. Meredith J. Kline affirms in this perspective that "man himself is the chief end-product of human culture. Genealogy is the primary genre of human historiography."[133] The book of the covenant is the book of Zion where Rahab, Babylon, Philistia, Tyre, and Cush are named in the registers of the people. Zion! "This one was born here" (Psalm 87), a place where one day is better than a thousand in the courts of the wicked and where even the sparrow finds a home (Psalm 84).

Pagan man "of the earth" is called to true humanity through the word of the Spirit in Scripture. "Man was invested with a God-like authority and majesty and charged, in imitation of God, to perfect the consecration of the world to his royal use and honor." Scripture renews the covenant in grace as a redemptive word, gives back dominion to man as the image of God, clothes him (2 Corinthians 5) in the righteousness of reconciliation, and calls him to appear in Zion. Scripture discloses God's kingdom polity, and its humanity is made for true humanity.

Third, the humanity of Scripture is Christ-centered, not in terms of the christological analogy, or because the Old Testament Scripture is *christotelic*, an interesting proposition made by Enns, but because *Christ is the conclusion of the whole historical process*.[134] As the "Alpha and Omega" he is the focus of God's works at the beginning, at the end, and in all that is between; Scripture bears witness to this fact in its unfolding story of redemption in three ways. Christ is the Creator (John 1; Col. 1:15–20; Heb. 1:1–2; etc.), he is the first and last who is promised by the prophets as the coming Messiah (Isa. 48:12–15), and he is the coming future glorious One who will judge the earth and establish the new creation (Rev. 1:1–8; 21:5–8; 22:12–15). Because we have the end of the story in the Revelation of John, we know the outcome and can trace the christotelic storyline right throughout history. Scripture is God's Word tracing his history with humankind and providing, in the completed canon, the key to the unity of God's redemptive purposes in Christ. Finally, Christ is the true image of God in the New Testament. Man, created in the image of his true humanity *in*

---

132. This will not be accomplished on a human timeline but by an action of *diastasis*, the wrenching of the new from the old when Christ appears in glory. Cf. K. Schilder, *Christ and Culture* (Winnipeg: Premier Press, 1977).

133. Kline, *Kingdom Prologue*, 69.

134. Enns, *Inspiration and Incarnation*, 154–56. Enns links the *christotelic* to an *ecclesiotelic* principle; the second is a function of the first, saying that the Old Testament is fulfilled in the body of Christ. This is an interesting suggestion. My own point of view is broader in a total eschatological sense. Christ is the consummation of all of creation, and its history and the story must be read back from its conclusion, an approach I proposed in an article "Eschatologie," *Dictionnaire Théologie Biblique* (Cléon d'Andran: Excelsis, 2006), 561–71. Cf. A. König, *The Eclipse of Christ in Eschatology: Towards a Christ-Centered Approach* (Grand Rapids: Eerdmans, 1989), from whom I learned this perspective.

princeps, is restored to it through adoption into the body of Christ.[135] The progression of humanity to this goal is described in the progressive human revelation of Scripture, with a divine purpose: salvation of the people of God through transformation according to the image of the second Adam.[136] This is an adequate context for the notion of accommodation.

Finally, there is no doubt a link that can be made between the humanity of Scripture and humanity in regeneration, a link to which Bavinck has already pointed:

> In revelation it is God's own purpose to mold people in whom his image is again fully restored. He gave us not only his Son but also the Holy Spirit in order that the Spirit should regenerate us, write his law in our heart and equip us for every good work. Regeneration, adoption, sanctification, glorification—are all proofs that God educates his children for freedom. . . .[137]

John Webster has made a similar connection between God's active self-presence in revelation through his Word and through sanctification. "The Spirit of Christ sanctifies and inspires creaturely realities as servants of God's presence."[138] Mark D. Thompson, in his monograph, *A Clear and Present Word,* is critical of Webster's proposition, and I share some of his reserves: "It is not enough to speak of human language as a creaturely phenomenon that is commandeered, or even 'sanctified' as a vehicle for divine self revelation. God is himself the source of language. He is the first speaker and invests language with a deep significance for generating and nourishing personal relationships."[139] Obviously this perspective on language and the divine action in Scripture would be fruitful for developing a theology of revelation in terms of a divine speech act, very much the fashion at present.

In more classic terms it seems that Bavinck's reference to the work of the Spirit in revelation and renewal is useful if the priority of the Spirit is maintained in both areas. God renews human language in inspiration and the inscripturation of his Word of revelation, and he renews human beings through his life-giving Spirit. There is a monergism of the Spirit in both instances; God is the author of Scripture and the author of salvation. He calls his prophets and apostles to speak his word, and he calls his people to confess his name. However, this is not all. As the Spirit who initiates the work of regeneration continues that work through the stages of the *ordo salutis,* so also the inspired Word continues to be the Word of God as the Holy Spirit

---

135. P. E. Hughes, *The True Image: The Origin and Destiny of Man in Christ* (Grand Rapids: Eerdmans, 1989) and my article "In Search of the Image of God."
136. Cf. R. B. Gaffin, "Speech and the Image of God: Biblical Reflections on Language and Its Usages," in D. Van Drunen, ed., *The Pattern of Sound Doctrine: Systematic Theology at Westminster Seminaries* (Phillipsburg, NJ: P&R, 2004).
137. Bavinck, *Reformed Dogmatics,* 1:473; cf. 1:443–46.
138. Webster, *Holy Scripture,* 40; cf. 17–30.
139. M. D. Thompson, *A Clear and Present Word,* 166. Cf. also Carson's critique "Three More Books on the Bible," 14–16.

speaks through it *hic et nunc*. The dynamic relation of Spirit and Word is not the property of Barthians! God is the perpetual author of Scripture, and his word remains a dynamic, penetrating, and redemptive force as the *viva vox Dei*.

The notion of the Word of God portrays a rich, manifold, and profoundly inter-related web of divine acts in which God as a communicating God spoke and continues to speak:

> *Verbum Dei*, the Word of God, signifies the virtue and power of God; it also indicated the Son of God, who is the second person of the most revered Trinity . . . But . . . the Word of God properly signifies *the speech of God* and the revelation of God's will; first of all uttered in a lively voice by the mouth of Christ, the prophets and the apostles; and after that registered in the writings which are rightly called "holy and divine Scriptures."[140]

Surely happy and exciting days lie ahead for the reconstruction of the doctrine of the humanity of Scripture, if evangelicals can shake themselves free from the shackles of negativity and break out of the stockade into which they have retreated because of the terror that flies on the wings of politically correct culture.

---

140. H. Bullinger, *Decades*, 51, quoted by R. A. Muller, *Post-reformation Reformed Dogmatics* (Grand Rapids: Baker, 1993), 2:186.

2

Sola Scriptura as an Evangelical Theological Method?

JOHN BOLT

~~~~~~~

The simple question I want to pursue in this chapter is whether the Reformational slogan *sola Scriptura* is an appropriate *methodological* framework for evangelical systematic theology today.[1] It is my contention that while fidelity to Scripture must always be a hallmark of orthodox Christian theology, "by Scripture alone" is not only an unduly restrictive criterion for a theological method but also, especially in our current situation, potentially harmful to the proclamation of the gospel's truth. Good, relevant, Christian theology, especially today, I will argue, must also be characterized by an explicit metaphysic that though it cannot arise directly from the biblical data—the Bible is not a book of metaphysics—is nonetheless consistent with Scripture and perhaps even coinheres with it.

I shall begin by highlighting some attempts to state a theological method in terms of the principle of *sola Scriptura*, indicate why this is a necessary but not sufficient condition for Christian theology, and illustrate from the great tradition why our greatest theologians—from Augustine to Thomas Aquinas to Francis Turretin to Herman Bavinck—were not strict biblicists in their theologizing but also serious metaphysicians. Sebastian Rehnman has given the reason for this clearly in the case of Francis Turretin as the model example of a seventeenth-century Protestant theo-

---

1. This chapter is a major rewriting of a key chapter of a work in progress on theological prolegomena. I gladly acknowledge my debt to Calvin Theological Seminary student David Sytsma who has served as my faculty assistant for the past two years. His mastery of the philosophical tradition in relation to theology far exceeds my own, and his help especially on the section dealing with "the great tradition" has been invaluable.

logian: "Although classic Protestant theology emphasized special revelation, it never claimed that revelation constituted a complete Christian theistic system. The slogan was *sola Scriptura,* not *nuda Scriptura.* For the perfection of Scripture does not, according to Turretin, exclude all human tradition and is inclusive of inferences."[2]

While revelation is received by faith rather than reason, Turretin is concerned that divine revelation be considered reasonable. If not, communicating the truth of the Christian faith would be impossible. "He was well aware of the fact that if a purported divine revelation was to be intelligible, if the Christian revelation was to be intelligible, the essential nature of the divine revealer had to be known (at least rudimentarily) prior to special revelation if that revelation should be possible to relate or identify with God."[3]

In sum: "The concept of deity then cannot be exclusively derived from special or supernatural revelation, but the philosophical or metaphysical inquiry into our idea of God is vitally necessary to Turretin's theology of revelation."[4]

In conclusion, for the same reasons, I shall state why it is crucial that we follow the lead of the great tradition represented by theologians such as Turretin, even though this proposal is the exact opposite of most contemporary pleas for renewing contemporary evangelical church and theology.[5]

The Meaning of "Method": Contemporary Discussions

We first need to clarify what we mean by "method." The word comes to us from the Greek, μετα + οδος' = (literally) "the way with." In this vein, physical scientists may refer to "the scientific method," philosophers to an "analytic method," and theatrical people to "method acting." What all these have in common is a *consistent pattern* of recognizable procedures or approaches that produce a specific result or effect. Theologian Bernard Lonergan stated it this way: "[Method is] a normative pattern of recurrent and related operations yielding cumulative and progressive results."[6]

Methods for gaining knowledge range from the simple to the very complex. For basic physical or chemical measurement such as determining the relative weights of three stones or when we want to know the chemical composition of a liquid, we subject our material to a well-defined and rigorous set of qualitative and quantitative tests. When designed properly and executed exactly, such tests performed on the same stones or liquid will yield the same conclusion whether done in Boston or Bo-

---

2. Sebastian Rehnman, "Theistic Metaphysics and Biblical Exegesis: Francis Turretin on the Concept of God," *Religious Studies* 38 (2001): 170; see 1.12.2, 8 in Turretin's *Institutes of Elenctic Theology,* 3 vols. (Phillipsburg, NJ: P&R, 1992–97).
3. Rehnman, "Theistic Metaphysics and Biblical Exegesis," 170; cf. Turretin, *Institutes,* 1.12.5.
4. Rehnman, "Theistic Metaphysics and Biblical Exegesis," 170.
5. These calls generally invite us to repudiate the classic theologically-based metaphysical tradition in favor of a postmodern epistemology. One example: Carl Raschke, *The Next Reformation: Why Evangelicals Must Embrace Postmodernity* (Grand Rapids: Baker Academic, 2005).
6. Bernard J. F. Lonergan, *Method in Theology* (New York: Herder and Herder, 1972), 5.

livia, by a male or a female, and regardless of the researcher's particular ethnicity or race.[7] It is important to emphasize this point here because the key to all scientific methodology is realizing that one must deal with universal reality and not individual subjective perception.[8]

It is true, of course, that it is more complicated when researchers consider the human person. Though there are certain tests that yield relatively consistent results when administered to the same person over time,[9] we know that subjective and temporal factors such as momentary stress directly affect the outcome of even basic physical measurements for such things as hypertension. When it comes to human internal states, we are not totally at a loss, but we are limited. We can do interviews of a person—how are you feeling?—but we know that interviewees don't always tell the truth. Artistic works—poetry, painting, music composition—are also useful in providing *indirect* access to a person's inner soul, but "reading" people through their works requires a sophisticated hermeneutical ability based on much training and experience. We are able to hide from each other, and it takes people of great skill to break through the numerous barriers we throw up to hide, distort, or resist being interpreted.

After that brief introduction it might seem that speaking about theology as a science and a proper scientific method to do *theology*, finding the right "way with" God, is presumptuous and impossible. "Who has known the mind of the Lord?" (1 Cor. 2:16, from Isa. 40:13, NASB). And it would be, were it not for one thing—God has revealed himself to humanity. I do not have the space to defend the following thesis in detail, but offer it here as a summary of the church's basic presupposition, a presupposition I am happy to also claim as my own: *"All theology as* λογός *about* θεός *would be presumptuous and impious if it were not for the fact that God has spoken to us first and revealed the truth about himself to us."*[10]

---

7. As will become apparent in the course of this chapter, I am assuming the validity of a realist epistemology and metaphysic. I do not have the space to defend this position in any detail, and readers who dispute the position's claim are encouraged to read my essay "An Emerging Critique of the Postmodern, Evangelical Church," *Calvin Theological Journal* 41, no. 2 (2006): 205–21, and the literature cited there. Also see, Kevin J. Vanhoozer, ed., *The Cambridge Companion to Postmodern Theology* (Cambridge and New York: Cambridge University Press, 2003). Anyone who is enamored of the current faddish postmodern epistemology should read New York University physicist Alan D. Sokal's spoof essay, "Transgressing the Boundaries: Toward a Transformative Hermeneutics of Quantum Gravity," which he submitted to the respected social science journal, *Social Text*, and actually had published. Sokal contended in this essay that postmodernism required a new nonreferential mathematics and physics and was taken seriously until he himself revealed it as a hoax. The article was published in *Social Text* 46/47 (1996): 217–52 and is available online at: http://physics.nyu.edu/facculty/sokal/transgress_v2/transgress_v2_singlefile.html.

8. Bavinck puts it this way: "The human mind . . . does not stop with . . . representations. Scientific knowledge is not produced by the senses but by the intellect. . . . The observation of phenomena is necessary and good, but it is not the only or highest activity of the mind. The object of science is not the particular but the universal, the logical, the idea" (*Reformed Dogmatics,* ed. John Bolt, trans. John Vriend [Grand Rapids: Baker, 2003], 1:229).

9. This is true of basic physical measurements (blood pressure, electrocardiograms, etc.), physiometric tests of strength and aptitude, as well as psychological tests such as the MMPI or Myers-Briggs.

10. Incidentally, the reality of revelation is also the reason why theology cannot be trapped into simply choosing between the two sides in the great modern epistemological debate, namely foundationalism *or* antifoundational-

So, then, our question is not whether theology as λογός about θεός is possible apart from biblical revelation; that question is settled and binding because of our conviction about revelation. Rather, we are asking whether theological method can be defined in terms of *Scripture alone*, whether Christian theology is in fact nothing else but good exegesis and interpretation of Scripture alone. Before we go on to consider some attempts to do contemporary systematic theology as essentially biblical theology, a few more words about method are in order.

A defining characteristic of modern thought is its preoccupation with questions of epistemology: "how do we know?" A corollary of this characteristic is that the modern era is also obsessed with questions of methodology, usually under the rubric of "hermeneutics."[11] The same is true of modern theology; methodological questions often overwhelm and even determine the content of theology.[12] We shall not intrude into this enormous body of debate but take as our starting point a more traditional understanding of method from Louis Berkhof: "Strictly speaking, however, the method of dogmatics concerns only the way in which the content of Dogmatics is obtained, that is the source or sources from which it is derived, and the manner in which it is secured."[13] It should be noted that in some cases the structure or pattern of organization of theological content itself is exactly what theologians mean by *method*. When informing readers about the *method* they will be following, they simply list possible options for the system's structure and then indicate their own preference.[14]

---

ism. Foundationalism is the view of modern thinkers such as Descartes who think that truth claims can only have universal validity if they are shown to be necessary or unchangeable and that the human mind can in fact find such unchanging principles. By contrast, the antifoundationalist claims that no such foundations exist. "They are all a matter of historical and cultural circumstances, and therefore lack universal validity. All claims, including theological claims, are social constructions" (Diogenes Allen, "Intellectual Inquiry and Spiritual Formation," in Ellen Charry, ed., *Inquiring After God: Classic and Contemporary Readings* [Oxford and Malden, MA: Blackwell, 2000], 26). Furthermore, "if antifoundationalism were true we would be left with a hopeless pluralism or relativism of religious claims. However, Christian teachings concerning our knowledge of God transform the situation. The entire framework of foundationalism and antifoundationalism is transcended by the conviction that God must manifest Godself [*sic*] and that we must become spiritually formed in order to respond to God's manifestations. . . . Warrant for Christian claims can be found because all claims about God are *suspended*, so to speak, from that which is not a member of the universe" (Allen, "Intellectual Inquiry," 27).

11. See Hans-Georg Gadamer, *Truth and Method*, 2d ed., trans. Joel Weinsheimer and Donald G. Marshall (New York: Crossroad, 1989); Gadamer, *Hermeneutics, Religion and Ethics*, trans. Joel Weinsheimer (New Haven: Yale University Press, 1999). For a recent attempt to recover hermeneutics from its philosophical captivity and for an orthodox, evangelical theology, see Jenz Zimmerman, *Recovering Theological Hermeneutics: An Incarnational-Trinitarian Theory of Interpretation* (Grand Rapids: Baker, 2004).

12. A good example is the three-volume *Systematic Theology* of Paul Tillich (Chicago: University of Chicago Press, 1951–1963), where the method of correlation affects the entire content. The same is true of Friedrich Schleiermacher's *The Christian Faith*, trans. H. R. MacIntosh and J. R. Stewart (Edinburgh: T & T Clark, 1989) for whom the methodological principle of deriving content from the experience of absolute dependence becomes the reason for relegating the Trinity—the core doctrine of the Christian religion—to an appendix.

13. Louis Berkhof, *Systematic Theology: Introduction* (Grand Rapids: Eerdmans, 1998), 61. Similarly, H. Bavinck, *Reformed Dogmatics*: "By the method of dogmatics, broadly speaking, one must understand the manner in which the dogmatic material is acquired and treated," 1:61.

14. See, e.g., A. M. Mills, *Fundamental Christian Theology*, 2 vols. (Salem, OH: Schmul, 1980), 1:24. Mills notes the two systems of Charles Hodge (*Systematic Theology*, 3 vols. [1872–1873. repr. Grand Rapids:

One more preliminary note: What follows in this essay is not a complete survey of theological methods used by evangelical theologians today. Furthermore, in identifying certain theologians and theological works as "biblical" theologians I wish to be clear that I am considering their *explicitly* stated theological method. As theologians explore such doctrinal areas as the person and work of Christ, the doctrine of salvation, they inevitably bring into consideration the conciliar decrees of Nicea, Ephesus, and Chalcedon, not to mention Dordt. However, all too often the explicitly stated theological method at the beginning does not acknowledge the substantive role of church tradition in the interpretation of Scripture; some theologians claim to be doing nothing more than good historical-grammatical exegesis of Scripture. One of the main points of this essay is to remind us that theological method is more complex than often allowed. As Lutheran theologian Carl Braaten has observed, "It should be evident from the division of theology as a whole into exegetical, historical, systematic, and practical disciplines that the method appropriate to theology is bound to be complex. . . . There is no one absolute approach that can do everything theology requires."[15]

Systematic Theology as Biblical Theology

We shall now consider theologians who claim that *methodologically* their only concern is with Scripture and its interpretation. Note that this places them in the same methodological sphere as the first generation or two of Christian theologians who had available to them as their source for doing normative theology only the apostolic testimony that eventually became the canonical texts of Scripture.[16] Today, however, we have some two millennia of Christian church reflection on Scripture along with certain received consensual dogmas such as the Nicene statement of the trinitarian character of the faith. We need to ask, therefore, whether anything forbids a theologian from beginning with the received consensual tradition, or even, in the case of an explicitly confessional tradition such as the Reformed or Lutheran, from taking the post-Reformation ecclesial documents as the starting point and framework for the theological system. A theologian who used the *Belgic Confession* or the *Book of Concord*, for example, as the basic structure and starting point for a theological text would be perfectly within his or her rights as an orthodox, confessional, and evangelical theologian. It is important to highlight this point because it is often forgotten today that these confessional documents are both a restatement of biblical truth and the normative *biblical* framework within which confessional theologians operate.

Eerdmans, 1982]) and John Miley (*Systematic Theology*, 2 vols. [New York: Eaton and Mains, 1892–1894]) and indicates he will follow the latter. No reasons are given, nor are we provided with a description of the method beyond the claim that creeds, mysticism, and rationalism are false sources for theology.

15. Carl Braaten and Robert Jenson, eds., *Christian Dogmatics*, 2 vols. (Philadephia: Fortress, 1984), 1:16.

16. "In the earliest period of the Christian church, it lived by the word of the gospel proclaimed to it by the apostles, which was clarified and expanded in the Epistles and Gospels" (Bavinck, *Reformed Dogmatics*, 1:62).

There are a number of distinct ways in which this basic approach of restating biblical doctrine is taken. We shall consider the following types:

a. Systematic theology as restatement of biblical doctrines.
b. Systematic theology as restatement via integrated biblical themes.
c. Systematic theology as restatement of the biblical narrative.
d. Systematic theology as restatement of the biblical-credal faith.

As Restatement of Biblical Doctrines

Notwithstanding the importance of confessional identities, even a theologian as confessionally attuned as Charles Hodge still states his theological method in terms of strictly biblical data. Hodge indicates his preference for the so-called inductive method thus: "The true method of theology is, therefore, the inductive, which assumes that the Bible contains all the facts or truths which form the contents of theology, just as the facts of nature are the contents of the natural sciences."[17]

Methodologically, thus, Hodge begins with the facts of Scripture as data, using these data to build up a structure of doctrine. However, Hodge's method is not *simply* biblical since he also has in mind a certain structure, albeit a structure derived inductively from the biblical data:

> It is also assumed that the relation of these biblical facts to each other, the principles involved in them, the laws which determine them, are in the facts themselves, and are to be deduced from them, just as the laws of nature are deduced from the facts of nature. In neither case are the principles derived from the mind and imposed upon the facts, but equally in both departments, the principles or laws are deduced from the facts and recognized by the mind.[18]

Here we see an implicitly realist epistemology, though Hodge, unlike say Bavinck, does not provide a *theological* ground for it. Incidentally, it is interesting to note that in spite of his insistence on a strictly biblical-inductive method, Hodge's organizational structure in his *Systematic Theology* turns out to be similar to the classic loci structure of the so-called "synthetic method."[19]

In his *Systematic Theology* Hodge does not delve into questions of theological encyclopedia in the same way his son Archibald Alexander Hodge did in his *Outlines of Theology,* namely distinguishing "systematic theology" from "exegetical theology" as well as three other branches in the "encyclopedia of theological sciences," namely

17. Hodge, *Systematic Theology,* 1:17.
18. Ibid.
19. See L. Berkhof, *Introductory Volume to Systematic Theology,* pt. 1 in *Systematic Theology,* new ed. (Grand Rapids: Eerdmans, 1996), 74–75; Bavinck, *Reformed Dogmatics,* 1:93–95, 112. The slight difference between Bavinck/Berkhof and Hodge is that the latter has only four basic loci—theology proper, anthropology, soteriology, and eschatology—with christology and ecclesiology discussed under the locus of soteriology.

"apologetics," "practical theology," and "historical theology."[20] In the younger Hodge's work we have a clear statement of systematic theology as biblical theology. He defines exegetical theology as "embracing the critical determination of the *ipsissima verba* of Divine Revelation, and the Interpretation [of] their meaning."[21] Exegetical theology, in other words, embraces textual criticism and basic exegesis along with hermeneutics. Systematic theology, however, also stays strictly within biblical limits when it is defined as embracing the development into an all-embracing and self-consistent system of the contents of that revelation, and its subsequent elucidation and defense.[22]

A more recent representative of that Princeton tradition, though he taught at Westminster Seminary, is John Murray, who in a seminal essay on the task of systematic theology makes the following distinction:

> Since the principal source of revelation is Holy Scripture, systematic theology must be concerned to be biblical not one whit less than biblical theology. The difference is merely one of method.
>
> Biblical theology deals with the data of special revelation from the standpoint of history; systematic theology deals with its totality as a finished product. *The method of systematic theology is logical, that of biblical theology historical.*[23]

Murray does acknowledge that systematic theology must deal "with the data of general revelation insofar as these data bear upon theology," but in definition and practice Murray sees its task much as the Hodges do: the systematic (rather than historical) ordering of biblical givens. Strictly speaking, both are forms of "biblical theology"; one is the comprehensive and logical structuring of biblical doctrine, the other is *historia revelationis.*[24]

This pattern is followed by a number of recent evangelical systematic theologies such as that of Reformed theologian Robert Reymond, who defines theology's proper method in terms of "Christ's own theological method," pointing to our Lord's sermon in Nazareth (Luke 4:16–21) and to his place in the Old Testament prophetic writings (John 5:46). Reymond concludes: "It is Christ himself then who establishes

---

20. Archibald Alexander Hodge, *Outlines of Theology*, rewritten and enl. (New York: Robert Carter and Brothers, 1880), 17–18.

21. Ibid., 17.

22. Ibid.

23. John Murray, "Systematic Theology," in John H. Skilton, ed., *The New Testament Student and Theology*, vol. 3, The New Testament Student (Nutley, NJ: Presbyterian and Reformed, 1976), 18. This essay was reprinted from the *Westminster Theological Journal* 26, no. 1 (1963).

24. This is essentially also the viewpoint of Geerhardus Vos to whom Murray makes favorable reference in his essay. Abraham Kuyper also speaks of *historia revelationis* in the third volume of his *Encyclopaedie der Heilige Godgeleerdheid*, 2d rev. edition (Kampen: Kok, 1908), sec. 17:166–79. For Kuyper this discipline belongs to the "pragmatic" division of the "bibliological group" (in contrast to the "canonical" and "exegetical" divisions of this group). In other words, it is more like archaeology than exegesis. For a fascinating discussion of similarities and especially key differences between Kuyper and Vos, see Richard B. Gaffin Jr., "Geerhardus Vos and the Interpretation of Paul," in E. R. Geehan, ed., *Jerusalem and Athens: Critical Discussions on the Theology and Apologetics of Cornelius Van Til* (Nutley, NJ: Presbyterian and Reformed, 1971), 228–37.

the pattern and end of all theologizing; the *pattern:* we must make the exposition of Scripture the basis of our theology; the *end*: we must arrive finally at him in all our theological labors.[25] A similar approach is advocated by Wayne Grudem in his *Systematic Theology.* According to Grudem, the distinguishing mark of systematic theology is that it answers the question, "What does the whole Bible teach us today about any given topic?"[26] Methodologically, this means essentially "collecting and understanding all the relevant passages of Scripture on any given topic."[27] The key tool for a theologian, in this view, is a biblical concordance.[28] Leaving aside the problem of using an English language concordance for the original Hebrew and Greek texts of the Old and New Testaments, this does not deliver on the promise of the "now," the "today," in Grudem's own definition. Methodologically, it is not at all clear how contemporaneity figures into the equation. Grudem simply assumes it. Furthermore, what factors lead a theologian to pick one topic over another and in what order? Why, for example, choose to discuss God before creation when the narrative of the Bible itself begins with creation? These sorts of questions are not even raised. Grudem's description of his method fails to explain adequately what he actually does as well as to provide any clue to the final structure and content he achieves.

Evangelical theologian Millard J. Erickson's popular *Christian Theology*[29] is also a biblical theology that begins with exegesis, and from this seeks to construct a body of topics. However, Erickson also includes nine additional steps after "collecting the biblical material," steps that incorporate history, culture, extra-biblical sources, contemporary expressions, and development of a central, integrative theme.[30] At the heart of the whole exercise, however, is "identification of the essence of the doctrine."[31] We are justified, therefore, in considering Erickson's *Systematic Theology* one of the more complete and thorough examples of a work that utilizes a *biblical-doctrinal method.* Demonstrating that he is not bound to the short traditional list of six or so loci, Erickson's method yields the following extended list of topics and organization, which does follow a fairly traditional order:

1. Studying God (Prolegomena)
2. Knowing God (Revelation)
3. What God Is Like

25. Robert L. Reymond, *A New Systematic Theology of the Christian Faith*, 2d ed. (Nashville: Thomas Nelson, 1998), xxviii.
26. Wayne Grudem, *Systematic Theology: An Introduction to Biblical Doctrine* (Grand Rapids: Zondervan, 1994), 21.
27. Ibid., 35.
28. "The process outlined above is possible for any Christian who can read his or her Bible and can look up words in a concordance," ibid., 37.
29. Erickson, *Christian Theology*, 2d ed., (Grand Rapids: Baker, 1998).
30. Ibid., 63.
31. Ibid., 75 (step 6).

4. What God Does (Creation, Providence)
5. Humanity
6. Sin
7. The Person of Christ
8. The Work of Christ
9. The Holy Spirit
10. Salvation
11. The Church
12. The Last Things

As Restatement via Integrated Biblical Themes

One of the steps in Erickson's biblical-doctrinal method as described above is the development of a central, integrative theme. Erickson himself chooses "the magnificence of God" for his theme.[32] Others choose different integrative themes. Stanley Grenz, who defines theology as "the conscious reflection—within the context in which we live and minister—on the faith commitment we share as Christians," then picks "community" as the integrative theme for his work. "Taken as a whole the Bible asserts that God's progress is directed to the bringing into being of community in the highest sense—a reconciled people, living within a renewed creation, and enjoying the presence of their Redeemer."[33] It is fair to ask whether this joining together and considering under one single theme the content of faith and the people created by faith in the gospel does not lead to some confusion. Is community the final goal of revelation? Why not choose as theme the glory of God, or covenant, or kingdom? Is community really as central as either of those other prominent biblical realities? What is theology all about? Is it not about God? Does this choice of community not conflate the *audience* for whom theology is done with the *content* of theology itself? When this is done, one risks exchanging the verticality of theology's object (to know God better) as well as the end of theology (the glory of God) for a horizontal goal—building up community. While the latter is of course a worthwhile goal, it is properly a derivative and subordinate goal—not the primary one. In fact, it could be argued that only when God is the primary object and end of theology can the goal of community be achieved.[34] To make community the primary goal is to be eternally frustrated in accomplishing it. What is interesting here again is that the method yields a fairly traditional organization with one important wrinkle: theology proper, anthropology, christology, *pneumatology*, ecclesiology, eschatology. What is not clear is how the one variant—pneumatology—arises specifically out of the integrative theme of community. If anything, it inverts the

---

32. Ibid., 82.
33. Stanley J. Grenz, *Community for the People of God* (Nashville: Broadman & Holman, 1994), 17–30.
34. According to Augustine in *De Doctrina Christiana*, 1:5–7; my thanks to David Sytsma for this reference.

order: the Holy Spirit creates community—the community does not generate a doctrine of the Spirit prior to that formation.

This critique is not given to suggest that one cannote write appropriate and useful books of theology with the stated method of using an integrated theme.[35] My point is simply to note that the stated method of summarizing biblical doctrine by means of an integrative theme in both of the cases considered (Erickson and Grenz) fails because though the theme does get picked up in the content of what is discussed in each locus or topic, it has no bearing at all on the structure and organization of the system as a whole. On this score, the next type we shall consider fares much better.

As Restatement of the Biblical Narrative

In this section we consider theological systems that are structured by the basic creation-fall-redemption-consummation narrative of Scripture itself. Only the first one (Gabriel Fackre) starts from an explicit commitment to narrative as such, as the structurally defining and determining category. The other two examples, Gordon J. Spykman's *Reformational Theology* and Hendrikus Berkhof's *Christian Faith* each state different prolegomena. We have chosen, nonetheless, to feature both Spykman and Berkhof here as examples of systematic theology as restatement of biblical narrative because the final *structure* of their theological system is essentially that of the biblical narrative.

Fackre relates "story" in a theological sense directly to "the narrower literary meaning: an account of characters and events in a plot moving over time and space through conflict toward resolution."[36] This is not to be identified with history, though history is of course at the base of the biblical story. Rather, a narrative orientation to Scripture seeks to "discuss the Christian faith in the context of a literary form—story in its delimited sense—with its characteristic features of tension and vision, pain and hope, movement and consummation."[37] Fackre's *The Christian Story* yields the following structure.

> Prologue: God
> 1. Creation
> 2. Fall
> 3. Covenant
> 4. Jesus Christ: Person and Work
> 5. Church: Nature and Mission
> 6. Salvation
> 7. Consummation

35. Although, in my judgment, the three-volume effort by Bruce Demarest and Gordon Lewis, *Integrative Theology* (Grand Rapids: Academie, 1987), does not succeed at the task either.
36. Gabriel Fackre, *The Christian Story*, rev. ed. (Grand Rapids: Eerdmans, 1984), 5.
37. Ibid.

The structure thus fits the stated method; the topics discussed follow the order of Scripture's own story. The structural logic is narrative.

Gordon Spykman's prolegomena, by contrast, is based on his commitment to the reformational philosophical work of Herman Dooyeweerd and Th. Vollenhoven (the Philosophy of the Cosmonomic Idea).[38] For Spykman, "the most fitting prolegomena to a Reformed dogmatics is a Christian philosophy."[39] However, the link between a Christian philosophy and Reformed dogmatics is indirect; it is bridged by a Christian worldview. "The deeper background to both [a biblically directed philosophy and a Reformed dogmatics] is a communally held Christian worldview, which binds scholars and the rest of the Christian community together as partners in faith. This jointly held worldview plays a bridging role between commitment to Scripture and the scientific enterprise in both philosophy and theology. It serves to integrate biblical faith and theoretical reflection."[40] Spykman describes this journey as a "normative movement from faith through worldview to philosophy and theology."[41] His summary statement: "Christian philosophy, grounded in the biblical faith and a Christian worldview, offers the most promising prolegomena to Reformed dogmatics."[42] What this yields is a "reordering of basic dogmas" with a deliberate aim "at overcoming the abstract and rationalist way of dealing with Christian doctrines which is inherent in the older 'loci' method, betraying as it does the influences of Protestant scholastic thought."[43] Spykman judges that his reordering—along the lines of creation-fall-redemption-consummation—is "a consistent follow-through on the spirit and thrust of [his earlier] prolegomenal discussion" and serves as an attempt "to give the historical-redemptive pattern of biblical revelation a firmer place in Reformed dogmatics."[44] At the same time, it also follows a trinitarian-credal line. The following structure is the result.

1. Foundations
2. The Good Creation
3. Sin and Evil
4. The Way of Salvation
5. The Consummation

Leaving aside for now the prejudicial language of "abstract" and "rationalistic" as descriptions of Protestant Orthodoxy, it must be said that in the actual content of

---

38. Gordon J. Spykman, *Reformational Theology: A New Paradigm for Doing Dogmatics* (Grand Rapids: Eerdmans, 1992), 100.
39. Ibid., 101.
40. Ibid., 102.
41. Ibid.
42. Ibid., 107.
43. Ibid., 135.
44. Ibid., 135.

Spykman's work he does deliver on the promise to make good use of the fruits of twentieth-century Reformed biblical theology with its emphasis on redemptive history (Geerhardus Vos, Herman Ridderbos, etc.). That is the strength of his work. What is not so clear, however, is exactly why this requires the circuitous journey from biblical faith to biblical worldview and then even to Christian philosophy, all in order finally to get to Reformed dogmatic theology. Why is it important to insert as an intermediate step the development of a Christian philosophy prior to doing theology itself? Herman Bavinck, it is worth noting, insisted that theologians not follow the lead of Schleiermacher and make the theologian dependent on letting philosophy be in any way determinative for theological method and task. Theology must go its own way; it has its own epistemology and metaphysic. Bavinck writes: "There is indeed no room for a philosophical theory of fundamental principles that must first lay the foundation for the study of theology and has the right to justify this pursuit. If dogmatics or theology in general did not, like other disciplines, have its own fundamental principles (*principia*), it could not lay claim to the name of being 'science concerning God'(*scientia de Deo*)."[45] This question is all the more pressing since it is not clear what the difference is between the worldview that is necessary *before* one does philosophy and the theology that comes *after* the philosophical inquiry. What Spykman describes as a Reformed worldview[46] looks for all the world like a Reformed *theological* statement in miniature. One could, therefore, just as well conclude that a Reformed theology is the prerequisite to doing Christian philosophy.

A final problem: the Christian philosophy Spykman describes is one that leads him to designate theology not as *scientia de Deo* but, like Schleiermacher, as a special science analyzing faith—pistology, in other words.[47] Not only does that have its own problems,[48] but there is no substantive link between Spykman's *definition* of theology as pistology and the *content* of his work. The content and its structure is derived from the worldview, a worldview that itself could be described as a piece of elementary theology. So, then, why do we need a prior philosophical definition *in order to do theology?* From Spykman's own example we could conclude that in fact we don't. It is possible to do theology without a prior explicitly stated and operational philosophical prolegomena.

Hendrikus Berkhof in his *Christian Faith* offers us a quite different method, though the organization of his content is not unlike Spykman's in many ways. He

---

45. Bavinck, *Reformed Dogmatics*, 1:209.
46. Spykman, *Reformational Theology*, 98ff.
47. Ibid., 102–4.
48. Ibid., cf. 104. *Pisto*logy, of course, really isn't *theo*logy at all; it is not about God but about faith. In its crudest form this would suggest theology as a kind of Gallup poll effort, taking the pulse of the Christian community and describing its beliefs at any given time. Here all normativity for theology flees; there is no right or wrong belief, just actual belief. This is no longer *logos* about *theos* but *logos* about *laos,* or better, *logos* about the *laos tou Theou* (speech about the people of God). Theology has become sociology. Acknowledging the role of faith in theology is important; the community of faith does play a vital role in theological formation and interpretation, but it is reductionistic to think of theology only as the science of faith.

explicitly tells us that "in broad outline," both in "method and task," he follows Schleiermacher.[49] Berkhof defines religion in general as *"the relationship to the Absolute"*[50] and insists that this relationship "cannot be reduced to another relationship or another aspect of man."[51] Here, too, he follows Schleiermacher who, in his On Religion: Speeches to Its Cultured Despisers,[52] argued against reducing religion to an intellectual or moral matter, insisting that it is a "separate province in the soul" characterized by an "apprehension and taste for the infinite" as "feeling."[53] Faith, in New Testament terms, is a matter of a "relationship to a person to whom man may entrust himself."[54] And though "faith" is a relationship while "study" is an objectifying activity so that "study of the faith looks very much like a contradiction in terms," Berkhof persists, with some reservation, to define dogmatic theology as "a systematic study of the contents of the relationship which God in Christ has entered into with us."[55] This yields the following division of topics:

1. Introduction [Prolegomena]
2. Revelation
3. God
4. Creation
5. Israel
6. Jesus the Son
7. The New Community
8. The Renewal of Man
9. The Renewal of the World
10. All Things New

My point here is not to be critical of the structure of either Spykman's or Berkhof's theology; on the contrary, I share a predilection for biblical-narrative structures. What I wish to point out, however, is that for both men the final narrative structure is not derived from the stated definition but is in many respects opposed to it. There is an interesting irony here: those theologians we considered first as representatives of a stated *biblical* method end up with structures and organizations that look like and are clearly dependent on other, perhaps even philosophical, presuppositions; by contrast, two theologians who explicitly state up front their philosophically-based methodology end up with the most explicitly biblical-narrative order of topics.

49. H. Berkhof, *Christian Faith*, trans. S. Woudstra, 2d ed. (Grand Rapids: Eerdmans, 1986), 25, 26.
50. Ibid., 6ff.
51. Ibid., 10.
52. Friedrich Schleiermacher, *On Religion: Speeches to Its Cultured Despisers*, ed. and trans. Richard Crouter (New York: Cambridge University Press, 1996). Published in German in 1799.
53. H. Berkhof, *Christian Faith*, 11.
54. Ibid., 21.
55. Ibid., 33.

As Restatement of the Biblical-Creedal faith

We now consider the last of our biblically-based attempts at doing doctrinal theology, namely, systematic theology as restatement of the biblical-creedal faith. While it is true that a detailed historiographical analysis reveals a detailed order that is far more complex,[56] it is fair to say that John Calvin's *Institutes of the Christian Religion* in its overall sweep follows a trinitarian-creedal structure.[57] What distinguishes Calvin's approach from that of the previously discussed theologians is that while Calvin has as his primary goal the exposition of Scripture, he does so with deliberate awareness of the church's creedal teaching as the framework. In his preface to the reader in the 1559 edition, Calvin states his intention forthrightly:

> Moreover, it has been my purpose in this labor to prepare and instruct candidates in sacred theology for the reading of the divine Word, in order that they may be able to have easy access to it and to advance in it without stumbling. For I believe I have so embraced the sum of religion in all its parts, and have arranged it in such an order, that if anyone rightly grasps it, it will not be difficult for him to determine what he ought especially to seek in Scripture and to what end he ought to relate its contents.[58]

If we are to describe the overall structure as biblical-creedal in a trinitarian way, we must note that this description is not exhaustive; it does not account for the inclusion of the law in book 2, for example. Nor does it really adequately describe the *duplex ordo* dimension of Calvin's epistemology.[59] My point here is only to say that as Calvin strives to provide a help for understanding and interpreting Scripture, the overall structure, including the descriptions of each book's content, looks very much like the creedal-trinitarian structure of the Apostles' Creed.[60] This is the result:

1. The Knowledge of God the Creator
2. The Knowledge of God the Redeemer in Christ
3. The Way We Receive the Grace of Christ [The Inner Work of the Holy Spirit]

---

56. See Richard A. Muller, "Establishing the *Ordo docendi*," in *The Unaccommodated Calvin: Studies in the Foundation of a Theological Tradition* (New York and Oxford: Oxford University Press, 2000), 118–39. Muller traces the development of the order in the *Institutes* from the 1536 edition to the 1559 edition and concludes that in addition to the creedal order—and the basic catechetical order of the 1536/7 edition—there is significant influence from Melanchton's Pauline *ordo* (taken from Romans) in the *Loci Communes*. Muller concludes with this comment on Calvin's expression of satisfaction with the order of the final 1559 *Institutes*: "What he probably meant was that, in 1559, the creedal model already resident within the *Institutes* had, for the first time, been successfully integrated with the remaining elements of the catechetical model and above all with the basic outline of the Pauline *loci* drawn from Melanchthon's *Disputio* and *Loci Communes*," 137.
57. John Calvin, *Institutes of the Christian Religion*, ed. John T. McNeill, trans. Ford Lewis Battles, 2 vols. (Philadelphia: Westminster, 1960).
58. John Calvin, "John Calvin to the Reader, 1559," in *Institutes*, 1:4–5.
59. For a more complete treatment of the shifts and divergences from a strict creedal order, see Muller, *Ordo Docendi*.
60. Though one should not forget that the creedal order is itself a narrative order.

4. The External Means or Aids by Which God Invites Us into the Society
   of Christ and Holds Us Therein [the Outward Work of the Holy
   Spirit]

What distinguishes Calvin from succeeding Reformed theologians such as Turretin, for example, is that Calvin includes no discussion of philosophical or metaphysical prolegomena; he simply begins with the twofold knowledge of God (and humanity) as confessed by Scripture and the Christian doctrinal tradition.

Is Summarizing Biblical Doctrine an Adequate Method for Systematic Theology?

Undoubtedly, the theological works discussed above have been a blessing to the church and helped Christians to understand their faith better and witness to their Lord more effectively. A few have rightly earned the designation of "classic." Why then raise questions about the wisdom of conceiving the task of evangelical systematic theology today as restatement of biblical doctrine? We have already raised a number of issues. One is the matter of consistency. We discovered that even explicit proponents of such a biblical-doctrinal method are inclined to qualify and nuance their own definitions by acknowledging the significance of general revelation (Murray) and the church along with broader human culture (Erickson). In addition, in spite of Grudem's definition that the theologian's task is to give us what the Bible teaches for "today," his stated method—get a good concordance!—really does not account for the need of theology to be contemporary and relevant.

Let us assume, for the sake of argument, that these concerns about the role of the church's tradition in an effort to speak to our contemporary world can be addressed and provide no real challenge to the basic understanding of systematic theology as biblical theology—where biblical theology is understood as summarizing the doctrine of Scripture rather than as *historia revelationis*. Since the Protestant Reformation was about *sola Scriptura*, among other things, it would seem that such a definition of the task of systematic theology would be self-evidently the proper one. Herman Bavinck addresses the same question: "Thus it seems the correct method is that followed by the so-called biblical theologians."[61] But Bavinck disagrees. Not only does the specific "school" of biblical theology he has in mind here with the term "so-called,"[62] suffer from "one-sidedness," it also ignores the important cultural, social, and confessional factors that shape all theologians and theologies. "While it thinks

---

61. Bavinck, *Reformed Dogmatics*, 1:82.
62. Bavinck mentions only the name of Ritschl here. It should be clear that I am not linking the names mentioned at the beginning of this essay—Hodge, Murray, Reymond, Grudem, Erickson, etc.—with the *content* of Ritschl's neo-Kantian liberal theology. The point of comparison is strictly with the claim to be a "biblical" theology and to eschew all metaphysics. At the same time, evangelicals who do eschew metaphysics should be aware that they are keeping company with modernist theologians who also reject any metaphysical basis for theological claims since the latter are only "value judgments." For an excellent, critical though

that it is completely unbiased in relating to Scripture and that it produces its content accurately and objectively, it forgets that every believer and every dogmatician first of all receives his religious convictions from his or her church. . . . All dogmaticians, when they go to work, stand consciously or unconsciously in the tradition of the Christian faith in which they were born and nurtured and come to Scripture as Reformed, or Lutheran, or Roman Catholic Christians. In this respect as well, we simply cannot divest ourselves of our environment; we are always children of our time, the products of our background."[63] We can say this in a different way by noting that "theology approaches the Bible as canon. This is a datum of prior understanding which cannot be derived from any philosophical theory or any result of historical research."[64]

Though we cannot delve into this in any detail, it is worth noting that Bavinck even applies this logic to biblical revelation itself. The Christian religion is not unique in the fact that it is based on revelation; on this score it is "similar to all other historical religions."[65] Even the forms and modes of revelation are similar. "Theophany, mantic, and magic, like offerings, temple priesthood, cult, etc., are essential elements in religion. Thus they occur in all religions, also in that of Israel and Christianity."[66] What is remarkable is that Bavinck not only acknowledges these similarities but he also insists that "this universal religious belief in manifestation, prediction, and miracle is certainly not—in any case not exclusively—to be attributed to deception or demonic effects nor to ignorance of the natural order but is a necessary element in all religion."[67] From this we are led to conclude that since an important responsibility of the theologian is to restate the content of the Christian faith for better communication to his or her own day, a biblical-doctrinal model is basic but inadequate. In addition to recognizing the importance of church tradition as a key presupposition for interpreting the Bible, the religious experience of the non-Christian also has to be considered at this point.[68] What this means is that a proper theology, as λογός about θεός, must explain how human beings who do not have direct access to biblical revelation still respond to the reality of God and his general revelation

---

sympathetic treatment of Ritschl, see H. Bavinck, "De Theologie van Albrecht Ritschl," *Theologische Studiën* 6 (1888): 369–403.

63. Bavinck, *Reformed Dogmatics*, 1:82.

64. Braaten and Jenson, *Christian Dogmatics*, 22.

65. Bavinck, *Reformed Dogmatics*, 1:326.

66. Ibid., 1:327.

67. Ibid., 1:326.

68. Bavinck's own *Reformed Dogmatics* provides a remarkable example of this. As Bavinck discusses various elements of Christian doctrine (e.g. incarnation, atonement, eschatology), he regularly begins with noting that there are universal religious experiences and expression that parallel the specifically Christian belief under consideration. He then proceeds to show how the specifically Christian article of faith is both similar to and yet distinctive from other expressions. One of the most remarkable examples is his discussion of conversion in volume 3 (where he incorporates a lengthy discussion of American psychologist G. Stanley Hall's empirical study of the psycho-sexual development of adolescents in the examination of the *ordo salutis*).

in ways that share common patterns with explicit biblical revelation. More than good communication is at stake; a perspective is needed that also does justice to the very *content* of the gospel. To state it in different words: a full and proper Christian theology must have an explicit epistemology that attempts to explain universal human experience. That is to say, Christian theology must incorporate an explicit metaphysic.

Why is this important? The answer depends in part on how one conceives the purpose of theology. If theology is only for the church, only for the already converted and committed, it would not be as necessary to address the metaphysical question. Systematic theology could then serve the limited but still useful purpose of helping those who already believe to understand the Bible better. However, if one also wants to serve the church in its missionary task of presenting the full truth of the Christian gospel to the world in understandable, credible terms, then more is needed. A simple appeal to biblical authority is not sufficient; to modern and postmodern people such an appeal is simply one more subjective, privileged form of knowledge. Christian theology, by contrast, insists that it is telling universal truth about God and his relation to his creation. Of course, theology is "faith seeking understanding"; we do not theologize ourselves into faith but grant that "as a rule faith precedes theological reflection."[69] At the same time, "theological ascertainment of the truth is not made superfluous by the certainty of faith."[70] As Pannenberg observes with respect to Anselm: "Anselm demanded that in the field of rational argumentation theology should examine what it believes subjectively by reason alone (*sola ratione*). It may not, then, make the subjective presupposition of the faith starting point of the argument. The force of the argument alone is what counts."[71]

To restate this in different terms: "Judgments about what is true or false, like all judgments, are undoubtedly subjectively conditioned. Nevertheless, in our judgments we do not control the truth. We presuppose it and seek to correspond to it. The truth in its binding universality precedes our subjective judgments."[72]

When one considers that our modern and so-called postmodern world is characterized by a radical questioning of the very idea of God as well as a growing epistemological relativism, it should be apparent that Christian theology which seeks to tell the truth about God cannot afford the luxury of biblicism. It must face the truth question about God head on. To see that this is not a lamentable concession but a richer, more thorough approach to theological work, let us consider the example of Herman Bavinck as one who explicitly rejects using *sola Scriptura* as a theological method.

---

69. Wolfhart Pannenberg, *Systematic Theology*, vol. 1, trans. Geoffrey W. Bromiley (Grand Rapids, Eerdmans, 1991), 50.
70. Ibid.
71. Ibid., 51.
72. Ibid., 52.

Metaphysics in Herman Bavinck's *Reformed Dogmatics*

By tackling the metaphysical question directly as a theological issue, Herman Bavinck's discussion of prolegomena in the first volume of his *Reformed Dogmatics* illustrates well the point we have been making. After exploring the twinned opposing epistemologies of rationalism and empiricism, Bavinck points out that these are not the only philosophical options. There is another epistemology—realism—that has as its starting point "ordinary daily experience, the universal and natural certainty of human beings concerning the objectivity and truth of their knowledge. . . . Every human being, after all, accepts the reliability of the senses and the existence of the external world, not by a logical inference from the effect, in this case the representation in his consciousness, to the cause outside of himself, nor by reasoning from the resistance his will encounters to an objective reality that generates this resistance. Prior to all reflection and reasoning, everyone is in fact fully assured of the real existence of the world."[73] It is this natural certainty about the reliability of the senses—"I *saw* her do it!"—and the reality of the external world that gives the lie to empiricists who claim that scientific, demonstrative certainty is the only certainty that there is.[74] The existence of such indemonstrable self-evident truths cannot, according to philosophic realism, be explained by the rationalist notion of innate ideas either. If the certainty we possess about the *external* world were based on *internal* states of affairs in the knowing subject, then there would still be a fundamental dualism between subject and object. According to Bavinck, the reason that the dualistic theory of innate ideas was rejected by Reformed theologians was their belief that it probably led inevitably to idealism. Instead they insisted, with empiricists, that sense perception came first, that "there is nothing in the intellect which is not first in the senses," and the reason they did so was "because, in distinction from the angels, man is corporeal, because his body is not a prison but belongs to his very nature and he is bound to the cosmos by that body."[75]

Realism begins with the conviction that not only is the external world real and perceptible to our senses but also that the perceptions we form are true to the reality perceived. The mind has its own power and "once it is activated, it immediately and spontaneously works in its own way and according to its own nature. And the nature of the intellect is that it has the power (*vis*), ability (*facultas*), inclination (*inclinatio*), and fitness (*aptitudo*) to form certain concepts and principles. . . . Thus the moment the intellect itself proceeds to act, it automatically knows itself bound to the laws of thought. In the activity of thought, the laws of thought inhere and come to expression. Thus experience teaches us what is a part and what is a whole, but the intellect

73. Bavinck, *Reformed Dogmatics*, 1:223.
74. Ibid., 1:224. Here we are in the ballpark of what more recent Reformed philosophers such as Alvin Plantinga and Nicholas Wolterstorff call "basic beliefs."
75. Ibid.

immediately grasps that a whole is greater than a part."[76] The crucial point here is
that "representations [in the mind] are faithful interpretations of the world of reality
outside us."[77]

What science, in this view, does is to reflect on particular sense experience and
seek out those things that are abiding and universal. In Thomas Aquinas's words,
"Science is not concerned with individual cases; the intellect concerns itself with
universal matters."[78] What the mind does is "to penetrate to the interior or essence
of a thing. Its true object is the quiddity, the real nature, of a material thing."[79] The
posture of realism is that universal concepts are real, "not in a Platonic or ontological
sense prior to the thing itself (*ante rem*), but in an Aristotelian sense in the thing itself
(*in re*) and therefore also in the human mind subsequent to the thing itself. . . . So,
in entertaining concepts we are not distancing ourselves from reality but we increasingly approximate it." Bavinck admits that the notion that in the process of forming
concepts and processing them in accordance with the laws of thought we are in fact
getting closer to reality itself seems odd, perhaps even counterintuitive. Here the
Christian doctrine of creation by the eternal Logos is crucial. "But that conviction
can only, therefore, only rest in the belief that it is the same Logos who created both
the reality outside of us and the laws of thought within us and who produced an organic connection and correspondence between the two. Only in this way is science
possible."[80] "The Logos who shines in the world must also let his light shine in our
consciousness. That is the light of reason, the intellect, which, itself originating in
the Logos, discovers and recognizes the Logos in things. . . . So, in the final analysis,
it is God alone who from his divine consciousness and by way of his creature conveys
the knowledge of truth to our mind—the Father who by the Son and in the Spirit
reveals himself to us."[81]

What this yields for theology is that God alone must be the principle of being,
the essential foundation (*principium essendi*) of theology. Theology is about the
knowledge of God. However, because of who God is and because of human limitation, God must make himself known to us. We cannot do without revelation, a
self-disclosure from God himself. Using the *principia* language, revelation is the
external principle of knowing, the *principium cognoscendi externum*. But if revelation,
both general and special, comes *to* a person there must also be an internal capacity
for receiving revelation (*principium cognoscendi internum*). "Corresponding to the
objective revelation of God, therefore, there is in human beings a certain faculty or
natural aptitude for perceiving the divine. God does not do half a job. He creates

76. Ibid., 1:225.
77. Ibid., 1:229.
78. T. Aquinas, *Summa theologica*, 1a.1.2; T. Aquinas, *Summa contra Gentiles*, 1:44; cited by Herman Bavinck,
Reformed Dogmatics, 1:229.
79. Bavinck, *Reformed Dogmatics,* 1:230.
80. Ibid., 1:231.
81. Ibid., 1:233.

not only the light but also the eye to see it. Corresponding to the external reality there is an internal organ of perception."[82] The human mind, in other words, is created in such a way that it has a built-in capacity for grasping the structure of reality; the truth of human representation depends on whether it corresponds to the reality of things outside the mind.

Rooted in faith, the theologian seeks to explore Scripture's testimony about God, the world, the human condition, God's provision for salvation in Jesus Christ, the end and goal of all things, and to describe this all in a coherent unity of thought. This unity may not be imposed from the outside; theologians search until the unity of biblical truth itself becomes present to the human mind. Here, too, the theologian is bound by the laws of thought itself. It is important that this search for the unified system of thought not be confused with full and complete comprehension. There are limits of human comprehension with respect to all created reality; how much more is this true of God and his ways with us. There must always be room in every theologian's work for wonder and mystery. "Christian theology always has to do with mysteries that it knows and marvels at but does not comprehend and fathom."[83]

From this Bavinck concludes: "Dogmatic theologians explicate the content of their faith as that is objectively exhibited by God himself before their believing eyes in revelation. They derive the principle of organization and the arrangement of the material, not from their own faith-life, but from the self-same object that it is their task to describe in their dogmatics."[84] Louis Berkhof follows Bavinck's lead in declaring that this method is the only way of doing justice to the fullness and unity of Scripture's own teaching:

> THE SYNTHETICAL METHOD. This is the only method that will yield the desired unity in dogmatics. It takes its starting point in God and considers everything that comes up for consideration in relation to God. It discusses the various doctrines in their logical order, that is, in the order in which they arise in thought and which lends itself to the most intelligible treatment. In such an order of treatment each truth, except the first, must be so related to preceding truths that it will be seen in the clearest light. God is the fundamental truth in theology, and is therefore naturally the first in order. Every following truth, in order to be seen in its true perspective, must be viewed in the light of this primary truth. For that reason anthropology must precede Christology, and Christology must precede soteriology, and so on. Proceeding according to this logical method, we discuss:
>
> I. The doctrine of God (theology).
> II. The doctrine of man (anthropology).

---

82. Ibid., 1:279.
83. Ibid., 1:619.
84. Ibid., 1:111.

III.   The doctrine of Christ (Christology).

IV.   The doctrine of applied salvation (soteriology).

V.   The doctrine of the Church (ecclesiology).

VI.   The doctrine of the last things (eschatology).[85]

We can quarrel with Berkhof's language of necessity here with respect to the topical *order*—"*must* precede"—but that must not obscure the crucial methodological point being made. In this understanding of theology it is the theologian's responsibility to present the full knowledge of God and his revelation as *reality, as a truth claim, as an argument for the truth about God and his world.* In other words, Christian theology is not only—and certainly not in the first place—a summary of what Christians *believe*, but an attempt to state what is really true about God and the world. Christian theology thus makes a *metaphysical* claim, and my burden is to argue that our theological method must reflect that metaphysical concern. Furthermore, on that score, I believe my contention is in keeping with the great tradition of Christian theology. We shall consider three key examples: Augustine, Thomas Aquinas, and Francis Turretin. In each case we shall notice the following common themes:

- All truth is from God; all truth is united in God.
- The human capacity for knowing the truth is universal; even after the fall all people have a rudimentary knowledge of God.
- There is a twofold truth about God—one that comes by reason; one that comes by special revelation; the former also requires faith; the latter is not unreasonable.
- Believers who have the benefit of special revelation and thus know God truly—but never fully!—are still obligated to search out God's truth beyond Scripture.
- Believers ought to use reason in their interpretation and explication of Holy Scripture.

Scripture and Metaphysics in the Great Tradition

Augustine

The important link between the truth about the world and the idea of God was made by Augustine.[86] Already in one of his earliest postconversion writings, the two books of *Soliloquies*, Augustine demonstrates the seeker's passion for God and for truth.[87] The form of this writing is important as Augustine searches for that which

85. Louis Berkhof, *Systematic Theology*, "Introduction," 75.

86. Pannenberg, *Systematic Theology*, 1:52; according to Pannenberg the key passage in Augustine on this point is *de lib. Arb.* 2.10; 12.

87. Augustine, *Soliloquies: Augustine's Interior Dialogue*, ed. John E. Rotelle, O.S.A., trans. Kim Paffenroth (Hyde Park, NY: New City Press, 2000).

is reliable and true in a world of change and decay. The *Soliloquies* are an inner dialogue between Augustine and his own reason as he searches for the only two things worth knowing: God and the soul.[88] Augustine's concern is whether it is possible to know the truth when the senses are obviously fallible and lead to deception. Heeding reason's argument, he comes to realize that the truth about all things must endure beyond the things themselves. Simply put, things endure because they are upheld by God; God's knowledge of them lasts; and the possibility of human knowledge of the truth depends on the immortality of the human soul in which the reception of the truth takes place.[89] He concludes by identifying "truth" with "being": "It seems to me that the 'true' is that which exists."[90] In the *Soliloquies* Augustine reflects more on the soul than on God, except for the opening prayer in 1:2–2, 7.[91] Boniface Ramsey notes that "when Augustine reflects on the soul in the *Soliloquies*, he is not reflecting on it in the way that moderns do. He is concerned with the soul not for the psychological but from the metaphysical perspective, not as the basis for the possibility of a relational existence but as a discreet entity subject to investigation in itself."[92]

Shortly after this Augustine pens another dialogue, *The Teacher*, in which he links the quest for truth directly with the quest for God. He describes the purpose of this work in his *Retractions:* "During this same period [at Cassiciacum, ca. 388] I composed a book called *The Teacher*, where, after some discussion and inquiry, we find that it is God alone who teaches men knowledge, all of which is also in accord with what is written in the Gospel: 'One is your teacher, Christ.'"[93]

Augustine insists that our understanding depends on "consulting" the "truth which presides over the mind itself from within" and that "He who is consulted and who is said to 'dwell in the inner man [Eph. 3:14–17],' He it is who teaches us, namely Christ, that is to say, 'the unchangeable Power of God and everlasting wisdom [1 Cor. 1:23–24].'"[94]

Finally, Augustine comes to the unambiguous claim that "truth itself is God."[95] In the previous chapter of *De lib. arb.* he celebrates the universal character of the truth, which is outside of us, greater than us, and shareable with all:

> In possessing truth, therefore, we have something which all of us can equally enjoy in common, for there is nothing wanting or defective in it. It welcomes all its lovers

---

88. Ibid., 1:2, 7.
89. Ibid., 2:18, 32.
90. Ibid., 2:5.
91. According to Boniface Ramsey, O. P., "Introduction" to *Soliloquies,* 13.
92. "Introduction" to *Soliloquies*, 13.
93. *Retractions*, 1.12; cited by Robert P. Russell, O.S.A., "Introduction," to "The Teacher," in Saint Augustine, *The Teacher, The Free Choice of the Will, Grace and Free Will*, The Fathers of the Church, vol. 59 (Washington, DC: The Catholic University of America Press, 1968), 3.
94. *The Teacher*, 12:38.
95. *On Free Choice of the Will*, 2:15.

without any envy on their part; it is available to all, yet chaste with each. No one of them says to another: step back so I may also embrace it. All cling to it; all touch the selfsame thing. It is a food never divided into portions; you drink nothing from it that I cannot drink. By sharing in it, you make no part of it your personal possession. I do not have to wait for you to exhale its fragrance so that I too may draw it in. No part of it ever becomes the exclusive possession of any one man, or of a few, but is common to all at the same time in its entirety.[96]

Augustine also applies this to the reading and interpretation of Scripture in *De Doctrina Christiana*[97] where he praises what is true in "pagan" learning and arts as valuable for Christians, even in Scripture study. "The discipline of rational discourse, indeed, is of the greatest value in penetrating and solving all kinds of problems which crop up in holy literature," he says.[98] All truth is God's truth, and Augustine defends the practice of "borrowing" from the pagans with his famous image of "plundering gold and silver from the Egyptians."[99]

Thomas Aquinas

With his customary exceptional clarity Aquinas incorporates Augustine's understanding of truth while also going beyond it. He begins his great treatise *De Veritate* by citing Augustine's definition from the *Soliloquies*: "It seems that the true is exactly the same as being, for 1. Augustine says: 'The true, therefore, is that which is.' But that which is, is simply being. The true, therefore, means exactly the same thing as being."[100] But Aquinas disagrees. To identify truth with being is to overlook the nature of the true as *knowledge about something*. Knowledge is not identical with being, it is a capacity of the soul to agree with being. To say that certain knowledge is *true* "expresses the correspondence of being to the knowing power [of the soul]." Truth is thus an adequate correspondence between a thing and the human intellect, the soul's capacity for knowing.[101] When we consider whether and how we know God, Aquinas has a twofold answer:

> There is a twofold mode of truth in what we profess about God. Some truths about God exceed all the ability of the human reason. Such is the truth that God is triune. But there are also some truths which the natural reason also is able to reach. Such are that God

96. Ibid., 2:14.
97. Ibid., 2:38–58.
98. Ibid., 2:48.
99. Ibid., 2:58.
100. St. Thomas Aquinas, *The Disputed Questions on Truth*, 3 vols., trans. Robert W. Mulligan, S. J., James V. McGlynn, S. J., and Robert W. Schmidt, S. J. (Chicago: Henry Regnery, 1952–1954), 1.1 (1.3).
101. Ibid., 1.1, "Reply" (1.6).

exists, that He is one, and the like. In fact such truths about God have been proved demonstratively by the philosophers, guided by the light of the natural reason.[102]

We must not misunderstand Aquinas here. He is under no illusions about natural reason and insists that "it was necessary for man's salvation that there should be a knowledge revealed by God, besides philosophical science built up by human reason," chiefly because "man is directed to God, as to an end that surpasses the grasp of his reason."[103] Furthermore, even the knowledge obtained by natural reason needs the correction of special revelation because it "would only be known by a few, and that after a long time, and with the admixture of many errors."[104] Later, in question 1, article 5, he insists that sacred science or theology is nobler than all other sciences in large measure because it both transcends all other forms of knowledge, including truths unknown and unknowable to reason, and at the same time incorporates truths known to human reason with greater certainty. In fact, "other sciences are called the handmaiden of this one." Finally, in the eighth article Aquinas is insistent that reason, logic, and argument are appropriate to theology. He does not claim that argument creates faith or that someone who denies the truth of Scripture can be argued into it:

> If our opponent believes nothing of divine revelation, there is no longer any means of proving the articles of faith by reasoning, but only of answering his objections—if he has any—against faith. Since faith rests upon infallible truth, and the contrary of a truth can never be demonstrated, it is clear that the arguments brought against faith cannot be demonstrations, but are difficulties that can be answered.

Argument can also be used internally, as a way of inference from certain truths of divine revelation to other truths. "Although arguments from human reason cannot avail to prove what must be received on faith, nevertheless this doctrine argues from articles of faith to other truths."[105]

There is, therefore, a twofold truth, but the key difference has to do with their source. Natural truth comes from God and is obtained by human reason though it is also a matter of belief.[106] Furthermore, the special revelation that comes by way of Scripture is nonetheless to be used as part of the reasoning process that is used to state the full implications of the faith. Even the truth that cannot be derived from human reason and that exceeds human reason is nonetheless reasonable.

---

102. Thomas Aquinas, *Summa Contra Gentiles,* 4 vols., trans. Anton C. Pegis, James E. Anderson, Vernon J. Bourke, and Charles J. O'Neil (Notre Dame, IN: University of Notre Dame Press, 1975 [1957]), 1.3.2 (1.63).
103. Aquinas, *Summa Theologica*, 1.1.1.
104. Ibid.
105. Ibid., 1.1.8 *ad* 1.
106. *Summa Contra Gentiles*, 1.1.4.

Of course much more can be said about Aquinas's theological metaphysics but for our purposes this is sufficient. I am trying to demonstrate that the great tradition of Christian theology is not only not adverse to metaphysics but rather considers it an indispensable part of the theological enterprise itself. Parenthetically, there is nothing so salutary for those inclined to fideism, not to mention postmodern anti-rationalism, as a careful look at the first question of Aquinas's *Summa Theologica* or, for those with more leisure available to them, book 1 of his *Summa Contra Gentiles.*

Francis Turretin

For those who might not yet be fully persuaded by an evangelical theological appeal to Thomas Aquinas, permit me to bring another Reformed witness to the stand—in addition to Herman Bavinck—the great seventeenth-century theologian Francis Turretin (1623–1687).[107] To the surprise of contemporary Reformed students of theology who have been tutored by Karl Barth (and, perhaps, G. C. Berkouwer), Turretin firmly posits not only a general revelation but a natural theology.[108] He judges this to be the clear teaching of Scripture (Romans 1 and 2) and confirmed by universal experience. Like Aquinas, Turretin affirms a twofold order of knowledge with respect to God and insists that this is not to be seen as somehow contradictory:

> It is not repugnant that one and the same thing in a different relation should both be known by the light of nature and believed by the light of faith; as what is gathered from the one only obscurely, may be held more certainly from the other. Thus we know that God is, both from nature and from faith (Heb. 11:6); from the former obscurely, but from the latter more surely. The special knowledge of true faith (by which believers please God and have access to him, of which Paul speaks) does not exclude, but supposes the general knowledge from nature.[109]

In the twelfth question (first topic) Turretin asks: "Are the doctrines of faith and practice to be proved only by the express word of God? May they not also be legitimately proved by consequences drawn from Scripture?" His answer: "We affirm the latter."[110] The next question (13) asks: "Is there any use of philosophy in theology?" and once again Turretin gives an affirmative answer. According to Turretin "the orthodox oc-cupy a middle ground" between those who "confound theology with philosophy" on

---

107. I am indebted here to Sebastian Rehnman's essay on Turretin ("Theistic Metaphysics and Biblical Exegesis") referred to in note 2. References that follow are to Turretin's *Institutes of Elenctic Theology,* 3 vols. (Phillipsburg, NJ: P&R, 1992–97). Also very helpful was David Sytsma's paper, "The Use of Reason in Francis Turretin's Arguments for God's Existence," in the Calvin Theological Seminary student body publication *Stromata* 47 (2006): 1–26.
108. Turretin, *Institutes,* 1:3.
109. Ibid., 1:3:9.
110. Ibid., 1:12.

the one side and the "fanatics and enthusiasts . . . who hold that philosophy is opposed to theology and should therefore be altogether separated from it, not only as useless, but also as positively hurtful."[111] Turretin describes the subtle relation between reason and faith thus:

> Although every truth cannot be demonstrated by reason (the boundaries of truth being much more widely extended than those of reason), yet no lie against the truth can be sheltered under the protection of true reason, nor can one truth be destroyed by another (although one may transcend and surpass the other) because whatever the one may be—whether below, according to or above reason, and apprehended by the senses, the intellect or faith—it has come from no other source than God, the parent of truth. So grace does not destroy nature, but makes it perfect. Nor does supernatural revelation abrogate the natural, but makes it sure.[112]

Turretin gives us four valuable helps that philosophy provides:

> 1. "It serves as a means of convincing the Gentiles and preparing them for the Christian faith."
> 2. "It may be a testimony of consent in things known by nature, by which (as from a twofold revelation) the truth and certainty of the things themselves may be better confirmed."
> 3. "It may be an instrument of perceiving things clearly, and rightly distinguishing between them—judging concerning that which is true and false, consequent and in-consequent, according to the rules of good and necessary consequence impressed upon our rational nature by God after it has been illuminated by the light of the divine word. . . . For although reason receives the principles of religion from the light of faith, yet (this light preceding) it ought to judge from these principles how the parts of the heavenly doctrine cohere and mutually establish each other, what is consistent with and what is contrary to them."
> 4. "The mind may be furnished and prepared by these inferior systems for the re-ception and management of a higher science."[113]

Finally, Turretin denies the validity of a "double truth" whereby something might be true in theology though it were false in philosophy. This is impossible "because truth is not at variance with truth, nor is light opposed to light."[114] Christian theologians are required, in faith, to use all the knowledge at their disposal to present the full truth about God. "Metaphysics is the highest of all sciences in the natural order, but acknowledges the superiority of theology in the supernatural order."[115]

---

111. Ibid., 1:13:1–2.
112. Ibid., 1:13:3.
113. Ibid., 1:13:4.
114. Ibid., 1:13:13.
115. Ibid., 1:2:4.

No philosophy or metaphysics can establish faith,[116] but at the same time, "the agency of reason is so far from making faith doubtful that it rather greatly assists and establishes the knowledge and certainty of it."[117] And this is especially the case in the interpretation of Scripture:

> Although Scripture is said to be perfect (as a foundation of things to be believed and done inasmuch as it contains all the doctrines and precepts of life necessary to salvation) this is not to deny the necessity of explication and applications. For a rule is perfect and yet we have to apply it. Nor does that application detract from the perfection of the rule, but rather proves and declares it.[118]

In sum, Turretin regards all truth as God's truth, and when stating the truth about God, one is obligated to use all the truth at one's disposal. In Sebastian Rehnman's words:

> Scriptural exegesis and metaphysical argumentation are ideally co-referential as special revelation, logic and metaphysics appropriately apply terms rooted in finite and contingent reality to ultimate reality because of the possibility of co-referentiality between the Creator and the creation. Hence, it is possible and desirable that biblical exegesis and metaphysical argumentation interact.[119]

Before concluding, one more witness for the prosecution demonstrates that the insistence on a biblical theology that is also metaphysically responsible is in fact a matter of confessional concern, at least for Reformed theologians. Turretin's assumption that God has implanted into humans basic principles concerning nature, God, and morality[120] is formulated by the *Canons of Dort*[121] in precisely those terms[122]: "There is, to be sure, a certain light of nature remaining in man after the fall, by virtue of which he retains some notions about God, natural things, and the difference between what is moral and immoral, and demonstrates a certain eagerness for virtue and for good, outward behavior."

The Problem with Evangelical Theology Today: Why We Need Metaphysics
I will not be able fully to deliver on the promise of the immediately preceding subheading—especially the first phrase—but my focus will consist of a defense of the

---

116. Ibid., 1:12:14–15.
117. Ibid., 1:12:17.
118. Ibid., 1:12:22.
119. Rehman, "Theistic Metaphysics," 175.
120. Turretin, *Institutes*, 1:8:1; 1:9.2; 11:1:7.
121. *Canons of Dort*, Main Point 3/4, art. 4.
122. For this I am indebted to David Sytsma, "The Use of Reason in Francis Turretin's Arguments," 13.

contrarian position I am taking with respect to truth and theological method.[123] First, however, let me provide a brief summary of my argument thus far.

My first point was that evangelical theological method should not be restricted to summarizing biblical doctrine. Such an understanding of the theological task today fails as claim of *truth* about God, a universal claim desperately needed today. I introduced a variety of approaches to illustrate the deep gulf that often exists between stated method and the content, structure, and organization of the work of those who attempt a strictly biblical doctrinal method. This method fails to do justice to the broader human experience of God outside the church, overlooks the key role of the church itself in any normative interpretation of Scripture, avoids addressing the key role of confessional and philosophical presuppositions, and does not account for theology's need to be contemporary, relevant, and able to speak to the issues of "today." Finally, a strictly biblical-doctrinal approach runs the risk of appearing to non-Christians as privileged communication; a kind of gnosticism that only communicates to the initiated. In short, this approach fails to make universal claims about the gospel of Jesus Christ and makes no argument about the universally true knowledge about God that is the church's mission to proclaim to the world.

As an alternative, I appealed to Herman Bavinck's Christian realism, the epistemology that is rooted in the creation of all things, including the human logos by the divine Logos. All truth is from God; we participate in the truth to the degree that our intellects adequately form concepts that correspond to the things of this world including our experience of God. We attempted to show, in broad strokes, that this view is characteristic of all the great theologians including Augustine, Thomas Aquinas, and Francis Turretin, as well as Herman Bavinck. Concretely this means that while the Bible is the final source and norm for Christian theology, the knowledge of God obtained by natural reason, reflected in the religions of the world, as well as legitimate, reasonable inferences from biblical truth, are all part of the theologian's thesaurus of truth.

I have taken some pains to demonstrate all this at length and with considerable repetition because there is a great deal at stake. I am quite aware that many current evangelical authors will not greet with approval this essay's claim(s) for a revitalized classic theological metaphysics . In fact, the case I have set forth is precisely what many judge to be the very problem that prevents evangelical Christianity from fulfilling its true contemporary calling. Why? Because many contemporary evangelicals are extremely nervous about truth claims in general. I do not have the space to docu-

---

123. I have dealt with aspects of this issue in, "An Emerging Critique of the Postmodern, Evangelical Church: A Review Essay," *Calvin Theological Journal* 41, no. 2 (2006): 205–21. The following volumes are especially relevant to the topic of this essay: Andreas Köstenberger, ed., *Whatever Happened to Truth?* (Wheaton, IL: Crossway, 2006); R. Scott Smith, *Truth and the New Kind of Christian: The Emerging Effects of Postmodernism in the Church* (Wheaton, IL: Crossway, 2005); David F. Wells, *Above All Earthly Pow'rs: Christ in a Postmodern World* (Grand Rapids: Eerdmans, 2006).

ment this in detail, but a recent essay in *Christianity Today* by Scot McKnight on the "emerging church" illustrates the point rather well.[124] "Emerging churches," we are told, "are communities that practice the way of Jesus within postmodern cultures."[125] What this means is spelled out in terms of prophetic rhetoric, accepting postmodernity, and concentrating on right living (orthopraxis) rather than right believing (orthodoxy). McKnight cites the following from Peter Rollins: "Thus orthodoxy is no longer (mis)understood as the opposite of heresy but rather is understood as a term that signals a way in the world rather than a means of believing things about the world." While some minister *to* postmoderns (e.g. David Wells), others embrace postmodernism and minister *as* postmoderns. According to McKnight this means "that they embrace the idea that we cannot know absolute truth, or at least, that we cannot know truth absolutely. They speak of the end of metanarratives and the importance of social locations in shaping one's truth. They frequently express nervousness about propositional truth."[126] McKnight then cites LeRon Shuts as example:

> From a theological perspective, this fixation with propositions can easily lead to the attempt to use the finite tool of language on an absolute Presence that transcends and embraces all finite reality. Languages are culturally constructed symbol systems that enable humans to communicate by designating one finite reality in distinction from another. The truly infinite God of Christian faith is beyond all our linguistic grasping, as all the great theologians from Irenaeus to Calvin have insisted, and so the struggle to capture God in our finite propositions is nothing short of linguistic idolatry.[127]

It is hard to know where to begin in responding to a diatribe that is filled with so much hostility and so many confusions. Of course we cannot know God absolutely; no responsible theologian has ever made such a claim. Nor have responsible theologians suggested that language is anything other than social. However, speaking of God with clear, thoughtfully-reasoned claims that are indeed intended to be universally true is not "linguistic idolatry" *when it is rooted in biblical revelation itself.* In fact, this self-celebrated epistemological humility—not making universal claims about God—when we do have revelation, should be seen for what it is: disobedience and a failure to give an account of the hope (and truth) that is in us (1 Pet. 3:15). If one were to take seriously the objection that the finite cannot represent the infinite, then the incarnation is impossible. Furthermore, nothing that we humans do could then possibly fit the requirement that we image God. There goes the Word become flesh; there goes the *imitatio Christi.*

124. Scot McKnight, "Five Streams of the Emerging Church," *Christianity Today,* February 2007, 34–39.
125. Ibid., 34.
126. Ibid., 37.
127. Ibid.

At the risk of piling on, I shall introduce one more example of the same genre that has become popular in evangelical circles. In a recent work celebrating postmodernism and calling on evangelicals to embrace it, Carl Raschke levels the accusation against a position such as the one advocated in this essay—with its indirect critique of postmodern thinking—that it is a species of gnosticism:

> The curious notion that the truths of the Christian faith can, and should, be argued in much the same way as one would prove a mathematical theorem—a notion that has gained momentum in evangelical circles in recent decades—reeks of Gnosticism. Like the ancient gnostics, the new antipomo apologists measure themselves by a false standard and try to be something they are not—secular philosophers—when they should instead be communicating and sharing the heart of Jesus.[128]

Appeals to metaphysics are part of a bad Greek legacy that is crippling evangelicalism, according to Raschke. "Like Peter we must decide whether we are going to flee to the safety of our Hellenic certainties, or whether we return with the Master on the *via dolorosa*."[129] The entire evangelical faith must be *dehellenized*, and the Bible's language recognized as *promissory* and *vocative*. What this means is that instead of thinking of the Bible in terms of contentful *propositions*, it must be seen as *relational*, as an *address* from an Other to whom we respond. The Bible creates an "I-Thou" relationship.[130] This new view, claims Raschke, takes us beyond liberalism and fundamentalism; moves us from hierarchy to relationality; will help create a new evangelical counterculture; turn us as worshipers into Pentecostals; and bring about the end of theology. By this last phrase Raschke has in mind a Copernican revolution, an end to metaphysics, the death of onto-theology, a setting aside of "the dualism of subject and object that has overshadowed the tradition of Western thinking."[131] Truth is now part of an intersubjective matrix in which the Other and all his or her mystery intrudes.[132] Here we meet God because the difference of otherness "is a difference that smashes though the stone walls of selfhood and the sufficiency of rational self-consciousness. It is the final challenge to predicative logic, because it is God's challenge. That is who God is. God is *tout autre*, 'wholly other.'"[133] What Raschke envisions, in hope, is "the power of God liberating evangelical, if not the whole of Christian thought and theology from its long captivity in the Egypt of metaphysics and the Babylon of modernism and drawing it back 'to God,' of 'letting God be God,' in the face-to-face relationship of faith and worship. After theology we must all get on our faces.[134]

128. Carl Raschke, *The Next Reformation: Why Evangelicals Must Embrace Postmodernity* (Grand Rapids: Baker Academic, 2005), 19.
129. Ibid., 131.
130. Ibid., 131–40.
131. Ibid., 212.
132. Ibid., 213.
133. Ibid.
134. Ibid., 215.

My own view is the direct opposite of Raschke's. I shall not engage his argument in any detail but only suggest that in fact evangelical theology has been insufficiently metaphysical instead of too much so. The accusations laid against so-called evangelical rationalism—too much philosophy; not enough relationality based on mystery and faith—are precisely the Achilles' heel of the postmodern enthusiasts. The epistemology and metaphysics I have been appealing to is not—quite unlike the pomo (postmodern) dependence on the antifoundationalist philosophers of the twentieth century—dependent on philosophical analysis as a foundation for its content; rather it begins with the ordinary, common-sense experience of the reality of God and the world. The attacks on propositions are really an attack on the realist definition of adequation[135] between a thing and the mind's understanding of it. To deny this adequation and insist on some privileged understanding based on social factors such as race, class, and gender, and to find the "truth" of the matter through those lenses—that is the real form of gnosis.[136]

Our concern ought to be for understanding the human condition better in order to be able to reach real and lost human beings with the gospel. The appeal I have made for a more classically metaphysical theology comes from that desire and goal. I believe that by coming to know better how God created us—how all human beings are constructed as image bearers of God; open to his presence; responding to his revelation—we are better able to meet them in their need and touch their hearts and minds with the truth of the gospel. The motivation of the pomo enthusiasts is laudable—they too want to address the children of our age. Unfortunately, it is my sad judgment that while they may succeed in being able to talk with those of our age who share their pomo enthusiasms, they will not reach them with the truth they need to hear: their universal need of a Savior from sin who claims their lives. To do this well we begin with Scripture as the infallibly true Word of God, adequately corresponding to the way things really are about God and the world. But we also make use of every tool granted to us—all truth is God's truth.

---

135. The classic term for a realist: *intellectus adequatio ad rem* [eds.].
136. Raschke's polarities are hardly new. The call for dehellenizing the Christian faith is hardly a postmodern development; its first and foremost spokesman was the decidedly modern church historian Adolf von Harnack. God as "wholly other" was elegantly and boldly proclaimed by the eccentric Dane, Søren Kierkegaard. And so one could go on. Raschke's 2004 published work overlooks the past 150 years of Christian thought and proclaims itself as a new word. It isn't. The "next reformation" he calls for has been tried, for more than a century, and in the judgment of most orthodox and evangelical Christian theologians, found wanting. Raschke does little to change that opinion, especially in his attack on Scripture and metaphysics. It is remarkable to see a philosopher using highly technical philosophical language to call for an end to metaphysics and theology and their replacement by intersubjectivity and Pentecostal worship.

3

No Easy Task: John R. Franke and the Character of Theology

PAUL HELM

~~~~~~

"Systematic Theology 'is no easy task.'"—Charles Hodge

The Christian world is presently being offered a number of "post-conservative," "postevangelical," and "emerging" theologies, or ways of doing theology. This chapter looks at one of these ways: John R. Franke's as we find it in his book, *The Character of Theology: A Postconservative Evangelical Approach.*[1] I will argue that Franke has seriously miscalculated what is involved in relating Christian faith to its cultural context, for he has overestimated the ease with which a nonfoundational Christian theology may be developed. By a happy irony, he has not succeeded in his project and (I shall imply) must fail to do so. What he offers remains a foundational theology. Nevertheless, it is a seriously deficient form of foundational theology. It is theologically unstable because it concedes too much to the culture and downplays the importance of truth. Theology is no easy task.

We shall consider these matters in order: first, Franke's idea of the shape of non-foundationalist theology, then its relation to the culture, and finally its relation to truth.

1. John R. Franke, *The Character of Theology: A Postconservative Evangelical Approach* (Grand Rapids, Baker, 2005).

93

Nonfoundationalist Theology

In common with many contemporary Christian revisionists, Franke turns his back on foundationalism, claiming that it cannot provide the appropriate theological method. He stresses his rejection of "strong" or "classical" foundationalism with these words: "At the heart of the foundationalist agenda is the desire to overcome the uncertainty generated by the tendency of fallible human beings to err and the inevitable disagreements and controversies that follow. Foundationalists are convinced that the only way to solve this problem is to find some universal and indubitable means of grounding the entire edifice of human knowledge."[2]

That is, theology cannot be a theological edifice in which the various doctrines and dogmas of the Christian faith—the superstructure—are grounded in a set of "indubitable beliefs that are accessible to all individuals."[3] In particular, contemporary culture has fiercely criticized the objectivity, the certainty, and the universality of the knowledge that theology claims to provide.[4] Franke accepts the cultural critique. Here we find run together three very different ideas: certainty, objectivity, and universality. Later, we shall consider each of these in turn.

Franke rejects more than merely strong or classical foundationalism, as exemplified in René Descartes, for example. It is perfectly possible to reject Cartesian foundationalism and yet subscribe to other sorts of foundationalism. For example, Alvin Plantinga's work, from which Franke takes the terms "strong" and "classical" foundationalism, is a case in point. Plantinga has espoused a form of what he calls weak foundationalism, based not upon indubitable truths recognized by any rational person but upon the "proper basicality" of certain beliefs. "Some beliefs are such that it is rational to accept them without accepting them on the basis of any other propositions or beliefs at all."[5] This is so-called "Reformed" epistemology, which by implication Franke also rejects. For he endorses the broader nonfoundationalist turn of postmodernism. "The heart of the postmodern quest for a situated and contextual rationality lies in the rejection of the foundationalist approach to knowledge along with its intellectual tendencies."[6] So he is concerned with more than the failings specific to strong or classical foundationalism. He is concerned with the foundationalist approach as a whole. To be clear, Franke objects to the idea that Christian theology involves a set of privileged truths, whether or not these are indubitably known, in terms of which other Christian beliefs are to be tested. Because of this, Franke bids farewell to foundationalism in both its liberal and conservative theological versions.[7]

---

2. Ibid., 26.
3. Ibid., 27.
4. Ibid.
5. Alvin Plantinga, "Reason and Belief in God," in *Faith and Rationality*, ed. Alvin Plantinga and Nicholas Wolterstorff (Notre Dame, IN: University of Notre Dame Press, 1983), 72.
6. Franke, *Character of Theology*, 27.
7. Ibid., 84–85.

Although he makes reference to the "entire edifice of human knowledge," it seems as if Franke is rather objecting to the edifice of Christian theology being founded on a set of indubitable propositions accessible to all. So we shall understand him in the following way: that in rejecting foundationalism he is principally interested in developing a nonfoundational Christian theology. According to Franke, a nonfoundationalist method in Christian theology is one in which no element of the theological enterprise is privileged, but which consists in a method that is an interplay between a number of different forces that exist in parity with each other. Franke initially defines theology very generally as "the orderly study and investigation of the truths of the Christian faith."[8] As he develops this view, paying particular respect to the context in which all theology is inevitably situated, he offers the following working definition: "Christian theology is an ongoing, second-order, contextual discipline that engages in the task of critical and constructive reflection on the beliefs and practices of the Christian church for the purpose of assisting the community of Christ's followers, in their missional vocation to live as the people of God in the particular social-historical context in which they are situated."[9]

This is quite a mouthful. Notice two things about it. The reference to "the truths" of the Christian faith made in the earlier more general definition disappears and is replaced by "beliefs." This may be thought to be a slip, but in view of what follows it has great significance. Franke later denies that his nonfoundationalist approach presupposes a denial of truth, and he distinguishes between ontological foundations—or sets of truths—and epistemological foundations—that is, our beliefs which may or may not be true. "While nonfoundationalist theology means the end of foundationalism, it does not signal the denial of foundations or truth."[10] But the critical question is: does the Christian, and the Christian church, have access to these ontological foundations, these sets of truths? If they are accessible to a degree, then according to Franke nonfoundationalist theology is a never-ending quest to gain access to these truths in the particular situations in which all theologizing must take place. In this quest, considerable prominence is given to "context" (there are two references to context in his definition), to situatedness. So the focus is on belief rather than on truth. Nevertheless, we may say that according to Franke nonfoundationalist theology aims at truth. Theology is a *contextual* discipline endeavoring to help the Christian community to form true beliefs about its faith in its particular socio-historical *context*. These beliefs are not simply the regulative rules of the Christian community, but they aim at truth. Franke seems to think that such nonfoundational theology, which must involve holding beliefs and so necessarily aims at

8. Ibid., 40.
9. Ibid., 44.
10. Ibid., 80.

truth, can never enable us to know (this side of the grave) whether or not we possess the truth or even to be reasonably certain that we do.

Besides the problem of privileging certain truths as foundational, Franke has another problem with foundationalism: "Attempts on the part of humans to seize control of these relations [viz. our epistemic relations with God] are all too common throughout the history of the church and, no matter how well intentioned, inevitably lead to forms of oppression and conceptual idolatry."[11]

These words are not altogether clear. For example, why must the claim to know something lead to the worship of concepts? But what Franke seems to endorse are the familiar postmodern claims that claims to knowledge are attempts to seize power, and that attention to the context in which knowledge-claims are made effectively neuters such attempts. The Christian theologian must avoid triumphalism, the claim that he, or the Christian church, possesses the truth. Here Franke endorses Merold Westphal's remarks. "If our thinking never merits the triumphalist title of Truth *and* there is no other knower whose knowledge is the Truth, then the truth is that there is no Truth. But if the first premise is combined with a theistic premise, the result will be: The truth is that there is truth, but not for us, only for God."[12]

The jigging about with the word "truth," now capitalizing it, now not, is a bit confusing, though the capitalizing is perhaps not confusing enough. Does Westphal know that there is no Truth for us, only truth; or does he Know it? For perhaps Westphal (and Franke) are saying that whereas God knows the Truth (or perhaps "Knows the Truth"), you and I only "know the truth" that "there is truth, but not for us." And where does that leave us? If one does not Know the Truth but only knows the truth that "there is truth, but not for us," are there any other truths that one knows, or do we only ever have beliefs, never knowledge? The capitalizing could be a rather irritating way of making the point that God's knowledge, being archetypal, is different from our human, ectypal knowledge. This would be quite consistent with the idea that human beings know things, though not in the way in which God Knows things. Or it could be the claim, familiar to students of absolute idealism, that it is impossible to have the truth unless one has the Whole Truth, and that it is only God, or the Absolute, that possesses, or who is, the Whole Truth. But somehow I don't think that it means either of these things.

Perhaps Franke, following Westphal, is committed to this: If someone knows (but does not Know), then such knowledge "inevitably leads to forms of oppression and conceptual idolatry"? Now consider Jesus. He is God the Son who has assumed human nature. He is situated in a context, first-century Palestine. Does he know, or Know? If he merely knows, then such knowledge leads inevitably to forms of oppression and conceptual idolatry. Not the sort of result we want, I take it. But if he

---

11. Ibid., 81.
12. Ibid., 80.

Knows, then it seems that Franke will have to say that Jesus did not have a context, or was somehow able to neutralize its epistemological effects. I leave the reader to sort out this tangled web. Whether or not these knots can be untied, I take it that Christians (including Franke) want in the main to say that claims to knowledge, if they are from the lips of Jesus, are not simply *claims* to knowledge but are rather more than that, but that they are not at all oppressive claims to power. But it's not clear how, under Franke's auspices, we are allowed to say this.

Yet of course beliefs (which, according to Franke's definition, is what theology is about) are also claims to have a grasp of the truth and therefore are potentially oppressive, too. Maybe the point is that beliefs, if they are tentatively expressed, will not be oppressive or idolatrous. At all events, the reader may agree that what exactly Franke is overall claiming and what he is overall denying is not altogether clear.

But it is clear that Franke intends to abandon any idea of there being foundations in theology. We must now explore his case for doing so.

Instability

What does nonfoundational theology look like? Franke characterizes it variously. "In nonfoundationalist theology, all beliefs are open to criticism and reconstruction. . . . Nonfoundationalist theology does not eschew convictions and commitments; it simply maintains that all such convictions and commitments, even the most long-standing and dear, remain subject to ongoing critical scrutiny and the possibility of revision, reconstruction, or even rejection."[13] Such an approach "promotes a theology with an inherent commitment to the reforming principle and maintains without reservation that no single human perspective, be it that of an individual or a particular community or a theological tradition, is adequate to do full justice to the truth of God's revelation in Christ."[14] "The adoption of a nonfoundationalist approach to theology accents an awareness of the contextual nature of human knowledge and mandates a critical awareness of the role of culture and social location in the process of theological interpretation and construction."[15] It "envisions theology as an ongoing conversation between Scripture, tradition, and culture through which the Spirit speaks in order to create a distinctively Christian 'world' centered on Jesus Christ in a variety of local settings."[16] It "seeks to nurture an open and flexible theology that is in keeping with the local and contextual character of human knowledge while remaining thoroughly and distinctly Christian." It also provides "a conceptual theological framework for the maintenance of the reforming principle."[17]

13. Ibid., 78.
14. Ibid., 79.
15. Ibid.
16. Ibid.
17. Ibid., 80.

Two or three matters are noteworthy. First, this nonfoundationalist approach to Christian theology sets up a three-way conversation between God's revelation in Christ, the church (in its local expression), and the cultural context in which the church is situated. Second, some of these descriptions, like the first cited, are so general that no Christian could dissent from them. Who could complain about the statement that no human perspective is adequate to do full justice to the truth of God's revelation? Who could deny that all our convictions remain subject to ongoing critical scrutiny? This has been the staple position of Christian thought throughout the centuries. Third, and most crucially, such theology is characterized largely in terms of its outcomes rather than its procedures or methods. The reader is told much more about what such theology will achieve than how it will achieve it. Structures are replaced by outcomes. But the important question is: how can these outcomes be guaranteed without a foundation for Christian belief?

Take the idea of a three-way conversation. Human conversations are notoriously open-ended and unpredictable. Who knows where they may lead? In the conversation held by the three conversation partners, Scripture, tradition (i.e. church tradition), and culture, who knows in advance what the outcome will be? In chapter 2 of *The Character of Theology*, Franke takes some pains to set out the subject of theology, which is the Triune God.[18] But once the three-way conversation gets going, how can he be confident that this will remain its subject matter? Why may not the conversation drift away from this? For he stresses that there is parity between the conversation partners. "Neither gospel nor culture can function as the primary entity in the conversation between the two in light of their interpretive and constructed nature; we must recognize that theology emerges through an ongoing conversation involving both gospel and culture."[19] Because the gospel is already interpreted and constructed by theologians in a culture, how can Franke be so sure that the theology will continue to be Christian theology? How can he "recognize" (that embraces a pretty strong epistemological claim, incidentally) that what will emerge from such a conversation will have a distinctively Christian character? For neither gospel nor culture is allowed to function as the "primary entity." If Franke really means this (and as we are seeing it looks to be contradicted by other things that he says about the gospel), then the gospel may be swamped by the culture, be taken over by it, and imprisoned within it.

Suppose that during the conversation the conversation partners are led to the conviction not that the glory of God is revealed supremely or exclusively in the face of Jesus Christ, but that (in John Hick's phrase) God has many faces. Then, on Franke's paradigm, that is the way things must go. We must follow our theological method wherever it leads, even if it leads in unforeseen directions. So here's the di-

18. Ibid., 46–47.
19. Ibid., 103.

lemma: if Franke says that things could not in Christian integrity go in such a direction, then he is committed to a foundationalist position. If he says that we must follow the conversation wherever it leads, then that is more consistently nonfoundational, but at the price of offering up the uniqueness of Christian theology in the interests of advocating a particular theological method.

Who knows whether or not tradition will succeed in radically reinterpreting the claims of Scripture, or if culture will succeed in neutralizing the claims of tradition? Franke knows. For as he describes this conversational process he specifies an outcome: a distinctively Christian world centered on Jesus Christ. It remains "thoroughly and distinctly Christian." But in a situation in which such conversations could go anywhere, how can he be sure? These questions are accentuated by the logic of nonfoundationalism. A nonfoundationalist theology is *one in which there are no foundations*. And, we might add, one in which there are no guaranteed outcomes either. No position, whether this is characterized in terms of starting points or of outcomes, is privileged. Franke seems to think that this three-way exchange provides three interacting intellectual forces in everlasting dialogue. But it may not happen. For conversation is dynamic and unpredictable. Who can tell where it will lead? If Franke says that the Christian subject matter of theology will and must be retained throughout the conversation, how does he know this? And if he does know that the outcome will be thoroughly Christian, is not the Christian element in the conversation then foundational? In a nonfoundationalist theological world it is not an accidental matter that the three-way conversations may go anywhere; this is a matter of theological principle. Otherwise the Christian conversation partner is privileged. If there is privilege from the start, then that heralds some kind of foundationalism. If there is privilege attached to one particular outcome, so that the conversation must move in only one direction, giving us only certain types of outcomes and not others, then certain possibilities are being ruled out from the start. But ruled out on what grounds?

The point is beautifully illustrated by something from Karl Barth, which Franke cites with approval:

> On this basis, Karl Barth concludes that the focal point and foundations of Christian faith, the God revealed in Jesus Christ, determines that in the work and practice of theology "there are no comprehensive views, no final conclusions and results. There is only the investigation and teaching which take place in the act of dogmatic work and which, strictly speaking, must continually begin again at the beginning in every point. The best and most significant thing that is done in this matter is that again and again we are directed to look back to the center and foundation of it all."[20]

20. Ibid., 81.

Franke does not seem to detect either the irony or the inconsistency of these remarks. Karl Barth appeals directly to the center and foundation of all theology,
the foundational character of God's revelation in Jesus Christ. Franke endorses
this, but in the course of promoting a nonfoundational theology! But if he endorses
what Barth says, then there is a foundation after all. And this foundation acts or
ought to act as the controlling material principle in Christian theologizing. Franke
may wish to retort: what Christian theology is, is what Christian theologians do.
But this is hardly satisfactory unless we can somehow specify some distinctive—that
is, foundational—feature that makes someone a Christian theologian in the first
place.

Further, nonfoundational theology presumably amounts to something more than
the need for Christian theologians to be cautious and modest in the way in which
they treat the divine mysteries. That note has resounded through the long centuries
of Christian foundationalism, though perhaps not heeded as often as it ought to
have been. Perhaps theologians have been over-confident, over-dogmatic, in claiming
or implying that theirs is the final word. It is certainly possible to have different
views on the truth about revealed mysteries. Protestants above all Christian people
have a stake in affirming human fallibility, even human theological fallibility.

Franke has not clearly seen what the implications of being "nonfoundational"
are for theological method, and I suspect that other nonfoundationalist Christian
theologians are in the same plight.

At this point, we may remind ourselves of something else that Franke says about
the nature of theology. In his definition, he emphasizes that it is a second-order
discourse:

> The doctrinal, theological, and confessional formulations of theologians and particular
> communities are the products of human reflection on the primary sources, teachings,
> symbols and practices of the Christian church. Therefore these formulations must be
> distinguished from these "first-order" commitments of the Christian faith. For ex-
> ample, theological constructions and doctrines are always subservient to the content
> of Scripture and therefore must be held more lightly.[21]

Is theology distinct from the content of Scripture? According to Franke, the answer
is: yes and no. There are two discourses, and in that sense they are separate. But at
any one time, if the second-order discourse of theology is taken seriously, then it tells
the church what Scripture means. It is the doctrinal and theological interpreter of
the first-order material. It must be held more lightly than the first-order material,
not because what Scripture says may trump what the theologian says, but only because
Scripture is the material on which the Christian theologian works.

21. Ibid., 104.

Theology, as he says, "has as its goal the setting forth of a particular understanding of the framework of meaning and the mosaic of beliefs that are at the core of the Christian community."[22] But can Franke consistently say this? The figure that characterizes the shape of theology has now changed: not foundations, but a framework, a core. It may be helpful to think of Christian belief in this way: like an apple, it has a core and outer flesh. It may be possible, in a relatively neutral manner, to discern a central set of claims, a framework of beliefs at the core of the Christian community. But Franke has to mean more than this. For at the core of the church's confession there are beliefs, and these already have meaning. The core is not a vague *substratum* to which the theologian gives meaning, but something that already *has* meaning. The theologian does not *give* this core of sentences—drawn from Scripture, and giving the church its Christian character—its meaning, but by his activities he vindicates this meaning, and so confirms or modifies the beliefs of the Christian community. That, at least, is how theology has classically been understood in the Reformed community.

"Foundations," a "core," a "framework"—despite himself, Franke continually returns to the foundational character of the Christian faith. It seems that he can't shake it off. The essential point is not affected by making one word, "core," do for another word, "foundation." To say that confessions of faith are activities through which the church binds itself "to the truth and hope of the gospel of reconciliation and redemption" and thus that such "confessional statements and formulas function as servants of the gospel"[23] is to be foundational. On the one hand, there is "the gospel of reconciliation and redemption." On the other hand, there is the work of confessing that gospel, the fallible, ongoing theologizing of the church, which "serves" the gospel. It is by virtue of its meaning that we become aware that it is a gospel of reconciliation and redemption, which then controls and adjudicates the thinking of the Christian theologian, or ought to. Because this meaning is fixed, the activity of the theologian relating this content to the vagaries of the culture, makes theologizing much more difficult than Franke seems to appreciate. Theology is not simply a three-sided conversation which has its own impetus. Something holds the conversation up, getting in its way. This is the gospel. The gospel is a difficult, awkward, conversation partner. That's because it has a foundational character. It is the fact that at all points the Christian theologian has to test his affirmations by "the gospel" that makes theology "no easy task."

Franke says that theology is a second-order activity. Indeed it is. But the distinction between the first-order character of Scripture and the second-order activity of doing theology is not hard and fast. The Bible is not simply a set of first-order data on which the theologian performs various second-order operations in order to pro-

22. Ibid., 105.
23. Ibid.

duce a theology. The Bible is also a theological document. The Bible is not simply a resource for the theologian; it is itself theological. So—to take obvious examples—when Paul is arguing in 1 Corinthians 15 about the nature of the resurrection body, or in Romans about the nature of justification, he is not simply providing data for the theologian; he is himself reasoning theologically, drawing theological conclusions and so giving the church a model of theological activity. Thus from the start, and not only when the Christian theologian has done some work, the Bible and particularly the New Testament, exercises its authority over the Christian mind.

How is this authority recognized and owned? In common with many who propound post-conservative or postevangelical theologies, Franke has little or nothing to say about this, though he implicitly recognizes that the theologian does not by his activity *confer* authority on Scripture, for Scripture already has that authority in the church. In fact, God himself confers that authority, as he witnesses by his Spirit to the spirits of his faithful people. This comes to the people of God in the form of an instinct, a gut-like instinct of recognition that God speaks in the words of Scripture. And how does this come about? Not by a fideistic leap of faith, or in simple acquiescence to the quasi-political authority of the church, but by the Spirit's testimony to the ways and works of God as they are found in Scripture. So it is intrinsic to the recognition of the authority of Scripture that it witnesses to its own God-given character in the very gospel to which it bears testimony. The Holy Spirit ratifies that testimony in our minds and consciences. The Bible has first-order meaning, which is the meaning that the Spirit witnesses to as the very truth of God.[24]

So Scripture is not simply sets of words or marks on a page, raw data that, when the theologian has got to work on it, will yield a theology which then exercises authority. Scripture inherently has authority because it is from the start a God-given theological document, containing a set of theological paradigms. The sentences that Paul wrote to the Corinthians, for example, do not require the intervention of theologians to make them "theology"; they already are theological. And so the inherently authoritative Scriptures are a theological document. Of course, this in no way disparages the ongoing work of Christian theologians, but it emphasizes that their task is circumscribed and bounded by the "biblical theology" that we already possess in the text of Scripture, which must always act as the criterion for testing subsequent theological efforts.

Franke may think that, because theology is, in his view, "an ongoing, second-order, contextual discipline,"[25] this somehow preserves the integrity of the first-order dis-

---

24. The *locus classicus* of the idea of the self-authenticating character of Scripture is John Calvin, *Institutes of the Christian Religion*, ed. John T. McNeill, trans. Ford Lewis Battles, 2 vols. (Philadelphia: Westminster, 1960), 1.7. For discussion of Calvin, see Paul Helm, *John Calvin's Ideas* (Oxford: Oxford University Press, 2004), chap. 9. For a first-rate modern exposition in the context of Christian epistemology, see Alvin Plantinga, *Warranted Christian Belief* (New York: Oxford University Press, 2000), chaps. 8–10.
25. Franke, *Character of Theology*, 84.

course of Scripture, allowing it to continue to speak in its own right and to exercise its own authority over the church. He sometimes seems to write like that. It may be that he thinks that whatever the theologian may make of this first-order material while developing a second-order discourse about it, the first-order material remains intact. In a sense this is true. The first order-discourse remains physically there, on the page, whatever the theologian makes of it. But yet on his view of the theological task, that first-order discourse has no prospect of being foundational for the work of the Christian theologian. Furthermore, the understanding of that discourse is constantly changing as the second-order discourse develops, for the second-order discourse, developed from the church and the culture, tells the theologian what that first-order discourse means, or at least what it means for the time being.

The Culture: What Is and What Ought to Be

A further factor that makes the task of theology much harder than Franke thinks is the need to make a sharp distinction between what *is* the case and what *ought* to be the case, between facts and values, descriptions and prescriptions. He hardly seems to recognize the need for such a distinction. But without it, when one bears in mind the heavily contextual and cultural emphasis that Franke makes, sociology triumphs over theology. In fact theology, if it endures in any such form, becomes sociology. I shall illustrate the dangers of not observing this distinction from what Franke says.

In his section "The Contextual Nature of Theology,"[26] Franke points to the obvious fact that all forms of thought are embedded in social conditions; they are "situated." Christian theology is no exception. It is a human activity that arises in particular contexts. That's true of course, of everything, including Scripture and the incarnation itself. But then he immediately follows this with something rather different: "It is not the intent of theology simply to set forth, amplify, refine, and defend a timelessly fixed orthodoxy."[27] This claim, right or wrong, does not at all follow from the point about situatedness. From the fact that theology is situated, inevitably situated, it does not follow that it may not have the *objective* or the goal of setting forth a timelessly fixed orthodoxy and that it may not, in a measure, realize that objective. What is to stop it from doing this? It is obviously no answer for Franke simply to repeat the point about situatedness, or to elaborate this point from the facts of Christian history, as in fact he proceeds to do.

As Franke says, Christian theology has taken shape from, been revised by, and navigated through, a number of cultural transitions in its history. But unless "theology" is simply the name of an activity, like whistling, then something must

26. Ibid., 84ff.
27. Ibid., 84.

have endured through these various vicissitudes.[28] Otherwise "Christian theology" is a wax nose. It is this enduring body of belief that ensures that the theology that endures is *Christian* theology—and not the theology of some other god or gods. Christian theology is transcultural.

Sometimes Franke appears to think that "contexts" are temporally and geographically confined, and fairly impermeable. In his approach to the task of theology he emphasizes that theology is "local," though it cannot be pursued in isolation from the universal church.[29] Yet paradoxically, his discussion of Origen (c. AD 185–254) is at odds with this contextual emphasis. Franke clearly has access to the thought-world of Origen. Among several other things, he tells us that Origen's work *On First Principles* "is an ordered and systematic account of Origen's theological and philosophical positions concerning God, creation, Jesus Christ, the Logos of God, and salvation."[30] So it must be possible for someone in one historical and cultural context to have access to the products of another context, to gain true beliefs about them, and to be able to criticize Origen, for example (as many others have), for accommodating his Christian thought to his own Hellenistic setting. In light of these reflections on Origen, Franke asks, "Have we too readily conformed our conception of the Bible and its interpretation to the assumptions and aspirations of our culture? Further, given our participation in our culture, on what basis are we able to make such an assessment?"[31] This is pretty rich for someone who wishes to ride bareback on postmodernism! But—more importantly for us—these questions reveal that, despite what Franke elsewhere says, it is an exaggeration to suppose that each of us is confined to the particularities of his or her own culture and that we cannot be addressed by saints and doctors of the church from other times and places. And it is an equal exaggeration to suppose that today's non-Christian culture cannot be addressed in the same way.

But Franke goes further. It is not simply that our context differs from Origen's. Rather, every understanding of the Christian message is "particular."[32] We too-readily assume a Christian constant or universal which "then functions as the foundation for the construction of theology, even though it will need to be articulated in the language of a particular culture."[33] This "translation" model of the relation between culture and the gospel is condemned by Franke because it is foundational. "Neither gospel nor culture can function as the primary entity in the conversation between the two in light of their interpretive and constructed nature; we must recognize that theology emerges through an ongoing conversation involving both gospel and cul-

28. Ibid., 84–85.
29. Ibid., 119.
30. Ibid., 93–94.
31. Ibid., 99.
32. Ibid., 103.
33. Ibid.

ture."[34] (Here is another expression of the parity between gospel and culture that Franke believes to be of the essence of nonfoundational theology.) So he favors an "interactive model."[35]

It is tempting to reverse the argument: Translation occurs, therefore translation is possible. We translate Aristotle, Origen, or Augustine. Do we translate every nuance? Clearly not. Are the translations faithful? Some are, some are not. How do we know which is which? By repeatedly consulting the original and anything we can find out about it. This happens with Origen, for example, as Franke clearly shows. Why may it not happen with the New Testament? We might pause to ask how Franke can be so confident about this approach to culture. How does he know that cultures are "particularities" in this sense? How does he know how cultures can be separately identified and counted like beans? What counts as one culture, what as two, or more? Isn't it much more likely that any one culture is a blend of several? We might press these questions. But it is sufficient for our present purposes to dismiss this appeal to cultural particularity by noting that his own discussion of Origen is a *reductio ad absurdum* of his own skepticism.

No doubt, Christian theology is contextual, which raises the following question: In any situation in which Christian belief is being assessed or evaluated, what elements of that belief ought we to accept because they cohere with, illuminate, and vindicate the sense of the sentences of the Bible, and what ought we to reject because they compromise that sense by being over-influenced by some feature of the context in which those beliefs were formulated and expressed? Some contexts are supportive of the Christian faith, others oppose it. But while all our activity is inevitably contextual, it by no means follows that we cannot attempt to minimize the effects of one kind of context, and maximize that of another.

Take, for example, moral contexts. Some contexts are deeply morally evil, others less so, others morally good. How do we assess the moral values of our particular culture? Suppose we can. We note that it has various moral aspects or elements, some of them in conflict with some others: for example, rights may conflict with duties. Which of these aspects ought we to indulge and allow to condition our theological thinking? The language of rights or the language of duties? Or neither? Which ought we to resist because they cut across our present understanding of Christian theology? More pointedly, which ought we to replace by our present understanding of Christian theology? Obviously, we ought to replace those that we believe undermine the gospel. Are there Christian moral values, set forth in Scripture, that have become lost to our culture, or obscured by it, or that as a matter of fact our culture has never recognized? Why can't the gospel judge the morals of our culture? Isn't the matter of judging the culture a vital aspect of the ministry of Jesus, or of the teaching of

34. Ibid.
35. Ibid.

Paul and the other apostles? When Paul writes to the Corinthians about their beliefs and their behavior, he is of course writing to them from a particular context. His readers are, presumably, in another context. Paul has beliefs, a place, a time, as do the Corinthians. Nevertheless, he does not scruple to criticize both their beliefs (about the resurrection of the dead, say) and their behavior (at the Lord's Table) by what he terms "my gospel." Of course, the Christian church lacks Paul's apostolic authority. Nevertheless, he sets a pattern of judging the context by the gospel. Is this an easy task? No, most certainly not. There are numerous pitfalls. Is it impossible? No, most certainly not. It cannot be. For if it were impossible, then we would be forced to accept that the culture, our situatedness, swamps the gospel, and what *is*—our context—becomes indistinguishable from what *ought* to be—our Christian commitment. The gospel then becomes a plaything of the culture.

If the gospel is able to stand over against the culture, as Paul stood over against the Corinthians, does this imply that the propositions of Christian theology are "timeless"? For more than half a century critics have charged that to accept the claim that at the heart of the Christian faith are true propositions is to make Christianity a matter of timeless truth. But as far as I know no one has ever succeeded in saying clearly what that charge amounts to.[36] So this is not only a red herring, a distraction from the main issue, but it's also a straw man.

Nevertheless, although its propositions may not be "timeless," the gospel and the theology that it gives rise to, and ought continually to be informed by, is abiding. The "core" of our faith remains through time, giving our theology its distinctively Christian meaning, though its manner of expression may vary. It is this balancing act between the abiding "orthodoxy"—the "form of sound words," the foundation that cannot be replaced by any other foundation—and its varied and ongoing expression in a variety of contexts that makes the practice of theology no easy task. Franke does not seem to appreciate this. Jesus Christ is the same yesterday, today, and forever. The faith is once delivered to the saints. There is "no other name." "For no one can lay a foundation than that which is laid, which is Jesus Christ" (1 Cor. 3:11)—there is the "foundation" (in the light of our discussion, an interesting New Testament word!) of the apostles and prophets, and of Jesus Christ the cornerstone (another interesting word!). And Paul makes plain that this foundation is accessible to us, that it may be built upon, as well as that some will do a better job of building on it than others.

A familiar fallacy must be avoided at this point. Let us grant, once more, that our present understanding of the Christian faith is "situated." To give an account of such situated understanding—of how people come to understand these things as they do in this time and this place—is to engage in the sociology of knowledge. But nothing follows from the fact that our present stock of beliefs can be studied sociologically

---

36. For a thirty-something contribution that tries to clarify this charge, see Paul Helm, "Revealed Propositions and Timeless Truths," *Religious Studies* 8 (1972): 127–36.

and certain valid sociological inferences can be drawn about how the present-day Christian community has come to hold its beliefs concerning whether this understanding of the Christian faith is true. The question of truth is not settled by noting sociological facts about how the church has come to have the beliefs she has, but rather by determining whether or not they are beliefs that faithfully—although no doubt fallibly—reflect the gospel. Otherwise skepticism follows. For since all human knowledge-claims of whatever kind are embedded in a culture, the claims of the sociology of knowledge included, the truth or otherwise of any such knowledge-claim would be dissolved by that fact. Is it "docetic" to maintain that the Christian faith is transcultural, fully divine, and only seeming to be human? Does it downplay and even ignore the reality of culture? Are we making insufficient allowance for the "incarnational" character of the revelation? Why might that be? The One who was incarnate had a situation too. But in deed and word he was nevertheless God's revelation. He was both human and divine. The situatedness of the gospel is real, but so is its transcultural character.

Downplaying Truth Claims

As we noted at the beginning, according to Franke postmodernism critiques the modernist project's quest for certain, objective, and universal knowledge.[37] And so it follows that postmodern theology will play down such claims, replacing them with something "situated" and tentative, or abandon them altogether. This is very much a corollary of our earlier discussion. But if this corollary is to be taken seriously, it also would fatally compromise the gospel. Let us see why.

First, a word on the "quest for certain, objective, and universal knowledge." Let us grant that this is an accurate characterization of the Enlightenment "quest." But to lay it aside for that reason is far too clumsy and indiscriminate a reaction. For one thing, the three epistemological goals—certainty, objectivity, and universality—are logically independent of each other. In particular, it is possible to have knowledge that is not accessible to everyone, or even to anyone. Perhaps everyone *could* have such knowledge, but not everyone *does* have it. I know that I now have the taste of grapefruit juice in my mouth while I am looking at the cliff face, but unless I tell you,[38] and you believe me in a way that justifies your belief, you don't know it, and never shall. I am certain that I have that taste now, and see the cliff face now, and the knowledge is objective (in at least one sense of that slippery term), since Helm's tasting grapefruit juice now while seeing the cliff face is a fact about the world, and knowing that I have that taste now while seeing the cliff face is knowing a fact about the world. (Of course there are differences. You could come here and see the cliff

---

37. Franke, *Character of Theology*, 15.
38. This raises the question of testimony and authority in epistemology, very important for the understanding of a truly Christian epistemology, since Scripture is testimony. Unfortunately (or fortunately, depending on your point of view) we don't have space to look into this issue here.

face even though it is impossible for you to have my taste of grapefruit juice. But the reader will understand if we do not pursue such niceties here.) So there can be knowledge that is certain and objective without its being universal. And perhaps I can know such facts without being certain that I know them. So it would be unwise to dismiss "certainty, objectivity, and universality" with a wave of a postmodernist hand.

In addition, it would be unwise for a Christian theologian to dismiss lightly objective knowledge, because knowledge, the knowledge of what God has revealed, is intrinsic to his quest. And some awareness of the character of that knowledge is a *sine qua non* for attempting Christian theology. In particular, Scripture testifies that there is knowledge that is not universal, at least not without adding a set of strong conditions. Both the modernist and the postmodernist are likely to be turned incandescent by the particularism of the knowledge claims of the Christian faith, but that cannot be helped. "To you it has been given to know the secrets of the kingdom of heaven, but to them it has not been given" (Matt. 13:11). Jesus is not saying that his disciples simply thought that they knew, or that "knowledge" is an honorific name or a kind of persuasive definition, for what he and the band of the disciples held in common. They knew what others did not know; in fact, what those others dismissed as piffle. And they knew these things because it had been given them to know them, willingly disclosed to them but not to everyone else. The fact that others may dismiss as piffle claims to know such mysteries did not affect the reality of the disciples' knowledge. Behind Jesus' claim, then, is a claim about the objectivity of truth. There are secrets of the kingdom. That's an objective fact. And the disciples were given to know those secrets.

The recognition that the revealed mysteries are truth has a long pedigree in Christian theology. (The objectivity of knowledge may have been a part of the Enlightenment *quest*, but it is most certainly not an Enlightenment *invention*). That knowledge is common to the disciples.

We have already noted that the fact that some goal is unattainable does not mean that we should not strive to approach it as nearly as possible. It is one thing to recognize that the quest for certain, objective, and universal knowledge is unachievable, quite another thing to maintain that we ought not to strive for it. No doubt the eliminations of disease, or hunger, or war are unattainable goals. But we do not and ought not to allow that fact to excuse a fatalistic attitude to the onset of disease, or to abandon the challenge of feeding the starving, or to cease to strive for peace. Rather, we should do all that we can to cure and feed and reconcile. We shall not revisit that point. But there is a related objection. Perhaps there are goals that are not finally attainable and that we cannot even begin to attain. Perhaps achieving objectivity and certainty in our beliefs are goals of this kind. Not merely goals that we cannot achieve, but goals that we cannot start to achieve.

As noted, fallibilism is inherent in Protestantism. Historically, this is due to the claims of the Roman church to possess an infallible *magisterium*. But more generally it acknowledges human finitude and sin, and error through willfulness and ignorance. Protestantism, and especially its Reformed segment, has willingly confessed that God alone is infallible. That infallibility no doubt transfers to the Word of God, but it does not transfer further to all human interpretations of Scripture. It cannot since these interpretations may and do conflict. So in drawing attention to human fallibility postmodernism is doing nothing new. Yet though this recognition of our all-too-human fallibility may be unsettling, we must put it or keep it in proportion. Fallibilism yes, but skepticism, certainly not. Being fallible, we are inclined to err, but fallibility—or on the other side, certainty—comes in degrees, as can be seen from some simple examples. I am fallible, but I know that I have a head; fallible, but pretty confident that this piece is being written in the United Kingdom; fallible, but less confident that the emission of carbon dioxide is responsible for current global warming, and so on. Certainty—not the mere subjective feeling, but certainty-on-evidence—comes in degrees. Some claims may be highly certain and thus more certain than their opposites, and so they may be strongly believed: I know I have a head, and thus am justified in rejecting the claim that I am headless; I am quite sure that I am writing this piece in the United Kingdom, and so can confidently reject the claim that I am writing it in Antarctica. How these degrees of certainty ought to be measured, whether by a probability calculus or in some other way, is a separate and more contentious matter. But the fact that there are degrees of certainty—or fallibility—cannot be doubted, or that there ought to be degrees of belief.

Earlier we noted the importance of the self-attesting character of Scripture in conveying to us its authority, and saw that such an instinct or intuition is the product of the Spirit's work testifying to the truth of Scripture. Let us now glance at some data for that, taken as it happens from John's Gospel, which speaks of truth and knowledge:

> If you abide in my word, you are truly my disciples, and you will know the truth, and the truth will set you free. (John 8:31–32)

> If anyone's will is to do God's will, he will know whether the teaching is from God or whether I am speaking on my own authority. (7:17)

> If I am not doing the works of my Father, then do not believe me; but if I do them, even though you do not believe me, believe the works, that you may know and understand that the Father is in me and I am in the Father. (10:37–38)

> I do as the Father has commanded me, so that the world may know that I love the Father. . . . (14:31)

These assertions come from a particular context, and are taken almost at random from the Gospel of John, and yet we seem to be able to understand what is being asserted. There may be nuances to "truth" and "knowledge" as used here that escape us, and yet it seems we may gain a fair understanding of these ideas. More importantly, it seems that, by God's grace, if what John says is true, men and women may themselves come into the same position of those about whom Jesus spoke, and to whom he spoke. What does post-conservative theology make of such assertions? The assertions occur in a very different context from that which we occupy, presumably, and so our understanding of these words, and our trust in them, must be seriously qualified. So perhaps the words "know," truth," "understand" ought to be given the post-conservative treatment. Is it not presumptuous for us to use them? Ought not the fallibility of these claims of Jesus to be emphasized? Is it not "docetic" to do otherwise? Or if it is not that, then at least the fallibility of our own understanding of them ought to be emphasized? If so, then perhaps we should place quotation marks around the relevant words. Not "know the truth" but "'know' the 'truth,'" and so on, as the quotation earlier from Westphal seems to suggest. Of course, that seals them off, placing them in a kind of theological museum. But if not that, then what? If not that, must not post-conservatism accept them at face value, as part of the "core" or "framework" or "foundation of truth" of the Christian faith? Let us hope that that is the reaction of Franke and the other post-conservatives. If it is, then one thing is sure: post-conservative theology is foundational theology after all.

But maybe we should simply call the bluff of the post-conservative. Do such people really mean to say that we cannot understand these words of Jesus, when he talks of knowing and believing and understanding? The fact that we might gain more and more understanding of the words as the scholars pore and pore over the text and then tell us what they've found cannot be denied. But don't we have a basic grasp? And doesn't that basic grasp depend on our grasp of our own uses of those words? Doesn't this include, for instance, our knowledge that we can understand something without believing it, and we can believe something without knowing it? That if we know something, then what we know is true? Isn't there a basic, accessible sense to Scripture, or to much of Scripture, particularly the New Testament writings that are so important for the life and work of Christians? And isn't this true, despite the fact that their original setting is fast receding into the past, and we are continuously suffering from (as we are told) "rapid cultural change"? So what's the problem?

The Christian church holds that it may reasonably claim a high degree of certainty about the meaning and truth of many biblical claims and that it may strive, by adopting practices familiar from non-theological areas, to increase the range of such propositions and the degree of certainty that it is possible to gain in them.[39] If this is so,

---

39. For a useful discussion of this question see D. A. Carson, *Becoming Conversant with the Emerging Church* (Grand Rapids: Zondervan, 2005), chap. 4.

then it is a short step to see that to the degree to which the meaning of some biblical statement is certain, it is objectively certain. It is objectively certain because the church holds that the biblical claims are objectively true and that by continuous efforts at Bible exposition and theological reflection upon them she may attain a closer and closer appreciation of them. Perhaps there are times of upheaval and reformation when the meaning, and hence the truth, and hence the certainty of some aspect of the truth, is called into question by some fresh proposal. But the point of principle remains, and the history of the church bears witness to it.

So the objectivity of Scripture is not to be understood in terms of some scholarly or popular consensus—if we took that line then once again we'd be treating theology as a branch of sociology—but by its God-given character. That objectivity is conferred on our theological statements to the extent that they reflect the meaning of Scripture but, given our inherent fallibility, our reflections do not have objective truth to the degree that the sentences of Scripture do. However, the objective truth, such as the church confesses it, is not merely privately or subjectively certain. It may be as certain for B as it is for A if B adopts the reasons, or similar reasons (or perhaps does not deny the reasons) that make A certain, or more certain than B. The same thing follows if A and B are in the same or a similar certainty-conferring environment. If it is certain for Jim that Jesus Christ came into the world to save sinners, then it may become similarly certain for Joanna. Would gaining more evidence from Scripture for the truth of that interpretation make it more certain than it is? Of course. Could the consideration of more evidence make it become less certain than it is? Of course, because sometimes, and paradoxically, we come to know less by becoming aware of more. But these are purely logical consequences of the fact that certainty ought to be based on evidence, and comes in degrees. So with certainty comes objectivity, not the objectivity of mere human consensus but objectivity whether we like it or not, or believe it or not.[40]

40. Thanks are due to Oliver Crisp and Mark Talbot for helpful comments and suggestions on an earlier draft.

4

Whosoever Will Be Saved: Emerging Church, Meet Christian Dogma

R. SCOTT CLARK

~~~~~~~~~

When our computers malfunction we simply hit the "reset" button and all is well. This act is a metaphor for late modern life. We live in an age that resists boundaries or resets them at will. Boundaries are elusive and eliding and there is a deep suspicion in "our time" of any attempt to reestablish them as little more than an exercise of the will to power.[1] Nevertheless, despite this formidable obstacle, I essay to reconsider and reestablish the notion of boundaries, arguing that there are objective, divinely revealed theological boundaries inherent and essential to Christianity. The argument is in three parts: our setting, the biblical revelation, and the creedal language.

Our Setting

Though proponents of the so-called emerging church seem to fancy themselves postmodern Christians, this first section argues that we are not in a genuinely post-modern time as much as we are in a late or liquid modern time. In Christian antiquity (from the patristic to post-Reformation periods), most everyone shared some basic assumptions about the nature of things: God is, he has spoken, his revealed will is

---

1. See David Wells's brilliant series of volumes indicting the evangelical movement for its capitulation to modernity. See David F. Wells, *No Place for Truth, or What Happened to Evangelical Theology?* (Grand Rapids: Eerdmans, 1993); *God in the Wasteland: The Reality of Truth in a World of Fading Dreams* (Grand Rapids: Eerdmans, 1994); *Losing Our Virtue: Why the Church Must Recover Its Moral Vision* (Grand Rapids: Eerdmans, 1998); *Above All Earthly Pow'rs: Christ in a Postmodern World* (Grand Rapids, Eerdmans, 2005).

normative, and it can be known. To be sure, there were massive disagreements as to what that revealed will is, but almost everyone was asking the same question: What has God said?[2]

From about the middle of the seventeenth-century until the late twentieth-century, much of the Western world came and remained under the influence of a very different set of assumptions until World War I in Europe and about 1968 in the USA. This set of assumptions produced a fundamentally different question: "Has God said?" During that period, the set of philosophical and theological ideas that dominated our thinking were described then as "Enlightenment" and have come since to be described as "modernity." According to modernity, we were said to have matured beyond the old supernaturalism. According to G. E. Lessing (1729–1781), in modernity we are on this side of an ugly ditch (the Enlightenment), by which we have been "emancipated from belief in the act of creation, revelation and eternal condemnation."[3] This antisupernaturalism manifested itself in two ways primarily: rationalism whereby autonomous human reason or empiricism whereby sense experience was said to be the measure of all truth and the arbiter of reality. In modernity, the real was the rational or empirical and the rational or empirical was the real. Modernity was a time of supreme certainty, grounded on autonomous foundations, in things human and a time of considerable skepticism about the old supernatural truths long held to be revealed by God to humanity. Rudolf Bultmann (1884–1976) summarized well the spirit of modernity:

> It is impossible to use the electric light and the wireless and to avail ourselves of modern medical and surgical discoveries, and at the same time to believe in the New Testament world of spirits and miracles. We may think we can manage in our own lives, but to expect others to do so is to make the Christian faith unintelligible to the modern world.[4]

This famous quotation strikes one today as quaint. By "wireless" he meant "radio," but we think of telephones or Internet access. More to the point, the passage reeks of modernist hubris.

Whereas, for the old Reformed and Lutheran orthodox, God was said to have unique knowledge (*theologia archetypa*) of which he had revealed an analogue to us (*theologia ectypa*) in Scripture.[5] God as he is in himself (*Deus in se*) is necessarily hidden from us. What is available to humans is what John Calvin described as reve-

---

2. The tripartite analysis of history, in this section of the essay, is borrowed and modified from Thomas C. Oden, *After Modernity What? Agenda for Theology* (Grand Rapids: Zondervan, 1990), 48–49.
3. Zygmunt Bauman, *Liquid Modernity* (Cambridge: Polity Press; Malden, MA: Blackwell, 2000), 28.
4. Rudolf Bultmann, *Kerygma and Myth: A Theological Debate*, trans. R. H. Fuller (New York: Harper & Row, 1961), 5.
5. See Willem van Asselt, "The Fundamental Meaning of Theology: Archetypal and Ectypal Theology in Seventeenth-Century Reformed Thought," *Westminster Theological Journal* 64, no. 2 (2003): 319–35.

lation that has been accommodated to human capacity.[6] Martin Luther made this same distinction by speaking of the "theology of glory" (*theologia gloriae*) and the "theology of the cross" (*theologia crucis*). In the Reformation and post-Reformation conception, what is revealed to us is objectively true and binding for all humans.

Under the influence of Immanuel Kant (1724–1804), however, modernity concluded that there is no objective reality (the noumenal), there is only our experience (the phenomenal) of it. Thus, whereas the Reformation and post-Reformation had it that God in himself is hidden, Kant argued that everything in itself (*Ding an Sich*) is hidden such that we cannot know things as they really are. In the modernist scheme, reality is not something "out there" established by God to which we must conform, but it is really a result of human experience or, in some cases, the human will. In other words, in contrast to Christian antiquity, which believed the Scriptures when they testified, "And God said . . . and it was," the modernists taught that it is we who speak, as it were, reality into existence. The predominant question of Christian antiquity was, what has God said? There were, of course, many different answers but most everyone agreed that God had spoken and revealed a deposit of objective truth to be known and confessed by the church.

The enlightened West, however, asked a radically different question: has God said? It begins not with God or some external authority, but with the self. It presupposes human autonomy and even superiority relative to all other authorities. Carl L. Becker reminds us that, in the eighteenth century, words such as sin, grace, and salvation, which the patristic, medieval, Reformation, and post-Reformation cultures used so frequently, came to be used less so. "In the eighteenth century, these grand magisterial words, although still to be seen, were already going out of fashion, at least in high intellectual society." Theologians "made much use of them," but they felt compelled to apologize to their rationalist critics on rationalist grounds for speaking like Christians.[7]

Liquidity

In the early part of the twentieth century in Europe, and since the late 1960s in North America, those antisupernatural certainties began to dissolve into what has often been called postmodernity or postfoundationalism. Just, however, as evangelicals have begun to come to grips with these developments, there is a move to re-assess the notion that the period in which we live is genuinely "post" modern. For example, Zygmunt Baumann, among others, has called our time "late," "liquidity" or "liquid

---

6. John Calvin, *Institutes of the Christian Religion*, trans. Ford Lewis Battles, ed. John T. McNeill, 2 vols., Library of Christian Classics (Philadelphia: Westminster, 1960), 1.13.1.
7. Carl L. Becker, *The Heavenly City of the Eighteenth-Century Philosophers* (1932; repr., New Haven: Yale University Press, 1968), 48. E.g., see Joseph Butler, *The Analogy of Religion* (London: George Bell and Sons, 1889).

modernity." Where solids are fixed, liquids are fluid and undergo constant change.[8] In continuity with earlier modernity, however, liquidity continues to be corrosive of all past loyalties and traditions, not in the interests of no "solids" whatever, which would be genuinely "post" modern, but in the interests of *new and improved solids.*[9] Liquid modernity has replaced the foundations of earlier modernity with the foundations of late modernity. In earlier modernity, the dominant metaphor was "space." Technology focused on overcoming space. In our time, however, the dominant metaphor is "time." Our technology (e-mail, cell phones, etc.) focuses on enabling us, allegedly, to do more, to overcome the limits of time.[10] We live and work on the move. We are become a nomadic society and late modern ecclesiastical life has not escaped this pattern.[11]

In liquidity, that reality is a human rather than divine construct has remained a basic assumption. Where earlier modernity found its certainty in rationalist or empiricist certainties, liquidity has turned to a plethora of personal, subjective certainties. The locus of certainty has moved from rationalist or empiricist foundations to subjectivist foundations. Liquidity has produced a considerable degree of skepticism—even cynicism—toward truth claims that purport to be universal. Nevertheless, since René Descartes (1596–1650), "I" remain the measure of all things. If there is no such thing as truth with a capital "T" that is universally binding, then all truth is really your truth or my truth but not "the" truth.

As Bauman has noted, because of this subjective turn, liquidity is particularly "inhospitable to critique."[12] In the biographical spirit of the age (*Zeitgeist*), permit me to illustrate this development from my own experience. When I left my congregation in the early 1990s to do doctoral work overseas, this cultural shift was well under way. In my university, however, I was permitted to speak my mind so long as my arguments were valid and sound. When I began teaching at an evangelical college a few years later, however, I found that a few students were offended by propositional discourse. In the years since, this experience has been repeated with increasing frequency. I finally realized that, for those who accept the premises of late modernity, any claim to truth is really nothing more than an attempt to impose one's personal views on another. All discourse is reduced to a Nietschean "will to power," that is, an attempt to impose rather than an expression of or search for truth.[13] If truth claims are really only a disguise for an act of the will, then any claim to truth is really

8. Bauman, *Liquid Modernity*, 1.
9. Ibid., 2–3.
10. Ibid., 9.
11. Ibid., 13.
12. Ibid., 23–24.
13. Friedrich Nietzsche (1844–1900) was a Prussian philosopher and classicist who concluded that traditional Christian morality was an outdated convention to be overthrown by the exercise of the will over self, to create a new self, to be consummated in the Übermensch.

an act of power.[14] It is not difficult to see how, from this point of view, traditional theological, ecclesiastical, and creedal boundaries have come to be seen not as not grounded in objective reality, but mere conventions to be overturned at will.

The broader evangelical church has not been untouched by these shifting cultural fault lines. Much of the old fundamentalist movement of the 1930s and 1940s and the broad evangelicalism since the 1970s was the conservative child of modernity. As such, it rooted certainty either in an illegitimate quest for religious certainty (in secondary and tertiary doctrinal and ethical points) or in an illegitimate quest for religious experience (i.e., the Schleiermachian quest for Jesus' religious experience or the unmediated encounter with the divine).[15]

Having rejected some of the assumptions of earlier modernity, as they have manifested themselves in fundamentalism and evangelicalism, elements of the emerging church movement have embraced the autonomous subjectivism of liquidity. This dual relation of the emerging church movement to modernity is evident in Brian McLaren's *A Generous Orthodoxy*.[16] Space does not permit me to summarize the entire work here, but it criticizes fundamentalism and sketches an outline for an inclusive, eclectic, synthetic approach to theology, piety, and practice.[17] He describes his Christian experience in terms of the various representations of Christianity he has experienced and then sets about to draw from each of them (and more) to create a new approach to Christianity that might attract those who are tempted either to leave the faith or investigate it for the first time.[18] He offers radical and sweeping proposals for the reconfiguration of Reformed theology including a reconfiguration of the heads of doctrine of the Synod of Dort (1519) and insists that reformed Protestants abandon "reductionism" by dropping the use of slogans such as *sola fide, sola gratia,* etc.[19] Perhaps the most provocative chapter in an intentionally provocative book is his proposal for how Christians ought to relate to other religions.[20] Though he does not embrace universalism, his language does not feature a *clear* articulation of the necessity of saving faith in Jesus as the only way to God and salvation.

There are obviously attractive qualities about McLaren's program and rhetoric. He has identified real problems, yet other writers have done the same thing without generating a movement of the same magnitude. His popularity and growing influence in broad evangelicalism and confessional reformed Christianity cannot be credited to the intellectual coherence of the book or to his grasp of history, theology,

14. Bauman, *Liquid Modernity*, 17, also points to Arthur Schopenhaur's notion that "reality" is created by the act of willing, which reinforces this worldview.
15. I explore these themes more completely in *Recovering the Reformed Confession* (Phillipsburg, NJ: P&R, 2008).
16. Brian McLaren, *A Generous Orthodoxy* (Grand Rapids: Zondervan, 2004).
17. E.g., he proposes a synthesis of Anabaptism and Anglicanism. See McLaren, *Generous Orthodoxy*, 223–38.
18. Ibid., 19–29, 49–74, 85–97.
19. Ibid., 221.
20. Ibid., 277–99.

or Scripture.[21] One possible explanation is that McLaren's program is in tune with the popular evangelical understanding of "postmodernism," which allows its adherents to define Christianity narcissistically and subjectively.[22] Its emphasis on personal religious experience and personal and corporate morality resonates with the pietist tradition in American evangelicalism. There is another, more profound, reason, however, for why the emergent movement is attractive. Though it markets itself as a counter-cultural movement, McLaren's *Generous Orthodoxy* is the product of the spirit of the age in important ways.

Options

It is no accident that the leader of the emergent movement is a baby boomer. He is part of a generational shift in evangelicalism that has resisted traditional boundaries for forty years. The cultural revolution symbolized by Haight-Ashbury on the West Coast, the 1968 Democrat National Convention in Chicago, and Woodstock on the East Coast has had its corollaries in evangelicalism. In 1968 Carl Henry lost control of *Christianity Today* magazine, the flagship of the evangelical movement. The pioneers of neo-evangelicalism were giving way to the baby boom generation who almost immediately began to revise the historic Protestant doctrines of Scripture, God, and the church. Why did the ascension of the baby boom generation signal such a "megashift"?[23]

To explain the broader social trends coinciding with this transition, Bauman has noted that where the dystopias of Aldous Huxley and George Orwell predicted a future without choice, we find ourselves besieged by options.[24] Anthropologist Thomas de Zengotita accounts for the contemporary resistance to limits by speaking of "representation," "virtualization," and "options."[25] By these three terms, he means that, in contrast to premodernity where reality was conceived as the result of divine Providence, in modernity we became "haunted by the knowledge that everything

---

21. To note just one egregious example, his account of the Reformation is unrecognizable to a historian, and his account of Calvin's life and theology is mystifying. For example, McLaren claims (ibid., 211–12) that Calvin began his pastoral ministry at age eighteen and then argues that we need to follow the example of the young Calvin. First, it is uncertain when Calvin became a Protestant, but it seems to have happened by 1534 at age 25. He was certainly not a pastor by age eighteen. Second, McLaren claims that Calvin published the first edition of his *Institutes* when Calvin was 25. In fact, Calvin was born in 1509, and the first edition appeared in 1536.

22. McLaren (*Generous Orthodoxy*, 324) seems to recognize this danger, but in my judgment, has not succeeded in avoiding it. See also Brian McLaren, "The Method, the Message, and the Ongoing Story," in Leonard Sweet, ed. *The Church in Emerging Culture: Five Perspectives* (Grand Rapids: Zondervan, 2003), which includes responses by Michael Horton; D. A. Carson, *Becoming Conversant with the Emerging Church: Understanding a Movement and Its Implications* (Grand Rapids: Zondervan, 2005), 57–70.

23. Robert Brow, "Evangelical Megashift," *Christianity Today*, February 19, 1990, 12–14.

24. Bauman, *Liquid Modernity*, 61.

25. Thomas de Zengotita, *Mediated: How the Media Shapes Your World and the Way You Live in It* (New York and London: Bloomsbury, 2005). This too-brief summary does not do justice to De zengotita's insightful work.

could be otherwise."[26] We became uniquely self-conscious that it has become increasingly difficult to distinguish the "mediated" from the "real," and that this mediated and virtual reality has created a panoply of choices to which we autonomous, reality-creating moderns have become accustomed. He calls the unending collage of options "the Blob."[27] The mediation of modern life ("the Blob") resists limits. "The Blob will not tolerate edges."[28] Modernity or mediation, that is, the self-constructed, self-conscious reality distinct to this age, authorizes eclecticism.[29] "The Blob is all about having it both ways. Or more."[30] In late modernity choice is ultimate and the chooser sovereign. Nietzsche was right about modernity: the point of the entire enterprise was to be done with God and limits.[31] Late modernism is high-tech narcissism.[32]

So, the emergent suspicion of theological and ecclesiastical borders is in tune with the spirit of the age as de Zengotita describes it. It is not that McLaren is unaware of the existence of boundary markers in the Christian faith. He makes reference to the catholic creeds and affirms them, but he is ambiguous about his relation to them and about their authority. This is clear when he defines his "generous orthodoxy" in moral rather than theological categories.[33] Where he allows a multiplicity of doctrinal views, he is rather stricter on what he finds morally acceptable. McLaren is latitudinarian when it comes to doctrine, but a precisionist when it comes to morals.[34]

Whether intended or not, the effect of McLaren's project is the weakening of creedal and confessional boundaries. This may be partly due to the fact that as much experience as McLaren has enjoyed in various parts of Christendom, to use his language, he does not seem to have met what one might call the Protestant confessional Jesus.[35] Nevertheless, according to Protestant confessionalism, Christianity is not

26. Ibid., 43.
27. Ibid., 23.
28. Ibid., 26.
29. Ibid., 259–60.
30. Ibid., 61.
31. Ibid., 265.
32. Ibid., 275.
33. McLaren, *Generous Orthodoxy*, 32–36, 148–49.
34. As an illustration of the resistance of liquidity to criticism, I note that McLaren is especially demanding of his critics. For example, having caricatured Calvinism and called for its overhaul along "emergent" lines, he cautions Calvinists to be generous in their criticism of him. See McLaren, *Generous Orthodoxy*, 221.
35. He might meet him in D. G. Hart, *The Lost Soul of American Protestantism* (Lanham, MD: Rowman and Littlefield, 2002). His juxtaposition of Calvin against the Calvinists has been thoroughly discredited by a mountain of modern scholarship. For example, See Richard A. Muller, *The Unaccommodated Calvin: Studies in the Foundation of a Theological Tradition* (New York and Oxford: Oxford University Press, 2000); Muller, *After Calvin: Studies in the Development of a Theological Tradition*, Oxford Studies in Historical Theology (Oxford: Oxford University Press, 2003); Muller, *Post-Reformation Reformed Dogmatics: The Rise and Development of Reformed Orthodoxy, ca. 1520 to ca. 1725*, 2d ed., 4 vols (Grand Rapids: Baker Academic, 2003); Carl R. Trueman and R. Scott Clark, eds, *Protestant Scholasticism: Essays in Reassessment* (Carlisle: Paternoster, 1999); R. Scott Clark, *Caspar Olevian and the Substance of the Covenant: The Double Benefit of Christ,* ed. David F. Wright, Rutherford House Studies in Historical Theology (Edinburgh: Rutherford House, 2005). McLaren's casual association of Calvinism with fundamentalism (*Generous Orthodoxy*, 208, 220–21) is puzzling. It is true that J. Gresham Machen made a tactical alliance with fundamentalism in the

the result of one's personal religious experience. Though capable of reasoned defense, the Christian faith is not first of all grounded in a universal truth evident to all reasonable persons nor is it defined by empirical truths, though it makes claim to empirical evidence of its truthfulness. Contra the suspicions of poststructuralism, Christianity is not a will to power, a convention, or a purely private truth. Rather, Christianity is a series of interrelated, public dogmas, grounded in the history of redemption, that must be taken up by faith in the tri-personal God who revealed them in Christ. McLaren seems, perhaps unintentionally, to have accepted assumptions about the nature of doctrine condemned by Dorothy Sayers (1893–1957):

> Teachers and preachers never, I think, make it sufficiently clear that dogmas are not a set of arbitrary regulations invented *a priori* by a committee of theologians enjoying a bound of all-in dialectical wrestling. Most of them were hammered out under pressure of urgent practical necessity to provide an answer to heresy.[36]

McLaren unhelpfully juxtaposes the dogmas of the faith with the drama of personal relations. To borrow further from Sayers, "the dogma *is* the drama."[37] According to the catholic church (i.e., the institutional church in all times and places) that dogma is delivered to us in Holy Scripture.

Scripture

The great difficulty in theological discourse with children of liquidity is the constant (often implicit) appeal to particulars over universals. Every assertion of a fixed truth is met with the response: "That is *your* tradition." Implied in any such response is a sort of skepticism about the existence of universals, that is, predicates that describe more than one thing at a time that are true for everyone at the same time in the same way. If there are no universals, then no one is bound to anything but his or her experience and perception or will (options).

Let us establish a starting point. For all its criticism of "modernity," it appears now that postfoundationalism is really only late or liquid foundationalism, and for all its shapelessness, liquidity continues to assume Enlightenment "givens," such as human autonomy relative to all other authorities and the centrality of the human knower relative to all knowledge.

As laudable as the war against Enlightenment foundationalism is, it does not follow that humans are capable of living in this world without *any* foundations. In

---

early twentieth century, but that alliance began to crumble even before his death and was dead by World War II. Historically, confessional Calvinism has had, at best, uneasy relations to fundamentalism.

36. Dorothy L. Sayers, "Creed or Chaos," in *Creed or Chaos* (New York: Harcourt, Brace, 1949), 34. This theme of doctrine as drama has been taken up by Michael S. Horton, *Covenant and Eschatology: The Divine Drama* (Louisville: Westminster John Knox, 2002) and by Kevin J. Vanhoozer, *The Drama of Doctrine: A Canonical Linguistic Approach to Christian Theology* (Louisville: Westminster John Knox, 2005).

37. Sayers, *Creed or Chaos*, 20–24 (emphasis added).

Christian thinking, instructed by divine revelation, it is understood that some foundation is essential, that no creature really starts from nothing. For creatures, in the nature of things, the question is not whether foundations, but whose? The great error of modernity was that it attempted to establish autonomous rationalist and empiricist (and sometimes, in reaction to those two, Romantic/mystical) foundations in defiance of and as a substitute for objective divine revelation as the starting point for human knowing and acting. The attempt by Descartes to find such a foundation in autonomous consciousness and rationality is symbolic and seminal of the modernist arrogance.[38] By the ruthless criticism of every other starting place, he found the reliable starting point *in himself*. Unlike most in Christian antiquity (e.g., Augustine and Anselm), he did not begin with God and reason thence; he began with himself and reasoned to God.[39] In Christian antiquity, we were said to be contingent upon God, but in modernity, whether earlier or late, God is said to be contingent upon us. The universe has been turned on its head.

As creatures, however, we are not entitled to begin with the self. We begin with revelation and we must begin where revelation begins, with the Creator and Revealer. It is true that this starting point assumes the beginning (*petitio principii*), but such is unavoidable for creatures: the finite is not capable of the infinite (*finitum non capax infiniti*).[40] Someone might object, "But revelation has to be interpreted." That is true, it does, but that is just the point. *Interpretation* is not creation. Creation is speaking into nothing and making something. Interpretation deals with that which is given. The act of submitting to revelation as the norm is, like the fear of Yahweh, the beginning of wisdom (Ps. 111:10). To paraphrase the psalmist, "The fool has said in his heart, I am autonomous" (Ps. 14:1). Because we are creatures, we may not think autonomously relative to God and revelation. Because we are creatures—there was when we were not—and therefore necessarily finite and contingent upon the Creator, any claim to autonomy relative to God is mere pretense. Further, because we are mere creatures, to understand ourselves and creation, we necessarily start with the God of Scripture. He alone is self-existent (*a se*) and autonomous. God's Word begins with his eternal, independent, self-existence: "In the beginning, God" (Gen 1:1).

38. See René Descartes, *Meditatio Secunda*, 2.3 in *Meditationes de prima philosophia/Meditations on First Philosophy,* bilingual ed., ed. and trans., George Heffernan (Notre Dame, IN: University of Notre Dame, 1990), 100–101. Though Descartes did not actually *say* "cogito ergo sum," it is a fair summary of his argument. He said, "So that—all things having been weighed enough, and more, this statement were—finally, to be established: '*I* am, *I* exist' (*ego sum, ergo existo*) is necessarily true so often as it is uttered by me or conceived by the mind."

39. Descartes' starting point in our experience is in stark contrast to Anselm (*Proslogion*, 3) who began with God's necessary existence: "God is that than which nothing greater can be conceived" ("*aliquid quo maius cogitari non potest*"). Anselm, *S. Anselmi Cantuariensis Archepiscopi opera omnia*, 6 vols, ed. F. S. Schmitt (Edinburgh: T. Nelson et filios, 1946–1961), 1.130.

40. Though often described in the secondary literature as a "rationalist" *a priori* from which Reformed theology is deduced, this expression is just a shorthand way of asserting an ontological distinction between the Creator and all creatures. See Richard A. Muller, *Dictionary of Latin and Greek Theological Terms Drawn Principally from Protestant Scholastic Theology* (Grand Rapids: Baker, 1985), s.v., "finitum."

By contrast, the same sort of existence is never predicated of us. We creatures were formed from the "dust of the earth" (Gen 2:7). It was God who animated us. We are contingent upon him, and his self-revelation defines reality (Gen 1:5). His self-revelation is embedded in creation and is known universally (Rom 1:19–20; 2:14–15) so that every human being is morally obligated to satisfy the righteous demands of his Creator and is without excuse for any failure to satisfy that righteousness. In his great apologetic discourse on the Areopagus, the apostle Paul quoted a pagan poet as evidence of the universal knowledge of God (Acts 17:28). From the beginning then, it is evident that all humans are bounded by two objective realities: God and his self-disclosure.[41]

Boundaries in Creation

From the beginning, humanity was circumscribed by divinely instituted limits. Yahweh Elohim placed Adam in a garden. His location relative to creation was limited. He was charged with specific responsibilities for that holy space.[42] He was to "keep" or protect the sacred space from violation (Gen. 2:15). The same terms and ideas are repeated at the end of the garden story (Gen. 3:24). Adam's choices were further narrowed. One of two symbolic trees was forbidden to him on pain of death (Gen. 2:17). When Adam failed, he was exiled from the paradise, excommunicated from the sacrament of life. It was with this foundational narrative in view that the apostle John declared that sin is "lawlessness" (1 John 3:4).

In Romans 5:12–21, the apostle Paul appeals to the limits (law) under which Adam was placed in order to contrast his refusal to submit to the divinely ordained boundaries with the last Adam's humble and willing submission (1 Cor. 15:45). He lived his human existence under the divinely imposed boundaries, indeed, he was "born of a woman, born under the law" (Gal. 4:4) for the very purpose of obeying and satisfying the righteous demands of the law. Paul was emphatic about the abiding force of these boundaries in Galatians 3:10, as he quoted Deuteronomy 27:26: "Cursed be everyone who does not abide by all things written in the Book of the Law, and do them."

Boundaries in Redemption

Beyond his existence, one of the most basic biblical declarations about God is that he is "one." Deuteronomy 6:4 says, "Hear O Israel, Yahweh our God, Yahweh is one." The God who delivered his covenant people out of Egyptian bondage is not like the

41. The emergent allergy to traditional theological categories notwithstanding, God's universal self-disclosure has always been understood as law, and his saving, gracious self-disclosure has been described as gospel. See R. Scott Clark, "The Letter and the Spirit: Law and Gospel in Reformed Preaching," in R. Scott Clark, ed. *Covenant, Justification, and Pastoral Ministry: Essays by the Faculty of Westminster Seminary California* (Phillipsburg, NJ: P&R, 2007).

42. That the garden was fraught with religious significance is made clear by the parallel in Ezek. 28:13 where the same noun is used to denote a sanctuary.

many Canaanite gods. He is without beginning (Ps. 90:2), he is not composed of parts, and he does not change (Mal. 3.6; James 1:17). He simply is (Ex. 3.14). None of these things could be said of the gods of the "nations." The New Testament writers echo repeatedly the theme of God's unity (Rom. 3:30; 1 Cor. 8:6; Eph. 4:6; 1 Tim. 2:5; James 2:19).

The apostle John was insistent that there are not simply *some* boundaries to Christian profession but *certain* and immovable boundaries to which all Christians must submit. Chief among these boundaries is Jesus the Messiah, whom John calls "the Word" or perhaps more pointedly, "the Revelation" (John 1:1). The Revelation was "with God" and "was God," that is, he sustains a personal relation to the Father and shares his essence. He is not only the Revelation of the knowledge of God, but is the Mediator of creation itself (John 1:3). The Revelation "became flesh" and lived in our midst (John 1:14).

It is because God the Son became incarnate that John is so insistent on the uniqueness of his mediation of the Father (John 14:6–9). No one has access to the Father except through Jesus the Revelation. Indeed, it is not possible for us to see the Father apart from the mediation of the Son. So complete is the Son's revelation of the Father that he who has seen him has seen the Father. One can see immediately why the apostle would be so hostile to those proto-Gnostics in the churches of Asia Minor, who were, by their denial of Jesus' humanity (and the reality of created matter generally) and their propagation of purported "secret" insights unavailable to the ordinary Christian, endangering the welfare of the congregations in Asia Minor.

In response to this threat, in 1 John 5:1–12, John posited a series of doctrinal and moral tests (5:13), universal affirmations of Christian truth that bind all Christians together. A Christian, one who is "born of God," believes that Jesus is the Messiah and loves others who are similarly begotten of God (5:1). He who belongs to this class of persons also loves and keeps God's commands (5:2–3). These lovers of God have conquered the "world" considered as an ethical rather than ontic category through faith. For the apostle John, it is inconceivable that anyone should reckon himself a "conqueror" of the world "unless" he actually believes and, by implication, confesses (John 9) that "Jesus is the Son of God." Though there is a distinction between theology and ethics and logical priority of theology over ethics, the two have a very close relation for John. Theology, that is, one's confession regarding Jesus' deity and humanity, has a necessary consequence in one's life, but without the divine birth and correct theology, one is not capable of loving God and other believers (1 John 5:5).

John's argument takes a very interesting turn in verses 6–9 where he reminds us again that the Savior is truly human. Jesus the Messiah came not only "through water but in water *and* blood," to which truth the Holy Spirit gives witness to the apostle John and through his ministry. He invokes the Old Testament law of "two or three witnesses" (Deut. 17:6). In this case, they are the water, the blood, and the Holy Spirit.

This language is most certainly a reflection of John's polemic against proto-Gnostics. For John, salvation is not a deliverance from matter nor does it entail a high-handed approach to createdness or giveness or situatedness. Our Savior has a created humanity. He has two natures, and became, for our sakes, "situated" in history with us and for us.

In the last section of the passage, John returns to the beginning: believing. The one believing has "the witness" (the testimony of the Spirit of 1 John 5:6–9). The unbeliever, in effect, calls God a liar, because he "has not believed in the testimony that God has borne concerning his Son" (5:10). The testimony is that God has given to believers eternal life in the Son (5:11), so that whoever "has" (i.e., believes in) the Son has life and whoever does not believe, does not have life (5:12).

I submit that the apostle's way of thinking is rather different from that of the emergent church movement, as represented by McLaren, in three ways. First, in McLaren's work I perceive an allergy toward the very idea of "nature" or "givens." McLaren quotes and agrees with Ken Wilbur on the sorts of dangers mentioned in this essay (e.g., pluralistic narcissism). Yet he also *affirms* the necessity for a sort of pluralistic narcissism and says he must make use of it as a sort of "chemotherapy."[43] Given the context of these remarks, it is not farfetched to imagine that it is the proponents of confessional orthodoxy who become the metaphorical "cancer" in view. The only alternatives McLaren seems to be able to imagine are what he calls "modern exclusivism/absolutism" and "pluralistic relativism."[44]

I submit that McLaren offers us a false dichotomy grounded in a misunderstanding of the nature of modernity (to which I think we are both opposed) and, as already suggested, a misdiagnosis of our present time. There is an alternative to McLaren's dichotomy: historic Christianity that never accepted the autonomous (rationalist, empiricist, or romanticist) premises of modernity of the "solid" (early) or liquid (late) varieties.

Rather, with the apostle John, we should affirm that there are boundaries, that there was a "beginning," and that there shall be an "end." There are also such things as natures. Our Lord Jesus has two. In the language of the Definition of Chalcedon, Christ has both a perfect "deity" and "manhood."[45] These are natures, givens. When we speak of Christ's "deity," we are speaking of something that is fixed and that cannot change. There is an immutable relation between the sign "deity" or "humanity" and the thing itself. The words "humanity" and "deity" are not mere conventions subject to continual revision and cultural change. They mean the same thing today in our post-everything culture that they meant in the fifth century AD when they were confessed at Chalcedon.

43. McLaren, *Generous Orthodoxy*, 324–25.
44. Ibid., 325.
45. Phillip Schaff, ed., *The Creeds of Christendom*, 3 vols. (Grand Rapids: Baker, 1983), 1:62.

Second, note how closely John connects the name "believer" to the thing named. There is, for John, a sort of *realistic* connection between the sign and the thing signified. This is important for several reasons. The emergent church, as represented by McLaren's book, takes a bivalent stance toward signs. On the one hand, the book is full of examples of "representation" or style, but it is both skeptical and casual about the relation between sign (*signum*) and thing signified (*res significata*). This analysis explains how McLaren is able to synthesize so effortlessly apparently opposing tendencies in theology, that is what we confess; piety (i.e., how we worship) and practice (i.e., how we live). For example, he attempts to synthesize theological liberalism with theological conservativism (ch. 8), fundamentalism and Calvinism (ch. 12), and most strikingly of all, Anabaptism and Anglicanism (ch. 13).

Since I have the least personal stake in the last example, let us turn briefly to it. As I understand the histories of Anglicanism and Anabaptism, they are radically opposed to one another in most significant ways. Anglicanism, whatever it has become since the rise of latitudinarianism, was a branch of confessional Protestant theology, piety, and practice. At its best, Anglicanism is represented by the piety of the prayer book and the orthodoxy of the Thirty-Nine Articles. Historic Anglicanism was churchly, public, and thoroughly Protestant, confessing the Reformation faith without equivocation.

Historic Anabaptism was almost none of these. Though sociologically anti-Roman, in theology all the major Anabaptist leaders rejected the material principle of the Reformation, justification *sola gratia, sola fide,* and its formal principle, *sola Scriptura.*[46] The piety of the Anabaptists was mystical. Indeed, Guido de Bres (1522–1567), the chief author of the *Belgic Confession* (1561) published an entire work in 1565 devoted in large part to criticizing what we would today call the Pentecostal or charismatic aspects of mysticism of the Anabaptist movement.[47] There could hardly be a sharper contrast between the rhythms and piety of the prayer book of historic Anglicanism and the mystical, subjective piety of Anabaptism. While some Anabaptists did confess their faith formally (e.g., the *Schleitheim Confession* of 1527), in the nature of the Anabaptist movement, that document binds only those individuals who signed it. The point of being an Anabaptist is that no one mediates anything to anyone and no one speaks for anyone else. In contrast, in theory at least, all Anglicans are bound to the Articles and the English Catechism. That McLaren believes he can synthesize these two movements suggests, whatever his personal experience with both movements, that he does not regard them as having particular, discrete "natures" and that he does not understand either of them very well. The only principle

46. That this is so is evident in a survey of the theology of the major leaders of the Anabaptist movements or in the masterful survey, G. H. Williams, *The Radical Reformation*, 3rd ed. (Kirksville, MO: Sixteenth Century Journal Press, 1992).
47. Guy de Brès, *La Racine, source, et fondement des Anabaptistes ou Rebaptizes de nostre temps* (Paris, 1565).

that really unites all the various "Jesuses" McLaren has known, with his other syntheses, is his religious experience. The claim to be able to synthesize them suggests a touch of the spirit of American religion, a religion that Harold Bloom describes as enthusiasm and Gnosticism.[48]

Finally, there seems to be a connection between McLaren's bivalent approach to signification and his ambivalence about Christian exclusivism. One does not find any hint of ambivalence in the apostle John about Christian exclusivism. Jesus is not *a* revelation of God, *an* eschatological truth, and *a* salvation, he is *the* Revelation (John 1:1–3, 18; 14:6). For John, as for Jesus, it is nearly blasphemous to ask to see the Father apart from Jesus. The Jesus of the Gospel and Epistles of John is "light," and "life," and "bread," and "the way, the truth, and the life" (John 8:12; 6:35; 11:25; 14:6). All these predicates are categorical and unequivocal and unambivalent.

Creeds and Catholicity as Boundaries

The language of the Definition of Chalcedon suggests a final consideration relative to McLaren's vision for theology, piety, and practice. I write as a representative of Reformed confessionalism, but my interest here is not to try to drag unwilling emerging Christians and churches into Protestant confessionalism; though it would be helpful if they would recognize this stream of historic Christianity as a distinct category.[49] Rather, my interest is to appeal to adherents of the emerging movement to consider the claims of catholic Christianity that bind all Christians together.

McLaren is correct to say that "catholic" is not a reference to the Roman communion,[50] but his account of what constitutes catholicity is a little misleading. He defines catholicity in terms of inclusiveness, liturgy, tradition, the Virgin Mary, and broadly, its humanity.[51] In at least three of these five characteristics (liturgy, tradition, humanity), however, this characterization could just as well describe important aspects of confessional Protestantism. By catholic, in this discussion, I do not refer to Rome. Rather, by catholic, I mean that public interpretation of Scripture, by the church in all times and places, that is universally binding on anyone who calls himself a Christian.

Historically, it has been the function of ecclesiastical creeds (e.g., the Apostles' Creed and the Nicene Creed) and confessions (e.g., the *Belgic Confession* and the *Westminster Confession*) to establish boundaries. Jaroslav Pelikan says,

> One of the most persistent features of all creeds and confessions of faith . . . so persistent as to be obvious and therefore in danger of being overlooked—especially in the after-

48. Harold Bloom, *The American Religion: The Emergence of a Post-Christian Nation* (New York: Simon and Schuster, 1992), see, e.g., 54.
49. On this see Hart, *Lost Soul of American Protestantism*.
50. McLaren, *Generous Orthodoxy*, 252.
51. Ibid., 253–59.

math of the modern controversies over liberal theology—is the utter seriousness with which they treat the issues of Christian doctrine as, quite literally, a matter of life and death, both here in time and hereafter in eternity.[52]

In the history of the church, the boundaries of biblical interpretation have been established not by modernity (in its liquid or solid states), but by the catholic church. This consensus about the teaching of Scripture is reflected in catholic or ecumenical creeds. One of the most important of these is the Athanasian Creed. Probably written in the sixth century, the Athanasian Creed summarizes the patristic consensus on the doctrines of the Trinity and Christ.

The Athanasian Creed is a witness against the arrogance of early modernity and the skepticism of liquidity. The opening line of the Athanasian Creed is and should be shocking to late modern pluralism: "Whosoever will be saved: before all things it is necessary that he hold the catholic faith."[53] The traditional name of the Athanasian Creed actually comes from the first two words of the Latin text, "*Quincunque vult*," that is, "whosoever will. . . ." This is the language of dogma, or ecclesiastical decree. This is not a proposition to be debated or discussed or viewed from an endless series of perspectives. By the nature of such language, options and choices are inherently limited. This is language from another time and place. It is the language of Christian antiquity. The sixth-century Latin church did not know Lessing's Ditch, Kant's phenomenal/noumenal distinction, nor did it know Foucoult or Derrida. It was not anguished by self-reflective obsession. It did not wonder how post-everything persons can affirm this or any dogma.

Pace McLaren, neither is this the language of intolerant Calvinism/Fundamentalism, nor of modern exclusivism. This is the language and stance of catholicity. In contrast to the *Zeitgeist*, where particulars overwhelm universals, catholicity teaches and requires universals. There are certain dogmas such as the Trinity (one God in three persons) and christology (one person, two natures) that transcend any particular place and time and that bind all Christians together. These universals make us, in the language of the Nicene-Constantinopolitan Creed, "one, holy, catholic and apostolic church." Universals and foundations are inherent in the very notion of a catholic faith.

Thus we should observe not only the exclusivity but also the severity of creedal language. The next line of the Athanasian says, "Which faith, unless everyone will keep whole and inviolate, without doubt he shall perish eternally."[54] Relative to this discussion the two adjectives "whole" and "inviolate" are most important. From the

---

52. Jaroslav Pelikan, *Credo: Historical and Theological Guide to Creeds and Confessions of Faith in the Christian Tradition* (New Haven and London: Yale University Press, 2003), 70.
53. Schaff, *Creeds*, 1.66.
54. My translation. "Quam nisi quisque integram inviolatamque servaverit: absque dubio in aeternum peribit" (Schaff, *Creeds*, 1.66).

point of view of catholicity, that is, from the historic Christian point of view, to which all Christians, even emerging Christians, are obligated, the faith naturally holds together, and we are not to undermine that coherence. The nature of the Christian faith is such that it contains its own boundaries, beyond which one may not travel and remain a Christian. According to the Athanasian Creed, despite McLaren's overt hostility to systematic theology, there are necessary and unchangeable internal relations in the faith between, for example, the doctrines of God (Trinity) and Christ. These ways of thinking and speaking militate against McLaren's eclecticism and selectivity.

Conclusions

Dorothy Parker once said, "You can't teach an old dogma new tricks." The absolutist language of the Athanasian Creed also testifies to the fact that the Christian faith is not *ours*, it is God's. It is inherently absolutist and exclusivist and antithetical to modernity in all its forms. In this chapter, I have contrasted Christian antiquity with modernity in two different forms, early or solid and late or liquid. I have argued that in certain important respects, the emerging church movement as represented by Brian McLaren's book *A Generous Orthodoxy*, though ostensibly *post*modern is really the product of the subjectivism of late or liquid modernity. Implicitly and explicitly, I have challenged McLaren (and everyone who subscribes his program) to reconsider his relations to authority, chiefly Scripture, as understood by Christian antiquity and especially as represented in the catholic creeds.

In response to the corrosive effects of late modernity on all fixity, I have reexamined the biblical witness to the existence of boundaries inherent in divine-human relations in creation and redemption (i.e., in the law and in the gospel). This argument for such boundaries finds its focus in the incarnation of God the Son and the apostolic proclamation of the absolute necessity of faith in him, orthodox confession about him, and congregational life in him. The reestablishment of such boundaries runs counter to McLaren's tendency to elide or call into question boundaries such as necessity of faith in Christ for salvation.

I have argued that Christian exclusivism and absolutism (as distinct from modern foundationalism) flow not from ecclesiastical convention or politics, but from the revelation of God in Christ, in Holy Scripture as understood and confessed by the catholic church.

In our time, that is, late or liquid modernity, the receiver/reader is said to be determinative of reality. Once speech/text has left the control of the author, the reader/ receiver is thought to be sovereign. In the biblical revelation, and subsequently in the premodern Christian world, however, quite the opposite was said to be true. As important as the receiver/reader is, it was reckoned that objective reality is constituted by God the Speaker through Christ his Revelation. Our responsibility with respect to revealed theology, piety, and practice is to "keep" (*servare*) or "protect" it. We do not name or constitute it, instead the faith names us. Thus, wherever McLaren might be at this moment theologically, what concerns me is the stance he has taken toward boundaries as revealed in Holy Scripture and confessed by catholic Christianity. There are implicit and explicit elements of McLaren's theological method that defy objective, revealed, and catholic boundaries, but the Christian faith cannot simply be rebooted. It has a nature, and certain universals are inherent in catholicity. I am not asking McLaren to become a confessional Protestant, though he certainly is welcome to join us, but I am asking him to decide whether he will be a catholic.

5

"Right Reason" and Theological Aesthetics at Old Princeton Seminary: The "Mythical Evangelical Magisterium" Reconsidered

PAUL KJOSS HELSETH

~~~~~~

In my contribution to the recent critique of post-conservative evangelicalism entitled *Reclaiming the Center: Confronting Evangelical Accommodation in Postmodern Times,* I argued that "postconservatism's repudiation of Old Princeton's 'propositionalist understanding of the theological enterprise' is based upon at least two profound misunderstandings of the Princeton mind."[1] In the second half of this chapter I expand upon the first of these misunderstandings, which is historical and related to Old Princeton's alleged indebtedness to "habits of . . . mind spawned by the Enlightenment,"[2] and in the first half I expand upon the second misunderstanding, which is theological and related to the nature of Old Princeton's opposition to the rise of theological liberalism. What I hope to establish is not only that the Princetonians were neither naïve theological realists nor rigid, uncompromising dogmatists,

1. Paul Kjoss Helseth, "Are Postconservative Evangelicals Fundamentalists? Postconservative Evangelicalism, Old Princeton, and the Rise of Neo-Fundamentalism," in Millard J. Erickson, Paul Kjoss Helseth, and Justin Taylor, eds. *Reclaiming the Center: Confronting Evangelical Accommodation in Postmodern Times* (Wheaton, IL: Crossway, 2004), 238. On the "propositionalist understanding of the theological enterprise," cf. Stanley J. Grenz, *Revisioning Evangelical Theology: A Fresh Agenda for the Twenty-First Century* (Downers Grove, IL: InterVarsity, 1993), 67.
2. Roger E. Olson, "Postconservative Evangelicalism: An Update after a Decade," ww.generousorthodoxy.net/thinktank/files/postconservative.pdf.

but that they weren't rigid, uncompromising dogmatists precisely because they weren't naïve theological realists, despite what the consensus of critical opinion would have us believe. As such, I hope to challenge a common assumption that is now an essential component of post-conservative evangelicalism's critique of the "received evangelical tradition" and thereby encourage readers to reconsider the "distinctive brand of conservatism" that post-conservatives insist forms the "mythical evangelical magisterium" at the heart of "establishment evangelical theology."[3]

The Dogmatic Habit of Mind and Theological Construction at Old Princeton Seminary

In *Reclaiming the Center,* I argued that the Princetonians were opposed to the rise of theological liberalism not simply because liberal theologians disagreed with their doctrinal formulations of revealed truth, but because liberals "reimagined" the essence of the faith and in the process emptied doctrinal formulations of real, enduring, objective substance.[4] Here is how I summarized the point, recalling the historical work of Richard Hofstadter and Ann Douglas:

> The Princetonians were opposed to the rise of theological liberalism . . . not simply because liberals advanced interpretations of doctrine that differed from their own dogmatic assertions, but more specifically because liberals conceived of doctrines in an "anti-intellectual" or "feminized" sense. Whereas the Princetonians conceived of doctrines as foundational summaries of biblical truth that must be believed in order

---

3. Ibid.

4. I am using the word "objective" in this essay not in the sense of Enlightenment foundationalism, i.e., to suggest that neutral, comprehensive, mathematically-indubitable knowledge is possible for finite human beings, but in the much less ambitious sense that affirms that at least some true knowledge of real states of affairs in the "world as it is" is possible for finite human beings, the influence of culture notwithstanding. In short, I am not convinced that the influence of culture is so profound that it precludes the Spirit from enabling believers to see reality more or less the way God would have his creatures see it. As far as I can tell, a text like 1 Corinthians 1 and 2 gives us warrant for concluding that either the apostle Paul should have done some graduate work in the sociology of knowledge or that at least some measure of "objective, transcultural" knowledge in fact is possible for finite creatures who have the "mind of Christ." Yes, theology is an enterprise in which finite human beings who are constitutive members of particular cultures engage; but when properly understood is the theological enterprise a merely human enterprise? Is it not also, in its best sense, a spiritual enterprise requiring a regenerated nature and all of the "stances" that entails? I don't see how we can conclude otherwise, and this is why I find it troubling when obviously gifted thinkers like John Franke affirm that "we simply cannot escape from our particular setting and gain access to an objective, transcultural vantage point" (*The Character of Theology: An Introduction to Its Nature, Task, and Purpose* [Grand Rapids: Baker, 2005], 90). For a helpful critique of Christian postmodernists who have endorsed the prevailing assumption that objective knowledge is impossible because there "is simply no way" for human beings "to get 'outside' of the influence of language to know the world as it actually is," see the incisive works of R. Scott Smith, including: *Truth and the New Kind of Christian: The Emerging Effects of Postmodernism in the Church* (Wheaton, IL: Crossway, 2005); and "Language, Theological Knowledge, and the Postmodern Paradigm," in *Reclaiming the Center,* 109–33. For an impressive affirmation of the possibility of objective knowledge that grounds the possibility of such knowledge in the activity of God rather than in the self either as an autonomous individual (modernism) or as a constitutive member of a particular, narrative-shaped community (postmodernism), see K. Scott Oliphint, *Reasons for Faith: Philosophy in the Service of Theology* (Phillipsburg, NJ: P&R, forthcoming).

for there to be faith, liberals conceived of doctrines as little more than expressions of an ineffable religious experience for a particular time and place. They considered doctrines to be true, in other words, not because they corresponded to real states of affairs in the external world, but rather because they captured the subjective experience of religion in the thought forms of a particular age.[5]

In the first half of this chapter I expand upon my discussion of post-conservatism's misunderstanding of this point by considering its implications for the practice of theology in general and the possibility of progress in theology in particular. With respect to the question of what is involved in theological construction, I establish that the debate between conservative and post-conservative evangelicals over the relative merits of the "propositionalist understanding of the theological enterprise" has less to do with an openness to progress of one group or another than it does with a disagreement about the nature of the progress to which believers should be open. As this portion of the argument unfolds I counter the notion that Old Princeton's understanding of the theological task leads necessarily to an uncompromising, arrogant, and "rigid dogmatism"[6] by demonstrating that even though the Princetonians were eager to maintain the realistic nature of religious language and the objectivity of established doctrinal truth, they never insisted that genuine believers would or necessarily should walk in lockstep with every proposition contained in the Westminster Standards.

The Dogmatic Habit of Mind at Old Princeton: A Case Study in Theological Hubris?

In an article published in 1894 entitled, "The Dogmatic Spirit," B. B. Warfield described the "habit of mind" that he thought should characterize theologians who were approaching the task of theology in a biblically faithful fashion.[7] "What is called the dogmatic spirit," he argued,

> is not popular among men. It is characterized by an authoritative method of presenting truth; by an unwillingness to modify truth to fit it to current conceptions; by an insistence on what seem to many minor points; and above all by (what lies at the root of most of its other peculiarities) a habit of thinking in a system, and a consequent habit of estimating the relative importance of the separate items of truth by their logical relation to the body of truth, rather than by their apparent independent value. Such a habit of mind seems to be the only appropriate attitude toward a body of truth given by revelation, and committed to men only to embrace, cherish, preserve, and propagate. It seems to be, moreover, the attitude toward the body of revealed truth

5. Helseth, "Are Postconservative Evangelicals Fundamentalists?" 239.
6. Olson, "Postconservative Evangelicalism: An Update after a Decade."
7. B. B. Warfield, "The Dogmatic Spirit," in *Selected Shorter Writings of Benjamin B. Warfield,* 2 vols., ed. John E. Meeter (Phillipsburg, NJ: P&R, 2001), 2:663.

commended to those who were to be its "ministers" and not its masters, by the Lord
and his apostles, when they placed it as a rich treasure in the keeping of stewards of
the mysteries of God. But it is irritating to men. They would discuss rather than receive
truth. And, if they must receive it, they would fain modify it here and there to fit
preconceived opinions or permit cherished practices. Especially in a busy age in which
Pilate's careless question, "what is truth?" represents the prevailing attitude of men's
minds, the dogmatic habit is apt to fare somewhat badly.[8]

Three years later, Warfield designated the systematic interpretation of revealed
truth that he thought should regulate the labors of believing evangelicals who were
approaching the task of theology in a dogmatic fashion. "The significance of the
Westminster Standards as a creed," he argued,

> is to be found in the three facts that: historically speaking, they are the final crystal-
> lization of the elements of evangelical religion, after the conflicts of sixteen hundred
> years; scientifically speaking, they are the richest and most precise and best guarded
> statement ever penned of all that enters into evangelical religion and of all that must
> be safeguarded if evangelical religion is to persist in the world; and, religiously speak-
> ing, they are a notable monument of spiritual religion.[9]

It perhaps goes without saying that just as the habit of mind manifest in these
quotations was not very popular in Warfield's day, neither is it very popular in ours,
particularly when its focal point is a confession that is thought by many to be a
rather sectarian and therefore narrow and exclusionary interpretation of revealed
truth. Indeed, especially for those who adopt "a constructionist view of the world,"
this habit of mind smacks of an arrogance that is nothing short of alarming, for to
them it betrays the kind of cocksure rigidity that is characteristic of those who
credulously deny the creatureliness and "situatedness of all human thought" while
simultaneously presuming that their doctrinal affirmations are just as authoritative
as "the language of the biblical text," or, to use the language of post-conservative
nonfoundationalism, that their confessional commitments "constitute a first-order
language of revelation."[10]

Certainly, if the previous quotations are taken in isolation from other things
Warfield wrote on the approach to theology advocated at Old Princeton Seminary

8. Ibid.
9. B. B. Warfield, "The Significance of the Westminster Standards as a Creed," in *Shorter Writings*, 2:660.
10. Franke, *Character of Theology*, 23, 78, 36, 35. According to Franke, "constructionists" maintain "that
humans do not view the world from an objective or neutral vantage point but instead structure their world
through the concepts they bring to it, particularly language. Human languages function as social conventions
and symbol systems that attempt to engage and describe the world in a variety of ways that are shaped by the
social and historical contexts and perceptions of various communities of discourse. No simple, one-to-one
relationship exists between language and the world, and thus no single linguistic description can provide an
objective conception of the 'real' world. Language structures our perceptions of reality and as such constitutes
the world in which we live" (ibid., 23; cf. 23–26).

and adopted by thoughtful conservatives in the twentieth century—the approach that champions the collection and systematic organization of revealed truths into doctrines that are thought to be both objectively true and subjectively compelling[11]—the post-conservative conclusion that "the propositionalist understanding of the theological enterprise" is an inherently arrogant enterprise entailing both an uncompromising dogmatism as well as the end to "constructive evangelical theology" could perhaps be justified.[12] But does wider reading in the primary sources of Old Princeton justify this conclusion? Were the Princetonians really convinced that the riches of God's revelation had been definitively exhausted in the Westminster Standards, and were they therefore opposed to the idea of more light and truth breaking forth from God's Word? Or, were they simply convinced that the light and truth that had yet to break forth needed to be in harmony with those doctrines that had already been "established" as definitively true throughout the "slow but ever advancing process" of church history?[13]

Theological Construction at Old Princeton Seminary
The answer to these questions largely depends, of course, upon what we mean by theological "construction." If our understanding of this word is informed by the nonfoundationalist assumption that human language "does not represent reality as much as it constitutes reality," then yes, the propositionalist enterprise as practiced at Old Princeton was rigidly opposed to theological "construction," for the Princetonians were unwilling to grant what is essential to nonfoundationalist approaches to the task of theology, namely, that in the process of contextualizing the language of Scripture in new social and historical settings "all . . . convictions and commitments, even the most long-standing and dear, [must] remain subject to ongoing critical scrutiny and the possibility of revision, reconstruction, or even rejection."[14] However,

---

11. In "Admiring the Sistine Chapel: Reflections on Carl F. H. Henry's *God, Revelation and Authority*" *(Themelios* 25, no. 2 [2000]: 48–58), Carl R. Trueman makes a number of helpful observations about the nature of the propositionalist enterprise. For example, he suggests: "To argue that revelation is propositional is not, despite apparent popular opinion, to reduce the Bible to a series of statements of the kind represented by, say, Pythagoras' Theorem or some other mathematical formulae. This is the charge that is often levelled [*sic*] against Henry and the classic evangelical position by advocates of neo-orthodoxy and by those who press for the importance of the (often very useful) contributions of speech-act theory" (56).
12. Olson, "Postconservative Evangelicalism."
13. B. B. Warfield, "The Idea of Systematic Theology," in *Studies in Theology*, vol. 9, *The Works of Benjamin Breckinridge Warfield* (1932; repr., Grand Rapids: Baker, 1991), 75.
14. Franke, *Character of Theology*, 26, 78. The reason that all convictions and commitments must remain open to critical scrutiny is found in the second-order nature of theological discourse. According to Franke, "The creeds and confessions of the Christian church are second-order interpretive reflections on the primary stories, teachings, symbols, and practices of the Christian faith that, under the guidance of the Spirit, provide a hermeneutical trajectory in which the discipline of theology is pursued in conversation with the normative witness of Scripture and the contemporary cultural situation. From this perspective, we can summarize the second-order nature of church confessions as subordinate and provisional, open-ended, and eschatologically directed" (ibid., 111). But does the second-order, provisional nature of theological discourse mean that all theological matters are up for grabs, so to speak? In other words, does "provisionality" promote a kind of "instability" (ibid.)? While Franke insists that it does not because creeds and confessions bear witness to

if our understanding of theological "construction" is informed by the traditional assumption that the Bible is "the sole foundation for theology" and that "objective, transcultural"[15] knowledge of its contents is possible for those who have been given the ability to discern the wisdom of its inexhaustible riches, then no, the propositionalist enterprise as practiced at Old Princeton was not opposed to theological "construction," for the Princetonians were convinced that progress in theology is possible not simply when "past achievements in theology" are "effectively spell[ed] out"[16] to a new generation of believers, but when the Spirit takes believers ever more deeply into the objective contents of God's Word as the history of Christian thought continues to unfold. The growth of the body of Christian truth, Warfield argued,

> has come down to us in the form of an organic growth; and we can conceive of the completed structure as the ripened fruit of the ages, as truly as we can think of it as the perfected result of the exegetical discipline. As it has come into our possession by this historic process, there is no reason that we can assign why it should not continue to make for itself a history. We do not expect the history of theology to close in our own day. However nearly completed our realization of the body of truth may seem to us to be; however certain it is that the great outlines are already securely laid and most of the details soundly discovered and arranged; no one will assert that every detail is as yet perfected, and we are all living in the confidence so admirably expressed by old John Robinson, "that God hath more truth yet to break forth from His holy Word." Just because God gives us the truth in single threads which we must weave into the reticulated texture, all the threads are always within our reach, but the finished texture is ever and will ever continue to be before us until we dare affirm that there is no truth in the Word which we have not perfectly apprehended, and no relation of these truths as revealed which we have not perfectly understood, and no possibility in clearness of presentation which we have not attained.[17]

---

gospel truth that will be objectively known in the eschaton (see Franke's discussion of "eschatological realism," ibid., 188–98), it seems to me that it cannot help but do so in the present without the willingness to affirm something close to what Warfield calls "progressive orthodoxy" (which presupposes that at least some measure of objective doctrinal knowledge is possible for regenerated human beings; see the forthcoming discussion). For example, if it is true that objective theological knowledge is completely beyond the reach of finite human beings due to "the social context . . . and the historicity of all theological reflection" (ibid., 102), then how can even the ecumenical creeds of classical Christianity—which bind together and unite the various traditions of the universal church and serve as the consensual basis for the ongoing theological reflection that takes place in particular believing communities (ibid., 191, 41, 193)—be beyond critical scrutiny and potential rejection? Since it seems that even these creeds aren't immune to such scrutiny, then what becomes the basis for the "principled theological pluralism" that postconservatives want to promote?

Franke suggests that "if we must speak of 'foundations' for the Christian faith and its theological enterprise, then we must speak only of the Triune God, who is disclosed in polyphonic fashion through Scripture, the church, and the world, albeit always in accordance with the normative witness to divine self-disclosure in Jesus Christ" (ibid., 78–79). But how can even "the Triune God" serve as the "foundation" for "a principled pluralism" when the doctrine of the Trinity is itself open to scrutiny given the contextual nature of all human thought?

15. Ibid., 88, 90.
16. Roger E. Olson, "The Future of Evangelical Theology," *Christianity Today,* February 9, 1998, 41.
17. Warfield, "The Idea of Systematic Theology," 75–76.

Thus, if we assume that Warfield is representative of his colleagues at Old Princeton Seminary, it follows that the Princetonians were open to more light and truth breaking forth from God's Word not because they were willing to jettison established doctrinal truths as they attempted to "state their Christian belief in terms of modern thought,"[18] but because they recognized that "the progressive men in any science are the men who stand firmly on the basis of the already ascertained truth."[19] As such, although they were clearly open to theological construction, they were zealous to distinguish the construction of theology from the destruction of theology, and it is this frank acknowledgement of the "increasing limitation" brought about by the establishment of theological truth that sets their view of progress apart from that of their contemporary nonfoundationalist critics.[20] "The prerequisite of all progress," Warfield argued,

> is a clear discrimination which as frankly accepts the limitations set by the truth already discovered, as it rejects the false and bad. Construction is not destruction; neither is it the outcome of destruction. There are abuses no doubt to be reformed; errors to correct; falsehoods to cut away. But the history of progress in every science and no less in theology, is a story of impulses given, corrected, and assimilated. And when they have been once corrected and assimilated, these truths are to remain accepted. It is then time for another impulse, and the condition of all further progress is to place ourselves in this well-marked line of growth.[21]

The Significance of Finitude and Fallenness at Old Princeton Seminary

But how is even this relatively modest understanding of theological construction compatible with the Princetonians' clear views on the significance of the Westminster Standards and the dogmatic nature of the theological task? In other words, how can Old Princeton's dogmatic habit of mind be reconciled with the notion that "as the orthodox man is he that teaches no other doctrine than that which has been established as true, the progressively orthodox man is he who is quick to perceive, admit, and condition all his reasoning by all the truth down to the latest, which has been established as true"?[22] The answer to this question is informed by the Princetonians' endorsement of two commitments that lie close to the heart of the Reformed worldview, commitments that together suggest that the Princetonians were ultimately open to progress in theology because they distinguished the essential truthfulness of the system of doctrine contained in the Westminster Standards from the truthfulness of every proposition that constitutes the Westminster Standards.

18. B. B. Warfield, "Review of *Foundations: A Statement of Christian Belief in Terms of Modern Thought*, by Seven Oxford Men," in *Critical Reviews*, vol. 10, *The Works of Benjamin Breckinridge Warfield* (1932; repr., Grand Rapids: Baker, 1991), 322.
19. Warfield, "Idea of Systematic Theology," 76.
20. Ibid., 79.
21. Ibid., 76–77.
22. Ibid., 79.

The first of these commitments has to do with the Creator-creature distinction in general, and the fact of creaturely-human finitude in particular. One of the more remarkable charges leveled by post-conservative critics of the "propositionalist understanding of the theological enterprise" is that conservative theologians remain smugly indifferent to the "hermeneutics of finitude"[23] despite the thoughtful prodding of irenic post-conservatives like Roger Olson.[24] Conservative evangelicals who claim to possess objective theological knowledge not only naïvely deny that the outlooks of human beings "are always limited and shaped by the particular circumstances in which they emerge,"[25] post-conservative evangelicals contend, but more importantly they arrogantly presume a kind of god-like omniscience by elevating themselves "above the conditions of earthly mortality" and suggesting that their knowledge of God and of theological truth is unbiased and comprehensive and thus essentially the same as God's knowledge of himself and of his revelation.[26]

While there is perhaps some merit to this critique in the case of "naïve theological realists"[27] who insist that "words and concepts must directly mirror the divine being,

23. Franke, *Character of Theology*, 27.
24. Olson, "Postconservative Evangelicalism." Painting with strokes that some might suggest are entirely too generous, Olson opines—but does not even attempt to demonstrate—that the critics of post-conservative evangelicalism are "ultraconservatives" who are gripped by an "inquisitorial spirit." These critics are "uninformed"—perhaps even "dishonest"—and "have created a straw man . . . only to tear it down and burn it." They are "really fundamentalists" with "a knee-jerk preference for the most conservative answers to theological questions and a tendency to defend the status quo . . . uncritically," and they lack "intellectual humility." In fact, these critics have accommodated modernity, and this accommodation is evident "in their insistence on tying evangelical thought inextricably with epistemological realism and the correspondence theory of truth as well as their slavish adherence to deductive logic in developing and criticizing theological systems." Would any conservatives out there like another helping of "generous orthodoxy"?
25. Franke, *Character of Theology*, 28.
26. Olson, "Postconservative Evangelicalism." It is clear that critics like Olson are primarily interested not in the qualitative difference between divine and human knowledge, but in the postmodern preoccupation with bias. While it is certainly true that the Princetonians would likely have been opposed to the frankly goofy notion of finitude that is daily on display in the ridiculous dramas of contemporary identity politics, it is also true that more than a few would likely have endorsed the chastened though no less robust "perspectivalism" of someone like Vern Poythress. In *Symphonic Theology: The Validity of Multiple Perspectives in Theology* (1987; repr., Phillipsburg, NJ: P&R, 2001), Poythress argues that the task of theology is enhanced by the contributions of theologians coming from a multiplicity of perspectives precisely because those contributions have the potential to enrich our understanding of objective, transcultural truths that are held in common. For evidence that Warfield was at least somewhat aware of the kinds of hermeneutical concerns that are of interest to post-conservatives, see these examples: His acknowledgement that "the temple of God's truth . . . is a miracle of art to which *all* ages and lands bring their varied tribute" ("Idea of Systematic Theology," 77–78; emphasis added); his insistence that the "truest" systematic theology is "framed out of the mountains and plains of the *theologies* of the Scriptures" (ibid., 66–68; emphasis added); his recognition that in the providence of God human "bias" serves to advance rather than obstruct "his gracious purposes" (B. B. Warfield, "God's Providence Over All," in *Shorter Writings*, 1:111–13); he opposed the racism of segregation, believing that "in Christ Jesus there cannot be Greek and Jew, circumcision and uncircumcision, barbarian, Scythian, bondman, freeman" (B. B. Warfield, "Calm View of the Freedman's Case," in *Shorter Writings*, 2:741; B. B. Warfield, "Drawing the Color Line," in *Shorter Writings*, 2:748).
27. Peter Hicks, *The Philosophy of Charles Hodge: A Nineteenth-Century Evangelical Approach to Reason, Knowledge and Truth* (Lewiston, NY: Edwin Mellen, 1997), 191. According to Hicks, "Naïve theological realism is the position of most unphilosophical people, past and present. If truth about God exists it may be known in essentially the same way as truth about anything else."

or they represent *untruth*,"[28] it is grossly unfair to evangelicals who have been significantly influenced by the Princeton theologians, for the Princetonians endorsed, at least in principle, what J. V. Fesko calls "a hallmark teaching of the Reformed faith, namely the difference between *theologia archetypa* and *theologia ectypa*."[29] In short, the Princetonians were open to progress in theology in part because they recognized that there is a qualitative distinction between archetypal theology and ectypal theology, that is, between "the knowledge of God which he has of himself" and the knowledge of God "which he has made available via revelation to humanity."[30] Whereas the Princetonians insisted that true theology is possible for finite human beings because God has condescended to make himself known to them in both general and special ways, they nonetheless acknowledged that "only God possesses *theologia archetypa*" because "only he is capable of knowing the object of theology, God Himself, perfectly."[31] Indeed, like the stalwarts of Protestant Scholasticism before them, the Princetonians maintained that although "true human theology" is possible, it is never more than "an ectype or reflection resting on but not commensurate with the divine self-knowledge [or archetype],"[32] for they recognized that there is a vast "epistemic gulf" separating creatures from the Creator.[33] "Only in God's mind . . . " Warfield argued, "does [theological] science lie perfect—the perfect comprehension of all that is, in its organic completeness. In the mind of perfected humanity, the perfected ectypal science shall lie. In the mind of sinful humanity struggling here below, there can lie only a broken reflection of the object, a reflection which is rather a deflection."[34]

The Princetonians were also open to progress in theology because they recognized, as the preceding quotation suggests, that not even regenerated sinners do ectypal theology perfectly. Warfield insisted that the task of theological construction in which systematic theologians are called to engage is a comprehensive discipline involving all the facts "concerning God and His relations with the universe," including "all the facts of nature and history."[35] Indeed, all science finds "its completion and ground in Him,"[36] Warfield argued, and for this reason the knowledge of God is "indispensable" to a "right knowledge" of all things: "Without the knowledge of God it is not too much to say we know nothing rightly, so that the renunciation of

28. Michael S. Horton, *Covenant and Eschatology: The Divine Drama* (Louisville, KY: Westminster John Knox, 2002), 189.

29. J. V. Fesko, "The Legacy of Old School Confession Subscription in the OPC," *Journal of the Evangelical Theological Society* 46, no. 4 (2003): 694; cf. Richard A. Muller, *Dictionary of Latin and Greek Theological Terms* (Grand Rapids: Baker, 1985), 298–301.

30. Trueman, "Admiring the Sistine Chapel," 58n12.

31. Fesko, "Old School Confession Subscription," 695.

32. Richard A. Muller, *Post-Reformation Reformed Dogmatics*, vol. 1: *Prolegomena to Theology*, 2d ed. (Grand Rapids: Baker, 2003), 225.

33. Fesko, "Old School Confession Subscription," 695.

34. B. B. Warfield, "A Review of *De Zekerheid des Geloofs*," in *Shorter Writings*, 2:119.

35. Warfield, "Idea of Systematic Theology," 72.

36. Ibid., 70.

the knowledge of God carries with it renunciation of all right knowledge."[37] Even
the knowledge of God, however, although it enables the "men of the palingenesis"
to reason "rightly" and thus to build the "edifice" of truth "better" than their unregenerate colleagues,[38] does not enable believing theologians to build perfectly, for
the gift of regeneration neither raises them above their creaturely status nor does it
completely remove the effects of sin on their faculties; it simply restores their "old
faculties" to "some measure" of their "proper functioning."[39] Since even "the regenerated man remains a sinner"[40] who is unable to lay hold of the revelation of God with
absolute perfection, it follows that the Princetonians were open to progress in theology
because they recognized that the ectypal theological task is an ongoing activity of
"the whole church"[41] that ultimately depends for its completion on the sanctifying
work of the Spirit throughout the progressively unfolding process of church history.
It is the "intrusion" of regeneration and regeneration alone, they argued, that prepares
believers "to build better, and ever more truly as the effects of regeneration increase
intensively and extensively, until the end comes when the regenerated universe becomes the well-comprehended object of the science of the regenerated race."[42] For
Warfield and his colleagues at Old Princeton, then,

> Systematic theology is thus . . . an attempt to reflect in the mirror of the human
> consciousness the God who reveals Himself in His works and word, and as He has
> revealed Himself. It finds its whole substance in the revelation which we suppose
> God to have made of Himself; and as we differ as to the revelation which we sup-
> pose God to have made, so will our systematic theologies differ in their substance.
> Its form is given it by the greater or less perfection of the reflection of this reve-
> lation in our consciousness. It is not imagined, of course, that this reflection can
> be perfect in any individual consciousness. It is the people of God at large who are
> really the subject of that knowledge of God which systematic theology seeks to set
> forth. Nor is it imagined that even in the people of God at large, in their present
> imperfect condition, oppressed by the sin of the world of which they still form a

---

37. B. B. Warfield, "The Task and Method of Systematic Theology," in *Studies in Theology*, 97. Note that the
comprehensive scope of the theological enterprise—which itself is based on the assumption "that all truth is
God's. All truth comes forth from him; all truth leads back to him"—makes it necessary for theologians to
have "[a]n attitude of eager hospitality" the truth claims of culture (B. B. Warfield, "Heresy and Concession,"
in *Shorter Writings*, 2:674). Thus it is not true that the Princetonians avoided "the thorny issues surrounding
the role of culture in theology" by "limiting the scope of theological reflection to the exposition of the biblical
text" (Franke, *The Character of Theology*, 89).
38. Warfield, "Review of *De Zekerheid des Geloofs*," 119.
39. B. B. Warfield, "Introduction to Francis R. Beattie's *Apologetics*," in *Shorter Writings*, 2:101.
40. Warfield, "Review of *De Zekerheid des Geloofs*," 118.
41. Warfield, "Idea of Systematic Theology," 81.
42. Warfield, "A Review of *De Zekerheid des Geloofs*," 119. Note that there is a postmillennial confidence that
pervades Warfield's writings on science and apologetics. Here is another example: "We may assure ourselves
from the outset that the palingenesis shall ultimately conquer to itself the whole race and all its products;
and we may equally assure ourselves that its gradually increasing power will show itself only as the result of
conflict in the free intercourse of men" ("Beattie's *Apologetics*," 104).

part, the image of God can be reflected back to him in its perfection. Only the pure in heart can see God; and who, even of His redeemed saints, are in this life really pure in heart? Meanwhile God is framing the knowledge of Himself in the hearts of His people; and, as each one of them seeks to give expression in the forms best adapted to human consciousness, to the knowledge of God he has received, a better and fuller reflection of the revealed God is continually growing up. Systematic theology is therefore a progressive science. It will be perfected only in the minds and hearts of the perfected saints who at the end, being at last like God, shall see Him as He is. Then, the God who has revealed Himself to His people shall be known by them in all the fullness of His revelation of Himself. Now we know in part; but when that which is perfect is come that which is in part shall be done away.[43]

"System" Subscription at Old Princeton Seminary

How, then, do these commitments suggest that we ought to think about the relationship between the Princetonians' dogmatic habit of mind on the one hand and their insistence that theological progress is not only possible but necessary on the other? Ought we to conclude that the Princetonians were hopelessly conflicted at this point? Or, ought we to acknowledge that both dogmatic certitude and openness to progress were compatible in their thinking? As far as I can tell, we ought to acknowledge that both of these emphases could peacefully coexist in the Princetonians' minds, for the commitments above suggest that the Princetonians were "system" rather than "strict" subscriptionists with respect to the Westminster Standards, and thus eager to distinguish between their theological interpretations of God's revelation on the one hand and God's first-order revelation of himself on the other. According to William Barker, system subscriptionists affirm that the "system of doctrine" taught in the Westminster Standards is essentially the system of doctrine taught in Scripture itself.[44] System subscriptionists do not necessarily affirm, however, that every proposition contained in the Westminster Standards is essential to the system, and thus they allow "for an ordinand to take exception, not merely to wording, but to doctrinal teachings of the Standards."[45] Charles Hodge, for example, was convinced that "there are many propositions contained in the Westminster Confession which do not belong to the integrity of the Augustinian, or Reformed System. . . . [Thus] we do not expect our ministers should adopt every proposition contained in our Standards. This they are not required to do. But they are required to adopt the

43. Warfield, "Task and Method of Systematic Theology," 104–5.
44. William Barker, "System Subscription," *Westminster Theological Journal* 63, no. 1 (2001): 10.
45. Fesko, "Old School Confession Subscription," 678. Note that for system subscriptionists, whether or not an exception subverts the Reformed system is a matter for the elected officials of the covenant community to decide: "The candidate professing to adopt the *Westminster Standards* should declare any exceptions that he may have, and then the Presbytery should decide whether his exceptions are such that he cannot be deemed as sincerely taking his ordination vow . . ." (Barker, "System Subscription," 7).

system; and that system consists of certain doctrines, no one of which can be omitted without destroying its identity."[46]

If the Princetonians in fact were "system" rather than "strict" subscriptionists—a point which continues to be hotly contested in Reformed circles but which seems plausible to me[47]—then it follows that they were simultaneously dogmatic yet open to progress because they adopted the Westminster Standards in what Warfield called a "liberal but conservative"[48] fashion: they did not require "the adoption of every proposition,"[49] thus allowing for progress as "the temple of God's truth" continues to be built throughout history,[50] but they required the adoption of "every doctrine essential to . . . [the Reformed] system,"[51] thus allowing for a kind of dogmatism that affirms essential, established truths. "There is, so far as we know," Warfield argued,

> no difference of opinion as to the import of the ordination vow in our Churches: it is everywhere understood and administered as binding those taking it merely to the system and not to the detailed manner of stating that system; but as binding them strictly to the system in its integrity and in its entirety. As such it has been justly lauded as combining in itself all reasonable liberty with all reasonable strictness— binding as it does to the great system of doctrine expressed in the Confession with absolute strictness, and yet leaving room for all possible individual preferences in modes of conceiving and stating this system. Under this combined strictness and liberty every genuine form of Calvinism has an equal right of existence under the Confession. . . . But beyond the limits of generic Calvinism the right of adoption ceases. Our vow of ordination is not a solemn farce: and the terms of our adoption of the Confession are not so phrased as to enable us to seem to adopt it while not adopting it at all.[52]

46. Charles Hodge, "What is Meant by Adopting the Westminster Confession?" in *The Confession of Faith,* by A. A. Hodge (1869; repr., Edinburgh: Banner of Truth, 1992), 420, 422.

47. In addition to the essays already listed in the notes, a few of the other essays that lead me to support this conclusion include: Charles Hodge, "The Constitutional History of the Presbyterian Church in the United States of America," in *Paradigms in Polity: Classic Readings in Reformed and Presbyterian Church Government,* ed. David W. Hall and Joseph H. Hall (Grand Rapids: Eerdmans, 1994), 365–92; B. B. Warfield, "Presbyterian Churches and the Westminster Confession," *Presbyterian Review* 10 (1889): 646–57; B. B. Warfield, "The Confession of Faith as Revised in 1903," in *Shorter Writings,* 2:370–410; J. Gresham Machen, "Premillennialism," *The Presbyterian Guardian* (October 24, 1936): 21; J. Gresham Machen, "The Second General Assembly of the Presbyterian Church of America," *The Presbyterian Guardian* (November 14, 1936): 41–45.

48. Warfield, "Presbyterian Churches and the Westminster Confession," 648–49.

49. Fesko, "Old School Confession Subscription," 686.

50. Warfield, "Idea of Systematic Theology," 77.

51. Barker, "System Subscription," 10.

52. B. B. Warfield, "The Proposed Union with the Cumberland Presbyterians," *Princeton Theological Review* 2 (1904): 314–15, quoted in Barker, "System Subscription," 11. Barker argues that there are four compelling reasons to endorse this form of subscription: (1) it "safeguards orthodoxy"; (2) it "promotes knowledge of the *Westminster Standards*"; (3) it "promotes honesty by avoiding mental reservations"; (4) it "promotes rule by Scripture" (ibid., 7).

Old Princeton's Endorsement of the Distinction between
First- and Second-Order Theological Discourse

A. B. Caneday has incisively argued that evangelical theologians "at their best" have always allowed for progress in theology because they have always distinguished between "first-order" and "second-order" theological discourse, that is, "between *Scripture* as God's Word and *interpretation of Scripture* as entailing theological formulations."[53] This was certainly true of the theologians at Old Princeton Seminary, and for this reason it is simply wrong to suggest that the Princetonians were narrow-minded fundamentalists who challenged the spiritual integrity of those who refused to endorse every jot and tittle of the Westminster Standards. Indeed, fair-minded interpreters must acknowledge that the Princetonians allowed for a measure of doctrinal diversity even within their own communion, for they recognized that there in fact is "a distinction between [the Westminster Standards] (which are subject to correction and revision) and Scripture (the very Word of God, the only infallible rule of faith and practice),"[54] and they conceded that even believing theologians are less than perfect interpreters of God's Word. Charles Hodge, for example, admitted,

> that theologians are not infallible, in the interpretation of Scripture. It may, therefore, happen in the future, as it has in the past, that interpretations of the Bible, long confidently received, must be modified or abandoned, to bring revelation into harmony with what God teaches in his works. This change of view as to the true meaning of the Bible may be a painful trial to the Church, but it does not in the least impair the authority of the Scriptures. They remain infallible; we are merely convicted of having mistaken their meaning.[55]

It is also true, however, that the Princetonians were convinced that objective doctrinal knowledge is possible, and this raises the question of how they discerned the difference between truth and error and thus distinguished between "progressive orthodoxy" and what Warfield called "retrogressive heterodoxy."[56] As the preceding quotation suggests, the Princetonians were convinced that, given the unity of truth, Scripture must be interpreted in accordance with "established" or "ascertained facts," that is, in accordance with what is known to be true from a variety of sources.[57] The difference between "progressive orthodoxy" and "retrogressive heterodoxy," then, is tied

---

53. A. B. Caneday, "Is Theological Language Functional or Propositional? Postconservatism's Use of Language Games and Speech-Act Theory," in *Reclaiming the Center,* 149. Note that conservative theologians like Caneday refuse to elevate second-order interpretations of Scripture to the level of first-order theological discourse: "To the degree that evangelical theologians view their understanding of Scripture as fused into one with God's revelation, as if their knowledge of God and of his ways were already perfected and absolute, postmodern epistemological correctives are helpful," ibid.
54. Barker, "System Subscription," 7.
55. Charles Hodge, *Systematic Theology,* 3 vols. (1872–1873; repr., Grand Rapids: Eerdmans, 1982), 1:59.
56. Warfield, "Idea of Systematic Theology," 78.
57. See Hodge, *Systematic Theology,* 1:56–59; Warfield, "Idea of Systematic Theology," 76–79.

to the status of the truth claims being considered by the systematic theologian as well as to the method of consideration. Whereas "progressive orthodoxy" is a constructive enterprise entailing the assimilation of modern learning to the established truths of Scripture, "retrogressive heterodoxy" is a destructive enterprise involving the accommodation of established biblical truths to truth claims that have yet to be established as true, or to truth claims that in fact are false.[58] "After all," Warfield asked,

> is it not enough to ask that "Christianity" and "its theology" shall be in harmony with truth? And if it is to be in harmony with truth, must it not be out of harmony with all the half-truths, and quarter-truths, and no-truths, which pass from time to time for truth, while truth is only in the making? A "Christianity" which is to be kept in harmony with a growing "science, philosophy, and scholarship," beating their way onward by a process of trial and correction, must be a veritable nose of wax, which may be twisted in every direction as it may serve our purpose.[59]

So how, finally, do believing theologians discern the difference between "God's truth and Satan's error," and how do they therefore know when an accepted interpretation of Scripture must be modified, abandoned, or retained?[60] This is the question that informs the discussion in the second half of this chapter. The answer will likely disappoint those who are reluctant to acknowledge that the theologians at Old Princeton Seminary were anything other than relatively unsophisticated devotees of either Scholastic or Enlightenment rationalism, for the answer makes clear that the Princetonians regarded the science of theology as an aesthetic enterprise involving the work of the Spirit on the whole soul—the head as well as the heart—of a moral agent.[61] Indeed, the Princetonians acknowledged that the task of theology is concerned with more than "a bare series of intellectual propositions, however logically constructed,"[62] for they recognized that the "true" theologian needs to be "a

---

58. On the difference between assimilation and accommodation, see Warfield, "Heresy and Concession," 2:672–79. Warfield was convinced that "the line of demarcation between the right-thinking and the willfully-thinking lies just here—whether a declaration of God is esteemed as authoritative over against all the conjectural explanations of phenomena by men, or whether, on the contrary, it is upon the conjectural explanations of phenomena by men that we take our stand as over against the declaration of God. In the sphere of science, philosophy, and criticism alike, it is the conjectural explanations of phenomena which are put forward as the principles of knowledge. It is as depending on these that men proclaim science, philosophy, and criticism as the norm of truth. We are 'orthodox' when we account God's declaration in his Word superior in point of authority to them, their interpreter, and their corrector. We are 'heretical' when we make them superior in point of authority to God's Word, its interpreter, and its corrector" (ibid., 679). Some would argue that a plausible case can be made that not even Warfield himself was faithful to the methodological principle that he here sets forth. Whether or not that is the case, it is certainly true that this principle is at the conceptual foundation of his understanding of "progressive orthodoxy."
59. Warfield, "Review of *Foundations*," 322.
60. I am indebted to the Rev. Ian Hewitson for framing the question in this fashion.
61. On the unitary operation of the soul, cf. B. B. Warfield, "Authority, Intellect, Heart," in *Shorter Writings,* 2:668–71.
62. B. B. Warfield, "Theology a Science," in *Shorter Writings,* 2:211.

divine."[63] By God's grace the true theologian needs to have, in other words, "a very sensitive religious nature, a most thoroughly consecrated heart, and an outpouring of the Holy Ghost upon him, such as will fill him with that spiritual discernment, without which all native intellect is in vain."[64] What I will establish, then, is that the Princetonians sought to discern the difference between truth and error not by appealing to the modern canons of universal reason—as if epistemological neutrality in fact were possible and absolute mathematical certitude in fact could be attained through the inductive analysis of Scripture using autonomous reason—but by hearing the message of the text with "right reason," which for them was a biblically-informed kind of theological aesthetic that presupposes the work of the Spirit on the whole soul of the believing theologian.

Theological Aesthetics at Old Princeton Seminary

In *Reclaiming the Center*, I challenged an assessment of the Princeton theology that has become an "article of faith" in historiography of American Christianity.[65] According to this assessment, the theologians at Old Princeton Seminary were thoroughgoing rationalists who compromised "the original spirit of the Reformation" by accommodating philosophical assumptions that fostered indifference to the subjective and experiential components of religious epistemology, thus encouraging an exceedingly "wooden" approach to the task of theology both at Old Princeton and in conservative evangelicalism more generally.[66] This assessment is now an essential component of post-conservative evangelicalism's religious historiography. Indeed, progressive evangelicals like Carl Raschke are convinced that the Princetonians' repudiation of Reformation theology is manifest in a kind of gnostic tendency. For the Princetonians, Raschke argues, "The 'heart,' which Luther and Wesley regarded as the seat of spiritual discernment, is of little bearing [in religious matters]. It is the mind that counts."[67] In *Reclaiming the Center* I responded to this line of thinking by arguing that despite what the consensus of critical opinion would have us believe, the Princetonians simply weren't rationalists. Rather, they "were committed Augustinians who conceived of reason in a moral rather than a merely rational sense. They recognized, in other words, that the reception of revealed truth is an activity involving the 'whole soul' rather than the rational faculty alone, and consequently they insisted . . . that the regenerate alone could apprehend this truth in

---

63. Warfield, "Idea of Systematic Theology," 87.
64. Ibid.
65. Helseth, "Are Postconservative Evangelicals Fundamentalists?" 223.
66. Carl Raschke, *The Next Reformation: Why Evangelicals Must Embrace Postmodernity* (Grand Rapids: Baker, 2004), 9. On theological "woodenness," see, for example, Mark A. Noll, "Charles Hodge as an Expositor of the Spiritual Life," in *Charles Hodge Revisited: A Critical Appraisal of His Life and Work,* ed. John W. Stewart, James H. Moorhead (Grand Rapids: Eerdmans, 2002), 191.
67. Raschke, *Next Reformation*, 128.

a 'right' or saving sense."[68] Here I develop this argument further by looking in more depth at the concept of "right reason" as it came to expression in the Christian tradition. After an overview of what the concept generally entails I isolate the historical strain of right reason that more than likely was at the heart of Old Princeton's religious epistemology, and suggest that since the Princetonians were faithful to what Robert Hoopes calls the "antihumanistic" heritage of the Reformation,[69] a key premise in post-conservative evangelicalism's critique of the "received evangelical tradition"—which presumes that the rationalistic bent of some conservatives represents a faithful appropriation of the Princeton theology—cannot be sustained.

The Place of "Right Reason" in the Postmodern World

"Right reason" is a philosophical concept with roots "both in [ancient] Middle Eastern and biblical culture, as well as in Greco-Roman antiquity"[70] that was assimilated by the Christian church, and that in many respects is still at home in the postmodern world. If we conceive of postmodernism as "a mindset" that, at its heart, "is tightly linked to . . . [the] denial that humans can know truth in any objective, universal sense" because they are thought to be "too historically situated and sociologically conditioned" to have anything approaching an unbiased, "God's-eye" view of reality,[71] "right reason" as a concept is remarkably at home in a postmodern world *not* because it lends credence to the truth-destroying notion that "'Knowledge' is [nothing more than] a construction of one's social, linguistic structures,"[72] but because it acknowledges that both objective and subjective factors are involved in the process of knowing. To vastly oversimplify the matter, while modernists are convinced that objective truth can be known *only* when "personal and subjective factors . . . [are] eliminated from the knowing process,"[73] and while postmodernists are persuaded that objective truth cannot be known *precisely because* personal and subjective factors are an essential component of each and every attempt to know, advocates of "right reason" recognize that although knowing does in fact involve the kinds of personal and subjective factors that many modernists naïvely presume have little if anything to do with our attempts to know, this does *not* mean that a more or less objective apprehension of reality is beyond our reach.[74]

---

68. Helseth, "Are Postconservative Evangelicals Fundamentalists?" 238.

69. Robert Hoopes, *Right Reason in the English Renaissance* (Cambridge: Harvard University Press, 1962), 97.

70. Brad Walton, *Jonathan Edwards, Religious Affections*, vol. 74, Studies in American Religion (Lewiston, NY: Edwin Mellen, 2002), 166.

71. Stephen J. Wellum, "Postconservatism, Biblical Authority, and Recent Proposals for Re-Doing Evangelical Theology: A Critical Proposal," in *Reclaiming the Center,* 163.

72. J. P. Moreland and William Lane Craig, *Philosophical Foundations for a Christian Worldview* (Downers Grove, IL: InterVarsity, 2003), 146.

73. Millard J. Erickson, *Truth or Consequences: The Promise and Perils of Postmodernism* (Downers Grove, IL: InterVarsity, 2001), 74.

74. I qualify this statement with the words "more or less" simply to acknowledge that although none of us sees any aspect of reality perfectly, some of us see various aspects of reality more clearly than others, and we do so for a number of reasons, including theological reasons.

The Concept of Right Reason

What, then, is "right reason"? In short, right reason is "not merely reason in our [modern] sense of the word; it is not a dry light, a nonmoral instrument of inquiry. . . . [Rather] it is a kind of rational and philosophic conscience which distinguishes man from the beasts and which links man with man and with God."[75] As a philosophical concept that was born in Ancient Greece and later assimilated "by the early Church Fathers and redefined in the Christian context of sin and grace," it denotes at once "a mode of knowing, a way of doing, and a condition of being" that is invested with "unique meaning" by two "controlling" assumptions.[76] In the first place, the concept assumes—in stark contrast to the fractured worldview that came to reign in the Age of Reason—that we live in a rationally ordered and organically-integrated universe that is comprised of truth that is simultaneously intellectual and moral as well as natural and supernatural in nature.[77] To put it differently, the concept affirms what Herschel Baker calls a "sacramental" as opposed to a "secular" view of the universe,[78] and thus it champions the notion that the right way for human beings to lay hold of the truth that comprises this organically-integrated universe is through the use of an "organic epistemology."[79] Since "Beauty, goodness, [and] love" are, according to this view, "a part of truth," it follows that reasoning itself is rightly regarded as an act of the whole soul that includes "faith, intuition, [and] feeling, as well as the more strictly rational processes."[80]

75. Douglas Bush, *Paradise Lost in Our Time* (Ithaca, NY: Cornell University Press, 1945), 37.

76. Hoopes, *Right Reason in the English Renaissance*, 1, 4.

77. S. L. Bethell, *The Cultural Revolution of the Seventeenth Century* (London: Dennis Dobson, 1951), 63–64.

78. A "sacramental" as opposed to a "secular" view of the universe presupposes *not* that "truth and piety" belong "to quite different orders of reality which permit no interaction," but that "every element in man's experience . . . [is] an object of cognition that . . . leads ultimately to God" who is both the cause and the end "to which the whole creation inexorably and teleologically strives" (Herschel Baker, *The Wars of Truth: Studies in the Decay of Christian Humanism in the Earlier Seventeenth Century* [Cambridge: Harvard University Press, 1952], 305, 5).

79. Ibid., 124. Note that the transition from a "sacramental" to a "secular" understanding of reality at the dawn of the modern age is a central theme of *Wars of Truth*. For Baker's initial discussion of the "sacramental" view, cf. 4–6. On this transition, see also Basil Willey, *The Seventeenth Century Background: Studies in the Thought of the Age in Relation to Poetry and Religion* (New York: Doubleday, 1955), 11–46. For helpful analysis of the intellectual history of the seventeenth century, see also: Gerald R. Cragg, *From Puritanism to the Age of Reason: A Study of Changes in Religious Thought within the Church of England 1660 to 1700* (Cambridge: Cambridge University Press, 1950); Cragg, *The Church in the Age of Reason, 1648–1789* (London: Hodder and Stoughton, 1960); Cragg, "Introduction," in *The Cambridge Platonists,* ed. Gerald R. Cragg (New York: Oxford University Press, 1968), 3–31; Perry Miller, *The New England Mind: The Seventeenth Century* (1939; repr., Boston: Beacon Press, 1961).

80. Bethell, *Cultural Revolution of the Seventeenth Century,* 57. Note that this organic view of reason was largely rejected in the Age of Reason when the epistemological realms of faith and reason were disastrously separated. According to Bethell, in the modern world, "the pattern of reasoning was mathematical deduction, combined with the inductive but strictly quantitative reasoning necessary for physical science. It is a process that ideally ignores the human element, though a large degree of unconscious faith actuated its exponents. . . . But faith, though a precondition, was not a part of the process; intuition, though useful in suggesting hypotheses, had no function in their demonstration; feeling, even a sort of austere aestheticism, could accompany, but could not enter into, the methods of reasoning; and the whole great range of human experience knowable

In addition to this affirmation of a "reasoning process" that involves the whole soul as opposed to "the quasi-mathematical reason" alone,[81] the concept recognizes, secondly, that since truth is simultaneously intellectual and moral in nature, it follows that both the depth and quality of an agent's apprehension of reality are largely dependent upon the kind of person the knowing agent is. According to Robert Hoopes, wherever advocates of right reason

> speak of the achievement of true knowledge . . . they invariably speak of a certain transformation that must take place in the character of the knower before that knowledge can be attained. . . . Since Truth in its totality is at once intellectual and moral in nature, the conditions of wisdom are for men both intellectual and moral. True knowledge, i.e., knowledge of Truth, involves the perfection of the knower in both thought and deed. . . .[82]

In both its classical and Christian manifestations, then, right reason is a kind of moral reasoning that "unites truth and goodness"[83] while combining both "natural and supernatural . . . into one picture of total reality."[84] That is to say, it is a kind of theological aesthetic that affirms a rationally ordered, "theocratic universe"[85] while insisting that because truth is not only true but good, in order for human beings to know truth in a more or less true or right sense "they must themselves *become* good."[86]

Right Reason in the Tradition of Christian Humanism

How, then, do human beings become good so that they can then know what is true? In his incisive analysis of Robert Hoopes's *Right Reason in the English Renaissance,* Jack Rogers correctly notes that the concept of right reason developed along "humanist" and "antihumanist" lines in the Christian church, in large measure because differing conceptions of philosophical psychology led to two different answers to this question.[87] Those who endorsed the "tripartite" psychology that originated in Ancient Greece and was later accommodated by Christian humanists in the Medieval and Renaissance eras viewed the human soul

---

only through faith, intuition, and feeling—spiritual experience, human passion, the beauties of nature and art—was no longer proper material for rational thought. The universe that reason could properly explore had narrowed to the calculable aspects of material existence: this was the real, the rest was epiphenomenon, manageable in part . . . by a 'common sense' which aped the categorical exactitude of true reason, but in the main left to the incalculable caprice of 'enthusiasts' and sentimentalists" (58).

81. Ibid., 55, 63.
82. Hoopes, *Right Reason in the English Renaissance,* 5.
83. Baker, *Wars of Truth,* 235.
84. Bethell, *Cultural Revolution of the Seventeenth Century,* 54.
85. Baker, *Wars of Truth,* 5.
86. Hoopes, *Right Reason in the English Renaissance,* 4, 6.
87. Jack B. Rogers, *Scripture in the Westminster Confession: A Problem of Historical Interpretation for American Presbyterianism* (Grand Rapids: Eerdmans, 1967), 84.

as an aggregate of autonomous functions ("faculties"), which were believed to operate discretely and in a prescribed order. Reason apprehended truth and recognized ultimate ends. The will, defined as a "rational appetite," sought the rationally defined good. [And] the affections, or passions, which constituted the "animal" part of human nature, followed sensually defined goods, such as food, sex or other sources of physical pleasure.[88]

In short, those who endorsed this understanding of the "faculty psychology" conceived of reason as a power that "was implanted by God in all men, Christian and heathen alike, as a guide to truth and conduct,"[89] and they insisted that men become good and thus reason "rightly" when they learn to follow the dictates of reason rather than of passion, the dictates of the head rather than of the heart. That is to say, moral agents become wise—they become virtuous knowers—when the affections or passions are self-consciously subordinated to the appetites of the rational will, and reason—which, though fallen, is still able to discern the good, the beautiful, and the true—is thereby exalted as "the ruler of the soul."[90] Hoopes

88. Walton, *Jonathan Edwards, Religious Affections*, 15. Walton suggests that the Aristotelian analysis of human psychology (cf. Nichomachean Ethics, bks. 2, 3, 6, 7, 10 in *Ancient Philosophy*, 3rd ed., ed. Forrest Baird, Walter Kaufmann [Upper Saddle River, NJ: Prentice Hall, 2000]) "passed to Thomas Aquinas, who identified the concept of rational choice, or 'rational appetite,' with the Latin word voluntas, or 'will.'" Walton summarizes Aristotle's views in the following fashion: "For Aristotle, human moral excellence lies in the subordination of the non-rational aspects of the soul to prudence, or practical reason, operating through deliberation and rational choice. The objects of deliberation and choice are normally presented by the senses, which combine percipience with affectivity, and which represent the animal aspect of the soul. Choice is thus carried out within a psychological environment of emotion, of 'sensitive appetite' and 'desire.' Emotion, or desire, competes with rational deliberation, to determine action. The 'uncontrolled' person . . . is not moved to act by the command of reason, but by sensation and desire. The self-controlled person . . . while experiencing sensitive appetite and desire, is not moved to act, except by the determination of the intellect. In the self-controlled person, the emotions and desires have been brought, normally by an elaborate and lengthy process of education, to a state of such tranquility and equilibrium as permit rational choice to operate without interference. Thus, the affections contribute to human moral excellence only negatively, by being so carefully controlled as not to overpower rational choice" (144).
    On the nature of Ancient Greek psychology, see also Norman Fiering, *Moral Philosophy at Seventeenth-Century Harvard: A Discipline in Transition* (Chapel Hill, N.C.: University of North Carolina Press, 1981), 147–48. For the primacy of reason in the thought of Aquinas, see, for example, *Summa Contra Gentiles* (Notre Dame, IN: University of Notre Dame Press, 1975), bk. 3, pt. 1, chap. 25.
89. Bush, *Paradise Lost in Our Time,* 37; cf. Hoopes, *Right Reason in the English Renaissance,* 3; John Spurr, "'Rational Religion' in Restoration England," *Journal of the History of Ideas* 49, no. 4 (1988): 570.
90. Fiering, *Moral Philosophy at Seventeenth-Century Harvard,* 113. On the anthropological optimism that is at the heart of Christian humanism, cf. Baker, *Wars of Truth,* 25–29, 90. Note that while classical and Christian humanists share a rather optimistic assessment of human nature, the assessment of Christian humanism is nowhere near as optimistic as that of classical humanism. According to Hoopes, whereas Christian humanists affirm the perpetual dependence of the creature upon the Creator, classical thinkers assume that "man by his own efforts may realize whatever ideal of perfection he sets for himself. The omnipresence of this assumption is, or ought to be, the meaning of 'the classical ideal,' for it is the one element fundamental to the thought of all classical thinkers whose systems otherwise conflict" (*Right Reason in the English Renaissance,* 65, 52; cf. 52–58). Thus, while classical humanists assert "man's essential independence" and insist that reason "possesses a potential infallibility *sui generis,*" Christian humanists assert "man's everlasting dependence" (ibid., 57, 56) and insist that reason's pursuit of the end for which we were created is dependent not only upon the law of God that is promulgated through and discerned by reason, but also upon the infusion of the theological virtues that make the achievement of this end possible. On the significance of the theological virtues, see

summarizes this "intellectualist" understanding of "right reason"—which sustained the Medieval synthesis and empowered Scholasticism's analogical investigation of reality[91]—as follows: "Right reason may thus be thought of as a faculty which fuses in dynamic interactivity the functions of knowing and being, which stands finally as something more than a proximate [or immediate] means of rational discovery or 'a nonmoral instrument of inquiry,' and which affirms that what a man knows depends upon what, as a moral being, he chooses to make himself."[92]

---

the helpful discussion in Jean Porter, *The Recovery of Virtue: The Relevance of Aquinas for Christian Ethics* (Louisville, KY: Westminster John Knox, 1990). For a helpful discussion of how this understanding of right reason informed patristic and medieval ethical theory, see Vernon J. Bourke, *History of Ethics* (Garden City, NY: Doubleday, 1968), 89–91.

91. On the relationship between analogical reasoning and the Medieval synthesis of faith and reason, of supernatural knowledge and natural knowledge, cf. Baker, *Wars of Truth,* 25–29, 309; Bethell, *Cultural Revolution of the Seventeenth Century,* 53–58.

92. Hoopes, *Right Reason in the English Renaissance,* 5 (emphasis added). The words "intellectualism" and "voluntarism" are being used in this essay in the way that Richard Muller uses them in his analysis of Calvin's theology. According to Muller, "The terms refer to the two faculties of the soul, intellect and will, and to the question of which has priority over the other: intellectualism indicates a priority of the intellect; voluntarism, a priority of the will. In a technical theological and philosophical sense, however, intellectualism indicates a view of soul that denominates intellect the nobler of the two faculties because it is the intellect that apprehends the final vision of God as being and truth, whereas voluntarism denominates the will as the nobler faculty and assumes that its ultimate cleaving to God as the highest good . . . addresses the highest object of human love" (*The Unaccommodated Calvin: Studies in the Formation of a Theological Tradition* [New York: Oxford University Press, 2000], 162). Muller argues that for Calvin the problem with the "intellectualism" of the Aristotelian-Thomistic psychology "is that its entirely correct definition of the relationship of intellect and will applies only to the prelapsarian condition of humanity. The philosophers did not understand grasp [*sic*] the problem of sin and therefore did not perceive the degree to which sin subverts the right ordering of the faculties" (ibid., 165). Muller therefore insists that what we find in Calvin is "not a philosophical but a soteriological voluntarism that not only recognizes the necessity of grace to all good acts of the will but also recognizes that, in the soul's present sinful condition, the will [—which "determines even the extent of our knowledge of any given object"—] most certainly stands prior to the intellect" (ibid., 166). In his recent analysis of Calvin's philosophy, Paul Helm amplifies the significance of the fall for understanding the basic differences between Calvin and Aquinas on issues relating to natural law and natural theology: "Calvin holds that there is an under-estimation of the noetic effects of sin possibly in the likes of Aquinas and certainly in the case of the classical philosophers more generally. He thinks that the idea that sin is solely a matter of sensuality prevails with them whereas for Calvin sin affects the understanding, not by destroying it but by depraving it. In particular the moral understanding is not completely wiped out, but it is choked with ignorance and prejudice, as a result of which without divine grace the will cannot strive after what is right" (*John Calvin's Ideas* [Oxford: Oxford University Press, 2004], 375; for elaboration of this point, see James K. A. Smith, *Introducing Radical Orthodoxy: Mapping a Post-Secular Theology* [Grand Rapids: Baker, 2004], 164–66). For helpful discussions of the "intellectualism" of the Aristotelian-Thomistic psychology, cf. Fiering, *Moral Philosophy at Seventeenth-Century Harvard,* 110–14; Walton, *Jonathan Edwards, Religious Affections,* 143–47.

Please note that one of the primary differences between the "intellectualist" view of "right reason" and the Augustinian view discussed below centers on disagreement over the effects of sin on our ability to know. Whereas advocates of the "intellectualist" view presume the "essential goodness" of man (Bush, *Paradise Lost in Our Time,* 39; cf. William J. Bouwsma, *The Culture of Renaissance Humanism* [Washington, D.C.: American Historical Association, 1973], 5–6) and affirm the ability of even unregenerated sinners to know rightly, advocates of the Augustinian view insist that the unregenerate are dead in sin and thus unable to know rightly. In her analysis of Augustine's anthropology, Carol Harrison summarizes the basic difference between Augustine's assessment of the moral agent and that of classical philosophy. While it would be unfair to suggest that Christian humanists endorsed the classical Greek view without qualification (please see n. 90) we can say that they shared, at least in some measure, the optimistic view of human nature that prevailed in Ancient Greece. According to Harrison, "The Christian doctrine of the fall, with its denial of man's capacity

Right Reason in the Tradition of Christian Antihumanism

While the affections or passions in this "intellectualist" view of the soul are separated from and thus are often at odds with the appetites of the rational will, the affections or passions are regarded as "an aspect" of the will in the psychology of "Augustinian voluntarism," the "bipartite, heart-centered psychology"[93] that Norman Fiering suggests is the "most enduring and persistent antagonist to intellectualism in [the history of] Western thought."[94] According to those who stand in the Augustinian tradition, the tradition that, in matters epistemological, came to be the object of near universal loathing in the sixteenth, seventeenth, and eighteenth centuries due to what its critics regarded as an "almost obsessive emphasis . . . upon the fact of human depravity,"[95] the soul is not "a mere aggregation of discrete faculties, but . . . an integrated totality of perception and volition, [that is] determined by the basic affective inclination, or fundamental amative orientation"[96] of "the inner essence of the whole man."[97] That is to say, Augustinian voluntarists conceive of the soul "not as a system of objectively distinguishable faculties" that have the ability to operate in more or less isolation from each other, "but as a 'mysterious organic unity'" that has "both an intellectual-

---

to attain the good through his own unaided efforts, of his inability to know or to do the good without God's grace, and of the unattainability of beatitude in this life marks the final break between classical and Christian understandings of virtue, the will, and the happy life. The startling optimism of classical philosophy, with its unerring conviction of man's autonomous will, his capacity for rational self-determination and for perfectibility through knowledge . . . , has been dealt a death blow by Augustine's uncompromising picture of man subject to Original sin following the fall of Adam. Without the help of grace man can do nothing to achieve salvation, his flawed and vitiated will can no longer do anything but sin, his grasp of the truth is marred by ignorance and blindness" (Carol Harrison, *Augustine: Christian Truth and Fractured Humanity* [Oxford: Oxford University Press, 2000], 100).

93. Walton, *Jonathan Edwards, Religious Affections*, 220, 181.

94. Fiering, *Moral Philosophy at Seventeenth-Century Harvard*, 117. In this psychology the soul is thought to consist of two rather than three faculties or powers—the understanding, which includes the powers of perception and speculation, and the will, which embraces the affections and the power of volition. Moreover, advocates insist that these faculties are not distinct, but act as a single substance that is united and governed by the "heart." Cf. Walton, *Jonathan Edwards, Religious Affections*, 43, 149, 220; Richard J. Gaffin, "Some Epistemological Reflections on 1 Corinthians 2:6–16," *Westminster Theological Journal* 57, no. 1 (1995): 120; J. Knox Chamblin, *Paul and the Self: Apostolic Teaching for Personal Wholeness* (Grand Rapids: Baker, 1993), 37–59; Peter T. O'Brien, *The Letter to the Ephesians* (Grand Rapids: Eerdmans, 1999), 320–22; T. Kermit Scott, *Augustine: His Thought in Context* (Mahwah, NJ: Paulist Press, 1995), pt. 3, especially 193–216. On the rise and subsequent decline of Augustinian voluntarism in the Renaissance, see William J. Bouwsma, *The Waning of the Renaissance: 1550–1640* (New Haven and London: Yale University Press, 2000), chaps. 2, 3, 11. Please note that I am using the term "Augustinian" largely in the sense that it is used by Perry Miller in his analysis of the New England Puritan mind. The Puritans in seventeenth-century New England were Augustinians, Miller argues, not because they "depended directly" upon the writings of Augustine, but because Augustine is the "arch-exemplar" of a kind of piety that "centered upon . . . God, sin, and regeneration" (*New England Mind*, 3–34). The various elements of "Augustinian voluntarism" can be found, for example, in: bk. 7:10, 17 of *The Confessions*, in *Nicene and Post-Nicene Fathers*, First Series, ed. Philip Schaff (1887; repr., Peabody, MA: Hendrickson, 1995), 1:109–10, 111–12; bks. 12–14 of *The City of God*, in *Nicene and Post-Nicene Fathers*, 2:226–83; bks. 8–13 of *On the Trinity*, in *Nicene and Post-Nicene Fathers*, 3:115–82; chaps. 1–5 of *The Enchiridion*, in ibid., 237–38; "Tractate 1," *On the Gospel According to St. John*, in *Nicene and Post-Nicene Fathers*, 7:7–13; bk. 1:1–4 of *Soliloquies*, in ibid., 7:537–38.

95. Hoopes, *Right Reason in the English Renaissance*, 98.

96. Walton, *Jonathan Edwards, Religious Affections*, 220.

97. Fiering, *Moral Philosophy at Seventeenth-Century Harvard*, 117.

percipient and a volitional-affective dimension," a two-dimensional unity that follows or takes its cues from the disposition or character of the "heart."[98]

What, then, is the "heart"? In the Augustinian tradition as in Scripture, the "heart" is "that mysterious organ which is the center of the personality" and "the single spring of thinking, feeling and acting."[99] The concept denotes the "bent" or "bias," the "inclination" or "fundamental amative orientation" of the personality "either toward the world of sin and self, or toward God and divine reality," and thus it indicates the underlying, preconscious "principle of psychic unity . . . [that] determines the manner in which one (1) perceives reality, and (2) wills, feels, and chooses."[100] Since the heart in this tradition is that principle which integrates and determines the "psychic totality" of the "whole soul," it has to do not with the emotions alone, but with "the simultaneous and interdependent operations of the cognitive and volitional-affective aspects of the personality, [aspects that are] unified, even fused, by its [inclination, or] fundamental amative orientation."[101] According to Augustinian voluntarists like Charles Hodge, it is this emphasis on the heart that

> forbids any such marked distinction between . . . [the soul's] cognitive and emotional faculties . . . , as is assumed in our philosophy, and therefore is impressed on our language. In Hebrew the same word designates what we commonly distinguish as separate faculties. The Scriptures speak of an "understanding heart," and of "the desires of the understanding," as well as of "the thoughts of the heart." They recognize that there is an element of feeling in our cognitions and an element of intelligence in our feelings. The idea that the heart may be depraved and the intellect unaffected is, according to the anthropology of the Bible, as incongruous, as that one part of the soul should be happy and another miserable, one faculty saved and another lost.[102]

For those who stand in the tradition of Augustinian voluntarism, what this emphasis on the heart suggests is that the rightness or wrongness of the manner in which an agent apprehends and interacts with reality is determined not by the natural competence of the agent's distinct faculties, but by the moral character or underlying disposition that unites the two dimensions of the agent's soul into an organic thinking-feeling-willing whole. What this means for Protestants who are like Augustine and take the fall and original sin seriously, then, is that moral agents who are dead in sin and inclined to the world of sin and self acquire the ability to reason "rightly" not by gritting their teeth and resolving to follow the appetites of the head rather than the passions of the heart, as in the intellectualist view of "right reason," but by

98. Walton, *Jonathan Edwards, Religious Affections*, 174, 227.
99. Ibid., 174, 184.
100. Ibid., 160, 227, 160.
101. Ibid., 177, 220, 160.
102. Charles Hodge, *A Commentary on the Epistle to the Ephesians* (New York: Robert Carter and Brothers, 1866), 249–50.

being given "hearts of flesh" (Ezek. 11:19)—that is, by being inclined to God and divine reality—in regeneration.[103] In regeneration, the Holy Spirit, working with and through the Word, becomes the new principle of life in the regenerated soul, and it is this new principle of life that inclines the soul to God and enables the moral agent to perceive, feel, and act "differently than before."[104] Among other things, the regenerated agent now not only sees all things in relationship to the God of the Bible because he looks at reality through the "spectacles" of Scripture,[105] but as an essential component of this seeing he also delights in and savors the spiritual excellence and beauty that is objectively present in and really radiating from the objects of his understanding.[106] In other words, he now recognizes with the likes of Charles Hodge that, "Truth is not merely speculative, the object of cognition. It has moral [and spiritual] beauty."[107] Jonathan Edwards, one of the most thoughtful defenders of the bipartite, heart-centered psychology in the history of the Augustinian tradition, summarizes the regenerated agent's ability to perceive what Hodge calls "the moral and spiritual excellence of truth"[108] as follows:

> Hence we learn that the prime alteration that is made in conversion, that which is first and the foundation of all, is the alteration of the temper and disposition and spirit of the mind; for what is done in conversion is nothing but conferring the Spirit of God, which dwells in the soul and becomes there a principle of life and action. 'Tis this is the new nature and the divine nature; and the nature of the soul being thus changed, it admits divine light. Divine things now appear excellent, beautiful, glorious, which did not when the soul was of another spirit.
>
> Indeed the first act of the Spirit of God, or the first that this divine temper exerts itself in, is in spiritual understanding, or in the sense of the mind, its perception of glory and excellency . . . in the ideas it has of divine things; and this is before any proper acts of the will. Indeed, the inclination of the soul is as immediately exercised in that sense of the mind which is called spiritual understanding, as the intellect. For it is not only the mere presence of ideas in the mind, but it is the mind's sense of their excellency, glory and delightfulness. By this sense or taste of the mind, es-

103. On classically Protestant conceptions of the life of the mind, see Mark A. Noll, *America's God: From Jonathan Edwards to Abraham Lincoln* (New York: Oxford University Press, 2002), 95–102; Theodore Dwight Bozeman, *To Live Ancient Lives: The Primitivist Dimension in Puritanism* (Chapel Hill, N.C.: University of North Carolina Press, 1988), 51–80.
104. Walton, *Jonathan Edwards, Religious Affections*, 187.
105. John Calvin, *Institutes of the Christian Religion*, 2 vols., ed. J. T. McNeill, trans. F. L. Battles (Philadelphia: Westminster, 1960), 1:70.
106. Cf. Walton, *Jonathan Edwards, Religious Affections*, 154–58, 189, 209, 222. Please note that by saying "objectively present in" I am *not* suggesting that the objects of the regenerated agent's understanding are themselves the ultimate *source* of the "spiritual excellence and beauty" that is perceived; I want to affirm with Reformed scholars generally that the glory of created things is *reflected* glory.
107. Hodge, *Epistle to the Ephesians*, 250.
108. Ibid.

pecially if it be lively, the mind in many things distinguishes truth from falsehood.[109]

Protestants who stand in the tradition of Augustine therefore insist that the regenerate alone "may rise to an understanding of the truth," because the regenerate alone have the moral ability to see revealed truth for what it objectively is, namely, glorious.[110] That is to say, regenerated knowers alone can know more or less "rightly" not only because they have an intellectual or speculative understanding of that which is true, but also because they have—as an essential component of their understanding—a love for the truth precisely because they see it declaring the glory, the moral excellence and beauty, of the One who is the source of truth and the epistemological key to interpreting all reality correctly (cf. Col. 2:3). For regenerated knowers, then, the eyes of faith—eyes that look at reality through the "spectacles" of Scripture—make a material difference not only in how they know, but also in what they know; they "are in a superior epistemic position"—that is, they are better knowers—because the Spirit, again working with and through the Word, helps them use "[their] natural epistemic faculties rightly."[111]

Old Princeton's Humanism of "the Broken Heart"

As I have tried to suggest in this chapter, and as I have tried to argue in my previous work on the Princeton theologians, there are good reasons for concluding that the theologians at Old Princeton Seminary stood squarely in what Robert Hoopes calls the "antihumanistic" heritage of the Reformation.[112] Although the Princetonians did

---

109. "Miscellanies" no. 397, in Jonathan Edwards, *The Works of Jonathan Edwards,* vol. 13, *The "Miscellanies," a–500,* ed. Thomas A. Schafer (New Haven: Yale University Press, 1994), 462–63.

110. Hoopes, *Right Reason in the English Renaissance,* 64. Please note that Augustinian voluntarists do *not* claim that the "right" knowledge the regenerate have is comprehensive knowledge; thus they are amenable to robust yet chastened understandings of "perspectivalism." For example, see Poythress, *Symphonic Theology*; John M. Frame, *The Doctrine of the Knowledge of God* (Phillipsburg, NJ: P&R, 1987).

111. William J. Wainwright, *Reason and the Heart: A Prolegomenon to a Critique of Passional Reason* (Ithaca, NY, and London: Cornell University Press, 1995), 42, 43. Note that if this is an accurate representation of how Augustinian voluntarists conceive of "right reason," then the work of Protestants who stand in this tradition ought not to be handled in a wooden, unimaginative fashion, for doing so will lead to serious misunderstandings, including the conclusion that such Protestants are rationalists. According to Carl Trueman, this is how progressive evangelicals have handled the Protestant scholastics. "As the work of scholars such as Richard Muller has indicated," Trueman argues, "confessional Reformed Orthodoxy . . . has theological moorings in an intelligent interaction with, and appropriation of, the best theological and exegetical work of the patristic and medieval authors, as well as the correctives of the sixteenth and seventeenth centuries. Yet this careful scholarship is so often aced in the evangelical culture by popular potboilers which tell a very different story. Thus, postconservative evangelicals may take the worst bits of Hodge, read them back into Turretin, mix in a faulty understanding of scholasticism as an adumbration of Enlightenment rationalism, repeat, Mantra-style, superficially learned and portentous phrases such as 'Cartesian dualism' and 'modernist mindset,' and extrapolate from there to dismiss the whole of confessional Reformed Orthodoxy; but that is just one more example of the cod-theology which passes for scholarship in some evangelical quarters" (review of *Is the Reformation Over?* by Mark A. Noll and Carolyn Nystrom [Grand Rapids: Baker, 2005], available at http://www.reformation21.org/Shelf_Life/Shelf_Life/127/?vobId=1466&pm=281).

112. In addition to the essay cited in note 1, please see the following articles for substantiation of this claim: Paul Kjoss Helseth, "B. B. Warfield on the Apologetic Nature of Christian Scholarship: An Analysis of His Solution to the Problem of the Relationship between Christianity and Culture," *Westminster Theological*

in fact affirm a kind of humanism, the humanism they affirmed was "antihumanistic" in both the Scholastic and Enlightenment senses because it was founded, as J. Gresham Machen argued in his classic work *Christianity and Liberalism,* "not upon human pride but upon divine grace."[113] That is to say, Old Princeton's humanism of "the broken heart" was founded upon "the consciousness of sin" rather than an essentially pagan confidence in the competence of "existing [or fallen] human faculties," and thus it championed the need for the regeneration of the whole soul as the necessary means to right reason and saving faith.[114] In short, the Princetonians—along with their most thoughtful descendants in the mainstream of the "received evangelical tradition"— recognized that since the "heart" is "that prevailing moral disposition that determines the volitions and actions" of the whole person,[115] regeneration is of necessity at the foundation of the ability to reason rightly because reasoning itself is an activity involving all the powers of the soul, not simply the rational faculty alone. As Archibald Alexander Hodge made clear in his *Outlines of Theology,* the Princetonians refused to grant a measure of autonomy to the rational faculty because they repudiated the foundational premise of both Scholastic and Enlightenment humanism. Indeed, they were simply not "rather bald rationalists,"[116] for they recognized that since,

> [t]he soul of man is one single indivisible agent . . . it is not true . . . that the understanding reasons, and the heart feels, and the conscience approves or condemns, and the will decides, as different members of the body work together, or as the different persons constituting a council deliberate and decide in mutual parts; but it is true that the one indivisible, rational, feeling, moral, self-determining soul reasons, feels, approves, or condemns and decides.[117]

This is the rather subtle point that has been overlooked by those who endorse the reigning interpretation of the Princeton theology, and this is the reason why the presumption of rationalism at the heart of post-conservatism's critique of the "received evangelical tradition" cannot be sustained.

Journal 62, no. 1 (2000): 89–111; Helseth, "'Right Reason' and the Princeton Mind: The Moral Context," *The Journal of Presbyterian History* 77, no. 1 (1999): 13–28; Helseth, "B. B. Warfield's Apologetical Appeal to 'Right Reason': Evidence of a 'Rather Bald Rationalism'?" *The Scottish Bulletin of Evangelical Theology* 16, no. 2 (1998): 156–77; Helseth, "The Apologetical Tradition of the OPC: A Reconsideration," *Westminster Theological Journal* 60, no. 1 (1998): 109–29.

113. J. Gresham Machen, *Christianity and Liberalism* (1923; repr., Grand Rapids: Eerdmans, 1990), 66.
114. Ibid., 65, 66.
115. A. A. Hodge, *Outlines of Theology* (1860; repr., Edinburgh: Banner of Truth, 1991), 459.
116. Cf. William Livingstone, "The Princeton Apologetic as Exemplified by the Work of Benjamin B. Warfield and J. Gresham Machen: A Study of American Theology, 1880–1930" (PhD diss., Yale University, 1948), 186.
117. Hodge, *Outlines of Theology*, 280–81.

6

Cornelius Van Til: "Principled" Theologian or Foundationalist?

JEFFREY C. WADDINGTON

~~~~~~~~

Postmodernism has called into question all sorts of certainties. Part and parcel of the postmodern critique of the modernist project is its rejection of foundationalism, the ostensible culprit behind epistemological certitude. In its desire to relativize knowledge, postmodernism rejects the privileging of some beliefs over others inherent in epistemological foundationalism with its distinction between basic and nonbasic beliefs. Rather, all beliefs are equally significant as they form a web-like noetic structure.[1] Unfortunately, the postmodern critique of noetic certainty has crept into the church, epitomized in such movements as post-conservative evangelicalism.[2]

1. I will discuss the relationship between foundationalism and contextualism/coherentism/holism with their distinct metaphors of a building and spiderweb later.
2. Those who hold to some form of post-conservative evangelicalism would include Nancey Murphy of Fuller Theological Seminary with her *Beyond Liberalism and Fundamentalism: How Modern and Postmodern Philosophy Set the Theological Agenda* (Valley Forge, PA: Trinity Press Int'l, 1996), Robert Webber, Roger Olsen, John Franke, and Stanley Grenz. Another favorable assessment of the intersection of postmodernism, truth, and the evangelical movement can be found in Henry Knight III, *A Future for Truth: Evangelical Theology for a Postmodern Age* (Nashville: Abingdon, 1997). One critical response to this movement is the helpful volume edited by Millard J. Erickson, Paul Kjoss Helseth, and Justin Taylor, *Reclaiming the Center: Confronting Evangelical Accommodation in Postmodern Times* (Wheaton, IL: Crossway, 2004). See also K. Scott Oliphint's appreciative review of this book in the *Westminster Theological Journal* 67, no. 1 (2005): 200–206. For further insight into the interaction of postmodernism and evangelicalism, see K. Scott Oliphint's "Something Much Too Plain to Say," *Westminster Theological Journal* 68, no. 2 (2006): 187–202 and a much fuller treatment of this and related issues in his *Reasons for Faith: Philosophy in the Service of Theology* (Phillipsburg, NJ: P&R,

For instance, Nancey Murphy has recently argued that liberals and fundamentalists were equally foundationalist in their respective epistemologies, albeit with different foundations. Liberalism built its theology upon experience and fundamentalism built its theology on the Bible.[3] In response to this apparent affirmation of noetic
relativism, some evangelicals have argued for a more chastened foundationalism.[4]
Given this context, the question has often been asked, was Cornelius Van Til a
foundationalist?[5]

That question can only be answered if we understand what foundationalism is.
So my goal is to offer a brief discussion of foundationalism. I will look at two forms
of foundationalism, its classical model as described by Alvin Plantinga and a modified form discussed by Nancey Murphy. After this look at the two forms of foundationalism I will examine Van Til's epistemology as derived from his Reformed confessional commitment involving both his doctrine of analogy and use of the model
of theological *principia*. By the time we reach the end of this chapter , we will see
that Van Til was not a foundationalist as that epistemological theory is normally
understood.[6]

What Is Foundationalism?

Our first concern is to determine the nature of foundationalism itself. The historical
origins of the theory are usually traced back to René Descartes, who, in the shadow
of the Thirty Years War, determined to find beliefs that were indubitable or incon-
testable.[7] The story is told about his looking out the window one day and thinking
that our noetic structure must be something like a building with a solid foundation.
Later, John Locke would develop the foundationalist model with his discussion of
the relation of belief and opinions.[8] Since our concern here is not with the pedigree
of foundationalism, we can move to the contemporary scene. We should recognize
that there are several varieties of this epistemological model. Alvin Plantinga has

---

2006). See also his book coedited with Lane G. Tipton, *Revelation and Reason: New Essays in Reformed
Apologetics* (Phillipsburg, NJ: P&R, 2007).

3. Murphy, *Beyond Liberalism*, 11–13.

4. Several of the chapters of *Reclaiming the Center* argue this way. Alvin Plantinga has argued for a modified
"Reidian" foundationalism in his *Warranted Christian Belief* (New York: Oxford University Press, 2000),
hereafter referred to as *WCB*.

5. I recognize Van Til's love-hate relationship with the broader evangelical movement in the United States,
but he would be classed by nonevangelicals and some evangelicals as an evangelical. However, I will show that
Van Til stood within the Reformed confessional tradition, especially with regard to his epistemology.

6. Again, I recognize that there are several forms of foundationalism, but we ought not to be misled simply
by the fact that we might occasionally talk in terms of the "foundation" of our theology being the Word
of God.

7. See Plantinga, *WCB*, 71, and Murphy, *Beyond Liberalism*, 12–15. See René Descartes, *Discourse on the
Method of Rightly Conducting the Reason and Seeking Truth in the Sciences* in *The Philosophical Works of Descartes*, ed. and trans. Elizabeth S. Haldane and G. R. T. Ross (New York: Dover, 1955). It should be noted
that the knowledge sought was not to be based upon any putative divine revelation.

8. See Plantinga, *WCB*, 71ff. See John Locke, *An Essay Concerning the Human Understanding*, ed. with
"Prolegomena" by Alexander Fraser (New York: Dover, 1959).

offered a detailed discussion of several varieties of foundationalism in his *Warrant: The Current Debate*.[9] However, it is his discussion of classical foundationalism that interests us here.

Epistemology is concerned with how we know what we know. It is concerned with the subject/object relationship and specifically with the relationship of ideas in the human mind with external (i.e., extra-mental) reality. Philosophers have long wondered what the difference was between opinions on the one hand and knowledge on the other. In other words, what is the difference between opinion or belief and knowledge? What is it that makes a belief real knowledge? After all, someone could think something and be accidentally or serendipitously correct. What is the difference between knowing something and just happening to hold a belief that turns out to be true? This leads us to the notion of justified true belief. Justified true beliefs are beliefs that an epistemic agent is within his rights to hold. It is within this context that foundationalism develops.

Plantinga unpacks classical foundationalism as part of what he calls the "classical package," which also involves deontology and evidentialism.[10] For the sake of accuracy we will look at all three elements, especially since Plantinga thinks they often travel together. Classical foundationalism, as we have already noted, develops a model of the human noetic structure based upon an analogy between that noetic structure and a building. Descartes noted that a superstructure was upheld by a solid foundation. If the foundation was faulty, the building was bound to fall. And so the human noetic structure also needed an unassailable foundation. Classical foundationalism therefore classifies beliefs as either basic or nonbasic.[11]

Only basic beliefs can form the foundation of a noetic structure. These are beliefs that are not based upon or derived from other more basic beliefs. Nonbasic beliefs are the superstructure and must be derivable from either basic beliefs located in the foundation or on other nonbasic beliefs that can be shown to derive from or depend upon the basic beliefs in the foundation. The question then naturally arises, what constitutes a basic belief? There is difference of opinion here, and these differences often lead to variations of foundationalism. Traditionally, as Plantinga describes it, in order for beliefs to be basic, to be a part of the foundation, they must be either (1) self-evident, (2) evident to the senses, or (3) incorrigible.[12]

---

9. Alvin Plantinga, *Warrant: The Current Debate* (New York: Oxford University Press, 1993), hereafter referred to as *WCD*. Plantinga continued his discussion in *Warrant and Proper Function* (New York: Oxford University Press, 1993) and his already noted *WCB*.

10. This evidentialism is similar to but not the same as evidentialism in apologetics. On the classical package, see Plantinga, *WCB*, 82.

11. I recognize that this is a characteristic common to the various forms of foundationalism and so is not unique to the classical form. See Plantinga, *WCD*, 68.

12. See Plantinga, *WCB*, 82–85, and *WCD*, 70–77, for a detailed discussion of proper basicality. Much of Plantinga's project (known as either "Reformed Epistemology" or "Warrantism") is geared toward expanding proper basicality to include belief in God.

We can conclude this brief look at Plantinga's discussion of classical foundationalism by mentioning the other two elements of his "classical package": deontology and
evidentialism. The deontological element has to do with the moral or ethical impera-
tive involved in properly knowing something. There are standards of proper knowing
such that if you transgress them, you have no epistemic right to hold a particular
belief. Evidentialism has to do with the notion that one should proportion his belief
to the significance and amount of evidence he has for a particular belief. Plantinga
cites the famous remark of W. K. Clifford that "it is wrong, always, everywhere, and
for anyone to believe anything upon insufficient evidence."[13]

As we have already had occasion to note, classical foundationalism is not the only
form of foundationalism, but as Plantinga himself puts it, the forms are analogous
and are lurking in the nearby row of bushes.[14] While I have no desire or intention
to catalog all the varieties of foundationalism, it will be useful to look at the discussion of foundationalism in Nancey Murphy's influential *Beyond Liberalism and
Fundamentalism* if for no other reason than that it has gained a hearing in the so-
called post-conservative evangelical movement and gives rise to our question as to
whether Cornelius Van Til was and ought to be considered a foundationalist.

Murphy discusses foundationalism within the context of a comparison/contrast
between liberalism and fundamentalism.[15] She traces the pedigree of foundationalism back to Descartes and Locke and their search for universal and indubitable
knowledge.[16] For Murphy, anyone who speaks of knowledge as involving "fundamental elements," of wanting to "build upon" a solid base, of "grounding" his theology
on certain principles is a foundationalist.[17] If anyone desires to discover, or believes
he already has, certain knowledge, he is a foundationalist.[18] Murphy is apparently
not concerned to limit foundationalism to those who explicitly embrace it in its
classical form or who intend to develop or augment it.[19] Murphy is concerned with
the use of metaphors, and so anyone who appears to use a construction or building
metaphor can be considered a foundationalist.[20]

13. Plantinga, *WCB*, 89, citing Clifford's essay "The Ethics of Belief" found in his *Lectures and Essays* (London: MacMillan, 1901), 183.
14. Plantinga, *WCB*, 85.
15. Murphy's usage of "fundamentalism" includes broader evangelicalism and confessional Reformed orthodoxy. In fact, she uses Charles Hodge as an example, even though I think he would be best construed as
a Reformed confessional theologian.
16. Murphy, *Beyond Liberalism*, 11–35.
17. Ibid., 12. She states, "Theologians have conceived of theology as a building needing a sturdy
foundation."
18. Ibid., 12–13.
19. In other words, Murphy doesn't appear concerned to relate her discussion to the kinds of discussions we
find in Plantinga and the philosophers with whom he interacts.
20. Murphy's concern for how the use of metaphors gives us clues to a person's epistemological theory
extends to herself and her use of the spiderweb idea as expressive of her form of coherentism or what she
calls "holism."

According to Murphy, both liberals and fundamentalists were locked into their respective theologies (or at least the epistemological aspects of them) because of the inherited foundationalist epistemic model. Both sought to ground their theologies on universal and indubitable knowledge.[21] For the liberal, this was a universal religious experience. For the fundamentalist, this was Scripture. So Murphy has something like a category of properly basic beliefs and beliefs that are nonbasic, although this terminology appears nowhere in her book. Additionally, she notes that reasoning in both forms of theology, given its foundationalism, was unidirectional.[22] That is, theologians in either camp reasoned *from* the foundations to other beliefs, so that there was apparently no give and take between the foundation and the superstructure of the liberal and fundamentalist theologies.[23]

In addition to the distinction between foundational and nonfoundational elements of theological structure in liberalism and fundamentalism and the unidirectional nature of the reasoning process, Murphy also discusses what distinguishes the two types of theology. The liberal followed an "inside-out" epistemology and the fundamentalist an "outside-in" theology.[24] That is, Murphy discusses the subject-object relationship in terms of liberalism's internal base of universal religious experience moving outward into the world and the relationship of God to the world and fundamentalism's external base of Scripture moving into the mind of the human knower.[25] Murphy then ties the foundationalism of liberalism and fundamentalism and their respective inside-out and outside-in epistemologies to a discussion of the use of language and understanding of how God relates to the world. Liberalism builds on an expressivist use of language and stresses God's immanence in the world (to the extent that we cannot distinguish particular divine acts from the rest of providence), while fundamentalism builds on a propositional use of language and understands that God has intervened in history on certain occasions.[26] Foundationalism, for Murphy, brings with it all these sorts of illegitimate binary oppositions to which she will oppose her form of "holism."[27] Ultimately, Murphy opposes epistemological certitude.[28]

21. What Plantinga calls properly basic beliefs, although Murphy evidences no awareness of Plantinga's discussion and certainly has not limited properly basic beliefs to the self-evident, evident to the senses, or the incorrigible. This is a continually irritating aspect of her work.
22. Murphy, *Beyond Liberalism*, 23.
23. Ibid., 23. Given Murphy's understanding of foundationalism, I would think she sees the very name "fundamentalist" as indicative of foundationalism.
24. Ibid., 28–35.
25. Ibid., 28–35. I hope to show how even this way of looking at things is overly reductionistic when we look at Van Til's use of the doctrine of analogy and theological *principia*.
26. Ibid., 36–82. Murphy is, of course, setting the reader up for her alternative of "holism" to the binary opposition of foundationalism as she has described it in the first part of her book. In the second part of her book where she advocates her holism, she will try to transcend the binary oppositions of foundation/ superstructure, outside-in/inside-out, expressive/propositional, and immanent/interventionist discussed throughout the first half of the book.
27. Ibid., 70–94.
28. That is, foundationalism is defective just because it privileges certain beliefs above others in that it sees foundational beliefs as certain. However, Murphy herself has been challenged, for instance, by J. Wetzel Van

To sum up what we have learned about foundationalism, we can see the following commonalities between the classical foundationalism described so fully by Alvin Plantinga and the foundationalism elaborated by Nancey Murphy: Both recognize a distinction between beliefs that are not based upon other beliefs (properly basic beliefs in Plantinga and foundational beliefs in Murphy) and beliefs that are derived from them (nonbasic beliefs in Plantinga and superstructures in Murphy). And they both recognize that the reasoning process moves from basic beliefs to nonbasic beliefs. Obviously there are other elements in each model that cause them to differ from one another: Plantinga talks about a "classical package," which ties classical foundationalism to deontologism and evidentialism, and Murphy ties foundationalism to the inside-out/outside-in subject/object relation, the use of either expressive or propositional language, and a particular understanding of how God relates to this world.[29] Now that we have looked at these representatives of foundationalism, we can move to an examination of Cornelius Van Til's Reformed biblical and confessional epistemology.

Van Til's Epistemology

Cornelius Van Til's epistemology arises out of his commitment to Scripture and the Reformed confessional tradition as the truest articulation of Scripture. He stands on the shoulders of giants who have gone before, while critically sifting this Reformed heritage. He does not merely parrot the past. Van Til appropriates, corrects where needed, and extends and develops the perspective articulated in the confessions of the Reformed churches. Given this critical appropriation and development, we can now look at his views.

Van Til articulates his epistemology in terms of his doctrine of analogy and theological *principia*. The doctrine of analogy is a rearticulation of the pervasive archetype/ectype distinction in Reformed theology going back at least to Franciscus Junius, professor of theology at the University of Leiden in the Netherlands.[30] Junius first

Huysteen of Princeton Theological Seminary, for still *privileging* her doctrine of God (i.e., it is foundational for her). I thank my friend and fellow Westminster Theological Seminary PhD candidate Brian Belh who brought Van Huysteen's assessment of Murphy to my attention.

29. Each of these aspects of the two descriptions of foundationalism deserves further treatment, but that is the work of another day. Also, there are other aspects of these views (I am particularly thinking of Plantinga here) that I haven't even touched upon here.

30. Junius's role in the formulation of the archetype/ectype distinction has been revealed in the following very helpful sources: Sebastian Rehnman, *Divine Discourse: The Theological Methodology of John Owen* (Grand Rapids: Baker, 2002), 52–89; Richard Muller in his "Scholasticism Protestant and Catholic: Francis Turretin on the Object and Principles of Theology," in *After Calvin: Studies in the Development of a Theological Tradition* (Oxford: Oxford University Press, 2003), 137–45 and *Post-Reformation Reformed Dogmatics: The Rise and Development of Reformed Orthodoxy ca. 1520 to ca. 1725*, vol. 1, *Prolegomena to Theology* (Grand Rapids: Baker, 2003), 113, 225–69; Willem van Asselt and Eef Dekker's *Reformation and Scholasticism: An Ecumenical Enterprise* (Grand Rapids: Baker, 2001); Van Asselt's article, "The Fundamental Meaning of Theology: Archetypal and Ectypal Theology in Seventeenth-Century Reformed Thought" in *Westminster Theological Journal* 64, no. 2 (2002): 319–35; Van Til's appropriation of this formulation is documented in R. Scott Clark's chapter, "Janus, the Well-Meant Offer of the Gospel and Westminster Theology," in *The*

articulated this distinction in his *De vera theologia*,[31] and it is believed that he was
building on Medieval theologian John Duns Scotus's distinction between God's
knowledge of himself (*theologia in se*) and our knowledge of him (*theologia nostra*).
Scotus is believed to have developed this formulation in contradistinction to the
analogia entis (chain or hierarchy of being) of Thomas Aquinas.[32] In other words,
Scotus was concerned to uphold the Creator/creature distinction. Between Scotus
and Junius stood such Reformers as Martin Luther who distinguished between the
hidden and revealed God (*deus absconditus* and *deus revelatus*) and John Calvin who
distinguished between God as he is in himself (*in se*) and as he is toward us (*quoad
nos*).[33] Of course, once the archetype/ectype distinction entered into Reformed
theological discourse, it became common property of the Protestant tradition.[34] The
tradition of the archetype/ectype distinction would most likely have come down to
Van Til through Dutch Reformed theologians such as Abraham Kuyper and Herman Bavinck.[35]

Van Til was concerned, as were his predecessors, to carefully and clearly uphold
the biblical distinction between God and his creation. God is original and humans
are derivative. Man is dependent upon God for both his existence and his knowledge.
While Van Til did not use as thoroughly the language of archetype and ectype
theology, his doctrine of analogy clearly is his own formulation of that very doctrine.
"In contrast to this, however, we should think of God as the ultimate starting point
of our knowledge, God is the archetype, while we are the ectypes. God's knowledge
is archetypal and ours ectypal."[36] In order for man to know anything truly he must
"think God's thought after him." That is, he must conform his thinking to God's
thinking. Now, man's knowledge cannot be a reflection of the knowledge God has
of himself (*in se*) for this is not available to man. However, Van Til recognized that

*Pattern of Sound Doctrine: Systematic Theology at the Westminster Seminaries: Essays in Honor of Robert B.
Strimple*, ed. David VanDrunen (Phillipsburg, NJ: P&R, 2004), 149–79; and in Michael Horton's *Covenant
and Eschatology* (Louisville: Westminster John Knox, 2002) and *Lord and Servant* (Louisville: Westminster
John Knox, 2004), and can be found in several of Van Til's own publications, a very small sampling of which
I will cite below.

31. Franciscus Junius, *De vera theologia*. This Latin work can be found in his *Opuscula Theologica Selecta*, ed.
Abraham Kuyper (Amsterdam: Miller and Kruyt, 1882), 39–101.

32. Rehnman, *Divine Discourse,* 58, 62ff.

33. For Luther, see Clark, "Janus," 154. For Calvin's view in this regard, see both Clark, "Janus," 156–57
and Paul Helm's "God *in Se* and *Quoad Nos,*" in his *John Calvin's Ideas* (Oxford: Oxford University Press,
2004), 11–34.

34. I was reminded of this salient point in a personal e-mail from Dr. Richard Muller.

35. For Kuyper, see his *Encyclopaedie* of which only a portion has been translated from the Dutch and is
available as *Principles of Sacred Theology*, trans. J. Hendrik de Vries (Grand Rapids: Baker, 1980), 248–92.
For Bavinck, see his *Gereformeerde Dogmatiek,* which is in the process of being translated into English. The
second volume contains the salient material: *Reformed Dogmatics*, vol. 2, *God & Creation* , ed. John Bolt,
trans. John Vriend (Grand Rapids: Baker, 2004), 107–10. It is not immediately clear what role, if any, the
theologians of Old Princeton may have played in this transmission. Examination of this remains the work
of another day.

36. Cornelius Van Til, *An Introduction to Systematic Theology* (Phillipsburg, NJ: Presbyterian and Reformed,
1974), 203.

God has revealed himself to his creatures in nature and history, in both natural and special revelation.

All of reality reflects its status of covenantal creatureliness. Man was dependent on God from the beginning, and this is true apart from any consideration of the fall. As Van Til has pointed out, God revealed himself in the garden of Eden through Adam's human nature and consciousness (i.e., Adam could reason and communicate with his wife Eve), and he spoke to him (specifically in the prohibition of eating from the tree of the knowledge of good and evil). The interaction of natural and special revelation came to a head when God commanded the man not to eat from the tree of the knowledge of good and evil. Adam had to be able to distinguish one tree from another (natural or general revelation) in order to obey God's command (special revelation). Man was dependent on God for his existence and knowledge in paradise.[37]

However, paradisiacal conditions didn't prevail. Adam and Eve disobeyed God and plunged themselves and their posterity into the estate of sin and misery. Our first parents failed to "think God's thoughts after him" when Eve was tempted by the serpent and Adam knowingly followed her lead.[38] Once Eve entertained the serpent's invitation to disobedience she set herself up as a judge between the so-called equal options of God and Satan. With the fall, special revelation would take on a redemptive or salvific color. Man is now not only dependent upon God for his existence and knowledge, he is now at war with God because of sin, and this animosity must be overcome if man is to be redeemed.

Van Til's discussion on these issues mirrors the earlier theological ruminations of his Reformed forebears. The Reformed Scholastics understood not only the archetype/ectype distinction, but they also recognized that ectype theology ought to be delineated in terms of a pre-fall and post-fall ectypal theology; a false theology (this would be natural theology as articulated by philosophers and false religions that failed to submit to God's Word); a theology of union within the person of Jesus Christ; a pilgrim theology; and a theology of vision (the beatific vision in the new heavens and the new earth).[39] Van Til would extend this archetype/ectype distinction within the Reformed tradition beyond theology proper, to which it appears to have been limited in the discussions of the Reformed Scholastics. Not only knowledge of God (i.e., theology) but also all other human knowledge would depend upon God.[40] Any kind of human knowledge, not just knowledge of God and the things

37. Cornelius Van Til, "Nature and Scripture," in Ned. B. Stonehouse and Paul Woolley, eds., *The Infallible Word* (Phillipsburg, NJ: Presbyterian and Reformed, 1946), 263–301.
38. Cornelius Van Til, *A Survey of Christian Epistemology* (Phillipsburg, NJ: Presbyterian and Reformed, 1969), 18–22.
39. Rehnman, *Divine Discourse,* 63–71. So we see that with the idea of *pilgrim theology* the Reformed tradition already possessed the idea that human (Christian) theology was by definition not infallible (i.e., *in via*) this side of the consummation. Postmodernism was not needed to come to a recognition of this reality.
40. Of course, Calvin can be understood this way in the opening of his *Institutes*. Knowledge of ourselves and God are intertwined, and Calvin could not determine which came first. See John Calvin, *Institutes of*

of God, depends upon the existence and character and revelation of the God of Scripture.

We now come to a consideration of what are called the theological *principia*. We have considered the doctrine of analogy (archetype/ectype distinction) in its broad outline. Christian theologians have often been concerned with what theology is— whether it is a science, and if it is a science, whether it is speculative, practical, or a mixture of the two and, if a mixture, which predominated. A science as traditionally understood was an organized body of knowledge that had its own object and method of study and organization of the results of that study. Theology is unique among the sciences (assuming it to be a science of some sort) in that its object (God) is not under the control of the human subject. As we have already noted, man is dependent upon God for his knowledge of him. God must reveal himself to man in order for there to be either true religion or true theology. God is then said to be the *principium essendi* or principle or ground of being of true theology.[41] For Van Til, God is this and more. He is the principle of all creaturely existence and, of course, of knowledge as well.

In order to bring out the nature of the *a priori* aspect of our method, we may discuss it in relation to what has in recent writings on theology been spoken of as the *principium essendi* of knowledge. In his monumental work on dogmatic theology *De Gereformeerde Dogmatiek*, Herman Bavinck has given a long discussion of the *principium essendi* of knowledge. What he means by this is that without the concept of God as self-conscious, as self-existent, we could not know anything. We must now develop this idea more fully. Before the world was, God existed from all eternity as a self-contained and self-sufficient being. From the Christian point of view, it is impossible to think of the nonexistence of God. It is very well possible to think of the nonexistence of the world. In fact, we believe that the world once upon a time did not exist; it was created by God out of nothing.[42]

While God is the *principium essendi,* this fact would be of little use to man epistemologically if he was not aware of it. True theology therefore depends not only upon God's existence, but also his communication with his human creatures. We have already noted that God has revealed himself in natural and special revelation. If God is the *principium essendi*, what is the *principium cognoscendi*? The principle of knowing in general is natural revelation, but for true theology, the *principium cognoscendi* is divided into the *principium cognoscendi externum* (external principle), which is Holy Scripture, and the *principium cognoscendi internum* (internal principle), which is faith, and the *testimonium internum spiritus sancti* (internal witness of the

---

the Christian Religion , ed. John T. McNeill, trans. Ford Lewis Battles (Louisville: Westminster John Knox, 1960), 1.1.1.

41. And, yes, *principium* also means foundation.

42. Van Til, *Introduction*, 9–10. See also Herman Bavinck, *Reformed Dogmatics*, vol. 1, *Prolegomena* (ed. John Bolt, trans. John Vriend, [Grand Rapids: Baker, 2003]).

Holy Spirit). True theology derives from and is dependent on God himself and his revelation and his activity in the lives of his saints. That Van Til builds upon this epistemological formulation is clear from his recurring references to the *principium*.[43] He often brings the *principium* to bear against autonomous unbelief in his apologetics.[44]

The "special principle" of Van Til (the theological *principia*) provides certainty because it is about God and comes from him. It involves both an internal and an external aspect, but in neither case is the certainty predicated upon a purely internal process within the human agent. The reader will note that human reason does not serve as a *principium*, or source of theology, as it does in several alternative theologies.[45] Reason is operative throughout this process, but it is instrumental. For true theology, reason is directed by faith and by the Holy Spirit. For false theology, reason is autonomous and becomes a source for error.[46] Additionally, the certainty of Scripture arises from its self-authenticating nature. It need not appeal to a higher authority for it derives its authority from its author, God. The internal testimony of the Holy Spirit is *not to be confused with* this self-authentication. Self-authentication is a quality of the Bible in itself. The witness of the Holy Spirit opens the heart and mind of a man to see the self-authenticated Scriptures for what they are.

Conclusion

So now we come to the conclusion of our study of classical and "Murphian" foundationalism and the question, was Cornelius Van Til a foundationalist in the light of his biblical and Reformed confessional epistemology? The short answer to the question is no.[47] However, I would like to offer some closing thoughts related to the relationship of Van Til and classical and Murphian foundationalism.

Classical foundationalism as described by Alvin Plantinga involves an internal process within the human mind or consciousness that accounts for the justification of belief. It is concerned with the nature of the human noetic structure and the production of justified true belief. Van Til's appropriation of the archetype/ectype formulation and use of the theological *principia* differ from this considerably. The archetype/ectype distinction (or doctrine of analogy) requires the conformity of the

---

43. A search for the word "principium" on the *The Works of Cornelius Van Til, 1895–1987*, ed. Eric Sigward (New York: Labels Army Co., 1997), CD-ROM, yields 104 hits in 48 articles, and a perusal of these will indicate Van Til's dependence upon and use of the formulation delineated above.

44. In this Van Til appears to be following in the footsteps of Abraham Kuyper, who in his *Principles of Sacred Theology* speaks of the antithesis between a "natural principle" and the "special principle," or autonomous human epistemology and a human epistemology dependent upon God and his revelation in nature and Scripture.

45. For instance, with the Anglican Lambeth Trilateral (Scripture, tradition, and reason) and the Wesleyan Quadrilateral (Scripture, tradition, reason, and experience). On this point, see Bavinck's discussion in *Reformed Dogmatics*, 1:288–89.

46. See Rehnman, *Divine Discourse*, 56.

47. This, of course, does *not* make Van Til a postmodernist born out of time, either.

human thinking process to God's revelation. And the certainty produced by the theological *principia* does not arise from some internal process inherent in the human mind (not even from the *process* involved in "thinking God's thoughts after him") but from the fact that the *principia* are God, on the one hand, and Scripture on the other (even though the Holy Spirit is at work within the human subject, the inner witness is not just some innate human epistemological process).

Classical foundationalism posits a distinction between properly basic beliefs and nonbasic beliefs and requires that the nonbasic beliefs be held on the evidentiary basis of the properly basic beliefs directly or indirectly. The model limits properly basic beliefs to beliefs that are self-evident, evident to the senses, or incorrigible. However one understands these categories, the *principia* do not fall into any of these categories, and even if we could somehow construe the *principia* so that they were consistent with these three categories, that would involve our concepts of the *principia* and not the *principia* themselves. And Plantinga's own project shows that those who are committed to this epistemological model consider belief in God to be something based upon other beliefs.[48] And, as Plantinga has pointed out, classical foundationalism is self-referentially incoherent.[49] Is the model itself a properly basic belief? It is clear that Van Til was not a foundationalist according to this model.

The matter is a little different with regard to Murphian foundationalism. Murphy equates the use of foundational and building metaphors with foundationalism as an epistemological model. This seems to me to be a rather facile equation. We have already noted that the archetype/ectype distinction and the theological *principia* are external to the human knower (even faith and the work of the Holy Spirit that gives rise to it cannot be reduced to mere subjectivity). This equation of the use of building metaphors with a foundationalist epistemology arises from her embrace of holism, which finds a distinction between *principia* and other beliefs untenable. All beliefs are equal and form a web. All is relative. And the relativism is not limited to beliefs within the system. There are no extra mental or extra linguistic standards to which different groups may appeal.[50] Even Murphy grants that one of the problems with her holistic epistemology is this relativism and its concomitant lack of standards by which to judge between two or more systems of belief.[51] And Murphy is reductionistic with her "inside-out" and "outside-in" epistemologies. While the *principia* are objective, there is the *principium cognoscendi internum* of faith and the witness of the Holy Spirit. In other words, there is both a legitimate objective and subjective aspect.

48. Plantinga, *WCB*, 81.
49. Ibid., 93ff.
50. This last statement should not be read as an appeal to common ground or a neutral zone of belief. The standards by which any and all epistemic systems are to be judged are the *principia*. These are not neutral, but they are objective.
51. Murphy, *Beyond Liberalism*, 155.

Cornelius Van Til worked within and advanced a biblical and Reformed confessional epistemology. Admittedly he may not have discussed the internal mechanism of the human mind to any significant degree. His concern was with bringing humans into conformity with God's Word. He was concerned with sinful autonomous human thinking, and he recognized that man must bring his thoughts into captivity to Christ. Any epistemological model that neglected to bring the Triune God of Scripture into the subject/object relation or that explored the internal mechanism of the human mind without reference to God or in opposition to Scripture was suspect, and rightly so. And epistemological models that failed to reckon with sin and its effects on the human noetic structure fell short as well. Van Til built his epistemology upon the theological *principia* of God, Scripture, and faith and the internal witness of the Holy Spirit. These do form a foundation, but one that is both outside the human mind and at work upon or within it. And when the Holy Spirit works internally, he cannot be reduced to human processes. However, use of building terminology does not make one a foundationalist in the technical epistemological sense. Cornelius Van Til was not a foundationalist, although he built on the solid foundations of God and his Word.

7

Church and Community or Community and Church?

RONALD N. GLEASON

~~~~~~~~~

The modern church, in both its megachurch as well as its "emergent" conversation, is a study in spiritual rigor mortis. Although the entire postmortem is not yet in, there are, and have been for at least a couple of decades now, signs that what has come to be known as "evangelicalism" has been dying a slow, but certain death.[1]

Around the time of the mid-1970s, the church growth movement got into full swing. By the 1980s, evangelicalism and the megachurch movement enjoyed unprecedented attention. Churches became disenchanted with "pastors" and began training and hiring CEO-types instead. The marketing of the church was moving along full steam ahead. Evangelical involvement in the political arena proved to be more difficult, messier, and required more compromise than was initially thought. D. G. Hart writes, "Electoral politics proved to be a difficult arena in which to persuade the breadth of the American public that the narrow way of faithfulness was best."[2]

---

1. For excellent monographs on this point see Mark Noll, *The Scandal of the Evangelical Mind* (Grand Rapids: Eerdmans, 1994); David Wells, *No Place for Truth, Or Whatever Happened to Evangelical Theology?* (Grand Rapids: Eerdmans, 1993); Wells, *God in the Wasteland: The Reality of Truth in a World of Fading Dreams* (Grand Rapids: Eerdmans, 1994); Wells, *Losing Our Virtue: Why the Church Must Recover Its Moral Vision* (Grand Rapids: Eerdmans, 1998); Wells, *Above All Earthly Pow'rs: Christ in a Postmodern World* (Grand Rapids: Eerdmans, 2005); and Wells, *The Courage to Be Protestant* (Grand Rapids: Eerdmans, 2008).
2. D. G. Hart, *Deconstructing Evangelicalism: Conservative Protestantism in the Age of Billy Graham* (Grand Rapids: Baker Academic, 2004), 14.

In the 1990s two pivotal works appeared in the United States: *No Place for Truth* by David Wells and *The Scandal of the Evangelical Mind* by Mark Noll.[3] On the British scene we could add Iain Murray's *Evangelicalism Divided*.[4] All of these works—plus a host of others—clearly documented, for all who were willing to listen, the fragile house of cards that evangelicalism was building.[5] Unfortunately, few were. The conventional wisdom was that "denominationalism" had divided Protestants for far too long and that evangelicalism "promised unity and more—unity *for action*."[6] The eradication of denominational lines was perceived as something to be desired rather than something detrimental.[7] After all, it was reasoned, couldn't Pentecostals and those who are committed to the historical Reformed faith just put their differences aside and peacefully coexist? In theory, according to some, they could put those differences aside, but the practice has demonstrated that this "unity for action," whether in the public arena or for the purposes of winning the lost or the world for Christ, has not been as easy as was first expected.[8] This is true for a number of reasons.

Historically, evangelicalism had to rise from the ashes of fundamentalism. Before long, the true distinctions between historic fundamentalism and what has come to be called neo-evangelicalism made it clear that cooperation was a complicated matter. The promises that the "coalition of the willing" made in terms of resolving the denominational ills of America have, in point of fact, produced precious few positive results. Hart is correct when he says, "But as useful as evangelicalism may have been, its *usefulness* is no longer obvious. In fact, its *harmfulness* may be what has become most apparent."[9] These harmful effects are either not seen or not admitted—or both—by the adherents of evangelicalism. John Stackhouse of Regent College has termed these deleterious spiritual effects as "perpetual adolescence," which is an apt phrase.

Landmarks of Evangelicalism's Decline

There are a number of "landmarks" in evangelicalism's development that we could point to as symptomatic of spiritual illness and the demise of evangelicalism, but for the present, I want to cite two that are fueled by its "perpetual adolescence": (1) a glaring lack of and disdain for the historical Christian tradition and (2) a thirst and desire for a "tangible" religion. I would add to this a third, which is not only admirable

---

3. Wells, *No Place for Truth* (Grand Rapids: Eerdmans, 1993) and Noll, *The Scandal of the Evangelical Mind* (Grand Rapids: Eerdmans, 1994).
4. Iain H. Murray, *Evangelicalism Divided: A Record of Crucial Change in the Years 1950 to 2000* (Edinburgh: Banner of Truth, 2000).
5. Compare Carl R. Trueman, *Minority Report* (Ross-shire, Scotland: Mentor, 2008), 43–67.
6. Hart, *Deconstructing Evangelicalism*, 177.
7. David Wells, *The Courage to Be Protestant* (Grand Rapids: Eerdmans, 2008), 4–12.
8. For a clear example of some of the major doctrinal differences that exist in evangelicalism, see Wayne Grudem, *Evangelical Feminism: A New Path to Liberalism?* (Wheaton, IL: Crossway, 2006).
9. Hart, *Deconstructing Evangelicalism*, 178 (emphasis added).

and desirable but also biblical: a hunger for genuine community and relationship. The last point has been strongly advocated by the emergent church movement in particular.

The Megachurch's and Emergent Church Movement's Disdain for Tradition

For decades, as far as the megachurch movement is concerned, and for almost as long as far as the emergent church movement (ECM) is concerned, there has been disdain for, a disregard of, and often a downright ridiculing of the value of the Christian church's history at all levels by its leaders. D. H. Williams, in his book *Retrieving the Tradition and Renewing Evangelicalism*, delineates that modern evangelicalism has "an acute problem of continuity."[10] According to Williams this acute problem is analogous to a case of amnesia where the patient not only forgets who his friends and relatives are, but also no longer knows who he is. Hart comments that, "as a result, new techniques for church growth and seeker-sensitive worship have filled the vacuum of memory loss."[11] With a view to 2 Timothy 1:13–14 ("Follow the pattern of the sound words that you have heard from me, in the faith and love that are in Christ Jesus. By the Holy Spirit who dwells within us, guard the good deposit entrusted to you"), Williams asserts that evangelicals "are no longer sure what this 'deposit' consists of, or where it can be found." Worse yet, for some evangelicals "finding this 'deposit' does not matter anymore."[12]

Brian McLaren, a prominent spokesman for the emergent church movement, makes it crystal clear that any acceptance of what might be viewed as Christian tradition is limited to the Apostles' and Nicene creeds.[13] By his own admission, McLaren desires to put doctrinal differences "in their *marginal* place."[14] He acknowledges that doctrinal distinctions have real value, but that their value is overrated.[15] He is also embarrassed that "nearly all orthodoxies of Christian history have shown a pervasive disdain for other religions of the world: Buddhism, Hinduism, Judaism, atheism, etc."[16] McLaren's aim, therefore, is to see members of others religions and nonreligions "as dialogue partners and even collaborators."[17] In evangelicalism's lineage and roots there is clear evidence as to how hostile evangelicalism is toward the historical Christian tradition. This being the case, it begs this question: "Is evangelicalism still evangelicalism once it aligns with any of the historic expressions of Christianity whose arguments extend across the millennia?"[18] The answer is a resounding no!

10. D. H. Williams, *Retrieving the Tradition and Renewing Evangelicalism* (Grand Rapids: Eerdmans, 1999), 1.
11. Hart, *Deconstructing Evangelicalism*, 181.
12. Williams, *Retrieving the Tradition*, 9–10.
13. Brian McLaren, *A Generous Orthodoxy* (Grand Rapids: Zondervan, 2004), 32.
14. Ibid. (emphasis added).
15. Ibid.
16. Ibid., 35.
17. Ibid.
18. Hart, *Deconstructing Evangelicalism*, 188.

A Thirst for "Tangible" Religion

Another phenomenon that has presented itself and has become a staple item in the ECM is an insatiable desire for the tangible as far as Christianity is concerned. This is probably more (self) evident in the emergent conversation than in the megachurch movement. For example, there is a return to elements found in medieval worship such as contemplative prayer, prayer labyrinths, votive candles, and a host of other accoutrements. Hart cites the example of Thomas Howard (*Evangelical Is Not Enough*) who converted to Roman Catholicism from High Church Anglicanism in his spiritual pilgrimage/quest. In his rejection of evangelicalism, Howard sought—as the title of his book states—for *more*. Howard believed that evangelicalism's articles of faith were sufficient as were its piety and zeal. "But Christianity offered so much more than the bare essentials of doctrine, a strict reliance on the Bible as opposed to the wisdom of the ages, or evangelicalism's strict morality."[19] The *more* that Howard yearned for was to be found in a return to the episcopate for both unity and accountability, the restoration of the Eucharist to the centrality of worship, which resolved itself in weekly communion, and the observance of the liturgical year. It comes as no shock then that Howard converted to Roman Catholicism.

Something similar to Howard's ecclesiastical change/conversion—without the in-depth thought—is to be found in the modern emergent movement.[20] McLaren admits that he is overly sympathetic to Roman Catholics, Eastern Orthodoxy, and theological liberals.[21] As the emergent conversation continues, there are increasing causes for deep concern and alarm such as its rejection of orthodox views of Scripture, the atonement, homosexuality, and the Christian tradition represented in, say, the Reformation *solas*, and his recent open disdain for what he calls a "violent" second coming that will culminate in God's judgment upon those not of the historical, biblical Christian faith, just to mention some. Therefore it should come as no surprise that McLaren's followers would be drawn to the same types of things—and they are.

A Desire for Community

The third component that is especially prevalent in the modern emergent church is a sense of and desire for community or relationship. In the aftermath of the megachurch movement and its crass anonymity, the pendulum has swung back to the side where churchgoers are weary of being lonely in the midst of the crowd. Therefore, this desire among the emergent folk is entirely understandable, but it also begs the question: will the community that is discovered actually comprise a biblical, cove-

19. Ibid., 179.
20. Perhaps the best and fairest analysis of McLaren and the emergent church movement is D. A. Carson's book *Becoming Conversant with the Emerging Church: Understanding a Movement and Its Implications* (Grand Rapids: Zondervan, 2005).
21. McLaren, *Generous Orthodoxy*, 35.

nantal community or will it be an amalgamation of both secular and biblical elements? At present, it appears that the emergent conversation is more akin to secularism than it is to historic Christianity.[22]

At the same time, it is both reasonable and understandable for congregational members to want to know and have contact with the pastor of the congregation where they are being shepherded.[23] For many in the megachurch movement even minimal contact with the "senior pastor" was next to impossible due to the size of the congregation of which he was, ostensibly, one of the spiritual overseers. This desire for intimacy and the aversion to large, ungainly megachurches has suffered from the problem of unintended consequences, however. Large evangelical megachurches have given way to large emergent conversations. As David Wells so aptly pointed out in the foreword, "The difference is that the Hybels faction marketed to Boomers, who were much more a part of modernity, whereas the emergents are marketing to Gen Xers who are much more attuned to postmodernity."[24] The unintended consequence is that a number of emergent congregations are large in number just like their megachurch predecessors.

In a very real sense, there is nothing new under the sun, and what is being done now has been done before. In fact, this is one of my major premises as it applies to the emergent movement. A similar movement occurred in Holland, led by a group of professors and pastors that came to be known as the "Ethical Theologians."[25] While claiming to hold to Scripture, these men concentrated their emphasis on the subjective life of the community/congregation. That is to say, the congregation was the body that determined what doctrine ought to be.

What I shall delineate in this chapter is the theological methodology of Dr. Herman Bavinck (1854–1921) and how it was applied vis-à-vis the Ethical Theologians, as well as how it can aptly be applied to the emergent movement today. As we shall see, Bavinck's interaction with these so-called Ethical Theologians centered, in large

22. See, for example, Carson, *Becoming Conversant*, 59–64; 68–78; 98–102.
23. Christopher J. H. Wright, *Walking in the Ways of the Lord: The Ethical Authority of the Old Testament* (Downers Grove, IL: InterVarsity, 1995), makes the valid point that biblical ethics are "covenantal." That is to say that "personal ethics are 'community shaped,' and the ethic of the redeemed community is that of a 'priesthood'—for the sake of the rest of human society" (ibid., 25). With this in mind, it becomes increasingly clear that a major stumbling block for the emergent conversation is the question of authority—even God's authority in Scripture. Wright offers this observation: "The heart of our complaint, then, against those who assert that morality is historically and culturally relative *per se* is that they themselves absolutize that which is relative (the historical process), and relativize that which is absolute (the order of creation). . . . The biblical authority, then, for our ethics in a world of moral relativism, is based on its twin affirmation of creation and history: creation as the fundamental order that shapes our existence in history, and which is destined for restoration in the new creation of the kingdom of God; and history as the stage on which we observe acts of the God whom we are commanded to imitate by 'walking in his ways'" (ibid., 54).
24. Cf. also Hart, *Deconstructing Evangelicalism*, 165–74.
25. See Jan Veenhof, *Revelatie en Inspiratie, De Openbarings- en Schriftbeschouwing van Herman Bavinck in vergelijking met die der ethische theologie* (Amsterdam: Buijten & Schipperheijn N.V., 1968), 141–249; 547–91, and Bavinck's analysis of de la Saussaye's theology in *De Theologie van Prof. Dr. Daniel Chantepie de la Saussaye: Bijdrage tot de Kennis der Ethische Theologie* (Leiden: D. Donner, 1884).

part, on the question of our priorities in terms of our theological methodology. In other words, does the Word of God (the Bible) have priority in Christian doctrine and life, or is the Christian life to be "spun out" from the "Christian consciousness" in the community first and foremost? In order to derive Bavinck's answer to this question, we shall have the occasion to examine his theological method, which, in point of fact, takes into account the place of three indispensable facets of the Christian faith: *Scripture, tradition, and the Christian consciousness.* Before we investigate Bavinck's paragraph on theological method, however, I want to make a few prefatory remarks regarding our current theological situation.

Who Are the Main Players in the Modern Church?

When what is touted as a "new" theological movement—or, as in the case of the emergent church movement, a "conversation"—appears on the theological radar, it typically takes a while to digest and analyze properly the various components of that movement. Such is the case with the Federal Vision (FV), the (so-called) New Perspective on Paul (NPP), and the emergent church movement. What began as a trickle in terms of writing has exploded exponentially, making it almost virtually impossible to keep abreast of the new works that are flooding the market.

Of course, as soon as such a prodigious quantity of articles and exegesis is produced and people begin to get a sense of the main components of the movement, a series of counterarticles and exegesis also makes its appearance. The instances of the FV, NPP, and ECM form no exceptions to the rule.

In the case of the NPP, for example, its origin can be traced back to E. P. Sanders's groundbreaking book *Paul and Palestinian Judaism.*[26] James Dunn picked up the ball regarding Second Temple Judaism and covenantal nomism as espoused by Sanders and actually coined the phrase New Perspective on Paul.[27] Currently, along with Sanders and Dunn, N. T. Wright is the best known and most articulate proponent of the New Perspective. Wright is a prolific writer whose very readable style has made him a much sought after theological commodity.

This is not to say that Sanders, Dunn, and Wright are the *only* advocates for the NPP. Within the ECM as well as some Reformed and Presbyterian churches some inroads have been made in favor of the NPP. In addition, the FV has infiltrated a number of Reformed and Presbyterian congregations, which is somewhat understandable since the FV and NPP are, in many regards, closely related. It is a rather interesting—as well as disturbing—phenomenon that the rise of the Norman Shep-

26. E. P. Sanders, *Paul and Palestinian Judaism: A Comparison of Patterns of Religion* (Minneapolis: Fortress, 1977).
27. See James D. G. Dunn, "The New Perspective on Paul," *Biblical Journal of Religious Literature* 65 (1983): 95–112; reprinted and expanded in James D. G. Dunn, *Jesus, Paul, and the Law* (London: SPCK, 1990), 183–214.

herd controversy at Westminster Theological Seminary in Philadelphia almost co-incided with the publication of E. P. Sanders's book on Paul.

Within the ECM camp, a number of theologians have exercised a rather profound impact, be it explicitly or implicitly. Names from the past such as Albert Schweitzer, William Wrede, Wilhelm Herrmann, Friedrich Schleiermacher, Albrecht Ritschl and his school, and Karl Barth are worthy of mention. In a more contemporary vein, the names of Jürgen Moltmann,[28] Wolfhart Pannenberg, the late Hans Frei (and the so-called Yale School), the late Stanley Grenz, Roger Olson, Krister Stendahl, the late John Howard Yoder, Robert Webber, Leonard Sweet, and possibly Clark Pinnock make up the partial list of devotees at the more technical level of theology.[29]

At the more popular, grassroots level, Brian McLaren remains the most prominent spokesman for the ECM. Step down to another level and names such as Donald Miller, Dan Kimball, Stephen Chalke, Doug Pagitt, Rob Bell, and Spencer Burke are familiar, household names. Anne Lamott is on a planet of her own and cannot be and is not taken seriously outside of the ECM tribe.

What all the movements, theologians, and pastors have in common is that they share, in general, a paradigm shift in their manner of "doing theology." What do I mean by this? Allow me to explain by using insights from J. I. Packer and David Wells. First, Packer warns us that simply because a movement is (relatively) new, we should not assume that it is necessarily *better.* Among the various fads and movements in theology today we should avoid the mindset, "for which the newer is the truer, only what is recent is decent, every shift of ground is a step forward, and every latest word must be hailed as the last word on its subject."[30] A little further, while describing the nature of systematic theology, Packer gives us this insight: "Nothing in this world is perfect, and it is not hard to find shortcomings in every theological

28. See David Wells, "The Future," in Mark Noll and David Wells, eds., *Christian Faith and Practice in the Modern World* (Grand Rapids: Eerdmans, 1988), 290–94.
29. The list of both adherents as well as detractors is compendious, but the following seminal works give a good introduction to both sides of the debate: D. A. Carson, Peter O'Brien, and Mark Seifrid, eds., *Justification and Variegated Nomism*, 2 vols. (Grand Rapids: Baker Academic, 2001–2004); A. Andrew Das, *Paul, the Law, and the Covenant* (Peabody, MA: Hendrickson, 2001); James Dunn, *The Theology of Paul the Apostle* (Grand Rapids: Eerdmans, 1998); John R. Franke, *The Character of Theology* (Grand Rapids: Baker Academic, 2005); Hans W. Frei, *Types of Christian Theology* (New Haven: Yale University Press, 1992); A. Donald MacLeod, "A Painful Parting, 1977–1983: Justifying Justification," in W. Standford Reid. *An Evangelical Calvinist in the Academy* (Montreal/Kingston: McGill-Queen's University Press, 2005); O. Palmer Robertson, *The Current Justification Controversy* (Unicoi, TN: Trinity Foundation, 2003); Peter Stuhlmacher, *Revisiting Paul's Doctrine of Justification* (Downers Grove, IL: InterVarsity, 2001); Guy Prentiss Waters, *Justification and the New Perspective on Paul* (Phillipsburg, NJ: P&R, 2004); Waters, *The Federal Vision and Covenant Theology* (Phillipsburg, NJ: P&R, 2006); Stephen Westerholm, *Perspectives Old and New on Paul: The "Lutheran" Paul and His Critics* (Grand Rapids: Eerdmans, 2004); N. T. Wright, *The Climax of the Covenant* (Minneapolis: Fortress, 1991); *What Saint Paul Really Said* (Grand Rapids: Eerdmans, 1997).
30. J. I. Packer, "Is Systematic Theology a Mirage? An Introductory Discussion," in John Woodbridge and Thomas McComiskey, eds., *Doing Theology in Today's World: Essays in Honor of Kenneth S. Kantzer* (Grand Rapids: Zondervan, 1991), 21.

system that has ever appeared. But defects in theology systems are of two sorts, some involving *wrong method* and others resulting from failure to meet the *demands of a right method.*[31] Since a great deal of this chapter will deal with theological method in general and the theological method of Herman Bavinck in particular, I want us to hold Packer's thought.

It should be kept in mind that Packer is not opting for an ivory tower theology that one only finds in academia, but rather wishes to follow the notion of "theology 'earthed' in life" advocated by William Perkins.[32] This too is important for our purposes, for a great deal of the emphasis in the ECM purports to be on "practical" as opposed to, say, "technical" theology. Even in the Presbyterian Church in America's magazine, *byFaith*, a new column has appeared entitled, "Theology for Ordinary Life." Of course, *all* theology is for ordinary life, but smokescreens are introduced to give the distinct impression that there is theology for those in academia or in the pastorate and there is theology for the man or woman on the street. This is simply incorrect.

David Wells expands upon these truths in his contribution to Kenneth Kantzer's *Festschrift* with an article entitled "The Theologian's Craft." He notes what he calls a "double estrangement" that has occurred between the church and the academy due, in part, to a "growing professionalization of theology."[33] It is Wells's conviction that theologians must pinpoint their audience, asking the question: "For whom is theology to be written?"[34] Until the nineteenth century, "theology was seen as a churchly activity, done by those *in* the church *for* those in the church."[35] Today, that is not always the case. In the face of a growing professionalization of the academy some theology has become so esoteric that only a few in academia even understand the concepts being discussed. In this case, the circle has narrowed *substantially*.

The late John Leith wrote a trenchant analysis of this problem in his book *Crisis in the Church.*[36] It was Leith's intention to emphasize "the overwhelming priority and significance in the life of the church of what God does and says, not what human beings do and say."[37] This is a double-edged sword for our purposes. It cuts against the "technical" theologians who disconnect the academy from the church as well as against the modern "pastors," such as McLaren, who boast of their lack of theological training and pretend to only be concerned about the "practical" matters of the faith. What matters most, what matters primarily, is what God says. As the ECM begins openly to question more and more biblical doctrines (Scripture, homosexuality, the penal substitutionary atonement, the environment, feminism), it falls more and more

31. Ibid., 22–23.
32. Ibid., 25.
33. Ibid., 189.
34. Ibid.
35. Ibid. (emphasis added).
36. John Leith, *Crisis in the Church: The Plight of Theological Education* (Louisville: Westminster John Knox, 1997).
37. Ibid., x.

under Leith's observation that liberalism is not the friend of the church, but rather her foe. He writes, "I have also become convinced that the left wing is a greater menace to the health of the Christian community than the right wing. . . . Certainly the left wing is more, not less, ruthless in imposing its will on the church."[38] This is a classic description of the iron fist in a velvet glove.

Wells suggests that "the purpose in thinking theologically, we must remember, arises from the nature of the enterprise itself and is not prescribed or proscribed by cultural considerations. If theology is about God, his character, his will, and his acts, then the most obvious audience is still those who, through Christ and their knowledge of his Word, know him."[39] In light of our contemporary situation, however, Wells makes this provocative point: "Theology does not fare well in the culture because it is not *believed*; it does not fare well in the church because it is not *wanted*."[40] And herein lies the crux of the matter and our modern dilemma. This leads Wells to conclude, "A church that neither is interested in theology nor has the capacity to think theologically is a church that will be rapidly submerged beneath the waves of modernity."[41]

A Theological Paradigm Shift

Our time has witnessed a paradigm shift that, to many in the emergent church movement, went largely unnoticed. Within the confines of the Norman Shepherd controversy, the advent of the New Perspective on Paul, and the Federal Vision, one has to believe that a number of the technical theologians not only saw the shift coming, but actually encouraged and facilitated it. This shift or change of trajectory, whether in the Federal Vision, New Perspective on Paul, or the emergent church movement, has been away from soteriology and toward ecclesiology. There are a number of theologians who have directed our attention to this shift, but I will cite only three to make my point.

First, Richard Gaffin argues from the standpoint of Pauline soteriology that "the salvation appropriated in union with Christ, by faith, consists of two basic, irreducible facets. These facets answer to sin's basic twofold consequences; one is *forensic*, the other, *renovative*."[42] It is not as if Gaffin believes that there are no ecclesiological implications in the doctrine of justification, as the book of Galatians makes abundantly clear, but it is, rather, a matter of emphasis.[43] Nevertheless, it is equally true

---

38. Ibid.
39. David Wells, "The Theologian's Craft," in *Doing Theology in Today's World: Essays in Honor of Kenneth S. Kantzer*, ed. John D. Woodbridge and Tom Edward McComiskey (Grand Rapids: Zondervan, 1991), 189.
40. Ibid., 190.
41. Ibid., 191.
42. Richard B. Gaffin Jr., *By Faith, Not by Sight: Paul and the Order of Salvation* (London: Paternoster, 2006), 44.
43. Ibid., 45. Gaffin writes, "For Paul, justification undoubtedly has inalienable ecclesiological implications and these are a prominent concern, especially in Galatians."

that justification is closely tied to the New Testament language of righteousness, which, in turn, is "realized in and constituted by Christ's work," which "answers to *sin.*"[44] Therefore, the "forensic transaction is in view ... not in *all* but in the *large majority* of Paul's uses of the corresponding verb (δικαιόω; *dikaióō*), with a transitive-active, not a stative, force and, as such, involves the notion of judicial reckoning or imputation."[45]

Guy Waters, who has performed extensive research on both the Federal Vision and New Perspective on Paul, discloses that within both camps the shift away from justification as primarily soteriological is clearly discernible. As was mentioned earlier, even though the Federal Vision and New Perspective on Paul adherents do not agree on every jot and tittle, there is sufficient evidence of their close reliance on each other. Waters writes, "Some FV proponents, consequently, have been critical of recent Reformed attempts to emphasize the differences between the NPP and Reformed theology. Yet, FV proponents are not all entirely agreed on which aspects of the NPP merit some degree of approval. Nevertheless, FV proponents have often been supportive of Reformed efforts to embrace Wright's and Dunn's insights on matters related to justification, particularly in their efforts *to recast the doctrine primarily as ecclesiological.*"[46]

Peter Stuhlmacher's book also sheds a great deal of light on some of the deficiencies of the NPP in particular. In his introduction, Stuhlmacher criticizes that there exists both a historical as well as theological one-sidedness in the New Perspective on Paul.[47] Albert Schweitzer, for example, viewed justification as a kind of "subsidiary crater" in Paul's theology in favor of a more mystical doctrine of redemption, which is clearly wrong.[48] To Stuhlmacher's mind, Paul understood justification as not only the forgiveness of sins but also "first and foremost the end-time *forensic* work of salvation. . . ."[49] Leaning upon Schweitzer, Sanders reasserted that "Paul considered participation in Christ and being in Christ to be much more important than justification. Sanders has recourse once again to Albert Schweitzer's distinction between a peripheral justification and a central Christ mysticism in Paul."[50] Viewing the New Perspective on Paul as a whole as well as its proponents leads Stuhlmacher to conclude that one of its many deficiencies is precisely that "the new perspective *fails to allow for any clear relationship between christology and justification.*"[51]

44. Ibid., 48 (emphasis added).
45. Ibid., 49 (emphasis added).
46. Guy Prentiss Waters, "Whatever Happened to *Sola Fide?*—Introduction," unpublished manuscript, Guy Waters and Gary Johnson, eds., *By Faith Alone: Answering the Challenges to the Doctrine of Justification* (Wheaton, IL: Crossway, forthcoming), 8.
47. Peter Stuhlmacher, *Revisiting Paul's Doctrine of Justification* (Downers Grove, IL: InterVarsity, 2001), 9.
48. Ibid., 29.
49. Ibid. (emphasis added).
50. Ibid., 38.
51. Ibid., 44.

Even though this and similar critiques recur, the Federal Vision, New Perspective on Paul, and emergent church movement continue to turn blind eyes and deaf ears even to their most competent and credentialed detractors. There are myriad reasons for this, some good; others quite bad. Some people, on a very simple plain, observed something happening in the churches that embrace any or all of the above-mentioned movements and they "liked" what was happening (an almost entirely subjective approach) or perceived, equally subjectively, that this new theological direction was "good" for them. Either way, the response was "me-oriented."[52] Wells correctly points out that in terms of contemporary theology or contemporary ways of "doing church" the traditional "four source" approach has been effectively reduced to but two: "Scripture and experience."[53] This can lead to a constituent of the so-called New Yale Theology, George Lindbeck, asserting the propriety of the biblical Word as a foundation for theology and then go on to say that the meaning of that Word is not self-contained but must be ascertained from the community of faith.[54] This is precisely the theological methodology of the emergent church movement.

For example, many of the children of parents who attended megachurches grew weary of the lack of community and longed for something substantially more personal and personable. The emergent church movement stepped in and filled that void. Never mind that there were egregious lacunae in doctrine and teaching. The emergent church movement promised more "community" and seemingly delivered on its promise.

On the other hand, it is difficult if not impossible to believe that those at the seminary and pastoral levels could not see the shift coming, especially in light of the almost unrelenting attack on justification by faith by the New Perspective on Paul and less direct attack on the same doctrine by the Federal Vision.

That is not to say that none of these groups speaks anymore about soteriology— they do. But it is also undeniable that with most of them ecclesiology has been shoved to the forefront at the expense of biblical soteriology. The emergent church movement has not announced this shift, therefore many within the movement do not know or even care that it has taken place. From a biblical, theological perspective, however, this shift is significant and posits a theological methodology that is untenable for a number of reasons that we shall now examine as we turn our attention to Herman Bavinck's theological methodology. Bavinck is a solid Reformed theologian with a substantial biblical methodology that corrects what is lacking in the modern trends about which we've been speaking. Therefore, I shall use him as a kind of springboard to point out the major deficiencies in the modern church.

52. For a comprehensive assessment of the modern church, see Wells, *Above All Earthly P'wers*.
53. Wells, *Theologian's Craft*, 175.
54. Ibid., 179.

Herman Bavinck's Theological Method

Until recently, the *magnum opus* of Herman Bavinck (1854–1921) was accessible only to those who understood the Dutch language. Now, however, we have a fine translation of the four-volume *Reformed Dogmatics (Gereformeerde Dogmatiek*; hereafter *RD)* into English.[55] This undertaking provides the English-speaking world with a long-awaited access to a giant among Reformed theologians.[56]

It is instructive that Bavinck encountered a theologian whose theological methodology was akin to what is now occurring in the emergent conversation. Therefore, I will make use of two key documents in delineating Bavinck's position on the place of the Christian community in formulating a theological methodology. In addition to the *RD*, I will also use Bavinck's debate with Daniel Chantepie de la Saussaye that appeared in the ecclesiastical newspaper, *The Free Church (De Vrije Kerk)* and was later published as a book.[57] I have chosen these two sources particularly because the *RD* clearly lays out a viable theological methodology that manifests the spiritual bankruptcy of the so-called emergent conversation, and because the debate contains Bavinck's critique of both the origins as well as the outworking of a theology that depends too much on the community.

The Material for Constructing Theology

Before we investigate Bavinck's second chapter in volume 1 ("The Method and Organization of Dogmatic Theology"), I want to make a few introductory remarks about the manner in which Bavinck ends the first chapter ("Introduction to Dogmatics"). In his criticism of theologians such as Schleiermacher, Rothe, Dorner, Frank, Wilhelm Herrmann, and Kähler, Bavinck writes, "All these distinctions suffer from the same defect: they all seek a fundamental difference between dogmatics and ethics. Such a fundamental difference is nonexistent."[58] In other words, "Theological ethics . . . is totally rooted in dogmatics."[59] The Dutch ethicist, Jochem Douma, said it this way: "Dogmatics without ethics is *empty*; ethics without dogmatics is *blind*."[60]

All of this is to say that for Bavinck the relationship between dogmatics and ethics is inextricable. The closing words to the first chapter of the *RD* function as a sort of hinge transitioning from the introduction into the methodology proper. Where

55. Herman Bavinck, *Reformed Dogmatics*, 3 vols. (Grand Rapids: Baker Academic, 2003–).
56. A special note of thanks is due to John Bolt, who did an outstanding job as the editor of the translation as well as John Vriend, who was in charge of the translation.
57. Bavinck, *De Theologie*.
58. Bavinck, *Reformed Dogmatics*, 1:58 (emphasis added). Note: All citations will be taken from the English translation except—obviously—where I cite from the fourth volume or from Bavinck's occasional writings. In those instances, the translation will be mine.
59. Ibid.
60. Jochem Douma, *Responsible Conduct*, trans. Nelson Kloosterman (Phillipsburg, NJ: P&R, 2003) from the Dutch work, *Verantwoord Handelen* (Amsterdam: Uitgeverij Ton Bolland, 1980), 38: "Dogmatiek zonder ethisch gehalte is leeg, ethiek zonder dogmatische gehalte is blind."

Bavinck's teachings have specific application vis-à-vis the emergent doctrines of "ecclesial" and "missional" is clearly seen in his desire to eradicate dualism as well as in his desire for organic unity. Separating dogmatics and ethics creates "a dualism between God and man, individual and community, salvation and life, rest and movement, intellect and will, and paves the way for ethics to go, by way of a speculative philosophy, in search of a principle all its own."[61]

Given the emergent conversation's characteristics (emphasis on community but not on doctrine; a highly ambiguous handling of God's truth, including non-Christian religions; disdain for Christian tradition; and being highly sympathetic to Roman Catholicism and Eastern Orthodoxy), there appears to be historical precedence for the emphasis on community at the expense of doctrine. In other words, there is nothing new under the sun; this has all been done before in another time and in another place.[62] In the history of the church, various theological methodologies have come and gone. In my estimation, the theological method of the emergent conversation will also be laid to rest in the theological cemetery within the not too distant future due to its shallowness and "faddish" nature.

Bavinck opens the third paragraph of his *Reformed Dogmatics* with these words: "By the method of dogmatics, broadly speaking, one must understand the manner in which the dogmatic material is acquired and treated. Three factors come into play in this acquisition: *Holy Scripture, the church's confession, and Christian consciousness.*"[63] What must be taken into consideration fully is the delicate balance that exists and must continue to exist among these three components. An imbalance will result in a lopsided theological method. It is against such an imbalance that Bavinck warns us. As we proceed, we shall see how Bavinck maintains the equilibrium among the three. It is precisely this balance that continues to make Bavinck's theology so viable and appropriate.

As S. Meijers has demonstrated in his doctoral dissertation, Bavinck strove, in the construction of this theology and theological method, for a biblical equilibrium

---

61. Bavinck, *Reformed Dogmatics*, 1:58.
62. One comment from Brian McLaren's book *A Generous Orthodoxy* will suffice to make my point. He writes, "To add insult to injury, nearly all orthodoxies of Christian history have shown a pervasive disdain for other religions of the world: Buddhism, Hinduism, Judaism, atheism, etc. A generous orthodoxy of the kind explored in this book, while never pitching its tent in the valley of relativism, nevertheless seeks to see members of other religions and non-religions not as enemies but as beloved neighbors, and whenever possible, as dialogue partners and even collaborators. . . . Beyond all these warnings, you should know that I am horribly unfair in this book, lacking all scholarly objectivity and evenhandedness. My own upbringing was way out on the end of one of the most conservative limbs of Christianity, and I am far harder on conservative Protestant Christians who share that heritage than I am on anyone else. I'm sorry. I am consistently oversympathetic to Roman Catholics, Eastern Orthodox, even dreaded liberals, while I keep elbowing my conservative brethren in the ribs in a most annoying—some would say *ungenerous*—way. I cannot even pretend to be objective or fair" (35). He's right: he cannot and should not pretend to be either objective or fair since he clearly ends up being neither.
63. Bavinck, *Reformed Dogmatics*, 1:61 (emphasis added).

between objectivity and existentiality.[64] What is of the utmost importance for Bavinck in this regard is that the Holy Scripture takes precedence and has preeminence in his entire method. In other words, "The whole of Scripture must prove the whole (theological) system."[65] Central to this notion is its correlation to an organic system of truths. Citing Jacob Böhme's contribution to this discussion, Bavinck writes, "He did not allow the things he found in the words to stand side by side in isolation from each other but conceived them as a *system*. In his mind God and the world, matter and spirit, nature and grace became a vital *unity*, an *organic system of truths*, in which the idea of life animated all the parts and every particular was viewed in the light of the whole."[66]

Return to the Subject and Subjectivism

There are a number of philosophers and theologians who were rather constantly being dissected by Bavinck. Among them are Schleiermacher, Kant, Hegel, and Ritschl. According to Bavinck, these men were instrumental in forming a method that was distinct—and often in blatant opposition to—both the traditionalistic and biblical methods.[67] What did their method look like? Bavinck describes it this way: "The method does not start out from the doctrine of the church or from the teaching of Scripture but from the believing subject, from the Christian consciousness. Kant, Schleiermacher, and Hegel were in agreement in no longer regarding religious truth as objectively given in Scripture or confession, and all three believed that it could be found in and derived from the religious subject."[68] It was upon these theologians that the "Ethical Theologians" of his day were dependent. In fact, it is next to impossible to read any of Bavinck's earlier works without finding him in interaction with one or more of these philosophers and theologians. When it came to the Ethical Theologians, Bavinck was convinced that de la Saussaye, for example, assimilated all of the negative aspects of Schleiermacher's theology into his own.[69] From Schleiermacher's theology, de la Saussaye focused truth in the consciousness of the congregation.[70] Bavinck describes De la Saussaye's methodology as follows: one of its primary tenets involved a strong rejection of the Reformed tradition in general and

---

64. S. Meijers, *Objectiviteit en Existentialiteit: Een onderzoek naar hun verhouding in the theologie van Herman Bavinck en in door hem beïnvloede concepties* (doctoral diss., Utrecht University [Kampen: Kok, 1979]).
65. Bavinck, *Reformed Dogmatics*, 1:617. Cf. Meijers, *Objectiviteit en Existentialiteit*, 43.
66. *Objectiviteit en Existentialiteit*, 64. Meijers writes concerning Bavinck's emphasis on "the organic": "De kracht van het begrip 'organish' is, dat het meer openheid kent dan het abstracte intellectualisme of dan het determinisme, omdat het de waarheidsmomenten daarvan te boven gaat en toch in zich kan opnemen. Bavinck kan het begrip organish dan ook promiscue gebruiken voor historisch en psychologish. Het bepleit immers een teleologische ontwikkeling..." (ibid., 90).
67. Bavinck, *Reformed Dogmatics*, 1:66.
68. Ibid. See also Helmut Thielicke, *Glauben und Denken in der Neuzeit: Die großen Systeme der Theologie und Religionsphilosophie* (Tübingen: J.C.B. Mohr, 1983), 177–257; 299–352; 353–92; 393–422.
69. Bavinck, *De Theologie*, 3. Bavinck writes that the influence of Schleiermacher on de la Saussaye and, in turn, the Ethical Movement was "great" (ibid., 2).
70. Ibid., 5.

John Calvin in particular. If there were any benefit to Calvin's theology, those kernels of truth had to be extricated from Calvin's metaphysical-scholastic methodology.[71] Bavinck is convinced that de la Saussaye was never really familiar with Reformed theology in any deep or substantial sense.[72]

The upshot of de la Saussaye's methodology surprises no one: he ended up choosing the so-called *Vermittelung theologie* of Albrecht Ritschl. This choice is tantamount to what the ECM is doing as well. Being misinformed about Reformed theology, the emergent conversation continually chooses a particular type of theology as others prior to them have. De la Saussaye chose Schleiermacher and Ritschl and McLaren, and his lieutenants have chosen Barth, Frei, Grenz, Olson, Pannenberg, Moltmann, Yoder, and others in the theological realm and Foucault, Derrida, Lyotard, and Rorty in the philosophical. What this constitutes is different choices with similar consequences.

In order to explain what I mean, I'll look at Bavinck's critique of Ritschl. Bavinck wrote a rather indepth criticism[73] of Ritschl's famous work *Rechtfertigung und Versöhnung* as well as Ritschl's theological method.[74] In a nutshell, Bavinck's assessment was that Ritschl's theology constituted value judgments without foundations.[75] Since Ritschl's theological method is heavily dependent upon the philosophy of Kant, certain consequences are inevitable. For example, Bavinck asks what Ritschl's epistemology is, for that is a crucial part of theological methodology. The *Ding an sich* is unknowable for us, according to Ritschl. We cannot know things as they are in and of themselves, but only things as they are *for us*.[76] But then we must ask the question: How do I decide what something is *for me*? The conception (*begrip*) of something is a formal conception without content; it is a representation (*voorstelling*) in which we summarize a series of perceptions.[77] Fundamentally, this means that

71. Ibid., 7. "De ethische CALVIJN moest uit den metaphysisch-scholastischen worden losgewikkeld." De la Saussaye discounted Reformed theology's appreciation for and use of proper philosophical and psychological categories, which sounds very much like the current emergent church movement methodology. What de la Saussaye and the Ethical Theologians envisioned was the following: "Van *al* het metaphysisch-scholastische moest de gereformeerde dogmatiek worden ontdaan; haar behoud en welvaren lag alleen in ethische verder-ontwikkeling, in overplanting uit het metaphysisch in het ethisch, christologisch gebied" (ibid., emphasis added).

72. Ibid., 6. Bavinck says that what knowledge de la Saussaye possessed about Calvin was, at best, secondhand.

73. Herman Bavinck, "De Theologie van Albrecht Ritschl," in *Theologische Studiën*, 6e jrg., blz. (1888), 369–403. Hereafter *TAR*.

74. Albrecht Ritschl, *Die christliche Lehre von der Rechtfertigung und Versöhnung*, 3 Bde. (Bonn: Marcus und Webers Verlag, 1903). Hereafter, *Rechtfertigung*.

75. You can order this twenty-three page unpublished work of mine from my Web site (www.rongleason. org). It is entitled *Value Judgments without Values: Dr. Herman Bavinck's Criticism of the Theology and Ethics of Albrecht Ritschl*.

76. Ritschl, *Theologie u. Metaphysik*, 30 (emphasis added). Bavinck continues to characterize Ritschl's epistemology in this manner: "Er is niets achter de verschijnselen en waarnemingen; en alle pogingen om daarachter te komen en de dingen op zichzelf te kennen, zijn ijdel en vruchteloos," *TAR*, 375. Cf. Ritschl, *Theologie u. Metaphysik*, 32ff.

77. Ritschl, *Theologie u. Metaphysik*, 18, 35.

there is no *being*. There is only *becoming*.[78] Bavinck makes this point, for it strikes at the very heart of Ritschl's epistemology. That is, if we change the word "thing" to "God," "Scripture," "Christ," "Holy Spirit," or something else, according to Ritschl we are left with the question of what they are *for us*.

It doesn't require much of a leap to see that the *for us* aspect is alive and well in the emergent conversation. This is part of the reason why major doctrines of the Christian faith are under attack in the emergent church, including Christ's penal substitutionary atonement, the doctrine of Scripture, what Scripture says about homosexuality, what the Bible teaches us about the use of foul language, the relativity of truth, the desire to see Christianity as an equal among other religions, and a host of other doctrines mentioned by McLaren, Chalke, Miller, Pagitt, and other adherents to the emergent conversation. Granted, these authors often deny they hold to ethical relativism or relativism in general, but their actual writings belie what their real position is. Their repeated (read: hackneyed, worn-out) caveat is: You just don't understand me! There are times when we do not understand our opponents, but there are other times when we understand them all too well and they refuse to acknowledge that we do.

Like Schleiermacher, Ritschl, and Ritschl's school of theology, the emergent conversation is rushing headlong down the path of classic liberalism and/or the Social Gospel. What Bavinck considers crucial about Ritschl's theology is that "nothing may be predicated about God apart from his relationship to us."[79] This is an important concept that Bavinck will return to repeatedly in his criticism of this paradigm shift in theology. He believes it forms a very weak link in the chain of Ritschl's theological method. It constitutes a thorough-going "subjectivizing" of his theology at the expense of the objective reality of God's Word. Flowing out of the doctrine of God is also the impact of Ritschl's methodology upon his christology. According to Ritschl there is nothing to say about the deity of Christ, his essential equality with the Father, or his pre- or post-existence. The question is not what or who Christ is *an sich*, but what his value and significance is for us.[80] Everything that Scripture and the doctrine of the church have to say about the person and work of Christ really does not describe his essential being, but is an expression of the religious consciousness of the Christian church (*gemeente*).[81]

78. Bavinck, *TAR*, 377.
79. Ibid., 379.
80. Ibid. Bavinck goes on to say, "De christologische dogmata dienden slechts, om aan deze waardering van den persoon van Christus door de gemeente uitdrukking te geven." Cf. Ritschl, *Rechtfertigung*, 371ff., Ritschl, *Theologie u. Metaphysik*, 22, 27ff.
81. More fully, Bavinck's critique consists of the following: "Indien er ernst gemaakt wordt met de leer van het kenvermogen, gelijk Ritschil die ontwikkelt, dat n.l. de onderscheiding van intelligibele en phnenomenale [*sic*] wereld moet verworpen worden; dat het Ding an sich geen realiteit heeft maar eene voorstelling is die uit het door ons ontworpen herinneringsbeeld is ontstaan; dat elk concreet ding, dat wij waarnemen, dus alleen in ons bewustzijn bestaat; dan is zonder hatelijke Consequenzmacherei licht in te zien, dat alle wetenschap, ook de theologie, op idealisme en illusionisme uitloopt. Wij hebben dan toch nooit met een zijn,

Analogously, the recent modern paradigm shift has placed ecclesiology at the center of the emergent conversation. *An sich*, this is not necessarily a bad thing, but the manner in which the emergent church has done this, as David Wells points out in the foreword, is merely to substitute one bad practice for another. In post-conservative evangelicalism, especially in the emergent conversation variety, we hear leaders such as McLaren, Bell, Bell's wife, Krisin, and others questioning the authority of Scripture, advocating "learning" from other world religions, and either claiming that the Bible is unclear about, say, homosexuality, or making nonsensical statements about the Word of God still being the "center" but just a different center. (There is an interesting parallel between de la Saussaye and the emergent church. Already in the nineteenth century, de la Saussaye was powerfully influenced by theologians such as Schleiermacher and Ritschl to the extent that he declared that here on earth nothing is absolute.[82]) Both biblically as well as culturally, the modern church has lost her bearings. The emergent reticence to honor God through his Word, rarely to speak of sin, and to equivocate on essential doctrines of biblical truth has shorn that movement of any true, helpful meaningfulness for life. Culturally, since all is relative and life is simply a journey, one's worldview must change as often as culture changes, which is like the wind. Little wonder that emergent church advocates have lost their "centeredness." That being the case, they have nothing to pass along to their adherents other than biblical and cultural disorientation.

Another striking similarity between the Ethical Theologians and our current situation with the emergent church is the former's desire for "authentic" living (*waarachtig menschelijke leven*).[83] The Ethical Theologians came to that desire by

---

eene natuur, eene substantie, maar altijd alleen met verschijningen, werkingen, verhoudingen te doen. God is dan geen absolute persoonlijkheid, is slechts de vorm, waarin ik mij Hem als de liefde denk. Christus op en voor zichzelf is geheel onkenbaar voor ons; maar voorzoover hij object onzer kennis is, is hij verschijning; alwat de Schrift en de Kerkleer aangaande Hem zegt, beschrijft niet zijn wezen, maar drukt alleen uit het religieuse bewustzijn der christelijke gemeente; Christus is niets anders dan die Christusverschijning in het bewustzijn der gemeente. De H. Geest is geen wezen, geen persoon, maar de grond voor het gemeentelijk bewustzijn van het kindschap God's En zoo met alle dogmata. De theologie wordt van het begin tot het einde gesubjectiveerd. Al het objectieve gaat te loor en wordt een product van ons bewustzijn. Het Ik schept en poneert het niet-ik. Zijn is bewustzijn." (*TAR*, 380). Cf. Barth, *Theologie*, 604: "Indem Jesus selber Träger der Gnade sowohl wie der Herrschaft über die Welt in ausgezeichneter Weise ist, ist er das Urbild der zum Reiche Gottes zu verbindenden Menschheit, und ist eben dies sein Beruf, den Gott, der die Liebe ist, zu offenbaren. Sofern er diesen seinen Beruf an uns ausübt bzw. sofern sein geschichtliches Dasein von uns als gottoffenbarendes Handeln erfahren und gewertet wird, ist er selber Gott. Nicht durch einen Befehl, nicht durch direkt göttliche Autorität, sondern als Prophet: durch seine moralisch wirkende Rede und als Priester: durch seine dienstfertige Handlungsweise hbt er als Gott das *munus regium*, macht er sein göttliches Herrenrecht an uns geltend. Er verwirklicht seinen Selbstzweck, der identisch ist mit dem Selbstzweck Gottes, der wiederum mit unserem eigenen Selbstzweck identisch ist. Indem dieser Zusammenhang erkannt und ausgesprochen wird, kommt es zu jenem entscheidenden, die christliche Theologie als solche begrhndenden Werturteil: Wir haben die Rechtfertigung, d.h. wir haben den Zugang zu Reiche Gottes, d.h. wir haben die Verwirklichung unseres eigenen Lebenszweckes nicht anders als durch Jesus in seiner Gemeinde und also und in diesem Sinne haben wir Gott in Christus."

82. Bavinck, *De Theologie*, 9.
83. Ibid., 22.

insisting that metaphysics is essentially ethical.[84] That is to say, the Ethical Theologians merged the metaphysical and the ethical, which left them with the problem of how to describe the epistemological. The second step—which is a sleight of hand because it is not based on exegesis—was to declare that the ethical is also *essentially* anthropological.[85] Similar to the theologians upon whom the Ethical Theologians were dependent, their theology led them in the following direction: they employed the methodology of Kant, Schleiermacher, Ritschl (and his school), and Hegel, which is adequately captured in the phrase, "Wende zum Subject."

In other words, the shift was away from doctrine being derived from Scripture to doctrine being construed from the "religious subject."[86] With particular regard to Ritschl, Bavinck points out that the cardinal flaw in this approach is the absence of an objective criterion by which the religious subject may verify his findings.[87] How can one ever derive—using Ritschl's method—that religion is founded upon truth; that there is an invisible reality that anchors our proclamations?[88] It is Bavinck's studied opinion that Ritschl's theology misses this key ingredient of having a true, *objective* standard, even though the Bible is mentioned frequently.[89] This means— among other things—that whoever rejects the *objective* standard of Scripture, both formally and practically—cannot have a solid *Erkenntnistheorie*.[90] Bavinck writes, "Accordingly, for Ritschl, the content of religion was limited to 'value judgments'; dogmas implied no theoretical or philosophical worldviews but *only that which corresponds to the religious need of the church. . . . It is restricted to what can be utilized in preaching and the relations of Christians among themselves*."[91] Couple this with Schleiermacher's desire to view "religion as subjective piety, as the mysticism of the heart,"[92] and a clear trajectory toward rampant subjectivism is clearly detectable. The remedy, as far as Bavinck is concerned, is to "emancipate the whole of theology from all subjective bias."[93]

Does this mean that Bavinck desires to ban the Christian consciousness from a valid theological methodology? The answer is an unequivocal no. It is simply that

84. Ibid., 21.
85. Ibid., 22.
86. Ibid. Bavinck says, "Naast de traditionalistische en de Bijbelsche methode is er tengevolge van den grooten omkeer in de nieuwere wijsbegeerte nog eene andere methode in de dogmatiek in gebruik gekomen, welke noch de leer der kerk noch van de leer der Schrift maar van het geloovig subject, van het Christelijk bewustzijn uitgaat. Kant, Schleiermacher en Hegel stemden hierin overeen, dat zij de religieuze waarheid niet meer beschouwden als objectief in Schrift of belijdenis gegeven, maar toch samen nog meenden, dat zij gevonden en afgeleid kon worden uit het religieuze subject."
87. Ibid., 42. "Al beriep Ritschl zich voor deze methode met voorliefde op Luther en Melancthon, hij vergat het criterium aan te geven, waarnaar de inhoud der Christelijke religie beoordeeld kon worden."
88. Ibid., 49.
89. Ibid., 55.
90. Cf. Bavinck, *Reformed Dogmatics*, 1:64–69.
91. Ibid., 1:67.
92. Ibid., 1:70.
93. Ibid.

the Christian consciousness cannot act autonomously. Our task is to think God's thoughts after him.[94] In order to do that, we must have as recourse his revelation to us especially as we find it in Scripture.

The Certainty of Theological Knowledge

One of the "sacred cows" of the emergent conversation is derived, in large measure, from secular philosophy and a reaction against the Enlightenment and its arrogance in relation to certainty. The mood of postmodernism is that certainty must be relinquished in order that man might live an authentic life, as messy as that might be (not to mention how postmodern man might know anything at all). David Wells is correct when he states that the postmodern mind "draws off pragmatism, existentialism, Marxism, psychoanalysis, feminism, language theory, and theories about science."[95] The emergent conversation has not remained unscathed or untainted and has, in fact, incorporated a number of these "-isms" into its life and worldview, and a clear trajectory toward rampant subjectivism is clearly detectable

One of the biggest axes the emergent church has to grind is with Enlightenment rationality and its accompanying certainty. Again Wells: "If Enlightenment rationality was logical, favored clean categories, and sequential thought, postmoderns, in casual and not so casual ways, like to juxtapose things that do not belong together in a kind of flippant, or maybe ironic, dismissal of logic: in architecture, styles of the past worked into parts of an otherwise very modern building."[96] If "certainty" aptly describes the Enlightenment, then "autonomy"—even though it is most often thought to apply to that time period—is an appropriate word to describe the postmodern and the emergent church. Wells is correct when he writes, "There are important threads of continuity between modernity and postmodernity and not least among these is the fact that at the center of both is the *autonomous* self, despite all the postmodern chatter about the importance of community. . . . In postmodernity, the autonomous being refuses to be fettered by any objective reality outside of itself."[97] To the postmodern, meaning has died, which leaves them—like it or not—in philosophical nihilism or religious anarchy, or both. The emergent conversation might attempt to salvage the (quasi-)Christian brand of postmodernity, but without some kind of metanarrative, meaning lies dead and personal consciousness or choice/preference is king of the hill.

Such an approach carries a hefty consequential price tag attached to it. Ultimately, the emergent conversation heralds the death of all worldviews, which is, no doubt, part of its agenda. Even if not all postmodern thinkers—Christian or otherwise—

94. Ibid., 1:59.
95. Wells, *Above All Earthly P'wers*, 61.
96. Ibid., 70.
97. Ibid., 68 (emphasis added).

hold to this verbatim, they do have "to resist this vortex."[98] Of course, Christians have rejected Enlightenment thinking for centuries, but that doesn't seem to affect the emergent conversation in the least.

To Bavinck's mind, faith does possess certainty.[99] But this faith must be "grounded in revelation, in a word from God that comes with his authority. Divine authority is the foundation of religion and therefore the source and basis of theology as well."[100] The place of God's revelation to us ranks so high in Bavinck's methodology that he insists, "A theologian can believe that there is no revelation, no greater and higher revelation, in Christianity (in the person of Christ, in the prophets and apostles, in Scripture) than can be observed elsewhere in nature of history. *Anyone* who so judges is then *no longer a Christian and is not qualified or able to write a Christian dogmatics.*"[101]

Knowing Bavinck's background, he made allowance for personal faith, but not the unbridled variety that has come down to us from the Second Great Awakening to the present. If Christians and Christian theologians are to take the stand that God's revealed will is Scripture, then three factors that Bavinck describes in the *RD* must be considered: Scripture, the church, and the Christian consciousness. Theologies and theologians derail when these three get out of balance or when the emphasis is only on one of these intricately related components of a solid theological methodology. For example, "The Reformation returned to Holy Scripture and, along with the ancient Christian church, acknowledged it as the sole foundation of theology. Rome by degrees elevated tradition to a level above Scripture, while mystics and rationalists alike draw the content of dogmatics from the religious subject."[102]

It is precisely within the context of the emergent conversation that we discover those strands of mysticism and rationalism—which go hand in hand—dominating its theology. Its overemphasis on experience in theology and "what works for me" in ethics provides the precise imbalance that is so detrimental to its theological methodology as well as to the adherents to the emergent conversation. Bavinck contends, "Since for many people authority in religion has totally faded from view and subjective religion was made independent of objective religion, the religious consciousness (conscience, feeling, reason, or whatever one wants to call it) has become the source and standard of religious ideas. Since Schleiermacher the whole of theology has changed, among orthodox as well as modern theologians, into a *theology of consciousness*. Though in treating the different dogmas Scholten, Schweizer, Biedermann, and Lipsius may still work on the basis of ecclesiastical formulations, what they offer

98. Ibid., 73.
99. See Bavinck's *De Zekerheid des Geloofs* (Kampen: Kok, 1901). The English version is *The Certainty of Faith*, trans. H. der Nederlanden (Jordan Station, Ont.: Paideia Press, 1980).
100. *Reformed Dogmatics*, 1:77.
101. Ibid., 1:78 (emphasis added).
102. Ibid.

finally is *nothing other than their personal faith.*[103] In other words, the personal character of our faith or theology "does not flow from our cutting all ties with its object and allowing every theologian to say and write what he pleases."[104]

If Christians do cut those ties, "then all we are left with is a body of subjective opinions in which one is as good as another."[105] Ironically, this is precisely our current situation in post-conservative evangelicalism. The megachurch led the way in distorting Scripture, taking a Madison Avenue, consumer mentality vis-à-vis "doing church" and forming its liturgy—which, at its root, wasn't truly a liturgy but rather entertainment disguised as liturgy. In terms of a spiritual legacy, the megachurch gave precious little for parents to pass along to their children with the net result being that the transition into the emergent conversation was almost seamless. The problem remains, however, that the emergent conversation is analogous to past movements and really brings nothing new to the table that's essential. What changes there are between the ECM and its historical counterparts are merely "window dressing" and cosmetic. What is severely lacking in the ECM and other post-conservative evangelical movements is a proper view—formally and practically—of Scripture and a full-orbed, robust theological method that places Scripture, the church, and the Christian consciousness into proper relationship and perspective.

Conclusions

In this chapter we have given a brief exposition of what has fueled and continues to fuel the megachurch and emerging church movements. We have examined the underpinnings and presuppositions that have driven and still drive those movements. We noted how many in the emergent conversation couple a disdain for Christian tradition with a thirst for "tangible" religion and a desire for "community." In note 23 Christopher Wright (the *other* Wright) is quoted as saying that according to Old Testament principles our ethics are to be covenantal in nature, that is, derived from God's covenant people and not individualistic.

We briefly traced the new trajectory of the modern paradigm shift into the "ecclesial" and "missional." Much has been written—rightly so—about the theological methodology or lack thereof in the emergent conversation. We disagree with the treatises and defenders of the ECM that say they have no clear-cut theological method. Granted—as the ECMers *always* want us to do—that their "conversation" is still in development, there is enough evidence from the writings of its leaders and from the actions of its adherents to surmise that there is definitely a delineated method.

We compared the tendency toward subjectivism and the penchant to have the "community" determine doctrine rather than receiving the faith once contended

---

103. Ibid. (emphasis added).
104. Ibid., 1:89.
105. Ibid., 1:90.

for (cf. Jude 3) in the emergent church movement with the Dutch theologian, Dr. Herman Bavinck, who posited a balance among Scripture, the church, and the Christian consciousness as a viable methodology. In essence, what Bavinck envisioned was giving due right to both objectivity and subjectivity. His descriptions of the philosophies of Hegel and Kant and the theologies of Schleiermacher and Ritschl directed us to a nineteenth-century shift back into subjectivism that has infiltrated and influenced subsequent theological movements. Clear traces of these philosophies and theologies are discernible especially in the ECM.

Using an article that Bavinck wrote about the so-called Ethical Theologians in general and one of its prominent leaders, Daniel de la Saussaye, in particular, we noticed several key similarities, proving the biblical dictum that there truly isn't anything new under the sun. As I conclude this article, I want to return to a a David Wells quote. When describing the postmodern mindset, he reminds us that it "draws off pragmatism, existentialism, Marxism, psychoanalysis, feminism, language theory, and theories about science."[106] Certainly and clearly all of these are easily discovered in the ECM. For the moment, however, I wish to concentrate on the role that feminism plays in the ECM, albeit not so explicitly. There is a great deal that has been inherited and incorporated into the modern church.

Rosemary Ruether gives us an insightful glance into what I'm talking about. In the following quote, substitue "emergent church movement" for "Women-Church" to observe the striking similarity: "Women-Church must form an ongoing commitment to establishing autonomous bases of community and cultural formation that are both in dialogue with the people of the churches, but outside their institutional control."[107] In addition, Ruether advocates the use of candles, repetitive chants, incantations, touch, dance, and rhythmic movement.[108]

But similarities can remain simply that; the main thesis of this article is not necessarily similarities, as instructive as they might be, but rather the utter disdain that the megachurch has shown (practically) and the ECM shows both formally and practically. Unless there is a genuine return to the authority and sufficiency of Scripture, post-conservative evangelicals will have nothing to say because they will have left nothing in terms of a spiritual legacy.

---

106. Wells, *Above All Earthly P'wers*, 61.
107. Rosemary Ruether, *Women-Church* (San Francisco: Harper & Row, 1989), 63.
108. Mary Kassian, *The Feminist Gospel: The Movement to Unite Feminism with the Church* (Wheaton, IL: Crossway, 1992), 200.

8

It's "Wright," but Is It Right?
An Assessment and Engagement
of an "Emerging" Rereading
of the Ministry of Jesus

GUY PRENTISS WATERS

~~~~~~

Brian McLaren has established himself as a leading spokesperson of what is being called the emerging church.[1] His influence, however, is not limited to congregations that have identified themselves with the emerging church. McLaren has achieved a hearing not only within broader evangelicalism, but also within the mainstream American media.[2]

Despite his occasional demurring,[3] McLaren has advanced a serious and articulate theological program for the church. He introduced this program in The New Kind

---

1. The term "emergent" is frequently distinguished from the term "emerging." As Justin Taylor observes, "*Emergent* is an organization (emergentvillage.us) or an official network of like-minded leaders and churches involved in one particular stream of the emerging 'conversation.' Tony Jones now serves as the first national coordinator in the United States. *Emerging*, on the other hand, is the term most often used to describe the much broader movement (or 'conversation') of those seeking to incarnate and contextualize the gospel for postmoderns," in "An Emerging Church Primer" (http://www.9marks.org/). McLaren has identified himself with the former movement (see http://www.emergentvillage.us/). In this chapter, however, we will use the term "emerging" because our primary concern is theological and not institutional in nature.

2. *Time* magazine has recently named him one of the "25 most influential evangelicals in America," February 7, 2005. See http://www.time.com/time/covers/1101050207/.

3. "I myself will be considered by many to be completely unqualified to write such a book of theology, being neither a trained theologian nor even a legitimate pastor if legitimacy is defined by ordination qualifications in a bona fide denomination. . . . In other words, I am a confessed amateur," in McLaren, *A Generous Orthodoxy* (Grand Rapids: Zondervan, 2004), 34.

of Christian Trilogy, a series of fictitious dialogues between a discontented evangelical pastor and a theological mentor.[4] In these dialogues, McLaren articulates and defends his call for the church to embrace postmodernism. He has offered a more formal statement of his theological views in *A Generous Orthodoxy*, subtitled *Why I am a missional, evangelical, post/protestant, liberal/conservative, mystical/poetic, biblical, charismatic/contemplative, fundamentalist/Calvinist, anabaptist, Anglican, Methodist, catholic, green, incarnational, depressed-yet-hopeful, emergent, unfinished Christian.*

What is evident from *A Generous Orthodoxy* and his more recent book, *The Secret Message of Jesus*,[5] is that McLaren's understandings of the teachings of Jesus in the Gospels are for him a key plank of his theological project.[6] McLaren is clear, however, that his readings of the Gospels are not altogether unique to him. He acknowledges dependence on such biblical scholars and theologians as Dallas Willard, N. T. Wright, Walter Wink, John Howard Yoder, and Walter Brueggemann.[7] One of these writers, N. T. Wright, is an accomplished moderate New Testament scholar whose publications have attracted a substantial following within American evangelical circles.[8] Among these writers, Wright is best known for his scholarship on the Gospels.[9] The influences of Wright upon McLaren in *The Secret Message of Jesus* offer an instructive theological snapshot of a movement that has postured itself at the vanguard of American evangelicalism.[10]

It is important to define precisely what we are and are not undertaking in this chapter. We are not attempting to offer a thorough critique of McLaren's writings.

---

4. *A New Kind of Christian: A Tale of Two Friends on a Spiritual Journey* (San Francisco: Jossey-Bass, 2001); *The Story We Find Ourselves In: Further Adventures of a New Kind of Christian* (San Francisco: Jossey-Bass, 2003); *The Last Word and the Word After That* (San Francisco: Jossey-Bass, 2005).

5. Brian D. McLaren, *The Secret Message of Jesus: Uncovering the Truth That Could Change Everything* (Nashville: W. Pub., 2006).

6. Eddie Gibbs and Ryan K. Bolger identify, in their eight-fold definition of emerging churches, "emerging churches as those (1) who take the life of Jesus as a model way to live," *Emerging Churches: Creating Christian Community in Postmodern Cultures* (Grand Rapids: Baker Academic, 2005), as quoted by Taylor, "An Emerging Church Primer." In other words, McLaren's interest in the life and ministry of Jesus is not unparalleled within the emerging church's theological project. Compare also the "Order and Rule of the Emergent Village," also quoted by Taylor.

7. McLaren, *Secret Message of Jesus*, 209.

8. *Christianity Today* identified N. T. Wright as one of five "top scholars [who] are believers who want to speak to the church," *Christianity Today*, February 8, 1999, 30. Wright is unquestionably moderate, particularly when measured against his peers within New Testament scholarship. His identity as an evangelical, however, is a matter of some dispute. See Gerald Bray, "Editorial," *The Churchman* 119, no. 3 (2005): 195–98.

9. Wright's most thorough work on the Gospels is *Jesus and the Victory of God: Christian Origins and the Question of God*, vol. 2 (Minneapolis: Fortress, 1996). A later and concise statement of his understanding of the Gospels may be found in *The Challenge of Jesus: Rediscovering Who Jesus Was and Is* (Downers Grove, IL: InterVarsity, 1999). A more accessible treatment is *The Original Jesus: The Life and Vision of a Revolutionary* (Oxford: Lion Hudson/Grand Rapids: Eerdmans, 1996). Valuable in the study of Wright's scholarship on the Gospels are the essays within Carey C. Newman, ed., *Jesus and the Restoration of Israel: A Critical Assessment of N. T. Wright's* Jesus and the Victory of God (Downers Grove, IL: InterVarsity, 1999).

10. This is not to say, of course, that Wright has given or would give his sanction to McLaren's work.

More comprehensive criticisms appear elsewhere.[11] Nor are we attempting to offer an exhaustive review of McLaren's understanding of the Gospels. Other contributors, for instance, will advance in this volume robust engagements of McLaren's doctrines of hell and of the atonement. Our purpose is to specify the points at which McLaren has either demonstrated dependence upon Wright's scholarship or evidenced strong affinity with Wright's scholarship. McLaren's debt to Wright is not a superficial one. He is close to Wright on a fundamental level. We will then be in a position critically to pose questions and concerns about some of McLaren's and Wright's characteristic positions with respect to the Gospels. These questions and concerns will, finally, enable us to broach further concerns about McLaren's theological project as a whole. Let us begin our study by offering a summary and critical engagement of Wright's and McLaren's understanding of Jesus and the Gospels.[12]

N. T. Wright and the Gospels

A Summary

For Wright, a regrettable theological dichotomy surfaced in the eighteenth century, "post-Enlightenment rationalism on the one hand, anti-Enlightenment supernaturalism on the other."[13] This "either-or" not only excludes "other alternatives" but also offers two essentially "modern positions."[14] Neither position, he argues, has been able to sustain the thoroughly Jewish character of the Gospel narratives. In this respect, the Enlightenment is also responsible for a christological dichotomy:

> Thus as long as the necessary question of the Enlightenment (the question of the historical Jesus) was addressed within the Enlightenment's own terms, it was inevitable not only that christology would collapse into warring camps of naturalist and supernaturalist—in other words, that Jesus-pictures would be produced in which the central character was either an unexceptionable first-century Jew or an inhuman and improbable superman-figure, but also that liberal and conservative alike would find it hugely difficult to reconceive the first-century Jewish eschatological world within which alone the truly historical Jesus belongs.[15]

11. Foremost in comprehensiveness is D. A. Carson, *Becoming Conversant with the Emergent Church: Understanding a Movement and Its Implications* (Grand Rapids: Zondervan, 2005). Well worth consulting is Mark Dever's review of *New Kind of Christian,* "Reformed or Deformed? Questions for Postmodern Christians," *Books & Culture,* March/April 2002, 26–27.

12. Two useful and concise overviews of Wright's *Jesus and the Victory of God* may be found at Robert H. Gundry, "Reconstructing Jesus," *Christianity Today,* April 27, 1998, 76–79; and Craig Blomberg, "The Wright Stuff: A Critical Overview of *Jesus and the Victory of God*," in Newman, *Jesus and the Restoration of Israel,* 19–39. The reconstruction that follows will rely especially on Wright's *Challenge of Jesus,* the particular work of Wright that McLaren has specifically cited as informing his own views in this area, *Last Word and the Word After That,* 191; *Secret Message of Jesus,* 227.

13. N. T. Wright, *The New Testament and the People of God: Christian Origins and the Question of God,* vol. 1 (Minneapolis: Fortress, 1992), 5.

14. Ibid.

15. Wright, *Challenge of Jesus,* 22–23.

Wright argues that contemporary conservative Christianity has fallen prey to a form of Gnosticism, not only in its conception of a "Jesus who only seemed to be human," and "a Bible that only seemed to have human authors," but also of a "salvation in which God's created order became quite irrelevant, a salvation thought of in almost entirely dualist fashion."[16]

To escape this complex of errors, and to grasp aright the central message of Jesus' teaching (the kingdom of God), Wright argues that we must give concerted attention to Jesus' Jewish context.[17] In fact, he contends that "until we know how Jesus' contemporaries were thinking, it will not just be difficult to understand what he meant by 'the kingdom of God'; it will be totally impossible, as generations of well-meaning but misguided Christian readers have, alas, demonstrated."[18] Jews, Wright contends, conceived themselves to be in a continued state of "exile." Even though they had returned from Babylonian captivity, the ongoing reality of foreign domination meant that, in some sense, their "exile" had not yet ended. The Jewish longing of deliverance from exile and, therefore, from Roman occupation came to be expressed in their understanding of the kingdom of God. Consequently, the kingdom of God did not mean—for Jesus or for his Jewish contemporaries—"a place, called 'heaven,' where God's people will go after death." It is, rather, the "rule of heaven, that is, of God, being brought to bear in the present world."[19] First-century Jews, however, disagreed "how, when, and through whom . . . the creator God intended to bring justice and peace to his world here and now."[20]

Jesus' alternative to the Jewish options of his day was drawn from the Old Testament and was "equally Jewish, if not more so" than they were.[21] Specifically, it was that "God's plan of salvation and justice for Israel and the world was being unveiled through [Jesus'] own presence."[22] In so doing, Jesus, as a prophet, proclaimed the end of exile and invited, without the sanction of the Jewish authorities of the day, men and women into the kingdom. This invitation into the kingdom ("repent and believe") has frequently been misunderstood, Wright claims. It is not a summons to "give up sinning and have a religious conversion experience."[23] In the first century, the call to faith and repentance had a "specific and indeed political meaning." It was a summons to "give up their agendas and to trust him for his way of being Israel, his way of bringing the kingdom, his kingdom-agenda."[24] Jesus' kingdom invitation, then, is essentially an invitation to break down culturally-established and sanctioned

16. Ibid., 24–25.
17. Ibid., 25.
18. Ibid., 34–35.
19. Ibid., 36–37.
20. Ibid., 37.
21. Ibid.
22. Ibid., 38.
23. Ibid., 44.
24. Ibid.

divisions and barriers. What follows is a lifestyle that markedly differs from that promoted by rival first-century Jewish kingdom agendas.

Jesus' kingdom agenda involved Jesus' "symbolic actions" against key symbols of Judaism—the temple, Sabbath, food, and the land.[25] In their place, Jesus offered alternative symbolic actions that evidenced the distinctive character of his kingdom agenda. Jesus supplants the Jerusalem temple by offering himself in its place—he would now be "where Israel's God was present and active in the same way as he normally was in the Temple."[26] Jesus also offers what Wright terms an "eschatological Torah," the "symbolic praxis" that followed from Jesus' kingdom teaching.[27] When understood in light of this Jewish kingdom context, Jesus' healings will not be seen to "evidence . . . his divinity," but to be the "symbolic expressions of Jesus' *reconstitution of Israel*," namely, the kingdom's "radical and healing inclusivism."[28]

Jesus' two greatest symbolic actions, Wright maintains, are his temple action (Mark 11) and his institution of the Lord's Supper. The former was not a "cleansing" of the temple in response to Jewish transgressions. It was, rather, "an acted symbol of judgment." As such it constituted an eschatological critique of the temple—the temple was soon to come to its appointed end.[29] In the institution of the Lord's Supper, "Jesus was deliberately evoking the whole exodus-tradition and indicating that the hope of Israel would now come true in and through his own death."[30] The Lord's Supper explains, then, why Jesus could symbolically enact judgment against the temple—"in his own work, in his own person, all that the Temple had stood for was being summed up in a new and final way."[31]

Why, then, was it *necessary* for Jesus to die? Wright indicates that one purpose of Jesus' death was to show his disciples that "he would himself travel the road he had pointed out to his followers. 'He would turn the other cheek; he would go the second mile; he would take up the cross. He would be the light of the world, the salt of the earth. He would be Israel for the sake of Israel.' He would defeat evil by letting it do its worst to him."[32]

Jesus' death, Wright maintains, was exemplary, but it was not strictly exemplary. Jesus believed that "YHWH would act through the suffering of a particular individual in whom Israel's sufferings were focused; that this suffering would carry redemptive significance; *and that this individual would be himself*."[33] His death would somehow result in the reconstituted people of God's reception of the "'forgiveness

---

25. Ibid., 54–67.
26. Ibid., 70.
27. Ibid.
28. Ibid., 68–69.
29. Ibid., 77.
30. Ibid., 85.
31. Ibid., 84.
32. Ibid., 85.
33. Ibid., 88–89.

of sins,' that is the end of exile."[34] Wright is insistent that the primary meaning of "forgiveness of sins" in Jesus' teaching is corporate in nature.[35] This does not mean that "forgiveness of sins" does not also have a private dimension. The man whom Jesus healed of paralysis, for example, "experience[d] his own personal 'return from exile,' in the form of healing from paralysis."[36] Wright tellingly acknowledges that "many details of this picture are not the same as the early church's atonement-theology, while they nevertheless offer themselves as the root from which that theology could have grown. . . ."[37]

Jesus' prophetic proclamation held out consequences for refusing his kingdom agenda. To remain aligned with other kingdom agendas and to refuse his call to join with him would result in judgment. The judgment of which Jesus primarily speaks, however, is not his return in judgment at the end of the world (although Wright does not wish to be heard denying the physical return of Christ). It is the Roman destruction of Jerusalem in AD 70.[38]

Some Reflections

In its respect for the historical integrity of the canonical Gospels, Wright's portrait of Jesus' life, ministry, and death is a good degree more conservative than many critical portraits and, in that respect, preferable to them. Nevertheless, Wright's specific portrait suffers from at least three deficiencies that are worth noting before proceeding to consider McLaren's understanding of Jesus' teaching and ministry. *First,* one must question the accuracy of Wright's claim that most first-century Jews conceived themselves to be in a continued state of exile.[39] The evidence points, rather, to a pluriformity of expectation.[40] In other words, it can be established that some Jews understood themselves to be in exile some of the time. It cannot be established that most Jews understood themselves to be in exile all of the time.[41] If this is so, then Wright's argument for the nature of Jesus' kingdom as restoration from Jewish exile is correspondingly compromised.

34. Ibid., 84. Note Wright's comment elsewhere, "Once again we must stress: in its first-century Jewish context, this [i.e. "forgiveness of sins"] denotes, not an abstract transaction between human beings and their god, but the very concrete expectation of Israel, namely that their nation would at last be rescued from the 'exile' which had come about because of their sins. Matthew is not suggesting that Jesus' death will accomplish an abstract atonement, but that it will be the means of rescuing YHWH's people from their exilic plight," *Jesus and the Victory of God,* 561, as quoted in Alister E. McGrath, "Reality, Symbol, & History: Theological Reflections on N. T. Wright's Portrayal of Jesus," in Newman, *Jesus and the Restoration of Israel,* 174.
35. "Forgiveness of sins is another way of saying 'return from exile,'" *Jesus and the Victory of God,* 268. Cf. ibid., 434.
36. Ibid., 272–73.
37. Wright, *Challenge of Jesus,* 91–92.
38. See ibid., 48–52.
39. See Gundry, "Reconstructing Jesus," 78.
40. See the discussion in Guy Prentiss Waters, *The End of Deuteronomy in the Epistles of Paul,* WUNT 221 (Tübingen: Mohr Siebeck, 2006), 29–79.
41. Richard B. Hays, "Victory over Violence: The Significance of N. T. Wright's Jesus for New Testament Ethics," in Newman, *Jesus and the Restoration of Israel,* 147–48.

Second, Wright's articulation of Jesus' conception of the nature and purpose of the kingdom is at the very least gravely imbalanced. Wright is certainly correct to affirm that Jesus' kingdom agenda had and has much to do with the terrestrial world and believers' lives in it. He is also correct to say that Jesus summons men and women to a repudiation of the agendas of this world and to a wholesale embrace of his own agenda. Wright unhelpfully, however, diminishes the spirituality of the kingdom that Jesus proclaimed. Heaven and hell—the ultimate destinies of men—were of paramount concern in our Lord's teaching. Jesus' proclamation of the kingdom in particular very much *did* bring to bear eternity upon his hearers. Those who, by divine grace, were admitted into the kingdom would enjoy fellowship and communion with God now and into eternity. They would do so on the basis of the work of Jesus Christ for them—a work that would be the sole basis for their pardon and acceptance before a holy God. Those who refused these gospel invitations would remain in their sins, justly subject to eternal punishment.

Wright maintains that many passages that have been mustered in support of this particular criticism have been misread. The "judgment" in view is not that of the end of the world. It is that of AD 70. It remains to be seen, however, how such an understanding of these passages can be reconciled with the pointed and pervasive expectation in the early church that Christ would return to judge wicked angels and men at the end of the age. How are we to explain this unexpected disjunction between Jesus' own teaching and the expectation of the early church?[42]

Third, Wright's articulation of Jesus' death leaves certain questions unanswered. Wright is clear in stating that Jesus' death was purposeful. In other words, Jesus was not the helpless victim of a Jewish-Roman conspiracy to end his life. Jesus resolved to go to Jerusalem precisely in order to die, and to die in order to carry out certain purposes. Wright is also clear that there is a patent connection between Jesus' death and his people's reception of the forgiveness of sins, which Wright defines in terms of the cessation of exile. We may, however, pose two questions to Wright. First, was it necessary for Jesus to be divine in order to accomplish his intended purposes in his death? Wright does appear to affirm the deity of Christ.[43] It is unclear, however, whether Wright sees a necessary connection between the deity of Christ and his substitutionary death. In other words, could a mere human have suffered and died as Christ died and still have accomplished through that death what Wright claims was accomplished?

Second, what was it about Christ's death that necessitated or permitted the extension of certain eschatological blessings to his people? Wright is clear *that* there is a connection between Christ's death and these blessings. He is unclear precisely *how*

---

42. Cf. here the comments of Hays, "Victory over Violence," 148.
43. See *Challenge of Jesus,* 96–125. Wright intentionally bypasses classical approaches to establishing the deity of Christ from the text of the Gospels. It is unclear, however, whether his own argument for Christ's deity is successful in establishing what it sets out to prove.

Christ's death resulted in the extension of these blessings.[44] Equally troubling is Wright's reticence in defining Jesus' understanding of his death in specifically atoning terms. We have already noted his comments on "forgiveness of sins" and his unwillingness to define forgiveness in the Gospels primarily in terms of the pardon of sin. How are we to relate Jesus' own understanding of his death to the apostle Paul's understanding of Jesus' death as atonement?

> There was, then, no such thing as a pre-Christian Jewish version of (what we now think of as) Pauline atonement-theology. There was a variegated and multifaceted story of how the present evil exilic age could be understood, and how indeed it could be brought to an end, through certain persons embodying in themselves the sufferings of Israel. Jesus, therefore, was not offering an abstract atonement theology; he was identifying himself with the sufferings of Israel. . . . What Jesus did and said stands out a mile from what early Christianity said about him and his execution, but early Christian atonement-theology is only fully explicable as the post-Easter rethinking of Jesus' essentially pre-Easter understanding. . . . In order to move, as historians, from the Jewish world to the very similar, and yet very different, world of early Christianity, we have to postulate a middle term. The gospels offer us one.[45]

Wright does not wish to sever the connection between Jesus' and the early church's understandings of his death. Neither, however, does he wish to identify them. As Alister McGrath summarizes Wright's position, "The suggestion (which is not fully developed in Wright's project thus far) would appear to be that Pauline atonement theology is an imposition upon the words and deeds of Jesus (although it should not be inferred from this that such a development is to be regarded as *improper*)."[46] This representation of Jesus' understanding of his death has many implications for the biblical doctrine of the atonement. We may, for the present, simply underscore the observation that the propitiatory, substitutionary atonement plays a negligible role in Wright's conception both of Jesus' self-understanding and of Jesus' proclamation of the kingdom.

We may also note that Wright purposefully marginalizes the atonement as an "abstract" or systematic consideration alien to the narrative within which Jesus is situated.[47] Wright more than once posits systematic formulations of atonement against the biblical narrative, as though the two exist in a necessarily antithetical relationship. We have observed him cautioning against conceiving the "forgiveness of sins" as an "abstract transaction" and urging us rather to see it within what he argues is the first-

---

44. We have noted similar imprecision in Wright with respect to his treatment of Paul's statements of the death of Christ in Waters, *Justification and the New Perspectives on Paul* (Phillipsburg, NJ: P&R), 139–42.
45. Wright, *Jesus and the Victory of God,* 592. See the similar quotation of this passage in Alister E. McGrath, "Reality, Symbol, & History," 171. Cf. Wright's comments on the parable of the rejected son (Matt. 21:33–46), *Jesus and the Victory of God,* 566; Luke 23:27–31, ibid., 570; and Jesus' predictions of his death, ibid., 575.
46. Ibid.
47. See ibid., 592.

century Jewish context of exile.[48] He elsewhere claims, "If the main purpose of Jesus' ministry was to die on the cross, as the outworking of an abstracted atonement-theology, it starts to look as though he simply took on the establishment in order to get himself crucified, so that the abstract sacrificial theology could be put into effect. This makes both ministry and death look like sheer contrivance."[49]

This purported dichotomy between history and theology is said to be traceable to the Reformers themselves. Wright argues that the Reformers were responsible for a dichotomy between history and theology that affected their reading of the Gospels. "Continuity with Christ [i.e. the orthodox doctrines of the person and work of Christ] meant sitting loose to the actuality of Jesus, to his Jewishness, to his own aims and objectives."[50] He chides post-Reformation theology—Protestant *and* Catholic—for "a general use of the gospels as sourcebooks for ethics and doctrine, for edifying tales, or, smuggled in behind the back of the *sensus literalis,* allegory. What else was there to do with them?"[51] In short, history was "conveniently ignored" by the Reformers and their heirs.[52] While Wright frequently and vehemently dissents from the critical conclusions of historical Jesus scholarship, he by no means wishes to be identified with many confessional Protestant readings of Jesus and the Gospels. Antithetically relating "history" and "theology," Wright is advancing a particular narrative-theological reading of the Gospels. This reading, as we have seen, yields results that radically distance Wright's understandings of Jesus' understanding of his death and of his kingdom from those of confessional Protestantism.

Brian McLaren, the Gospels, and Resonances with Wright

At this juncture, we are prepared to examine where McLaren and Wright evidence commonalities with respect to their readings of the Gospels. In so doing, it is important to stress that not all commonalities evidence McLaren's expressed dependence upon Wright. In the following survey of McLaren's presentation of the life and ministry of Jesus, we will endeavor to highlight the points at which McLaren either specifies or manifests dependence upon Wright's scholarship.

Jesus and the Political Message of the Kingdom
1. Summary. In a discussion where he expressly acknowledges his debt to Wright, McLaren insists that the church has failed to grasp appropriately the political message of Jesus.[53] The term "good news" was "itself a public term that evoked the

48. Ibid., 561.
49. Ibid., 14.
50. Ibid., 15. In this sense, Wright argues, Kähler and Bultmann are the legitimate heirs of Luther, ibid.
51. Ibid.
52. Ibid., 16.
53. McLaren, *Secret Message of Jesus,* 9–25. At the outset of the chapter, McLaren states, "much of the historical material here comes from N. T. Wright's writings, including *The Challenge of Jesus* (London: SPCK, 2000 [*sic*])," *Secret Message of Jesus,* 227n2.

political announcements of the Roman emperors." Consequently, Jesus' proclamation of the gospel can be understood only in its specifically Jewish historical and political context.[54] Following Wright, McLaren argues that first-century Judaism was consumed with the problem of Roman occupation. Various Jewish groups posed different solutions to this problem. Jesus' solution, which differed radically from those proposed by the Herodians, Essenes, and Pharisees, was articulated in his proclamation of the kingdom of God.[55]

The kingdom, McLaren insists with Wright, was not "heaven after you die."[56] The Johannine "translat[ion]" of "kingdom of God," or "eternal life," does not mean "life in heaven after you die" but "an extraordinary life to the full centered in a relationship with God."[57] Jesus is positing an alternative to the "oppressive empire of Caesar and the oppressed kingdom of Israel."[58] This alternative is "to see, seek, receive, and enter a new political and social and spiritual reality [Jesus] calls the kingdom (or empire) of God, or the kingdom (or empire) of heaven."[59] The kingdom therefore is a "direct challenge to the supremacy of the empire of Caesar centered in Rome, for in the kingdom of God, the ultimate authority is not Caesar but rather the Creator. And you find your identity—your citizenship—not in Rome but rather in a spiritual realm, in the presence of God (which is what *heaven* means . . .)."[60]

To what is McLaren responding when he claims that "the secret message of Jesus isn't primarily about 'heaven after you die'"?[61] He is distancing Jesus' proclamation of the kingdom from what he perceives to be a popular misunderstanding: "[The kingdom] doesn't give us an exit ramp or escape hatch from this world, rather, it thrusts us back into the here and now so we can be part of God's dreams for planet Earth coming true."[62] The ultimate hope articulated in Jesus' kingdom message was the resurrection of the body. Following Wright, McLaren argues that we must distinguish "heaven" from "resurrection."[63] This distinction, for McLaren, seems to be between a "timeless *disembodied* state away from the earth" and "an embodied state within this creation in a new era or age when present wrongs would be made right."[64]

The kingdom, then, is primarily focused on this world—both in this age and in the age to come. Specifically, the kingdom is a political reality that is an alternative to what is offered by Israel, Rome, or any other would-be Caesar, including "the tyran-

54. Ibid., 11.
55. Ibid., 14.
56. Ibid.
57. Ibid., 36–37.
58. Ibid., 14.
59. Ibid., 17.
60. Ibid.
61. Ibid., 183.
62. Ibid.
63. Ibid., 184–85. McLaren cites N. T. Wright, *The Resurrection of the Son of God* (Minneapolis: Augsburg Fortress, 2003), esp. 417ff., *Secret Message of Jesus*, 234n3.
64. Ibid., 184.

nical trinity of money, sex, and power."[65] It is in this context that Jesus' warnings are to be properly understood. His words in Matthew 24–25 must not be understood in reference to the "literal end of the world"—this would be a mistaken reading of Jewish apocalyptic.[66] They refer rather to the impending Roman judgment on Jerusalem in AD 70. This does not mean that Jesus' words have no application to the present day. We are daily faced with the decision to "seek," "enter," receive," and "live as citizens" of the kingdom. Jesus' warnings remind us that "our future hangs in the balance no less than it did for Jesus' original hearers in AD 30 or so. We can invest in today's conventional futures or counterfutures, or we can seek the creative future offered by Jesus."[67] This future, McLaren insists, is not "more or less determined," for the Bible does not "give us a timeline of the future" (this is said to violate human "freedom").[68] Rather, we have set before us "the ultimate warning that evil and injustice will lose and the ultimate promise that God and good will win."[69] Presumably, just as ultimate reward will be experienced in the resurrection body, so too ultimate loss will be experienced in some fashion in this world as well. McLaren, however, has here and elsewhere refused to specify this ultimate loss in terms of a resurrection unto judgment coupled with subsequent eternal torment with the devil and his angels forever.[70]

   2. Reflections. We have observed McLaren's debt to Wright in his political definition and conception of the kingdom of God; in his positing Jesus' conception of the kingdom as a radical and this-worldly alternative to Roman and Jewish conceptions of "kingdom;" and in his emphasis upon "resurrection" as an alternative to a popular modern conception of "heaven" as the destination of the denizens of the kingdom of God. In its main lines, then, McLaren's understanding of the kingdom suffers similar deficiencies as those of Wright's understanding of the kingdom.

   McLaren is surely correct to desire to counterbalance certain evangelical descriptions of the kingdom as that which has little or nothing to do with life in this world. He is also surely correct to emphasize the resurrection of the body unto glory as the chief and consummate hope of the believer. McLaren seems, however, to have attenuated Jesus' repeated warnings of eternal torment for the impenitent and unbelieving (Matt. 8:11–12; 24:25–51; 25:29–30, 45–46; Mark 9:42–48). Jesus, to be sure, extends the promise of "eternal life" to his people. To "eternal life," however, is juxtaposed "eternal punishment" (Matt. 25:46). The "life" and "punishment" in

---

65. Ibid., 134.
66. Ibid., 180.
67. Ibid., 180–81.
68. Ibid., 173.
69. Ibid., 174–75.
70. "[L]ike the prophets before him, Jesus spoke of coming judgment on injustice and hypocrisy. For the ancient prophets, judgment didn't mean that people would be thrown into hell. Rather, it meant that their evil would be exposed and named, and they would suffer consequences of their evil in history, in this life," McLaren, *Secret Message of Jesus,* 23. For McLaren's more extended reflections upon the doctrine of hell, see his *Last Word and the Word After That.* For a critical discussion of McLaren's doctrine of hell, see Greg Gilbert's contribution to this volume.

view are fixed and permanent states into which all persons must enter and from which no inhabitant will depart. In view of this pairing, McLaren's gloss of "eternal life" ("an extraordinary life to the full centered in a relationship with God") is markedly understated if not altogether misdirected.

If we were to inquire why eternal punishment plays such a meager role in McLaren's telling of the kingdom, the answer is not difficult to locate. Observe how McLaren represents what Christian theologians have historically termed "the fall":

> [Adam and Eve's] noble status quickly deteriorates as they disconnect from God and reject any limits placed upon their freedom by their Creator. The results of their disobedience are visible as the story unfolds—a sense of shame and alienation from God and one another, violence of brother against brother, disharmony with creation itself, misunderstanding and conflict among tribes and nations. (This second episode we call *Crisis*).[71]

Absent from McLaren's description of the fall is the *guilt*, or obligation to divine justice, that Adam incurred for himself and his ordinary posterity in his first sin. McLaren's description focuses, rather, upon the psychological and social consequences of sin—a sense of shame and breach of fellowship with God, fellow human beings (as individuals and as nations), and the creation itself. The redemptive solution naturally consists of a remedy of this breach, "God constitutes a 'crisis response team' in the form of a family—a lineage of people who will, through the generations, remember their Creator and their original purpose, and who will seek to bring truth, blessing, wisdom, and healing to all people so that God's creation can be rescued from human evil."[72] Notably absent from this description is any hint of the necessity of satisfaction made to divine justice in order to permit reconciliation between God and the sinner. When McLaren defines the human plight chiefly in terms of breach of relationship, we are not surprised to see the redemptive solution defined primarily in terms of a remedy of that breach. The questions that we posed to Wright above naturally emerge: why was it necessary that Jesus Christ die? and, what is it about what Christ's death accomplished that required Jesus Christ to be divine? To answer these questions, we will need to probe further into the message and actions of Jesus during his earthly ministry.

Jesus and the Jewish Message of the Kingdom
1. Summary. McLaren follows Wright in insisting that Jesus was "a Jewish prophet of some sort" who found himself not only in the midst of but at the climax of a Jew-

---

71. McLaren, *Secret Message of Jesus,* 27. For McLaren's animadversions against the term "fall," see *Story We Find Ourselves In,* 50–55. He describes "crisis" in the following fashion: "Wherever we go, we fail to respect the limits, the boundaries, the balance and harmony, and so we keep expanding episode two—chaos, or crisis, or whatever you want to call it," *Story We Find Ourselves In,* 59.
72. McLaren, *Secret Message of Jesus,* 27–28.

ish story extending back to the creation.[73] Jesus, as a prophet, heralded a kingdom
that brought this story to its appropriate climax and conclusion.[74] Whereas other
Jewish groups conceived the kingdom to be future, Jesus proclaimed it as "here and
now." This message, as we have seen, is fundamentally one of reconciliation and
principled inclusivism.[75] As such, this message directly "threaten[ed] the status quo"
and communicated to the religious leadership that "they have lost their way, forgotten their identity, and proven unfaithful to God."[76] Jesus' revolutionary proclamation
of the kingdom was, therefore, a direct albeit nonviolent affront to the Jewish leadership of his day. How did this confrontation express itself?

One significant means of articulating the confrontational message of the kingdom
was the parable. In fact, McLaren argues that "God's kingdom advances by stories,
fictions, tales that are easily ignored and easily misunderstood."[77] In this respect,
McLaren evidences affinity with Wright, who claims that story—and specifically
parable—occupies a unique and privileged role in the advancement of the kingdom,
which itself is the announcement of the climax of a story originating at the creation
of the world.[78]

Jesus also performed certain symbolic actions that communicated the termina-
tion of the exclusivity of the old order and the inclusiveness of the kingdom. Signs
and wonders, for example, were important signposts of the kingdom. In terms similar
to those adopted by Wright with respect to healing, signs and wonders denote, among
other things, the "invasion" of the kingdom. They are "dramatic enactments of his
message," namely that the kingdom is "available to all, here and now."[79] In other
words, signs and wonders communicate the inclusivity of the kingdom, the openness
of the kingdom to all sorts of persons without regard to the exclusivist social structure
of first century Judaism.[80]

McLaren briefly comments that Jesus' overturning of the tables in the temple
was a specifically "prophetic action."[81] It is clear that McLaren does not invest the

---

73. Ibid., 19. For McLaren's exposition of this "deep and grand story," the "story Jesus found himself in," see also 26–34. McLaren's story contains several discrete stages: creation, crisis, calling, and
conversation/covenant/conflict.

74. Ibid., 30–31. McLaren describes Jesus as "a kind of second Adam who seeks to bring people together
after so many centuries of distrust and division," 31.

75. By *principled* inclusivism, we mean that McLaren rejects what he terms "naïve inclusion," *Secret Message of
Jesus*, 165. Jesus' inclusivism, he argues, excludes "people who rejected [the kingdom's] purpose," ibid., 168. "To
be truly inclusive, the kingdom must exclude exclusive people," and "not gather those who scatter," 169.

76. Ibid., *Secret Message of Jesus*, 24, 25.

77. Ibid., 49.

78. "[Jesus] told stories whose many dimensions cracked open the worldview of his hearers and forced them
to come to terms with God's reality breaking in their midst, doing what they had always longed for but doing
it in ways that were so startling as to be hardly recognizable. The parables are Jesus' own commentary on a
crisis—the crisis faced by Israel, and more specifically, the crisis brought about by Jesus' own presence and
work," Wright, *Challenge of Jesus*, 38.

79. McLaren, *Secret Message of Jesus*, 59.

80. See Wright, *Challenge of Jesus*, 68, 69.

81. McLaren, *Secret Message of Jesus*, 22.

temple action with the significance within Jesus' ministry that Wright does.[82] It is also clear that, whereas Wright conceives the temple action to be a strictly eschatological critique of the temple, McLaren is willing to see it in terms of Jesus' critique of the "religious greed" and "hypocrisy" of the day.[83] Nevertheless, McLaren conceives Jesus' temple action to have been a denunciation of "exclusion."[84] In other words, consistent with other prophetic actions of Jesus, the temple action is a means of communicating the kingdom message of inclusivity as displacing first-century Jewish exclusivism.

McLaren terms the death and resurrection of Jesus to be the "most profound sign and wonder of all."[85] What do the death and resurrection of Jesus mean? They "show the scandalous truth that no human system can be trusted, that all —*isms* are potentially demonic and idolatrous 'graven ideologies.'"[86] While McLaren may not have intended this to be a comprehensive statement of the atonement, it nevertheless illustrates what McLaren understands to be at the core of both Jesus' message and his death and resurrection. At this core is the demonstration of the poverty and ultimate demise of human ideological divisions, including even the "sacred theologies" of the church.[87]

McLaren sees essential continuity between the apostle Paul's and Jesus' conception of the death of Jesus:

> Somehow, for [Paul], the defeat of Christ on that Roman cross—the moment when God appears weak and foolish, outsmarted as it were by human evil—provided the means by which God exposed and judged the evil of empire and religion, and in them, the evil of every individual human being, so that humanity could be forgiven and reconciled to God. And the reconciling movement resonating out from Christ's life, teaching, death, and resurrection is what we mean by the kingdom of God.[88]

For Paul, then, the cross entails the exposure and judgment of institutional and personal evil. By "judgment," does McLaren mean the exactment of a penalty in keeping with the demands of justice? In *The Story We Find Ourselves In,* the character Kerry (at the time an unbeliever) makes the following observation concerning the doctrine of substitutionary atonement: "For starters if God wants to forgive us, why doesn't he just do it? How does punishing an innocent person make things better? That just sounds like one more injustice in the cosmic equation. It sounds like divine

---

82. For Wright, the temple action, coupled with the Last Supper, are the two paramount symbolic actions of Jesus' ministry.
83. McLaren, *Secret Message of Jesus,* 22.
84. Ibid.
85. Ibid., 70.
86. Ibid.
87. Ibid.
88. Ibid., 71.

child abuse. You know?"[89] "Dan" (the protagonist of the book) does go on to say in response that substitutionary atonement is "just one of six theories . . . it's like trying to see the whole beautiful, majestic sky from one of your hospital windows."[90] The objection, however, is alarmingly permitted to remain unanswered. The implication is that McLaren has granted its legitimacy.

In *A Generous Orthodoxy,* McLaren, in his discussion of the "Conservative Protestant Jesus," describes an Arminian doctrine of satisfaction as one "metaphor" (among four) that explains, for evangelicals, how Christ's "innocent self-sacrifice somehow cancels out human guilt."[91] He concludes his discussion of those metaphors by stating, "the full answer includes and yet eludes all these metaphors, analogies, and diagrams."[92] McLaren criticizes this view for its inadequacy rather than for its error. "Conservative Protestant emphasis on the death of Jesus" can "marginalize" the teachings of Jesus, and makes the gospel to be "simply an individualistic theory, an abstraction with personal but not global import. It became about the solution to a cosmic legal/business/political problem, real and serious, but a bit dry, removed from real life."[93]

What then of our initial question? By "judgment," does McLaren mean the exactment of a penalty in keeping with the demands of justice? Certainly one cannot exclude from McLaren's understanding of judgment what he terms the "cosmic legal/business/political problem" (he calls it "real and serious").[94] Nevertheless, McLaren pointedly states in *The Secret Message of Jesus,* "like the prophets before him, Jesus spoke of coming judgment on injustice and hypocrisy. For the ancient prophets, judgment didn't mean that people would be thrown into hell. Rather, it meant that their evil would be exposed and named, and they would suffer consequences of their evil in history, in this life."[95] For Jesus, the judgment to which men and women are justly subject does not consist in the eternal torment of hell. It is profoundly *this*-worldly.[96] Historic Christian orthodoxy has maintained that Christ's sufferings on the cross correspond, on behalf of the people of God, to the eternal judgment that is their due. Because Christ has suffered in his room and stead, the justified believer can know that he will not bear in his own person the strokes of eternal judgment—Christ, to whom he is united, has borne them for him. It is difficult to see—from the above statement—how McLaren could defend Jesus' understanding of his own death in terms of a penal, substitutionary atonement.

89. McLaren, *Story We Find Ourselves In,* 102.
90. Ibid.
91. McLaren, *Generous Orthodoxy,* 46.
92. Ibid., 48.
93. Ibid., 49.
94. Ibid.
95. McLaren, *Secret Message of Jesus,* 23.
96. I have, on this point, been sharpened in my reflections through correspondence with Greg Gilbert.

We find in other of McLaren's statements in *The Secret Message of Jesus* both reticence and imprecision in expressing precisely how Christ's death results in the forgiveness of sinners. We have observed him state that the cross "provided the means by which God exposed and judged the evil of empire and religion, and in them, the evil of every individual human being, so that humanity could be forgiven and reconciled to God."[97] He elsewhere states that "the peace of God's kingdom comes not through the violent torture and merciless extermination of the king's enemies, but rather through the suffering and death of the king himself."[98] While such statements would theoretically accommodate a doctrine of the substitutionary atonement, they do not require that doctrine. Given McLaren's criticisms of judgment in terms of eternal punishment, and his definition of judgment in terms of temporal exposure or unmasking, it is unlikely that substitutionary atonement is in view in such statements.

We have observed, however, McLaren acknowledging that what he terms the "cosmic legal/business/political problem" is a legitimate component of the Scripture's teaching on the death of Jesus. Even so, this particular dilemma does not occupy center stage in McLaren's understanding of the problem that exists between God and sinful humanity. The problem to which McLaren gives the most concerted attention in his exposition of Jesus' understanding of the kingdom is the problem of alienation and division—between God and individual humans, to be sure, but especially among human individuals and groups:

> In refusing to draw or respect racial, religious, moral, ethnic, economic, or class barriers, in welcoming non-Jews and treating them with kindness and respect, in eating with both Pharisees and the prostitutes hated by the Pharisees, Jesus shows his primal kinship with all people—a kind of second Adam who seeks to bring people together after so many centuries of distrust and division.
>
> In healing the sick and raising the dead . . . Jesus even identifies himself with the story's original and ultimate hero—God—stating that those who had seen him had in some real way seen God, declaring that he and God were one, and suggesting that through him, God was launching a new world order, a new world, a new creation.[99]

Jesus' message, then, concentrates on God's establishment of a "new creation." This new creation is evidently chiefly, in the above statement, in the breaking down of conventional barriers and the establishment of lines of "kinship with all people."

The strength and persistence of McLaren's concern for horizontal reconciliation is also evident in his treatment of the Pauline gospel. For McLaren, many see Paul's gospel as consisting of "a select few escaping earth and going to heaven after they die."[100] This, however, is not Paul's gospel. For Paul, "kingdom" is at the heart of his

97. McLaren, *Secret Message of Jesus*, 71.
98. Ibid., 99.
99. Ibid., 30–31.
100. Ibid., 91.

message. Paul takes Jesus' kingdom message and, without merely "repeating the words and imagery of Jesus," is "dealing faithfully with the new situation Jesus has created."[101] This involves, for Paul, two matters at the heart of the apostle's gospel. First, "Paul's oft-repeated language of Jesus being Lord resonates with kingdom language . . . to say Jesus is Lord is to declare one's allegiance to a different empire or kingdom . . ."[102] Second, Jesus' message was that "the kingdom of God will be radically, scandalously inclusive." The "old distinctions" do not apply in the kingdom. For Paul, "these very issues of inclusion played out time and again: How can Jews and Gentiles be brought together in one kingdom, one network of relationships?"[103] While McLaren acknowledges that Christ's death, for Paul, plays a necessary (albeit undefined) role in the forgiveness of sinner's sins and these sinners' reconciliation to God, McLaren is most concerned to unfold the cross's significance in effecting reconciliation among "all the at-odds individuals and groups that comprise humanity." "What is this set of reconciled relationships," McLaren queries, "other than the kingdom of God?"[104]

We may, in concluding this portion of our discussion, note a formal similarity between McLaren and Wright—one to which McLaren gives some credence.[105] Both Wright and McLaren conceive the heart of Paul's message to consist in the proclamation of the lordship of Christ.[106] McLaren explicitly states this proclamation to be Paul's reformulation (not mere reiteration) of Jesus' kingdom message for a largely Gentile context. In similar fashion, Wright argues that Paul has likewise contextualized Jesus' kingdom message.[107] This contextualization consisted of Paul's proclamation of the lordship of Jesus to the whole world.[108]

Connected to this Pauline kingdom proclamation of Jesus' lordship, for McLaren, is the reconciliation that Christ has effected at the cross. A vital component of the

101. Ibid., 94.
102. Ibid., 97.
103. Ibid., 95.
104. Ibid., 99, 100. Compare McLaren's question two pages further in response to his exposition of Philemon, "Can you see how the secret message of Jesus is meant not just to be heard or read but to be seen in human lives, in radically inclusive reconciling communities, written not on pages in a book, but in the lives and hearts of friends?" ibid., 102.
105. In reference to his own understanding of the theological relationship between Jesus and Paul, McLaren cites Wright's *What Saint Paul Really Said: Was Paul of Tarsus the Real Founder of Christianity?* (Grand Rapids: Eerdmans, 1997), *Secret Message of Jesus*, 230n2.
106. For Wright, the gospel is not "a system of how people get saved," *What Saint Paul Really Said*, 45. Rather, "Jesus, the crucified and risen Messiah, is Lord," ibid., 46. The gospel is not "a message about 'how one gets saved,' in an individual and ahistorical sense. It is a fourfold announcement about Jesus," ibid., 60, and a "double and dramatic announcement about God," *viz*. God is "the one true God," and "the God of Israel is now made known in and through Jesus himself," ibid., 60.
107. "[W]e are forced to realize that for Paul to be a loyal 'servant of Jesus Christ,' as he describes himself, could never mean that Paul would repeat Jesus' unique, one-off announcement of the kingdom to his fellow Jews. What we are looking for is not a parallelism between two abstract messages. It is the *appropriate continuity* between two people living, and conscious of living, at different points in the eschatological timetable. . . . *When Paul announced 'the gospel' to the Gentile world, therefore, he was deliberately and consciously implementing the achievement of Jesus*," *What Saint Paul Really Said*, 181.
108. Ibid.

kingdom message, then, is the proclamation of reconciliation, especially in view of the estrangements and separations owing to human division. For Wright, while "justification by faith alone" is not itself the gospel, it is an implication of the gospel.[109] Justification, for Wright, is not the pardon and acceptance of a sinner before a holy God. It is chiefly the declaration that one is already a member of the people of God.[110] As such, justification is a declaration that "faith"—not such exclusive Jewish identity markers as circumcision and dietary laws ("works of the law")—would publicly mark and distinguish the people of God, inclusive of Jew and Gentile. It is for this reason that Wright can term justification "the great *ecumenical* doctrine."[111] Although Wright and McLaren use different terms to describe the message (for Wright it is "justification;" for McLaren it seems to be Paul's "kingdom" message), both theologians see a message of radical inclusivity coupled with the lordship of Christ as resting at the heart of Paul's proclamation. Neither Wright nor McLaren denies the forgiveness of sins through the penal, substitutionary atoning death of Jesus Christ. Neither theologian, however, conceives that doctrine to sit at the heart of Jesus' message of the kingdom or of Paul's gospel.

2. Reflections. With respect to the Gospels, McLaren evidences affinity with Wright at a number of points. Both theologians understand Jesus as a prophet who advanced the message of the kingdom through the medium of story, particularly parable. Both conceive the signs and wonders of Jesus to illustrate the principled inclusivity of the kingdom. Both understand the essential continuity between the teachings of Jesus and the teachings of Paul to consist in the proclamation of the kingdom. Paul has taken Jesus' message of the kingdom and presented it in a manner appropriate to his eschatological situation. The result is a message proclaiming the lordship of Jesus and reconciliation: both God's reconciliation to human beings and the reconciliation of human beings to one another.

We may raise two general areas of concern with respect to McLaren's particular reflections on Jesus' message of the kingdom. *First,* McLaren's conception of judgment as the exposure and identification of evil as evil is defective. As we have observed above, such a definition restricts judgment to this present age. John the Baptist, Jesus, and Paul, however, all speak of a judgment at the end of the age. John the Baptist proclaims the "wrath to come" and bids men to repent in advance of that day when Christ "will burn up the chaff with unquenchable fire" (Matt. 3:7, 12, NASB). Jesus spoke of a general and final judgment of angels and men at the end of the age (Matt. 24:29–31, 36–41, 25:31–32; John 5:25–29). At this judgment, Christ "will then repay every man according to his deeds" (Matt. 16:27, NASB). This judgment will be punitive for the wicked, who will experience eternal torment for their

109. Ibid., 132.
110. Ibid., 119, 133.
111. Ibid., 158.

sins (Matt. 18:23–35). The judgment of the last day will furthermore evidence that the righteous are in fact righteous (cf. Matt. 12:36–37).

Preaching in Athens, Paul pointed his hearers to a "fixed . . . day in which [God] will judge the world in righteousness through a Man whom He has appointed . . ." (Acts 17:31, NASB). There is a future day—"the day of wrath and revelation of the righteous judgment of God" (Rom. 2:5, NASB)—when "God will judge the secrets of men through Christ Jesus" (Rom. 2:16, NASB). Paul likewise speaks of Christ, at the last day, "dealing out retribution" to the wicked, who "will pay the penalty of eternal destruction, away from the presence of the Lord and from the glory of His power" (2 Thess. 1:8–9, NASB). The believer has yet to appear before the "judgment seat of Christ"—not to receive in his own person a punitive return for his sins, but to give an "account of himself to God" (Rom. 14:10, 12; 2 Cor. 5:10, NASB), "knowing that whatever good thing each one does, this he will receive back from the Lord, whether slave or free" (Eph. 6:8, NASB).

We could multiply examples elsewhere in both the New Testament and the Old Testament. These suffice to demonstrate how the doctrine of the judgment to come pervades the teaching of Jesus Christ and of Paul. The absence of any substantial discussion of this doctrine in McLaren's evaluation of Jesus at the very least gravely distorts his overall portrait of the message of Jesus Christ.

Second, McLaren's discussion of the gospel according to Paul compromises the integrity of that gospel. McLaren, we have observed, defines the gospel in terms of the proclamation of the lordship of Christ *and* in terms of a message of reconciliation between God and human beings, but chiefly among human beings. We may address each of these two components in turn.

McLaren is surely correct to insist that the lordship of Christ is a *sine qua non* of Christian proclamation (Rom. 10:9). It is difficult, however, to place that doctrine definitionally at the very heart of the gospel itself. The maxim "Jesus is Lord and Caesar is not" will be affirmed by every man and woman at the day of judgment (Phil. 2:9–11). One cannot define the gospel in terms of affirming the lordship of Christ when many who will affirm that truth will perish. To be sure, McLaren insists that one must not simply declare Jesus' lordship, but also align oneself with his kingdom.[112] McLaren's exposition of Jesus' teaching, however, does not adequately account for the reality that some who appear to be earnest for the Lord and his kingdom agenda will nevertheless be condemned by Jesus for their hypocrisy. This state of affairs indicates that McLaren's definition of the gospel is defective.

McLaren's discussion of Paul's teaching on reconciliation does not neglect the reconciliation between God and sinners that is made possible by the death of Christ.[113] We might observe, however, that McLaren's understandings of the nature and con-

---

112. McLaren, *Secret Message of Jesus*, 97.
113. Ibid., 99–103.

sequences of Adam's first sin; of the nature of the divine and eternal judgment of human beings; and of the nature of Christ's death for sinners conjoin to raise serious questions regarding how McLaren conceives the character of that divine-human reconciliation.

The overwhelming emphasis of this discussion on reconciliation, moreover, is the fact that Jesus' death makes possible the reconciliation of alienated human groups and individuals. It is true that horizontal reconciliation and principled inclusion within the church is a legitimate consequence of the death of Christ (Rom. 15:7–13; Phil. 2:5–11). It is misleading, however, to identify that reconciliation with the gospel itself.

It is when we turn to Paul's most extensive definition of his "gospel"—the epistle to the Romans—that we most clearly see McLaren's imbalances and deficiencies. For Paul, the chief problem humanity faces is sin and the necessary divine response ("wrath") to that sin (Rom. 1:18). Unfolding the sins of Jew and Gentile alike, Paul concludes that all alike are "under sin" (Rom. 3:9), that is, alike under its guilt and condemnation. To remedy this state of affairs for his people God has sent his Son, who has died an atoning, propitiatory death for them (Rom. 3:21–26). The death and life of Jesus Christ—his "righteousness" accounted to the sinner in union with him, and received by the sinner through faith alone—is the basis of his justification, or his pardon and acceptance before a holy God (Rom. 4:6–8; Rom. 5:18–19). In union with his risen Savior, the believer is transformed—imperfectly yet truly—after the image of Jesus Christ (Rom. 6:1–7:25). The believer, thus progressively sanctified, possesses, through the pledge of the Spirit given to him, a solid assurance of consummate communion with Jesus Christ in glory and a firm hope of a creation from which the veil of futility will have been lifted (Rom. 8:18–25).

These great truths Paul deemed to rest at the heart of the gospel. Paul can therefore claim that in his gospel "the righteousness of God"—the imputed righteousness of Jesus Christ—"is revealed from faith to faith" (Rom. 1:17, NASB). This is why Paul can classify the death of Christ "for our sins" and the resurrection of the body as among the matters "of first importance" delivered to the church (1 Cor. 15:3, NASB). Paul can therefore summarily speak of the "appearing of our Savior Christ Jesus, who abolished death and brought life and immortality to light through the gospel" (2 Tim. 1:10, NASB). The gospel, to be sure, must not in its fullest sense be identified with justification by faith alone. Neither, however, can the place of justification by faith within the gospel be diminished or marginalized. It is this latter error into which McLaren appears to have fallen. In the absence of any robust discussion of justification by faith alone, McLaren's discussion of Paul's kingdom message in terms of horizontal reconciliation risks confusion with a moralistic appeal for inclusivity.

We should note in conclusion that on more than one occasion, McLaren represents, as the alternative to his own position, what he deems to be a widespread understanding of the gospel: "a select few escaping earth and going to heaven after they die."[114] McLaren is correct to critique any expression of biblical salvation that neglects due emphasis upon the proper role of the body particularly and of the creation generally. McLaren, however, has erected a most unhelpful dichotomy: either one can identify with a gospel that proclaims salvation to sinners (and therefore abandon the creation) or one can embrace McLaren's understanding of Jesus' and Paul's teaching concerning Christ's kingdom (and consequently mute biblical teaching on sin and redemption). Neither option accurately represents contemporary evangelicalism as a whole. Neither option is biblically satisfactory. The biblical doctrine of salvation by grace alone does not warrant wholesale withdrawal from the creation. Nor does proper and thoughtful Christian engagement and service in the creation at all compromise or attenuate the doctrines of grace. "Godliness is profitable for all things," says the apostle, "since it holds promise for the present life and also for the life to come" (1 Tim. 4:8, NASB). McLaren, however, offers us in *The Secret Message of Jesus* a picture of the kingdom of God that has negligible interest in the world to come. Consequently, McLaren's exposition of the kingdom is of minimal value to human beings seeking relief from what the Bible declares is their real problem—sin and God's just displeasure with them as sinners.

Concluding Reflections

One is struck in reading both McLaren's and Wright's published writings on Jesus by their reactive tone. McLaren and Wright are palpably in dialogue with their understanding of mainstream evangelical Christianity.[115] Both theologians offer trenchant critiques of contemporary evangelicalism. These critiques, while not always evenly informed, nevertheless can be useful in highlighting imbalances that surface in evangelical teaching on the Gospels. In this respect, one can genuinely learn from McLaren's and Wright's writings.

It would be a mistake, however, to understand McLaren and Wright as summoning their audience to traditional Reformational orthodoxy. Each proposes a new *method* by means of which the gospel is to be articulated. Both writers maintain that the church needs to grasp "story" or narrative as the medium within which the biblical gospel is articulated and as the medium by means of which the church must articulate the biblical gospel. This claim is of itself unextraordinary. Reformed theology in particular has maintained the place and importance of biblical narrative to the gospel and its proclamation. This is evident from such individual treatises as Jonathan Edwards's *History*

---

114. Ibid., 91, compare McLaren, *New Kind of Christian*, 82–83; McLaren, *Generous Orthodoxy*, 91–101.
115. Neither author restricts his criticisms, however, specifically to evangelical Christianity. Both target criticisms at Protestantism in general. See McLaren, *Secret Message of Jesus,* 209–18; Wright, *Jesus and the Victory of God,* 13–16.

of Redemption and John Owen's *Biblical Theology.*[116] It is also evident from such creedal statements as the *Westminster Confession of Faith*, much of which is structured along the lines of the biblical pattern "creation—fall—redemption—consummation."

The difficulty comes in both McLaren's and Wright's frequent dichotomizations of narrative and systematic formulation. Narrative is posed as a pure biblical alternative to what is said to be abstracted systematic formulation. What have never properly been rivals are now posed as mutually exclusive alternatives. At least two problems attend such a proposal. First, it denies what is an inevitable enterprise. The human mind can no more cease to think systematically than it can cease to think. The question is not *whether* we will reflect on the biblical narrative systematically but *how* we will think on the biblical narrative systematically. Second, in our survey of McLaren's work we have registered concern regarding the lack of needed precision in Jesus' teaching on judgment and the atonement. McLaren offers severe criticisms of eternal punishment and of the penal substitutionary atonement, but his criticisms do not extend to their explicit and wholesale rejection. McLaren at points employs language that is sufficiently broad to include those doctrines. If it is greater theological precision that the interested reader seeks, McLaren is methodologically predisposed against it. His particular conception of narrative and his criticisms of systematic theological reflection militate against such a request. The question must be asked whether McLaren's particular approach toward narrative represents an opportunity for progression or regression for evangelical theology. Regrettably, this method appears unable to sustain the precision of the teaching of the Scripture.

McLaren and Wright have both argued that the mainstream evangelical church has lost sight of what the "gospel" is. McLaren proposes that Jesus proclaimed, in his preaching of the kingdom, a radical and scandalous inclusion of persons who were excluded or condemned by the religious hierarchy of first-century Judaism. The apostle Paul, in appropriating Jesus' kingdom message, heralded the doctrine of Christ's lordship and the doctrine of reconciliation—especially the reconciliation of disparate and alienated persons to one another. At the core of the teaching of both Jesus and Paul, then, is a message of radical and principled inclusivity. The overwhelming emphasis of the kingdom proclamation of both Jesus and Paul was not "heaven after you die" but life lived in this world, in the here and now. Their proclamation, in other words, was profoundly temporal.

In *The Secret Message of Jesus*, McLaren has undoubtedly presented an accessible and disarming attempt to describe Jesus' message and ministry to an unbelieving audience. It is precisely in view of this fact, however, that we must register concern. McLaren's exposition is overwhelmingly concerned with horizontal reconciliation,

---

116. Jonathan Edwards, *A History of the Work of Redemption* in Edward Hickman, ed., *The Works of Jonathan Edwards*, 2 vols. (1834; repr., Edinburgh: Banner of Truth, 1974) 2:532–619; John Owen, *Biblical Theology, or the Nature, Origin, Development, and Study of Theological Truth, in Six Books . . .* , trans. Stephen P. Westcott (1661; repr. Morgan, Pa.: Soli Deo Gloria, 1996).

inclusivity, and this world. Little is heard of the sinner's native depravity; of the sinner's guilt before a holy God; of reconciliation between God and the sinner through the atoning, propitiatory, and substitutionary death of Jesus Christ; and of the eternal state. It is not that McLaren expressly denies these points. It is that they occupy no appreciable position within McLaren's overall discussion of the teaching of Jesus and Paul. McLaren's primary concerns—horizontal reconciliation among human beings, and principled inclusivism within the church—stand more or less independently of them. It is here that Wright's influence upon McLaren's exposition of Jesus' and Paul's teaching is most palpably observed, and it is here that Wright's influence is most disconcerting.

One must ask whether it is likely or even possible that an unbelieving inquirer will read *The Secret Message of Jesus* and be sufficiently confronted with his sinfulness before a holy God, the danger of a Christless state, and the necessity of repentance and faith in Jesus Christ to escape the wrath to come. We must answer in the negative. *The Secret Message of Jesus*'s concern with this world to the practical exclusion of the world to come effectively sidelines the chief concerns of the Bible—the unblemished holiness of God and the guilt borne by every ordinary son and daughter of Adam. It is these concerns, however, that occupy the heart of the biblical message. It is when this message is preached in its fullness and clarity that sinners may be brought to the full realization both of the depths of their condition and of the riches of divine grace in Jesus Christ. May God be pleased in this generation to bring multitudes "having no hope and without God in the world" (Eph. 2:12, NASB) to the point where they, "having been justified by faith," and thereby having entered into "peace with God through our Lord Jesus Christ," proceed in word and in life to "exult in hope of the glory of God" (Rom. 5:1–2, NASB).

9

Joyriding on the Downgrade at Breakneck Speed: The Dark Side of Diversity

PHIL JOHNSON

~~~~~~

I can't remember a fad or phenomenon in the past four decades that has captured the imagination of evangelicals as quickly or as powerfully as the emerging church movement (ECM). Various ECM-style trends have been leaching into evangelical thought and practice more or less quietly for about two decades. Internet forums promoting "postmodern Christianity" were appearing as early as 1994. The growing influence of Brian McLaren was evident by the start of the new millennium. His books (and others in the same vein) stood out as one of the remarkable success stories in Christian publishing in the first half of the decade. The Emergent Convention in 2003 also garnered quite a bit of publicity. I watched all those trends with interest.

But when *Christianity Today* published its first major story about the movement in November of 2004,[1] many of my evangelical friends and fellow ministers said they had never heard of the ECM before. That article seemed to introduce the ECM to many in the evangelical mainstream for the very first time. By then, the ECM was already an amazingly widespread phenomenon, but most evangelical pastors and church leaders seemed completely caught off guard by it.

The following March I attended a major evangelical pastors' conference, and questions about the emerging church were raised at least once in every question-and-answer session. Just two years later at the same conference, it seemed like the ECM

1. Andy Crouch, "The Emergent Mystique," *Christianity Today*, November 2004, 36–41.

211

was practically the *only* topic anyone wanted to talk about. If my perception is accurate, from the ECM's first blip on the evangelical radar screen to the point where it utterly dominated the evangelical conversation was a short enough time span to be measured in months.

Analysis and critique of the ECM is no easy task. The movement is a typically postmodern phenomenon—deliberately diverse, perplexingly amorphous, and constantly in flux. It has no clear homogeneity in doctrine, philosophy, or practice. In early 2006, Ed Stetzer, who has studied and written about emerging trends in a Southern Baptist context, identified three distinctive strains of emerging style.[2] Shortly after that, Mark Driscoll (unquestionably the most conservative leading figure within the movement) essentially borrowed Stetzer's taxonomy and added a fourth category that better characterized his own position.[3]

A year later, Scot McKnight, who describes himself as a participant in the ECM (and who functions alternatively as a sympathetic critic and an apologist for the movement), wrote an article in *Christianity Today* identifying *five* streams of influence in the ECM.[4] That same month, Zondervan released a book-length symposium discussing various doctrinal perspectives within the ECM, featuring five contributors ranging from Driscoll on the far right to Doug Pagitt at the opposite end of the spectrum.[5] There was so much ambiguity and so little consensus among the participants that in a summary at the end of the book, general editor Robert Webber wrote, "For those who have read this book to gain clarity on emerging beliefs, I have to say that what you are looking for is not here, except in Mark Driscoll."[6]

Diversity may well be the only descriptor that can be used without asterisks or qualifiers to describe the many theological currents that keep the ECM in a constant swirl. Read a generous sampling of ECM books or blogs and you will soon realize

---

2. Ed Stetzer, "Understanding the Emerging Church," First-Person column, *Baptist Press News*, January 6, 2006, http://www.bpnews.net/. Stetzer's article, first posted online and widely circulated, identifies three strains of emerging churches: the *relevants* (who are merely trying to contextualize the church's message for a postmodern culture), the *reconstructionists* (who want to restructure the church and corporate worship while holding to a more or less "orthodox view of the Gospel and Scripture"), and the *revisionists* (who are questioning "and in some cases denying" the most essential evangelical doctrinal convictions). Stetzer concludes that the emerging "conversation" is strategic and that evangelicals should jump in and participate. "Many 'emerging' evangelicals are distancing themselves from the revisionist leaders," he writes. "Let's affirm the good, look to the Scriptures for answers to the hard questions, and, yes, let's graciously disagree when others hold views contrary to our best scriptural understanding of God, Bible and church" (ibid.).
3. In a videotaped interview promoting the 2006 Desiring God conference, Driscoll described the same three categories of ECM types Stetzer had named, but Driscoll then placed himself in a fourth category, which he characterized as essentially Reformed *theologically*, but *methodologically* emerging, i.e., striving to contextualize Christianity for postmodern culture. http://desiringgod.org/media/video/2006_National/national2006_driscoll_interview1.mov.
4. Scot McKnight, "Five Streams of the Emerging Church," *Christianity Today*, February 2007, http://www.christianitytoday.com/ct/2007/february/11.35.html.
5. Robert Webber, ed., *Listening to the Beliefs of Emerging Churches: Five Perspectives* (Grand Rapids: Zondervan, 2007). The five contributors to the volume were Driscoll, Pagitt, John Burke, Dan Kimball, and Karen Ward.
6. Ibid., 200.

that there are many *more* than five streams of influence feeding into the movement. With all due respect to Stetzer, Driscoll, McKnight, and Webber (and other friends of the ECM who have bravely attempted to explain ECM beliefs to the rest of us), five categories—or ten or a hundred—are not nearly enough to do justice to the breadth and variety of theological opinions represented within the movement. Perhaps the only accurate way to depict the ECM's vast doctrinal diversity would be to have as many categories as there are persons who identify with the movement.

Indeed, it might be even more accurate to say that one of the principal aims of the ECM seems to be the elimination of categories and boundaries altogether. In the words of one ECM blogger, "We love it when people begin thinking for themselves and value intellectual diversity. We distrust systems of moral and doctrinal boundaries precisely in the way that the New Testament distrusts religious legalism."[7] That seems a fair way to characterize the dominant ECM perspective on doctrine. Clarity, harmony, and precision are held in high suspicion because such values invariably establish "boundaries." Boundaries (by definition) mean someone is being marginalized—and that reeks of "legalism" (or even worse).

Diversity, on the other hand, though missing from every *biblical* list of virtues, is esteemed within the emerging movement even more highly than unity. The many clear New Testament pleas to "be of one mind"[8] are effectively set aside in favor of the more postmodern and politically-correct ideal of liberal-minded "tolerance."

Three major motives seem to drive the passion for diversity within the ECM. One is the unwitting (or, in some cases, intentional) adoption of *postmodern values.* Anyone who watches the evening news will have noticed that "diversity" is one of the few remaining virtues of secular postmodern society. The general tide in the ECM is clearly and profoundly swayed by that point of view.

A second reason the ECM fosters such unbridled theological diversity stems from a gnawing *doctrinal indifference* that has been spreading like leaven through the evangelical movement for several decades. The trend seems to have begun in the mid-twentieth century as a radical overreaction to the fundamentalist idea—especially in the wake of the fundamentalist movement's failure to maintain focus on the truly essential doctrines of the Christian faith.[9] But the accrued apathy of at least four-plus decades of neo-evangelical influence has left evangelicals virtually defenseless against doctrinal error—especially the subtle varieties. The ECM has aggressively exploited that weakness, challenging on various fronts practically every historic evangelical

---

7. Isaac Everett, "Kimball, MacArthur, and Me" on the "Transmission" blog (27 January 2007), http://www.transmissioning.org/?m=200701.

8. 2 Cor. 13:11; cf. Rom. 15:5–6; 1 Cor.1:10; Phil. 1:27; 2:2; 3:16; 4:2; 1 Pet. 3:8.

9. For my own brief assessment of the fundamentalist movement's meltdown, see "Dead Right: The Failure of Fundamentalism" (seminar transcript, Shepherds' Conference, Grace Community Church, Sun Valley, CA, March 3, 2005). http://audio.gracechurch.org/sc/2005notes/JohnsonDeadRight.pdf.

doctrinal distinctive. The ECM has therefore become practically the mirror opposite of what fundamentalism was supposed to be.

A third motive for so much stress on diversity in the ECM seems to be *self-defense.* Individuals within the movement are essentially free to deny or assert anything they like while the larger movement remains effectively impervious to doctrinal criticism—because "Not everyone in the movement believes like that" works well as an easy, all-purpose reply. Heresies and false doctrines of all types can and do percolate freely within the movement (often coming from some of the ECM's best-known figures[10]), but emerging devotees usually dismiss legitimate concerns about the erosion of doctrine in their midst with a shrug and a wave of the hand at the ECM's broad diversity.

In this chapter, I want to highlight and examine those three factors—and attempt to explain why a celebration of theological diversity per se augurs disaster for the movement's inevitable drift.

Postmodernism

Proponents of the ECM and their critics alike frequently use the expression *postmodernism.* It's hard to make much sense of the ECM without some idea of what that term refers to. The word is notoriously difficult to define succinctly, because postmodernism truly *is* a complex and enigmatic idea—involving, for example, ingenious theories about how language works, how ideas are formed, and how texts should be interpreted. Various trends in art, philosophy, epistemology, education, and literature have all been labeled "postmodern"—and a thorough definition of the term would need to account for all of them.

To complicate things further, postmodernists tend to think of reality as a socially-constructed concept (meaning we determine what is "real" by perceptions that are influenced by our interaction with one another). Postmodernism does not (as is often supposed) deny that absolute or objective truth exists. (Such a categorical denial would entail too obvious a self-contradiction.) But the typical postmodernist points out that if objective reality does exist somewhere, we could never see it objectively. So the only "truth" we can apprehend is inherently subjective, ever-changing, and always different depending on our perspective when we see it. Our knowledge of what's true should therefore always be tentative and indefinite, never settled and confident.

---

10. To cite just one specific example of this, Spencer Burke, former pastor of the ten thousand-member Mariners Church in Irvine, CA, issues a press kit in which he boasts of his reputation as "a heretic." His recent book, *A Heretic's Guide to Eternity* (San Francisco: Jossey-Bass, 2006), denies the personality of God (195); is skeptical about the exclusivity of Christ; and champions a broad kind of universalism that fatally alters the gospel ("I don't believe you have to convert to any particular religion to find God," [197]). The Web site Burke founded, TheOoze.com (http://www.theooze.com/), is one of the most-trafficked ECM portals on the Web, and despite his aggressive advocacy for doctrinal opinions that (by his own admission) are rank heresy, he remains one of the most influential figures in the ECM.

In practice, of course, this means that even if the most sympathetic scholar produced a large tome attempting to explain *postmodernism* as thoroughly, as carefully, and as favorably as possible, the typical postmodernist would still insist the definition isn't quite right yet. All of this makes the postmodernist idea seem arcane and esoteric to anyone whose thinking isn't already well-mulched with postmodernist presuppositions.

Furthermore, classic postmodernism involves a theory about language and literature that is inherently hostile to unambiguous definitions anyway. To define *that* word crisply is to contradict it. It is also tantamount to lobbing a personal taunt at every postmodernized college student and blogger who reads the definition. All such definitions are therefore guaranteed to be met with the most ruthless kind of deconstruction.

Fortunately, postmodernism has been explained with a fair degree of thoroughness and analyzed on numerous levels in several helpful evangelical resources,[11] so someone who still has no idea what postmodernism is can refer to those resources.

But with those caveats, here's a simple description of what is most relevant about postmodernism in any discussion of the ECM: *Postmodernism has at its heart a nagging suspicion that at the end of the day, no one can really know with complete certainty or settled assurance what is true and what is not.* It might not be too far-fetched to say that's virtually the distilled essence of the whole postmodern idea.

Postmodernists modestly refer to their own invincible lack of certainty as "epistemic humility." To anyone who has something to be certain about, the postmodernist's refusal to be definitive looks, sounds, and acts like old-fashioned cynicism. From the postmodernists' own perspective, however, that kind of skepticism is the new meekness—while the very epitome of ugly arrogance is any notion that we actually do know something with conclusive and categorical certainty. Dogmatism of any kind is equal to the most diabolical kind of cruelty; anyone with strong moral convictions is deemed particularly judgmental; and even quiet faith has a kind of uppity feel to it. Thus the "humility" of perpetual ambivalence has become postmodernism's one supreme and cardinal virtue.

Postmodernism (as the name itself suggests) is supposed to entail a radical renunciation of the *modern* mentality, and in one sense, it does. The central belief of so-called modern thinking was that our only *sure* knowledge is whatever is scientifically verifiable. In other words, modernity still made room for certitude, but modernists maintained that the only reliable test of what's true is scientific rationalism.

---

11. See, for example, D. A. Carson, *The Gagging of God* (Grand Rapids: Zondervan, 2002); D. A. Carson, *Becoming Conversant with the Emerging Church* (Grand Rapids: Zondervan, 2005); David Wells, *Above All Earthly Pow'rs: Christ in a Postmodern World* (Grand Rapids: Eerdmans, 2005); Gene Edward Veith, *Postmodern Times: A Christian Guide to Contemporary Thought and Culture* (Wheaton, IL: Crossway, 1994); David S. Dockery, *The Challenge of Postmodernism: An Evangelical Engagement* (Grand Rapids: Baker, 1995); and John MacArthur, *The Truth War* (Nashville: Thomas Nelson, 2007).

Modernity is often traced to the *foundationalism* of René Descartes in the early seventeenth century. Descartes sought an unassailable foundation for human certainty. Noting that virtually all human beliefs are subject to skeptical arguments, Descartes was left with one invincible certainty: his own conscious existence. And he concluded that nothing but his own mind gave him certainty of *that*. His famous maxim, *Cogito, ergo sum* ("I think, therefore I am") reflects that singular certainty. Using it as his starting point and foundation, he argued for the existence of God and the reality of the physical world. A genius as a mathematician, Descartes approached epistemology like someone solving a mathematical problem. His work was seminal in bringing epistemology to the forefront of philosophical debates.

But modernity was unleashed in its full fury by Darwin's theory that men are only animals who evolved from lower creatures. In Darwin's system, of course, everything hinges on the survival of the fittest. Humanity is not really accountable to any higher moral being. The predictable results included Marxism, fascism, and various other social experiments that had Darwinism as a main ingredient and the survival of the fittest as their goal and justification. Modernity thus spawned two world wars and a long cold war—until communism finally collapsed under its own weight.

Modernity died with the last communist superpower—or thus many postmodernists allege. By the end of the 1980s, the certainty supposedly guaranteed by science and human reason had been unmasked as a cheap illusion. The hubris of scientific modernism was utterly exposed; Cartesian foundationalism was summarily discredited; and modernity itself was suddenly regarded as academically unfashionable. Postmodernism—borrowing ideas made popular by existentialism and cultural and ethical relativism, and blending them with values made politically correct by secular humanism—stepped into the gap.

The ECM is fundamentally a self-conscious attempt to adapt the church and frame the gospel message in a way that meets the unique challenges postmodernism presents. There's nothing wrong with trying our best to communicate more effectively with postmodern people, of course. In fact, it is right for Christians to grapple with the question of how the church should respond to postmodernism. That's a serious and vitally important issue that too many old-style evangelicals are blissfully oblivious to (and too many evangelicals who are aware of the problem seem unwilling to face it seriously). The ECM deserves credit for recognizing the megashift and sounding a wake-up call. The evangelical movement desperately needs to be stirred from its own apathy and oblivion.[12]

12. One genuine contribution the ECM has made is in its analysis of the many failures of the contemporary evangelical mainstream. The ECM *critique* of the evangelical movement is for the most part right on target, especially when emerging critics decry contemporary evangelicals' infatuation with everything frivolous, superficial, and self-centered. As a matter of fact, one major catalyst that seems to be propelling young people into the ECM is their loathing for the unbridled shallowness and self-absorption of modern evangelicalism.

Unfortunately, the emerging movement has an extraordinary knack for adapting to and embracing the very aspects of postmodern culture that most need to be confronted with the truth of the gospel. In the process of contextualizing the Christian message for a postmodern culture, the ECM has rather uncritically assimilated a postmodern value system. Postmodern "virtues"—such as uncertainty, ambiguity, mystery, latitudinarianism (masquerading as "tolerance"), and above all, *diversity*—have somehow made it to the head of the ECM's hierarchy of moral values. These inevitably crowd out and eliminate more biblical values, such as assurance, boldness, conviction, understanding of the truth, and the defense of sound doctrine.

Read any book, blog, or essay from ECM sources, and you can hardly help noticing how postmodern moral values—especially diversity and ambivalence—dominate practically every page. Brian McLaren, for example, starts one of his books with this caveat: "A warning: as in most of my other books, there are places here where I have gone out of my way to be provocative, mischievous, and unclear, reflecting my belief that clarity is sometimes overrated, and that shock, obscurity, playfulness, and intrigue (carefully articulated) often stimulate more thought than clarity."[13] Robert Webber sums up his symposium on emerging beliefs with this: "Emerging leaders do not want a closed theological system all neatly tied together by reason and logic. They call us to a more open view of theology with room for mystery. Theology is 'an adventurous exploration of new horizons.' Theology is more like a 'mysterious adventure than a mathematical puzzle.'"[14]

Qualities like diversity, ambiguity, mystery, and novelty—as well as qualms about expressing our own certainty—will sound like positive virtues to almost anyone steeped in postmodern entertainments and mass media. But from a biblical perspective, those things are not inherently virtuous at all. In fact, they are all fraught with serious and significant dangers, especially when applied with lavish abandon to biblical theology and hermeneutics.

Sober, careful consideration of the biblical exhortations for Christians to guard sound doctrine would soon peel the mask of "virtue" off the postmodernist value system. Specifically, a better understanding of the *biblical* concept of humility would

---

The publisher's ad copy for Russell Rathburn's *Post-Rapture Radio* (San Francisco: Jossey-Bass, 2005) expresses a typical sentiment: "Frustrated with the shallowness of the American Evangelical Movement of the past few decades, and seeing that many of his friends wanted to have nothing to do with Christianity, Russell . . . decided to create a church that his friends would want to come to." Rathburn and friends are absolutely right in their negative assessment of contemporary evangelicalism, but their solution could hardly be more wrongheaded. Redesigning the church to suit one's own cultural or generational preferences (as opposed to taking a *biblical* approach to church order) is the very thing that caused the evangelical movement to run aground in the first place. It has already bred a completely different, and perhaps more dangerous, kind of superficiality in the ECM, too.

13. Brian McLaren, *A Generous Orthodoxy: Why I am a missional + evangelical + post/protestant + liberal/ conservative + mystical/poetic + biblical + charismatic/contemplative + fundamentalist/calvinist + green + incarnational + depressed-yet-hopeful + emergent + unfinished Christian* (Grand Rapids: Zondervan, 2004), 22–23.

14. Webber, *Listening to the Beliefs of Emerging Churches,* 199.

help correct the most glaring, fundamental flaw in the ECM's approach to Scripture and doctrine: an almost impenetrable apathy about what's really true.

Doctrinal Indifference

In biblical terms it is anything but *humble* to imply that God's Word is not sufficiently clear—as if we can't possibly be sure what the Bible means and as if we should never be so "arrogant" as to defend its truths against the enemy's relentless attempts to twist and subvert what God has said. For Christians blithely to accept (or even defer to) the postmodern premise that certainty and arrogance are essentially the same thing is to surrender a major portion of the very ground we are called to defend. This is no minor or incidental matter. John MacArthur writes,

> What is *really* at stake are the very same truths the serpent sought to subvert when he asked Eve, "Has God indeed said . . . ?" (Genesis 3:1). They are the same truths that have *always* been at the heart of the Truth War—the inspiration, authority, inerrancy, sufficiency, and perspicuity (clarity) of Scripture. . . . Surely *those* are issues that cannot be swept aside or discounted as marginal in the name of a twisted notion of charity or false humility.[15]

No one would argue that everything in the Bible is crystal clear. The inspired text itself contains an acknowledgment that "some things [in it] . . . are hard to understand" (2 Pet. 3:16). We're not to imagine, however, that *most* of the Bible is sheer mystery—so lacking in clarity that every interpretation and every opinion about every doctrine deserves equal (or automatic) respect.

In fact, Christian leaders in particular are charged with the task of defending the truth against those who would twist it (Acts 20:28–31). As politically incorrect as this might sound to postmodern ears, there are abroad and within the church "many who are insubordinate, empty talkers and deceivers. . . . They must be silenced . . ." (Titus 1:10–11). Or, in the more picturesque imagery of King James parlance, "[Their] mouths must be stopped."

How false teachers are to be silenced is one of those things in Scripture that *is* crystal clear. It is not by physical force or auto-da-fé. They are to be refuted and rebuked by qualified elders in the church who are skilled in the Scriptures, "able to give instruction in sound doctrine and also to rebuke those who contradict it" (Titus 1:9). That presupposes that vital truth is clear enough to know for certain. And it prescribes a clear remedy involving exhortation, reproof, rebuke, and correction.

This is to be done patiently, not pugnaciously: "The Lord's servant must not be quarrelsome but kind to everyone, able to teach, patiently enduring evil, correcting his opponents with gentleness. God may perhaps grant them repentance leading to

15. MacArthur, *Truth War,* 38–39.

a knowledge of the truth, and they may come to their senses and escape from the snare of the devil . . ." (2 Tim. 2:24–26).

And yet even within those boundaries, the defense of the faith sometimes requires a kind of spiritual militancy (1 Tim. 1:18; Jude 3). The Christian life—especially the duty of the leader—is frequently pictured in Scripture as that of warfare (2 Cor. 10:3–6; Eph. 6:10–18; 1 Tim. 1:18; 2 Tim. 2:3–4).

So the defense of the faith is no easy task. But it is an *indispensable* duty for faithful Christians. Again, Scripture is not the least bit vague or equivocal about that.

Nevertheless, the defense of the faith is a duty the evangelical movement as a whole has mostly shirked for at least two decades. Since the formal dissolution of the International Council on Biblical Inerrancy in September 1987,[16] evangelicalism as a movement has never fully mobilized for the defense of any point of doctrine— even in the wake of seismic challenges to the doctrine of God in the form of Open Theism[17]—and despite recent assaults on the penal, propitiatory, and substitutionary aspects of Christ's atoning work.[18] It is no longer safe to assume that someone who calls himself an evangelical would even affirm such historic evangelical nonnegotiables as the exclusivity of Christ or the necessity of conscious faith in Christ for salvation.[19] Recently, it seems, the evangelical movement's standard response to that kind of doctrinal slippage has looked like nothing more than cynical insouciance.

16. ICBI, founded in October 1978 (at the height of the controversy spawned by Harold Lindsell's landmark book *The Battle for the Bible* [Grand Rapids: Zondervan, 1976]), was never meant to be a permanent organization. At the beginning, they laid out a strategy, stuck to that strategy until the task was finished, and then in September 1987, the organization was formally disbanded.

17. See Greg Boyd, *God of the Possible* (Grand Rapids: Baker, 2000); John Sanders, *The God Who Risks: A Theology of Providence* (Downers Grove, IL: InterVarsity, 1998); and Clark Pinnock, ed., *The Openness of God: A Biblical Challenge to the Traditional Understanding of God* (Downers Grove, IL: InterVarsity, 1994). All of these books deny that God knows the future perfectly. After lengthy debates about the issue, the Evangelical Theological Society issued a statement in 2002 disavowing Open Theism. Yet three years later the Society declined to remove Pinnock and Sanders from membership, in effect embracing theologians who deny the foreknowledge of God and who regard inspired prophecy as merely "probabilistic." They are welcome in the ETS as long as they profess to hold to some form of "inerrancy"—or at least the profession thereof. The evangelical movement's leading periodical quickly heralded the development as a triumph for "grace and truth." See David Neff, "Open to Healing: Anxieties and Attack Turn to Grace and Truth at ETS Meeting" (*Christianity Today,* January 2004, 21–22). The title and tenor of that article reflect contemporary evangelicalism's deep-seated discomfort with the thought of any polemical defense of the faith.

18. Steve Chalke in the UK and Brian McLaren in the US have both strongly criticized the historic evangelical belief that God's wrath against his people's sin was satisfied when Christ bore their guilt as their substitute on the cross. Chalke referred to that view as "cosmic child abuse," in *The Lost Message of Jesus* (Grand Rapids: Zondervan, 2003), 182. McLaren had the protagonist in one of his fictional dialogues echo the same idea, dismissing the idea of penal substitution as just "one more injustice in the cosmic equation. It sounds like divine child abuse. You know?" Brian McLaren, *The Story We Find Ourselves In* (San Francisco: Jossey-Bass, 2003), 102. Canadian theologian Robert Brow attacked penal substitution in the pages of *Christianity Today* more than fifteen years ago, and he correctly predicted that the evangelical movement would be rocked by a "megashift" in which historic evangelical doctrines ranging from the atonement to the exclusivity of Christ would be abandoned on a widespread basis. Everything he predicted has come to fruition, and most of the opinions Brow was advocating then are now staples in the ECM. See Robert Brow, "Evangelical Megashift," *Christianity Today,* February 19, 1990, 12–14.

19. No less an iconic figure than Billy Graham, for example, has made numerous public statements in recent years suggesting that he no longer believes personal trust in Christ is necessary for salvation. When asked

Yet such trends represent nothing less than the abandonment of true evangelical principles. *Historic* evangelicalism has always had the gospel at its center. The name itself reflects that, and it also denotes a particular stress on the *doctrinal* content of the gospel message.[20] Yet the typical message proclaimed in many mainstream evangelical churches—including some of the best-known and most influential megachurches—was long ago reduced to a set of selfish and simplistic aphorisms ("God loves you and has a wonderful plan for your life"; "accept Jesus as your personal Savior"). The message is sometimes overlaid with moralistic platitudes and a conservative, mostly-secular political agenda. In fact, a lobbyist's commitment to a handful of morally-related political issues is about as close to anything serious as you will find in the average evangelical community. So the message communicated to the world at large sounds like a social and cultural commentary driven by Republican party politics. Gone are the clarion notes of personal guilt, the redemption of the soul, and the real meaning of the cross—which, after all, Scripture says is the one message worth proclaiming (1 Cor. 2:2).

Why *fight* for a message that doesn't even have Christ crucified at the center anyway? Contemporary evangelicals have utterly neglected and virtually forgotten almost everything truly distinctive about *historic* evangelicalism. They have broadened their boundaries to include beliefs they once viewed as beyond the pale. They have now forgotten what the boundaries were all about in the first place. Meanwhile, with the gospel no longer at evangelicalism's heart and hub, the entire evangelical subculture has begun to seem like a kind of spiritual black hole, where bad ideas spawned at the fringes are sucked one after another into the void at the center.

The typical young person coming out of an evangelical background and into the ECM most likely has never really been exposed to all that much serious biblical preaching or theological precision. And yet many of them are convinced an undue preoccupation with propositional truth and doctrinal correctness is one of the chief reasons for contemporary evangelicalism's pathological commitment to shallowness. They are therefore determined to avoid rigid boundaries at all costs. No wonder the emerging movement itself is so diverse and all-inclusive. "The fathers have eaten sour grapes, and the children's teeth are set on edge" (Jer. 31:29).

---

whether he believes heaven will be closed to good Jews, Muslims, Buddhists, Hindus, or secular people, Graham says, "Those are decisions only the Lord will make. It would be foolish for me to speculate on who will be there and who won't . . . I don't want to speculate about all that. I believe the love of God is absolute. He said he gave his son for the whole world, and I think he loves everybody regardless of what label they have." Jon Meacham, "Pilgrim's Progress," *Newsweek*, August 14, 2006, 36.

20. The *Oxford English Dictionary* traces the earliest recorded usage of the term *evangelical* to William Tyndale. The original meaning of the word was simply "of or pertaining to the gospel," but *evangelical* then came to be used in a more technical sense, referring to "that school of Protestants which maintains that the essence of 'the Gospel' consists in the doctrine of salvation by faith in the atoning death of Christ, and denies that either good works or the sacraments have any saving efficacy." ("Evangelical," *The Compact Edition of the Oxford English Dictionary* [New York: Oxford, 1971], 1:905.)

Looked at from that perspective, the ECM is not really a surprising development at all. It's just another revolution in a steady downward spiral that has been carrying the evangelical *movement* away from historic evangelical *principles* for several decades. It follows a predictable pattern of decline and disintegration that should be familiar to anyone who knows evangelical history.

More than a century ago, Robert Shindler (a fellow Baptist pastor and close friend of C. H. Spurgeon's) traced the path from apathy to apostasy through several cycles, beginning with the Socinian heresy that arose in the first generation of the Protestant Reformation. Shindler noted that the pattern is always the same. It begins when otherwise good men grow careless with regard to the defense of the faith. They usually begin to stress the moral teachings of the New Testament and neglect or downplay the "great central truths" of the gospel.[21] When that occurs, Shindler said, it's like being on a steep downgrade. The next steps always involve questioning or redefining the atonement, softening the difficult parts of the gospel, balking at the exclusivity of Christ—and ultimately putting every vital truth of Christian orthodoxy up for grabs. The further you move, the more you gain speed—and the harder it is to stop the descent.

Describing the rise of deism and unitarianism at the end of the Puritan era, Shindler wrote,

> As is usual with people on an incline, some who got on "the down grade" went further than they intended, showing that it is easier to get on than to get off, and that where there is no brake it is very difficult to stop. [They] may not have dreamed of denying the proper deity of the Son of God, renouncing faith in his atoning death and justifying righteousness, and denouncing the doctrine of human depravity, the need of Divine renewal, and the necessity for the Holy Spirit's gracious work, in order that men might become new creatures; but, dreaming or not dreaming, this result became a reality.[22]

Shindler was drawing a comparison between earlier apostasies and the modernist drift that was beginning to derail the late nineteenth-century evangelical movement. The emerging wisdom of Shindler's and Spurgeon's time insisted that if the church did not adapt her methods and message to accommodate modern thought and style, Christians would lose their influence and their religion would become irrelevant.

Shindler and Spurgeon strongly opposed that idea, of course, and sounded a shrill warning about the dangers of such a strategy. They were written off or decried as alarmists and unsophisticates by the Christian mainstream of their era.

---

21. Robert Shindler, "The Down Grade," *The Sword and the Trowel* (March 1887), 122. Charles Spurgeon, of course, was the publisher of *The Sword and the Trowel,* and this was the first of a series of articles that launched the infamous "Down Grade" controversy, which consumed the final years of Spurgeon's life and ministry.
22. Ibid., 124.

But before the twentieth century was half over, the bitter fruits of modernism completely vindicated both the substance and the shrill tone of every warning Spurgeon, Shindler, and like-minded evangelicals ever published.[23] The mainline denominations in America, virtually all of whom embraced modernist principles in quest of greater relevance, actually lost influence and membership as a result. Churches that fought modernism and held onto evangelical principles invariably grew and gained influence—until they began to forget the dangers of the downgrade and started on the downward path themselves—some via the path of neo-evangelical compromise; still more through the avenue of seeker-sensitivity; and now even more by way of the ECM.

The similarities between nineteenth-century modernism and the ECM of today are uncanny. Some of the most popular bromides of the ECM are ringing echoes of arguments that were used by Victorian modernists—including the suggestion that penal substitution is too harsh a model for understanding the atonement; the claim that too much stress on orthodoxy undermines orthopraxy; and the incessant pleas for liberality and tolerance—even while leading voices in the movement are systematically attempting to dismantle the biblical foundations of evangelical belief.[24] The only thing remarkable about the current descent is the astonishing speed and utter heedlessness with which the downgrade is now being traversed.

The ECM's tenacious commitment to unbridled diversity is one of the major factors making that downward inertia so difficult to arrest. It is practically impossible to make any defense of the faith or refute error when diversity is deemed virtuous and certainty is written off as inherently arrogant. How can faithful shepherds keep wolves at bay—or indeed, why should they—if being tolerant is truly a higher virtue than being right?[25]

Perhaps that is why the New Testament commands Christians to pursue unity, not diversity.

23. A comprehensive collection of documents regarding the "Down Grade" controversy, taken mostly from *The Sword and the Trowel* and other primary sources, is available in paperback from Pilgrim Publications, Pasadena, TX. A similar collection of documents is freely available online at http://www.spurgeon.org/misc/dwngrd.htm.
24. Spurgeon's replies to the modernist proposals of his day work remarkably well as answers to ECM arguments—with no revision whatsoever. I have posted excerpts from Spurgeon at my blog almost weekly for nearly two years, showing how perfectly he answered the rhetoric of the ECM, and I'm nowhere close to running out of material. Spurgeon often sounds remarkably like someone replying to Brian McLaren. A careful reading of his "Down Grade" writings should convince any reasonable reader that the ECM phenomenon is really nothing new. I have suggested elsewhere that even *postmodernism* is a complete misnomer. It really ought to have been called Modernism 2.0.
25. Doug Pagitt (founding pastor of Solomon's Porch, an ECM congregation in Minneapolis) gave his perspective on the ECM's hierarchy of Christian virtues: "To meet face to face, to create our own language, to create our own expression really matters to us. To have creativity and art and beauty matters. It's more important for us to feel like we're representing a beautiful expression of our life with God than it is to be right about everything. . . . We would just as soon be careful about being a people of peace and of beauty and of goodness and not have to be right." Quoted in Kim Lawton, "Interview: Doug Pagitt,"*Religion & Ethics Newsweekly,* July 8, 2005, http://www.pbs.org/wnet/religionandethics/week845/interview4.html.

Self-Defense

The same broad diversity that has virtually eliminated doctrinal boundaries in the ECM is also the movement's favorite self-defense. As we've seen, classifying subgroups or currents within the ECM is nearly impossible and only marginally helpful because the movement is full of people who don't fit nicely into *any* category. In good postmodern fashion, they consciously resist labels and try to live outside the margins as much as possible anyway. Some of them seem just as irked by those who merely attempt to categorize them as they are by those who aggressively criticize them.

That means almost any *general* criticism leveled at the ECM can be deflected or dismissed by saying the critic is painting with too broad a brush. On the other hand, *specific* criticisms cannot possibly apply equally to everyone in the ECM. So whatever complaint the critic makes, the critique is judged invalid. When critics notice liberal tendencies in the ECM, someone will point out Mark Driscoll's crypto-fundamentalism as a significant exception. If, on the other hand, the critic is a liberal or egalitarian who thinks Driscoll sounds misogynistic or reactionary, he will be assured that Driscoll is an anomaly who by no means represents the overall direction of the movement. Practically every critical analysis of the ECM can be—and has been—deconstructed by similar means.[26] But those are evasions, not answers, and meanwhile, the menagerie of errors continues to circulate and be sampled by people in the ECM, as if all this diversity is a wonderful and positive development.

It's not. Nowhere does Scripture suggest that diversity—least of all, *doctrinal* diversity—is a virtue. Quite the opposite. "Diversity" at Corinth was the source of most of that church's difficulties—which is the reason Paul wrote, "I appeal to you, brothers, by the name of our Lord Jesus Christ, that all of you agree, and that there be no divisions among you, but that you be united in the same mind and the same judgment" (1 Cor. 1:10).

The ECM's thoughtless celebration of unbounded diversity is a deadly trait. The idea that diversity is somehow intrinsically virtuous is rooted in postmodern principles rather than biblical truth. It fosters apathy toward sound doctrine and a passive attitude toward error. It makes wayward Christians impervious to correction. It's an idea borrowed from the world, and it has no business in the church.

---

26. The ECM's renunciation of D. A. Carson's *Becoming Conversant with the Emerging Church* (Grand Rapids: Zondervan, 2005) is a case in point. The book is a helpful and perceptive critique, explaining the ECM's contempt for most kinds of certitude and tracing the movement's postmodern roots. It is generally well-documented, understandable, thorough, and thought-provoking. Carson makes many strong points against commonly-held ECM viewpoints. But within the ECM, the book is usually disregarded or treated with a kind of sneering contempt. Yet the one argument most frequently made against the book is that Carson focused too much of his criticism on Brian McLaren, who (as we are constantly reminded by some of the same people who enthusiastically recommend his books) doesn't speak for the whole movement. Scot McKnight, for example, began his *Christianity Today* article about the ECM with this offhand dismissal: "Carson's book lacks firsthand awareness and suffers from an overly narrow focus on Brian McLaren and postmodern epistemology" (McKnight, "Five Streams of the Emerging Church," 35).

10

Entrapment: The Emerging Church Conversation and the Cultural Captivity of the Gospel

MARTIN DOWNES

~~~~~~~~

Ideology of a Dictatorship

It is said that the triumph of a dictatorship is not when it has to censor its subjects, but when its subjects are willing to censor themselves. This happens to the church when it accepts the ideology of a dictatorship above its confession of Jesus as Lord. But the form of the dictatorship need not be represented by a nation state. It can also be found in the way that the thought forms of the age exert control over their subjects. When this happens, the gospel becomes a lost message. It no longer sounds distinctive but resonates with the sound of the culture. This does not necessarily mean that people are kept from hearing about Jesus, the good news, the Bible, or the cross. The words themselves may remain, but their content is altered by, and adapted to, the dominant cultural worldview. And the frightening thing is that this can be done willingly and with the best of motives. In seeking to communicate the gospel to the culture it is possible for the church to be assimilated by the mindset of that culture.[1]

---

1. I suspect that this will be a key controversy in the twenty-first century not only as the present relationship of gospel and culture is being examined but also in the assessment of the relationship between them in church history. This is evident in present rejections of penal substitution as an alleged product of Western culture and in the general assessment of evangelical theology as the product of modernism.

In this chapter I will argue that prominent figures in the emerging church conversation have already crossed a line on this issue and that this has entailed the cultural entrapment of Christian doctrine.[2] I believe that this has been done sincerely and out of a genuine desire to reach the emerging culture with the gospel. In saying this I am not accusing them of outrightly denying all essential doctrines at this moment. Neither am I applying this criticism to everyone who identifies with the emerging church movement. Yet it is the case that some doctrines have received sharp criticism and rejection, such as substitutionary atonement, God's righteous retributive justice, inerrancy, and eternal hell. And if they have not been denied outrightly, a case could be made for the blurring, downplaying, and recasting of other doctrines. Neither for that matter am I proposing the logical fallacy of the slippery slope argument—that these leaders will deny essential doctrines if they keep moving in this direction.[3] Rather, by adopting a mindset that undermines our confidence in holding to any doctrines in an unequivocal way, or that gives changing culture the lead role in determining the shape of the gospel, essential Christian doctrines have already effectively become imprisoned by the culture. The very idea of dogma, of doctrines that are definite, decided, and fixed, is under question. What I will argue is that a wrong move has been made from the start in relating the gospel to the culture that carries with it the entailment of cultural captivity. Or to state the matter in a different way, the relationship between divine revelation, culture, and theology has been wrongly configured so that doctrine is no longer believed, taught, and confessed as it once was or now ought to be.[4]

The accusation of cultural entrapment has of course been made against evangelicalism by one of the most well-known of emerging thinkers, Brian McLaren. He made this point in a 2005 PBS interview:

> We think that the church has, in many ways, already accommodated to modernity. And so the Christian message has become a product almost, and it and the methods of spreading it are like sales pitches. We feel that it has been individualized. It's almost

2. I chose the adjective *prominent* because there is simply no plausible way to deny that there are well-known, easily recognizable figures associated with the emerging church movement and emergent village. The protestation that the views of certain figures (e.g. Brian McLaren) on specific issues should not be equated with the position of all who identify with the emerging church (as if we could lump them all together) is a valid point, since no one figure ever speaks for a whole movement (not even John Calvin), but is not sufficient to deflect all criticism and concern. I appreciate also that quoting Brian McLaren has an emotive effect on defenders of the emerging church conversation.

3. The slippery slope argument suffers at the hands of friends and critics alike. It is made to explain and do too much in prosecuting error. Likewise opponents of it are quick to point out its logical limits (what may happen, what is possible, not what will happen). But error is not merely a matter of being intellectually wrong but includes the "rectitude of the heart." For all its alleged logical inadequacies the slippery slope argument has demonstrable historic precedent and is undermined by an approach to orthodoxy that limits it to a checklist of affirmatives.

4. Although evidence could be provided of the orthodoxy of the authors I will cite on several points, it is the qualified nature of their positive comments that causes concern. It is as if what is given with the right hand is taken away by the left.

like we have personal computers, and now we have personal salvation. And there's not so much attention to what's going on in our world. What about the social dimensions of our faith, that sort of thing? What we're trying to do is say, "We've already overaccommodated to modern culture. We've commodified our message; we've turned our churches into purveyors of religious goods and services."[5]

Some of this criticism of evangelicalism is both valid and entirely appropriate. To the degree that sectors of evangelicalism have adopted a dominant marketing philosophy toward church, evangelism, and doctrine, it is true that they have accommodated themselves to the mindset of the culture and not the Word of God. Doubtless this too has been done out of a sincere desire to reach the culture with the gospel. But in that process, how the gospel has been heard (form and style) and what has been heard (content) have both been negatively impacted. Which is another way of saying that the culture has been allowed, willingly by the church, to influence the church's message and doctrine. The reality is that in seeking to faithfully pursue mission, *all churches* face the same challenge of relating their confession of Christ in the gospel to the culture that they are seeking to reach.

McLaren of course is not alone in making this charge about evangelicalism's cultural compromise. It seems to be a common critique among those who participate in the emerging church conversation, and it is a point that has been made well by many evangelicals concerned about the doctrinal state of the movement.[6] But the emerging critique of evangelicalism is not confined to church growth methods; some of it also extends to the doctrinal heritage of evangelicalism. This too is charged with being tainted and compromised by modernism.[7] Nonetheless, the answer to how we should respond to emerging postmodern culture is not to be found in becoming a new kind of postmodern Christian. In fact we may be surprised to find that postmodernism is not the only factor behind some emerging alternatives to the traditional evangelical position. It is the presenting issue, but in and of itself it does not explain some of the key distinctives found in the emerging movement. We will see that some of the proposed theological changes have deep affinities with the response of a former generation to modernism and their appraisals of evangelical orthodoxy. My contention is that along with a cultural adaptation to the emerging postmodern culture it is possible for us to discern in the emerging movement some of the theological distinctives of liberalism.[8] Of course there are significant discon-

5. A transcript of the interview is available at http://www.pbs.org/wnet/religionandethics/week846/interview.html.
6. See for example David F. Wells, *Above All Earthly Pow'rs: Christ in a Postmodern World* (Grand Rapids: Eerdmans, 2005), 263–309.
7. Tony Jones, Brian McLaren, Nancey Murphy, John Franke, and the late Stanley Grenz have all made this charge.
8. Of course in making this argument I am not suggesting that all who wish to identify with "emerging" approaches to ministry are predisposed to embracing liberal or post-liberal theologies. People participate in this broad movement for many reasons and from different theological backgrounds.

tinuities as well as continuities at work here. Nonetheless, I will argue, the relationship between the gospel and culture for some has been a recapitulation of the liberal methodology.

Responding to the Rise of the Emerging Postmodern Culture

It goes without saying that we are living in a period of massive cultural change at many levels. As the tide of Christendom has receded over the last two hundred years, the church in the Western world no longer holds its privileged cultural position. This decline, most notably in Europe, with the additional impact of multiculturalism, has forced upon the church the need to rethink mission. It can no longer be assumed that people in the West know even the basic story line of the Bible or basic Christian doctrines. Analyzing this transition and responding to it has become something of a preoccupation for evangelicals. How this has been conducted over the last ten years by emerging church thinkers is fascinating in itself. The shift has been away from thinking in terms of generational approaches to ministry and toward grappling with the advent of postmodernism. We could characterize this as a shift from focussing on ministry methods to a realization that the changes that the church must face have more to do with philosophy and worldview. Of course there is no unanimity in all of these assessments as to exactly what postmodernism is, or even if it exists.

Recognizing this, it will not be essential in this chapter to pin down a precise definition of postmodernism or even to establish that we are in fact in a new postmodern culture. Rather, the questions to be explored are bound up with our disposition toward the culture and the gospel. If we are in a period of significant cultural change, from modernism to postmodernism, how should the church respond to this new situation? Should there be a change of message as well as a change in methods as the church continues its mission in an emerging culture?

A deliberate change of approach, because of a change in the culture, seems to me to be a central idea to the emerging church. As Carson has written, "at the heart of the emerging reformation lies a perception of a major change in culture."[9] Furthermore, he asks the question that ought to be on our lips as we assess emerging church proposals: "Is there at least some danger that what is being advocated is not so much a new kind of Christian in a new emerging church, but a church that is so submerging itself in the culture that it risks hopeless compromise?"[10] The position adopted by some prominent figures in the emerging church movement seems to entail much more than merely recognizing changes in culture and working out their implications for mission. Rather it is that the emerging postmodern culture has radical implica-

9. D. A. Carson, *Becoming Conversant with the Emerging Church: Understanding a Movement and Its Implications* (Grand Rapids: Zondervan, 2005), 42.
10. Ibid., 44.

tions for how we think about knowledge, faith, and doctrine. It raises questions about what we can be certain about. In fact it legitimizes raising questions about everything. As one leader put it, "there should be nothing that is not on the table for reconsideration."[11] This transition has irrevocable consequences for the church since this change in the culture, from modernism to postmodernism, effectively demands a change in theological method and in theology.

In the film *Awakenings*, Robert De Niro's character, Leonard Lowe, wakes up from a thirty-year coma, the result of a mysterious sleeping sickness that afflicted him as a child. His doctor, played by Robin Williams, has to help him adjust to the world that he now finds himself in, a world that has changed dramatically and irreversibly over those decades. In many ways this is a suitable picture of the concerns of the emerging church. The church, especially in the West, has to wake up to a new situation. However uncomfortable and disconcerting it may be, the church has to change radically if it is to survive. As we will see, this cultural analysis seemingly acts as a nonnegotiable authority. For some it appears to act as a theological control through which the faith is perceived. If postmodernism burst the bubble of modernity and exposed the deception of universal reason, it has put in its place the recognition of a vast number of perspectives. None of these are privileged vantage points. All of them are "situated" in language and culture.

Consider the following observations from the widely acclaimed book, *Emerging Churches*, by Eddie Gibbs and Ryan Bolger: "If the church does not embody its message and life within postmodern culture, it will become increasingly marginalized. Consequently, the church will continue to dwindle in numbers throughout the Western world."[12] And,

> A major transformation in the way the church understands culture must occur for the church to negotiate the changed ministry environment of the twenty-first century. The church is a modern institution in a postmodern world, a fact that is often widely overlooked. The church must embody the gospel within the culture of postmodernity for the Western church to survive the twenty-first century.[13]

Now, if by "embody" they mean something like becoming or being "culturally appropriate," then we would easily be able to identify a spectrum of approaches among evangelicals with both good and bad practice. If we infer that they mean that churches really need to pay attention to the world and lifeview of those they are seeking to bring the gospel to, and then communicate the gospel to that intended audience, this would be good mission practice. There is no clearer example of this than Paul's ap-

11. Doug Pagitt, "Also, Doug Does…" December 29, 2004; Tony Jones, "De Trinitate," Theoblogy Weblog, December 29, 2004, http://theoblogy.blogspot.com/2004/12/de-trinitate.html.
12. Eddie Gibbs and Ryan K. Bolger, *Emerging Churches: Creating Christian Community in Postmodern Cultures* (London: SPCK, 2006), 8.
13. Ibid., 17.

proach to the Jews in Antioch and to the pagan intelligentsia in Athens recorded in the book of Acts. After all, we ought to know and care about the way that the people we are seeking to reach think and live, if we want to be faithful to Scripture. But it seems that Gibbs and Bolger are saying more than this. Their conclusion also includes the embodiment of the church's "message" within postmodern culture. But what will this mean for the gospel? How can the gospel be embodied in a postmodern view without being governed by that worldview? This is a point that we will need to return to once we have felt the force of their conclusion for the future of the church.

On this analysis it would be fair to say that the advent of postmodernism has precipitated something of a crisis for the church. Even if we grant that the assessment of Gibbs and Bolger is a genuinely sober realization that the church finds itself in a new world facing new challenges, does their certainty of demise follow from this? Notice that they insist that the church *must* embody the gospel in a new way to survive. Is this not altogether too shrill a sound, given that it rests on their perspective on cultural change? And what if their reading of culture is wrong? As Michael Horton notes, "Postmodernism is the new code word for mission, a new way of enforcing not just change but particular changes that have particular ideological assumptions. One can detect a note of fatalism in challenges that verge on bullying: 'Get with it or get left behind.'"[14] The fear of obsolescence itself can easily be transformed into a coercive dogmatism once a movement discovers the way forward, the "magic formula," for reaching the culture. But there is nothing new in this situation, despite claims to the contrary.

Retreading the Path of Protestant Liberalism

The challenge of responding to a changing culture is precisely what confessional churches faced first in Europe and then in America during the Enlightenment. As with our own day, the pressure was felt acutely in the realm of knowledge, although (again as in our own day) the changes were at the same time being felt in every area of life. Perhaps it should not surprise us to find J. Gresham Machen documenting the profound effect of cultural change in the 1920s and the inevitable effect this had upon the church:

> The rise of modern naturalistic liberalism has not come by chance, but has been occasioned by important changes which have recently taken place in the conditions of

14. Mike Horton, "Better Homes and Gardens," in Leonard Sweet, ed., *The Church in Emerging Culture: Five Perspectives* (Grand Rapids: Zondervan, 2003), 110. Frederica Mathewes-Green adds that "in the 1970s we Episcopalians in the charismatic renewal used to say similarly that parishes would be 'charismatic or dead in 10 years.' Boy, were we wrong," ibid. Likewise Dan Kimball writes that "I also don't think that the 'emerging' way is the new great way, or that if you aren't 'emerging' you are submerging, sinking, and useless. Or that some are 'in' or 'out,' depending on if you are emerging or not," Dan Kimball, "The Emerging Church and Missional Theology," in Robert Webber, ed., *Listening to the Beliefs of the Emerging Churches: Five Perspectives* (Grand Rapids: Zondervan, 2007), 84.

life. The past one hundred years have witnessed the beginning of a new era in human history, which may conceivably be regretted, but certainly cannot be ignored by the most obstinate conservatism. . . . *What is the relation between Christianity and modern culture; may Christianity be maintained in a scientific age?* It is this problem which modern liberalism attempts to solve.[15]

There are of course clear discontinuities between the route chosen by liberals and by the choices facing the church in the twenty-first century. The submission of supernaturalism in general, and the miraculous in particular, to rationalism is clearly one of these differences. Our own time has seen an increasing return to spirituality and less optimism being placed in unbiased human reason.[16] Yet we do encounter in this comparison the same fear of the church being left behind as the culture moves on. This is the very same challenge to the church now posed by the emerging postmodern culture. Consider the words of Doug Pagitt:

> It seems to me that our post-industrial times require us to ask new questions, questions that people 100 years ago would have never thought needed asking. Could it be that our answers will move us to re-imagine the way of Christianity in our world? Perhaps we as Christians today are not only to consider what it means to be a 21st Century church, but also—and perhaps more importantly what it means to have a 21st Century faith. The answers to all these questions will have an impact on how our faith communities are structured . . . and even how we understand the gospel itself.[17]

The advent of modernism, however, proved to be nothing short of disastrous for confessional churches. It would seem that the anxieties expressed by Gibbs and Bolger were felt a century ago by George Tyrell, the Catholic modernist. David Wells writes that Tyrell

> believed that if the Church did not adjust to the modern world it would be destroyed. She "seems like some little Alpine village," he once remarked, "doomed by the slow resistless progress of a grinding glacier. Can she change now, even at the eleventh hour, and plant herself elsewhere?" How could the Church do this and avoid its demise? The answer, Tyrell said, was that it had to adapt itself to the thought forms of the age, creating a synthesis out of "a careful criticism of Catholicism on the one hand and of the modern culture on the other."[18]

15. J. Gresham Machen, *Christianity & Liberalism* (Grand Rapids: Eerdmans, 1923), 2–3, 6 (emphasis added).
16. But not exclusively; there is clearly still a market for books like Richard Dawkins's *The God Delusion* (Boston: Houghton Mifflin, 2006).
17. Doug Pagitt, *Reimagining Spiritual Formation: A Week in the Life of an Experimental Church* (Grand Rapids: Zondervan, 2004), 4–5.
18. Wells, *Above All Earthly Pow'rs*, 278.

And it is not too much to claim that the solution offered by Gibbs and Bolger resonates with this earlier response to cultural change. The same mindset could also be found in Shailer Mathews, theology professor at the University of Chicago. Again Wells summarizes: "Shailer Mathews devoted a chapter in his *The Faith of Modernism* to the question: 'Is Christianity Outgrown?' He went on to speak of modernism as the 'projection of the Christian movement into modern conditions,' as moving from the outside to the inside of culture."[19]

It is worth quoting Shailer Mathews's observations on "Current Religious Tendencies" and the changes that the scientific worldview was making upon the church:

> Older churches and theologies are not passing away, but religion, while conserving the elements of the past, is experiencing readjustment of emphasis upon doctrines. . . . This elevation of vital rather than dogmatic interests makes it possible for men of different views to co-operate in expressing their common faith in Jesus as the revealer of the salvation of God the Saviour. Religion, even among those most loyal to doctrinal regularity, is finding active expression in social service, the removal of injustice, the attempt to abolish war, and the fusion of the Gospel of Christ with the expansion of Western civilization.[20]

It is not hard to see parallels with the emphases of the emerging churches.[21] Is there really a significant difference in the mindset of those who wanted to replant the church in an emerging modern culture and those who want to embody the gospel in the emerging postmodern culture? If there is no significant difference, then confessional Christianity has once more been subverted by the tyranny of culture.

Is This Comparison Fair?
By drawing an unfavorable comparison with the mindset of Protestant liberalism my critique is open to the challenge that I am demonizing the emerging churches. After all, accusing someone of looking and sounding like a liberal could be a rhetorical ploy for emotive purposes. This is after all what happens when the comparison is drawn between conservative evangelicals and the Pharisees. However valid the analogy may be, you cannot help but feel that it creates prejudice as much as it informs. Knowing that, for those who value orthodoxy, liberals are the pariahs of the Christian world, is it fair to be claiming an identification between them and some emerging thinkers? In the first part of this chapter I set out to show the comparable

---

19. Ibid., 278–9.
20. Shailer Mathews, "Current Religious Tendencies," in A. S. Peake and R. G. Parsons, eds., *An Outline of Christianity: The Story of Our Civilization*, vol. 3, *The Rise of the Modern Churches* (London: Waverley, n. d.), 333–34.
21. Well illustrated by the words of Holly Rankin Zaher, "We partner with others who seem to embody kingdom values and are doing kingdom work, even if they are not 'orthodox' Christians," quoted in Gibbs and Bolger, *Emerging Churches*, 53.

situation of liberal and emerging church responses to significant changes in the culture. In the next section I will show that there are well-known and influential figures who have in fact destabilized orthodoxy by taking their lead from the culture instead of from Scripture. But before I demonstrate the validity of this comparison, it is worth hearing from some voices that have raised the same concerns from within emerging church circles, and to consider how the pressure to conform to the wisdom of the world has been a constant danger for the church.

Listening to the Beliefs of the Emerging Churches

In his assessment of the five written contributions from Mark Driscoll, John Burke, Dan Kimball, Doug Pagitt, and Karen Ward, on emerging church beliefs, Robert Webber admits "the language of the writers does not have the clarity most desire. They do not speak in familiar categories. Their thoughts on theological issues seems slippery and difficult to pin down."[22] This is a little wide of the mark since Driscoll is robustly evangelical on the Trinity, Scripture, and the atonement.[23] Kimball is likewise clearly evangelical in many of his views and stakes his flag on an inspired Bible and the importance of the Nicene Creed. Furthermore John Burke not only stresses the importance of Scripture but is strongly, and perhaps surprisingly, evidentialist in his approach to apologetics.[24] Nonetheless, Webber poses some key questions as he summarizes the five views: "So we ask, 'Are they really evangelicals?' or *'Are we witnesses to an emerging evangelical liberalism?'* if indeed those two words can be comfortably used together."[25] At least three times in his final analysis Webber links the contributors together, "except Driscoll," noting that "the other four do not deny the faith, they simply ask you to join the quest to figure out how the faith speaks in a new culture."[26] However, this does not prevent concerns being raised by the contributors to the concessions being made to the emerging culture. In his chapter John Burke articulates the right relationship between gospel and culture, when he says that "theology must seek to answer the questions of the culture without conforming to the culture. We must let our culture's questions help us better conform to truth and God's revelation."[27] Later he adds an ominous warning: "One fear that I have for the emerging church is that we will cut loose from the anchor of the authority of the Scriptures in hopes of relating to our relativistic culture."[28] He then adds, "I think the emerging church will find itself stranded on the shoals of post-

22. Ibid., 195.
23. His chapter is entitled "The Emerging Church and Biblicist Theology."
24. Burke seeks to demonstrate from biblical and extra-biblical history the validation of Jesus as the Messiah through fulfilled prophecy, Webber, *Listening to the Beliefs*, 61.
25. Ibid., 195 (emphasis added).
26. Ibid., 200.
27. Ibid., 54.
28. Ibid., 61.

modernity if we separate from Scripture as our final authority."[29] But as we will see, there is no hypothetical "if" at all. This is precisely the kind of embodiment of the gospel in the emerging culture that is going on. Driscoll has stated the matter bluntly elsewhere:

> I had to distance myself, however, from one of many streams in the emerging church because of theological differences. Since the late 1990s, this stream has become known as Emergent. The emergent church is part of the Emerging Church Movement but does not embrace the dominant ideology of the movement. *Rather the emergent church is the latest version of liberalism. The only difference is that the old liberalism accommodated modernity and the new liberalism accommodates postmodernity.*[30]

The Perennial Problem Facing the Church

The entrapment of the gospel by the culture is not a relatively new phenomena in the history of the church. It is much older than the capitulation of confessional churches that went on during the Enlightenment. In one form or another it has been a perennial problem. When the church faces the pressure of open, external persecution, it is something like the unsubtle attack made in *The War of the Worlds*. There is the direct contrast of the world and the church, and the active destruction of the church by physical attack. But the church also faces an internal pressure that is often hidden. This is the pressure of theological compromise. The attack upon the church from within, by heretics who reconfigure and redefine the faith, is like *The Invasion of the Body Snatchers*. This point was made by Tertullian: "Heresies, at the present time, will no less rend the church by their perversion of doctrine, than will Antichrist persecute her at that day by the cruelty of his attacks, except that persecution makes martyrs, [but] heresy only apostates."[31] Heresy is the takeover of the gospel by an alien worldview. A foreign element subverts, regulates, and determines a new shape to Christian belief. But this does not happen openly; it happens under the guise of orthodoxy. As G. P. Fisher put it:

> When Christianity is brought into contact with modes of thought and tenets originating elsewhere, either of two effects may follow. It may assimilate them, discarding whatever is at variance with the gospel, or the tables may be turned and the foreign elements may prevail. In the latter case there ensues a perversion of Christianity, an amalgamation with it of ideas discordant with its nature. The product then is a heresy. But to fill out the conception, it seems necessary that error should be aggressive and

---

29. Ibid., 62.
30. Mark Driscoll, *Confessions of a Reformission Rev.* (Grand Rapids: Zondervan, 2006), 150 (emphasis added).
31. Tertullian, *Prescription against Heresies*, chap. 4, http://www.earlychristianwritings.com/text/tertullian11.html.

should give rise to an effort to build up a party, and thus to divide the Church. In the Apostles' use of the term, "heresy" contains a factious element.[32]

We see this impulse at work within the New Testament. It is the root cause of the Corinthian error about the resurrection. Paul counters this local manifestation of error by showing its implications for the resurrection of Christ, the integrity of gospel proclamation, and the future judgment of believers. Interestingly, he also counters it by asserting the catholicity of belief in the resurrection. We are led to infer from this that the fact and explanation of the resurrection of Christ and his people was under duress from an interpretation of the resurrection that had not originated from the apostolic preaching. It was, therefore, attributable to an alien worldview. And as long as some in the Corinthian church viewed the resurrection through the framework of this alien worldview, they would not believe, confess, or teach it truthfully.

Another example from the Corinthian church is the preaching of the super apostles. Paul makes it quite clear that although their vocabulary was orthodox—after all they spoke of Jesus, the gospel, and the Spirit—the content of those words had been radically changed. Paul writes "For if someone comes and proclaims *another* Jesus than the one we proclaimed, or if you receive *a different spirit* from the one you received, or if you accept *a different gospel* from the one you accepted, you put up with it readily enough" (2 Cor. 11:4). The signs remained (Jesus, Spirit, gospel) but the things signified were not the same as in the apostolic gospel. Irenaeus, in his monumental work, *Against Heresies*, warned about the danger of being "carried off" by false teachers because "*their language resembles ours while their sentiments are very different.*"[33] And Tertullian, again, attributes this subversion of Christian doctrine to the influence of pagan philosophy, "The same subject-matter is discussed over and over again by the heretics and the philosophers; the same arguments are involved."[34]

Furthermore, Hippolytus of Rome makes the same connection between heresy and pagan philosophy: "For from philosophers the heresiarchs deriving starting-points, (and) like cobblers patching together, according to their own particular interpretation, the blunders of the ancients, have advanced them as novelties to those that are capable of being deceived."[35] In addition,

It now seems to us that the tenets of both all the Greeks and barbarians have been sufficiently explained by us, and that nothing has remained unrefuted either of the

---

32. Quoted in B. B. Warfield, "Heresy & Concession," *The Presbyterian Messenger,* May 7, 1896, 672.
33. Alexander Roberts and W. H. Rambaut, trans., *The Writings of Irenaeus*, Ante-Nicene Christian Library, vol. 5 (Edinburgh: T. & T. Clark, 1868), 2.
34. Ibid., chap. 7.
35. Hippolytus, *Refutation of all Heresies*, bk. 5, chap. 1.

points about which philosophy has been busied, or of the allegations advanced by the heretics. And from these very explanations the condemnation of the heretics is obvious, for having either purloined their doctrines, or derived contributions to them from some of those tenets elaborately worked out by the Greeks, and for having advanced (these opinions) as if they originated from God.[36]

From Paul's warning about being taken captive by "philosophy and empty deceit" (Col. 2:8) through Tertullian's argument that "heresies are themselves instigated by philosophy,"[37] and the words of Hippolytus, it is fair to say that Christianity has had a desperately uneasy relationship with philosophy. Doubtless it is the case that the *language* of the ecumenical creeds is indebted to language borrowed from Greek culture. For the sake of clarity and precision this was done. However, that is far different from the approach that took *concepts* derived from pagan philosophy and dressed them up in biblical language. Philosophy terminology has been made into a servant in expressing biblical doctrines, but it has always become a tyrannical master when it has intruded upon the content of Christian faith.[38] Peter Leithart has made some valuable observations on this point: "It would be a distortion to say that classical theism is Hellenism in Christian garb. . . . The simple fact that the Church fathers formulated the doctrine of the Trinity shows that Greek philosophy did not function as a straight-jacket that theologians were unable to escape. If Greek philosophy had exercised veto power, we would be Arians."[39] When the presuppositions of the culture control the embodiment of the gospel, the decision has already been made to reconfigure what the gospel really means. This is the perennial danger for the church.

Relating the Gospel to the Emerging Culture
The first priority of the church is not mission but confession. Any emphasis on being missional that is not already clear on what it means to be confessional will misrepresent the person and work of Christ and hinder the work of the church. And without a true confession there is no authentic mission. The liberal theologians and preachers of the nineteenth and early twentieth centuries did not intend to destroy the church. Many of them felt compelled to adopt new theological positions because of the impact of new scientific knowledge. And many of them were seeking to reach their generation with the gospel, or what they considered to be the gospel. So, we return to the issue at hand. Has orthodoxy been destabilized by key emerging church leaders tak-

36. Ibid., bk. 9, chap. 26.
37. Ibid., chap. 7.
38. This is perhaps particularly misunderstood in the post-Reformation period. For the distinction of scholasticism as a method and not a way of determining theological content, see Richard A. Muller, *Post-Reformation Reformed Dogmatics*, vol. 1, *Prolegomena to Theology* (Grand Rapids: Baker, 2003), 34–37.
39. Peter J. Leithart, "Trinity, Time and Open Theism," in Douglas Wilson, ed., *Bound Only Once: The Failure of Open Theism* (Moscow: Canon, 2001), 126.

ing their theological lead from the culture instead of from Scripture just as the liberals did? The form that the cultural entrapment of the gospel takes, of course, differs according to the dominant thought form of the day. We will explore this by examining the representative views of Doug Pagitt and Brian McLaren.

Doug Pagitt on Theology and Culture

Doug Pagitt was one of the contributors to the recent volume *Listening to the Beliefs of the Emerging Churches*. For Pagitt theology is essentially both personal and confessional. He says that there is "no way to remove ourselves from our theology."[40] Indeed "theology is the living understanding of the story of God in play with the story of our lives."[41] The plural is important, too, since "the true nature of one's theology is in the life lived and the community it is lived within."[42] This insight makes Pagitt question just how accurately his theology can be understood apart from his community.

As he articulates the shape of his theology, Pagitt emphasizes two controlling principles in his thinking: the dynamic nature of theology and the role of context or culture in forming theology. The dynamic principle is that theology really is "the story of God *in play* with the story of our lives." Theology is not the story of God, and it is not our story.[43] Our stories change and our understanding of God's story changes. When this happens our theology should change too.[44] Theology, he says, is "explanatory—answering certain questions or addressing certain issues. But it must never be confused with the life of God or the story of God."[45] Theology then must be living, dynamic, and ever changing. If it is not, it becomes "dogma, history, or a collection of random facts."[46]

The second principle at work is the cultural context. Pagitt explains the importance of recognizing this: "Theology is always human. It is people who create theology as a tool of our culture to explain reality as we see it. So we all operate from a context. We think in categories given to us by our language and culture. Theology is not a culturally neutral act."[47] It would be fair to say that Pagitt has an aversion to the Bible being handled apart from the recognition of the way it is embedded in a culture. He says that "many of us who hold the Bible in high regard have the unfortunate habit of trying to theologize, or moralize, the Bible to serve our context."[48] Moreover, he says, "What I find objectionable about this is that it

40. Doug Pagitt, "The Emerging Church and Embodied Theology," in Webber, *Listening to the Beliefs*, 120.
41. Ibid., 121.
42. Ibid.
43. Ibid., 123.
44. Ibid.
45. Ibid.
46. Ibid., 121.
47. Ibid., 123.
48. Ibid., 125.

removes the context and places authority in the fact that a statement is in the Bible rather than considering the faith and lives of the people involved."[49] What we need, says Pagitt, is a "more contextual understanding of what the Spirit is saying to us in our day in order to live into it."[50] The canonical Scriptures certainly have authority in our lives and faith,[51] but "Christians have never been intended to be a people only of a book but a people who are led by the ever present God, active in our lives, communities and world."[52]

Doug Pagitt on the Way That the Gospel Changes

Given the dynamic and contextual principles for theology, where does that leave our understanding of the gospel? Does the gospel change? Pagitt is careful to stress that his community (Solomon's Porch, Minneapolis) takes seriously the faith of those who came before them. Moreover, even when one has factored in the influence of culture, he says, this does not mean that there was a "total undoing" of the Christian understanding from the first to the third century, but the change was *immeasurable*.[53] There was a change in the understanding of the gospel, specifically what makes it good news. We would be "unwise and uninformed to consider it to be simply saying the same things with new words."[54] Lest we misunderstand the implications of what this means for the way that the gospel changes over time, it is worth weighing the following words that set the agenda for church life and gospel proclamation. He writes, "We are called to be communities that are cauldrons of theological imagination, not 'authorized re-staters' of past ideas. What we have in our communities are not simply people who need to have the gospel applied to their lives, but people who need to know their situations and what the Good News of God means for them."[55] Finally, not only do we need to figure out what the gospel means for us now, we also need to bear in mind that the ever changing nature of the gospel has a bearing on how we view and relate to past statements of the gospel: "The development of creeds, refined statements of belief, and explanation was not driven by a desire to keep the news the same. It was driven by a desire to allow the story of God to make sense in their day to a people with a story different from the Hebrews, and most certainly different than many of our stories today. The Greek converts to Christianity in the first through third centuries had to understand the gospel in their setting and not only in the first-century Hebrew setting."[56]

49. Ibid.
50. Ibid.
51. Ibid.
52. Ibid., 126.
53. Ibid., 127.
54. Ibid., 126–27.
55. Ibid., 129.
56. Ibid., 127.

The Cultural Context for Doing Theology

While there are many interesting issues that Pagitt raises I will focus on those directly related to the relationship of gospel and culture. My argument has been that, faced with modernism, Protestant liberals let the culture control their theology. In the end, as Francis Schaeffer contended, "liberal theology is only humanism in theological terms."[57] What if the proposal being offered here is more like postmodernism in theological terms? What will this do to the gospel?

There is a certain ambivalence in Pagitt's approach. He claims that his view of atonement is shaped more by ideas similar to those prevalent during the time of the biblical story than it is by the Greco-Roman understanding that so influenced some of the early church's understanding. He characterizes the Greco-Roman view as being built around a "judicial model of separation."[58] But is this biblical view itself the product of ancient culture? Is this culture normative for today? Was it normative for the early church or was the church just contextualizing the atonement for its culture when it proposed a judicial model? Was the early church wrong to do that? Is it part of God's story? Quite simply, if Pagitt's view of the atonement corresponds in some way with the biblical view, as he claims, then would it not be misguided, if not malicious, for us not to be "authorized re-staters" of the gospel? Or is he treating this Greco-Roman view of the atonement as a theological corruption that replaced an authentic biblical view? Was this the insidious effect of the culture on the gospel? If so, does this not chasten his appeal for us to change when the worldview changes?

In his response to some of the other authors in *Listening to the Beliefs of the Emerging Churches*, Pagitt is quick to attack appeals to the Bible and just as quick to defend the controlling influence of culture. He is troubled by Driscoll's use of the Bible (but without offering any alternative explanations, it seems) and argues that "such a view denies the reality of the development of language and the pressure of culture."[59] Furthermore he says, "I am not advocating a postmodern reading of the Bible for everyone [unless that is your culture and then there is nothing more one can do], but I am suggesting that people cannot legitimately operate with no cultural lens."[60] The statement in brackets is problematic. It amounts to a prison cell for the gospel. Of course we must grant the presence of culture, and be aware of it. It is neither possible nor desirable to deny the presence of culture. But will revelation not be able to critique culture, even postmodern culture? This takes us back to how we configure God's story and theology. David Wells, speaking about the recent trend in writing contextualized theologies, has said that, "somewhere in the making of each of its

---

57. Francis A. Schaeffer, from *A Christian Manifesto*, in *The Complete Works of Francis A. Schaeffer: A Christian Worldview*, vol. 5, *A Christian View of the West* (Wheaton, IL: Crossway, 1994), 442.
58. Ibid., 134.
59. Ibid., 43.
60. Ibid., 44.

works the fatal step was taken to allow the culture to say what God's story should sound like rather than insisting that theology is not theology if it is not listening to God telling his own story in his own way."[61] Of course we can take wrong turns in theology. But unless our story is the story of God, in Scripture, all we have is the sound of our own voices. Just how much does our understanding of God's story change? Pagitt seems to be saying that it changes from culture to culture and age to age. If that were so then we would only have gospels to tell and no gospel at all, no faith once delivered to the saints that the saints in every age confess.

Creeds, Confessions, Orthodoxy, and Heresy

We encounter further problems with Pagitt's view of culture when we consider his handling of creeds and theological error. In response to Dan Kimball's claim that the conclusions of the Nicene Creed transcend any time period, and would be the same conclusions that we would draw if we were grappling with the issues, Pagitt stresses that creeds are statements of belief made in certain contexts and that they do not "constitute some sort of timeless doctrine of finality."[62] From a certain point of view this is true. The fathers who met at Nicea and formulated a confessional statement of the Trinity used the language of their culture as they sought to confess what the Scriptures taught about God. The Niceno-Constantinopolitan Creed has a context in the debates of its own day. But that is simply to state the obvious. What is more disconcerting is that Pagitt consistently criticizes the other contributors for their use of the Bible, and stresses the discontinuity of theological formulations. Despite what he claims about the development of the creeds not being driven by a desire to keep the news the same, this is precisely what the succeeding generations who compiled the ecumenical creeds understood themselves to be doing.[63]

Another area of concern is Pagitt's explanation of the debate between Augustine and Pelagius. He sees this as largely personal and political, not doctrinal. Moreover, he wants to explain the doctrinal conflict as a clash of cultures, with Pelagius's Celtic spirituality and druidic understanding of God and humanity born with "the Light of God aflame within them, if even dimly lit" clashing with Augustine's Greek understanding of God "taken primarily from the Greek Pantheon imagery" that viewed human beings as born separate from God. These two approaches were bound to conflict, the one "finding the goodness in creation and organizing the church to live in harmony with the God of the earth," the other for "the Greeks of Augustine's land" with their "Roman spirituality" calling for "an explanation of how one might

---

61. Ibid., 7.
62. Ibid., 114.
63. Jaroslav Pelikan, *Credo* (Yale: Yale University Press, 2003), 9–14, and see also Brett Kunkle's paper "Essential Concerns Regarding the Emerging Church," given at the Evangelical Theological Society's Annual Meeting, November 2006.

appease the removed God living in an 'elsewhere heaven.'"[64] Pagitt illustrates this with different dances being appropriate for different songs, with songs and dances working together, and dances changing when the songs change. This helps to understand the relationship of the cultural worldview and religious understanding. Augustine and Pelagius had a different song in their head and different steps on the dance floor. And he concludes from this that "we must never get to the place where we allow our worldview to be stagnant; it must always be changed by the dance," and "so it is with cultural worldviews and understandings of theology."[65]

Yet Pelagius and his followers also held to the orthodox view of the Trinity as expressed in the Nicene Creed in common with Augustine and the catholic church. The role of culture in forming Pelagius's view of human nature was recognized at the time. But this was not thought to be attributable to druidic origins. Jerome said that Pelagianism was the heresy of "Pythagoras and Zeno." In other words this was an instance of the takeover of Christianity by an alien worldview. Herman Bavinck summarized the origins of the Pelagian view of humanity: "In voicing these ideas, Pelagius did little more than take over the views that had been promulgated long before by Greek and Roman philosophers and had found acceptance in popular philosophy."[66] Far from being an instance of the way that theology cannot help being shaped by culture it was in fact the paganizing of Christian doctrine. Culture did have a role in this, but Pagitt's explanation of it is inaccurate. Pelagianism was later, but not too much later, condemned as heresy. This interpretation of such a well-known and clear-cut controversy goes against Pagitt's comments elsewhere concerning the way that Solomon's Porch looks to church history in order to handle heresy.[67] And surely Pagitt's explanation of the influence of Greek culture on the theology of the Latin speaking, North African, Augustine is also inaccurate. Is he suggesting that Augustine's orthodoxy was a product of culture? That the decisive element in his doctrine of God was borrowed from paganism? At the least Pagitt's use of this incident is historically misguided. But if he thinks that culture can give such explanatory power to the orthodox and heretical sides of this controversy, it seems that we cannot avoid concluding that essential Christian doctrines are entrapped by the culture. And that would make orthodoxy variable and unstable across time and culture, and without authority to be believed on the sole authority of the Word of God.

Brian McLaren on Changing the Message as Well as the Methods

Like Doug Pagitt, Brian McLaren argues that the message of the gospel changes and not just the methods that we use to communicate it. McLaren relates how discon-

---

64. Ibid., 128–29.
65. Ibid., 129.
66. Herman Bavinck, *Reformed Dogmatics,* vol. 3, *Sin and Salvation in Christ* (Grand Rapids: Baker, 2006), 86.
67. Quoted in Kunkle, "Essential Concerns," 9–10.

certing this realization was as he read church history, fielded questions from post-modern seekers, and interacted with Christians from other backgrounds.[68] Previously, he had thought that only our methods should change. In relaying his story, McLaren highlights his realization that the theory of the atonement celebrated by his tribe as the heart of the atonement, namely penal substitution, was largely unknown before Anselm and was not central for other Christians.[69] We are also told of his encounter with a card-carrying "liberal Christian" who pointed out to him the "obvious difference between the gospel of Jesus and the gospel about Jesus."[70] Today McLaren's gospel pays more than a passing resemblance to this description.

With all this in mind McLaren has come to the conclusion that the gospel is a story that is cumulative, performative, catalytic, many-versioned, many-faceted, many-layered, and Christ-centered. He says:

> If you ask me about the gospel, I'll tell you, as well as I can, the story of Jesus, the story leading up to Jesus, the story of what Jesus said and did, the story of what happened as a result, of what has been happening more recently, today even. I'll invite you to become part of that story, challenging you to change your whole way of thinking (to repent) in light of it, in light of him. Yes, I'll want you to learn about God's grace, God's forgiveness, about the free gift of salvation. . . . But for me that will just be a footnote to a gospel that is much richer, grander and more alive.[71]

For McLaren, when the gospel stops being about Jesus, it stops being the gospel. But what each culture hears about Jesus varies according to its own distinctives. The culture determines the gospel it hears, or needs to hear. So liberation theology was an articulation of the gospel for the poor in Latin America,[72] and ecology is important for the gospel McLaren now preaches. The gospel of heaven instead of hell, he says, may have been the answer people in the Middle Ages needed when they were faced with death daily, but may be a ghost of the "real gospel that Jesus talked about."[73] Although he does believe that the gospel has facets that deal with the forgiveness of sins, he feels that it would be unfaithful to define the gospel by that one facet when

68. Brian D. McLaren, "The Method, the Message, and the Ongoing Story," in Sweet, *Emerging Culture*, 194–98. Incidentally Tony Jones also uses the rhetoric of changing the message as well as the methods we use. He has said, "We do not think this [the ECM] is about changing your worship service. We do not think this is about . . . how you structure your church staff. This is actually about changing theology. This is about our belief that theology changes. The message of the gospel changes. It's not just the method that changes," quoted in Kunkle, "Essential Concerns," 10.

69. Ibid., 195. He has since attacked and repudiated penal substitutionary atonement. For counter evidence that penal substitution has historic pedigree well before Anselm see Steve Jeffery, Michael Ovey, and Andrew Sach, *Pierced for Our Transgressions: Rediscovering the Glory of Penal Substitution* (Wheaton, IL: Crossway, 2007), 161–204.

70. Ibid., 197.

71. Ibid., 214–15.

72. Ibid., 211–12.

73. Ibid., 213.

other gospel concerns like "justice, compassion, sacrifice, purpose, transformation into Christlikeness, and hope," are not addressed.[74]

But if the culture shapes the expression of the gospel this much, a fact that naturally would lead us to reimagine and "figure out the gospel" for our own day, why did Jesus direct his apostles to his suffering, death, and resurrection foretold in the Scriptures and command them to preach repentance and forgiveness of sins in his name to the nations (Luke 24:44–48)? McLaren's foil in all this is the stylized gospel of his own church background. He refers to this reduced gospel several times and sees it summed up in the sinner's prayer, four laws, and decisions for Christ limited to getting into heaven. It is tempting to excuse McLaren's excess as a reaction against his conservative church background. But for several reasons this should be avoided. For one he is far too old to be blaming his church background. For another he is far too well-read to have simply followed the pendulum in the other direction.

By giving changing culture the lead role in how the gospel is expressed, McLaren has transferred the word *gospel* away from what God has done in Christ and freely used it about matters that are, at best, consequences of the impact that the gospel makes when it is believed. But this move is illegitimate since the biblical gospel defines the very reason why it is needed, and it does so in such a way that deals with the redemption of a new humanity and the coming of a new creation. The biblical gospel deals with the cosmic effects of sin and the curse and not just the eternal destiny of individuals.

One of the reasons why culture has been given a free hand to shape the gospel is that the many-versioned, Christ-centered gospel story McLaren offers has not been shaped sufficiently by the Bible. For example he says that there are facets or layers that deal with sin and guilt and others that deal with hope, the future, justice, compassion, individuals, humanity, and politics:

> But all of these versions, facets, and layers center in Jesus Christ. If Christianity has anything to say at all, if it has a message worth repeating at all, then at the core is Christ. And not just a facet of Christ or an idea about Christ, not just a theory about Christ's birth or death or resurrection or teaching or deity, but Christ himself, Christ the person, Christ the figure who came to us in the story we call the gospel.[75]

This is a somewhat confused, and confusing, statement to make. How can we speak of Christ apart from what we know about him? The Christ we are meant to know and who saves us is never an "uninterpreted Christ." He is either rightly interpreted or wrongly interpreted. How can he be the *object* of saving faith unless we know things about who he is and what he accomplished? A false faith would be faith placed in a wrongly interpreted Christ. Isn't that Paul's point about the super apostles in

74. Ibid.
75. Ibid., 200.

2 Corinthians 11? They preached *"another* Jesus." By a rightly "interpreted Christ" I mean that the Christ of the Bible and the apostles' proclamation is never separated from what God has said about him (his person and his work). Take away God's interpretation of Christ from our experience of him and you are left with either a mystical Christ, of whom we know nothing and whose name serves merely as a religious word, or a false Christ (and there are many in history who have fit this description). Detach right ideas from Christ and his work and you are left either with nothing, or with a false Christ. There is no uninterpreted Christ. We need God's explanation of him in order for us to call on him.

In a sense this is what McLaren has concluded since he locates Christ "in the story we call the gospel." But precisely because the story in the canonical gospels explains and interprets Christ, it makes no sense to speak of Christ himself apart from "facets," "ideas," or "theories." Not that these are interpretations that we are free to create, evaluate, or embrace as we see fit according to our culture or location in history. When the apostle Paul in 1 Corinthians 15 records the apostolic testimony about the gospel that was universally proclaimed and believed, he stresses that this is the authorized interpretation of Christ. He gives the facts. That Christ *died*, was *buried*, and was *raised on the third day*. He gives the meaning of those facts. That Christ died *for our sins*, and that without his resurrection from the dead we would still be in our sins. And he tells us where that meaning is authoritatively interpreted for us. Christ died for our sins *according to the Scriptures*.[76] There simply is no other Jesus than this one. And since that is the case, what we may say about him in the gospel is nonnegotiable. It cannot and must not change. It is certainly not amenable to the whims of human thought and cultural change.

How then does McLaren view those who don't change the gospel message? Are they doomed to face obsolescence?

> This view means that those who stick by old methods and old formulations are not wrong; they may in fact be doing exactly what Jesus wants them to do, addressing the gospel to enclaves that need it exactly as they are expressing it. Or—perhaps more importantly—they may be preserving certain facets of the gospel that will be needed in a decade or century or two. Again, you never know when or how much you'll need something you almost threw away or cut down and burned.[77]

Notice that this unchanged gospel is suited to "enclaves" while presumably the new message addresses the new emerging culture. Let us be clear: on this view the audience is king.

76. I owe this helpful division and explanation of the text to an insightful sermon by Dick Lucas.
77. Ibid., 215.

Orthodoxy, Orthopraxy, and Culture

G. K. Chesterton once wrote that "heresy always affects morality, if it is heretical enough." It is true to say that any form of error, and not just heresy, will show itself in some form of deficiency or delinquency in the life of the church and the Christian. If we follow the logic of Paul in the Pastoral Epistles, we should expect false theologies to produce ungodly behavior. But there is a subtle danger with Chesterton's observation. The danger is that we will form in our minds a narrow and set idea of what that immorality could look like. And, based on that assumption, we will then expect those who are theologically compromised to be immoral only in that particular way. Yet in the history of the church there have been those who clearly and definitely embraced and taught error who were known for their personal moral integrity. In fact men as notorious as Pelagius and Faustus Socinus were respected in just this way. You would expect the opposite to be true. But there is more to it than a simple, straightforward, personal moral failure.

Recent writings on orthopraxy have stressed the outworking of orthodoxy in terms of changed Christian behavior along the lines of the fruit of the Spirit. Sometimes this has been married with an affirmation that this kind of orthopraxy is in fact what orthodoxy is really all about. What has been neglected, in my estimation, is the stress on orthopraxy at the very point where it connects to orthodoxy. This is the kind of orthopraxy that values guarding the good deposit, of being found trustworthy with the mysteries of God, of rightly handling the word of truth, of keeping the faith, of holding firm to the trustworthy Word as taught. These things are also included in biblical orthopraxy—so much so that a failure here may have eternal consequences for preacher and listener alike. Such a failure is exacerbated when those guilty of it continue to exhibit this kind of ungodliness. A refusal to be corrected and to hold onto views that deviate from the gospel is itself a form of immorality and ungodliness. If we do not hold firmly to the gospel, then we will have a chronically misshaped orthopraxy at a vital point. And, it should be said, it is a failure that will only be corrected by repentance.

Have you ever been waiting at a train station, sitting patiently at your seat, while next to you another train is likewise waiting to leave? And then, as the train starts to move, for a few seconds you are not sure if your train is the one moving or if it is the next train that is starting to pull off. The way to be sure is to look at the platform. The platform, after all, doesn't move. So it is in an age of cultural change. Our ultimate authority here is Scripture. This is exactly where Paul directs Timothy as he seeks to be faithful in an age of change. He is to continue in what he has learned and has firmly believed (2 Tim. 3:10–17). This is the fixed point for doctrine.

11

Saved from the Wrath of God: An Examination of Brian McLaren's Approach to the Doctrine of Hell

GREG D. GILBERT

~~~~~~

No small number of books and articles has been written lately on the subject of hell. Some of these treatments are attempts to rethink and perhaps even reformulate the traditional Christian doctrine of hell as a real place of eternal conscious torment for unbelievers. Others are written to defend that traditional understanding. The main contours of the argument are fairly easy to identify and follow. Those who would reformulate the traditional doctrine fall broadly into two camps: *universalists*, who argue that Scripture teaches the final salvation of everyone without exception, and *annihilationists,* who argue that unbelievers are finally destroyed, or otherwise go out of existence altogether. Of course there are various positions and nuances within each of these general categories. Annihilationists, for instance, may argue that the destruction of believers is due to the direct punitive action of God, or they may argue for a position called "conditional mortality," according to which a special act of God's power is necessary to maintain a soul in existence after it is separated from the body. In the case of unbelievers, then, that special act of sustaining power is withheld, and the soul returns to nonexistence.

However numerous the positions in this argument, the common thread among them is that they are all attempting to say something about hell's ontology, or substance—whether or not it is real, and if so, what it might be like. Yet it is precisely the desire to stop having that conversation that makes the work of Brian McLaren unique and worth a careful look. A widely-read author and a recognized leader in the emergent church, McLaren has articulated a sweeping vision of the gospel of Jesus Christ, one which challenges the traditional understanding of Christ and the meaning of his life and death on many different levels.[1] One of the more important charges he makes is that the traditional Christian doctrine of hell is simply insufficient. What he finally proposes is that the church should stop focusing on the question of whether hell is real, what it will be like, and who will be there, and start focusing instead on the doctrine's practical effects.

In this essay I hope to offer an accurate, concise summary of McLaren's approach to the doctrine of hell and then make a number of critiques about both his theological method and his conclusions. I conclude that it is McLaren's reimagining of hell, not the traditional doctrine, that proves insufficient. His attempt to turn the doctrine of hell primarily into a rhetorical tool fails both biblically and philosophically, and when he is finally forced to confront hell's substance, what he proposes is wholly insufficient when compared to the Bible's teaching. Moreover, McLaren's deficient rethinking of hell seems to have sprung from his deficient rethinking of the gospel, and there is the most serious problem. For in the end, his struggle to be rid of the traditional doctrine of hell is finally only a symptom of his having misunderstood the gospel of the kingdom.

A Summary of McLaren's Treatment of the Doctrine of Hell

While McLaren writes about hell occasionally in several of his books, the vast majority of his thinking on the subject is found in the third book of his A New Kind of Christian trilogy. *The Last Word and the Word After That* brings to a close the story of Daniel Poole, a fictional pastor who in the first book of the trilogy met an affable Jamaican man named Neil Edward Oliver (Neo), who leads him over the course of the story to rethink his understanding of the entire Christian faith and gospel. In this final book, it is Daniel's discomfort with hell that comes to the fore, and Neo (who is now going by simply "Neil") helps him discover a new way of dealing with the Bible's teachings about it.

Before moving on to a summary of McLaren's ideas about hell as articulated in his books, it is worth pausing to note that any project of critiquing McLaren's work is an inherently dangerous enterprise. That is because a good deal of his writing is fictional, and his theological views are placed in the mouths of characters with whom McLaren himself sometimes agrees, and with whom sometimes he does not. In fact, he is careful to warn that the total viewpoint of any one character should not be understood as being his own. Sometimes he even has a character say something with much assurance in the book's text, and then only in the notes at the back of the book says something

---

1. Other chapters in this volume have dealt ably and at length with McLaren's views about the kingdom of God and its relation to the gospel of Christ. See especially Guy Waters's contribution.

like, "The situation is a bit more complex than Dan and Neil realize."[2] Similarly, McLaren several times in his fictional writing cites books by authors called "Maundet" and "Berton and Chase," and only in the endnotes does the reader find out that no such authors exist. The words attributed to them are written by McLaren himself, though they are cited amidst dozens of other real authors of widely varying viewpoints.[3] In one sense, that is all very well. The author of fiction is king in the world he creates. Nevertheless, the distance McLaren has constructed between his written words and his own thoughts by doing his theology in fiction calls for an extra degree of care. So I have tried to be careful to note in my reading when I think McLaren may be exaggerating through the words of one of his characters, or when I think he might not hold as strictly to a certain idea as one of his characters might seem to. On the other hand, McLaren is dealing with very real ideas, and he is obviously writing in order to persuade. So I have not hesitated to impute the ideas of McLaren's characters to McLaren himself when it has seemed justified to do so. When one of his characters offers an idea or makes a statement that is allowed to stand without objection or refutation, I have taken that idea to be one which McLaren himself would be willing to espouse.

At various places in his books, McLaren mentions several different reasons for his discomfort with the traditional doctrine of hell. Sometimes he puts the matter in stark emotional terms, other times more philosophical. One reason McLaren would rather be rid of the traditional doctrine is that, in his view, it implies a capricious, vindictive, and almost sadistic God. The idea that God is love and yet would "fry your butt in hell" is simply "wacky" and unworthy of Christianity.[4] So McLaren dedicates his book *The Last Word* to those who are "seeking for a God to love but have been repulsed by the ugly, unworthy images of a cruel, capricious, merciless, tyrannical deity." In a similar vein, McLaren cannot seem to imagine that Jesus would allow for any person to spend eternity in conscious torment: "Everything I know about Jesus," says one of McLaren's characters, "tells me he would go down there and get them out."[5] Furthermore, he objects to the traditional doctrine of hell because of its effects on Christians' behavior. By putting so much emphasis on the afterlife, he argues, the doctrine of hell minimizes human injustice, shifts focus from justice in this world to salvation in the next, and in the process allows people to take the name "Christian" and still commit atrocities of ostracism and even genocide.[6]

In light of all this, McLaren wants desperately to move away from questions about what hell is, or who might be there. In short, he wants to avoid the debate about hell's substance that I briefly described above:

2. See, for example, Brian McLaren, *The Last Word and the Word After That* (San Francisco: Jossey-Bass, 2005), 189.
3. Ibid., 195.
4. Ibid., 75.
5. Ibid., 32.
6. Ibid., 61, 83, 85, 135, for example.

Personally, while I believe these reflections [on annihilationism, universalism, etc.] are valuable, I lean toward the conclusion that they are trying to answer questions that aren't the best questions to ask, even though those questions do inevitably energize our curiosity. The language of hell, in my view, like the language of biblical prophecy in general, is not intended to provide literal or detailed fortune-telling or prognostication about the hereafter, nor is it intended to satisfy intellectual curiosity, but rather it is intended to motivate us in the here and now to realize our ultimate accountability to a God of mercy and justice and in that light to rethink everything and to seek first the kingdom and justice of God.[7]

In other words, to ask what finally happens to the wicked in eternity is not the right question, nor is the debate between traditionalists, annihilationists, and universalists the right conversation to be having. Instead, Christians ought to be talking about how the idea of hell functions in our lives. Does it lead us to ostracize and hate other people, or does it spur us on to realize that God wants no one to be an outcast from his kingdom? As Neo puts it sharply, "It's none of your business who does and does not go to hell. It is your business to be warned by it and to run, not walk, in the opposite direction! . . . Now stop speculating about hell and start living for heaven!"[8] McLaren calls this idea, learned from Lesslie Newbigin, "predicamentalism."[9] Instead of leading Christians to speculate on the eternal fate of other people, it focuses them on their own lives, their own predicaments.

"Its Best Good Work": The Rhetorical Purpose of Hell
In order to arrive at this "predicamental" understanding of the Bible's teaching on hell, McLaren embarks on a project of deconstructing the traditional doctrine. He is entirely straightforward in saying that this is his goal, and contrary to its popular reputation, he understands the process of deconstruction to be a good thing. "The word *destructive* is often associated with the word *deconstructive*, but the association is erroneous. Deconstruction is not destruction; it is hope."[10] By clearing away the accumulated traditions, customs, and expectations about certain ideas, he argues, we may be able to see something much better than that with which we started. "It's like taking apart a cheesy billboard that somebody built along the highway so that people can see the beautiful view the billboard was hiding."[11] The best way to do this work of deconstruction is by doing history. By tracing the development of an idea through time, one can perhaps get behind current formulations of that idea to the original motivations and forces that gave rise to it in the first place.

---

7. Ibid., 188–89.
8. Brian McLaren, *A New Kind of Christian* (San Francisco: Jossey-Bass, 2001), 126. See also Brian McLaren, *A Generous Orthodoxy* (Grand Rapids: Zondervan, 2004), 122–24.
9. McLaren, *New Kind of Christian*, 126. See also McLaren, *Last Word*, 103.
10. McLaren, *Last Word*, xvii.
11. Ibid., 106.

McLaren begins his project of deconstructing the idea of hell by asserting that the ancient Jews thought very little about the subject:

> One thing was clear to me, I explained: hell was not "revealed" in the Old Testament. Nowhere did a Hebrew prophet have a vision or dream that revealed the reality of hell. It's never mentioned once in the whole Hebrew Bible. Even the latest books of the Old Testament, thought to have been written about 450 B.C., have no reference to hell. Instead, the idea appears suddenly—to us, anyway—in the Gospels, on the lips of Jesus.[12]

In fact, McLaren asserts, the Old Testament is characterized by a "persistent Jewish disinterest in afterlife."[13] So where did Jesus's idea of hell come from? If not from the Old Testament, where did he get it, and why did it form such an important and frequent part of his teaching?

McLaren proposes that the idea of eternal torment in hell that prevailed in Jewish thinking at the time of Jesus was actually an amalgamation of ideas drawn from four different "threads" of history and belief, as well as one other idea called "the scapegoat factor." Those four threads were the Babylonian (Mesopotamian), Egyptian, Zoroastrian (Persian), and Greco-Roman cultures, each of which represented an important point of contact for the Jews during the intertestamental period. It was from these cultures, McLaren says, that the Jews learned and appropriated ideas about a disembodied afterlife, rewards and punishments after death, and eternal conscious torment. Here is how McLaren, through his character Dan, summarizes the original development of the idea of hell:

> So, it all comes together in the intertestamental period when many Jews, to greater and lesser degrees, are attracted to a belief in life after death. Since they don't have the resources for that in their own religion, they start weaving together elements from the first four foreign threads—the Mesopotamian [Babylonian], the Egyptian, the Zoroastrian or Persian, and the Greco-Roman—with their own key fifth thread: the Messianic.[14]

McLaren adds one other thread, one that "helps explain the prevalence of hellfire rhetoric at several other times in history"—the "scapegoat factor."[15] When people have an enemy they need to ostracize or weaken, he explains, they often make that enemy a scapegoat for whatever is wrong with the world, blaming them for society's ills. Anti-Semites have used Jews for this purpose, he says, and whites have

---

12. Ibid., 45.
13. Ibid., 46.
14. Ibid., 60.
15. Ibid., 61. McLaren credits the "scapegoat factor" to Elaine Pagels, *The Origin of Satan* (New York: Random, 1995).

used blacks. In fact, the scapegoat factor is a universal theme in the history of humankind. In the time of Jesus, the scapegoat factor was in wide use as the Jews tried to explain how they, as God's chosen people, could possibly be languishing under the domination of the Roman Empire. One group in particular, the Pharisees, believed that God had abandoned the nation because of rampant sin in the lives of the people. Thus the Pharisees "scapegoated" the prostitutes and drunks in society, blamed them for Israel's problems, and then brandished the idea of eternal conscious torment to frighten the sinners into stopping their sin.[16]

"Into this scenario," Neil says, "Jesus came. He didn't create the beliefs about hell promoted by the Pharisees and embraced by many of the common people, and he didn't endorse them either."[17] In other words, the doctrine of hell did not come from Jesus, nor was it revealed by God in the Old Testament. It was rather an outgrowth of Israel's contact with pagan cultures. Yes, Jesus appropriated the language of hell for his own purposes, but he did not necessarily accept that language as corresponding to reality.[18] Instead, he took the Pharisees' threats against "sinners" and turned their words back on them. "He was like a practitioner of jiu jitsu—he turned the force of the argument back on the heads of the Pharisees."[19] Jesus' reasons for doing this were many, McLaren says. Besides wanting to protect the old scapegoats, he uses the language of hell to redefine "goodness" and "righteousness" over against the Pharisees. Instead of the "cold, exacting, heartless, merciless" righteousness that the Pharisees demanded, God's righteousness was a matter of mercy and kindness and inclusion, especially for the outcast and the sinner.[20] Through this process, then, Jesus "deconstructs" the Pharisees' idea of hell, "fulfills" it, and "sows the seeds for its own demise and replacement."[21] Where the Pharisees used hell to ostracize undesirables, Jesus used it to teach the folly of exclusion. In other words, "Jesus uses the power language of hell to disempower the injustice of the powerful and to empower the disempowered to seek justice."[22]

Here is where McLaren's deconstruction of hell comes to its point. "Neil," says Dan, "we Christians use the whole doctrine of hell exactly as the Pharisees did! We're

---

16. McLaren, *Last Word*, 62.
17. Ibid., 62.
18. See ibid., 73, and especially 57, where Dan is relieved to realize that Jesus is not "to blame" for the idea of hell. "I guess I'm kind of relieved," he says. "I used to believe that Jesus must have invented all the talk about hell, you know, since it isn't overtly found in the Old Testament. I think a lot of people feel that way: since Jesus is the first to talk about it in the Bible, he was revealing it. But now I realize hell has this long and . . . fascinating history. Jesus isn't to blame for thinking it up" (ellipsis in original). Why is Dan relieved? The only sensible explanation is that his relief comes from his realization that the doctrine of hell is not part of special revelation, neither by God the Father nor by Jesus. Therefore, presumably, he no longer has to believe in it.
19. Ibid., 63.
20. Ibid., 63.
21. Ibid., 74–76.
22. Ibid., 136.

playing on the wrong side!"[23] While we follow the Pharisees' example of using hell to threaten sinners, divide humanity, and mark out those who are excluded from God, Jesus used the rhetoric of hell to threaten the very ones who were doing the excluding, and to show them that God's kingdom is kind, merciful, and compassionate, not cold and exacting. At bottom, McLaren argues, Jesus' use of hell-rhetoric is meant to teach believers the evil of excluding and ostracizing others, and stir them up to "bear fruit now . . . especially in the area of compassion for the weak and needy and vulnerable."[24]

If he were able, McLaren really would like nothing more than to stop the conversation there. Over and over again in his books, he drives home the point that this, the rhetorical *use* of hell, is the point, not whether it really exists or who will be there. To ask such questions is to miss the point of hell entirely. "Daniel!" Neo shouts—and the reader gets the distinct impression that he could just as well insert his own name there—"That's not the point! Can't you see? . . . The point is not whether there is a hell: the point is God's justice! The point isn't whether Jesus—by using the language of the construction—confirms it. The point is, for what purpose does he use the language?"[25] Or as another character writes in verse:

> Hell is not my condition or my destiny. . . .
> Hell is neither state of mind nor lake of literal fire. . . .
> Hell is a warning, and like all warnings, issues
> From love, from wisdom, from better judgement—
> Whether God's or from our own best selves,
> It does not matter.[26] Its purpose, not its substance, is the point. . . .
> Do justice, love kindness, walk humbly with your God,
> And hell has done
> Its best good work, like Nineveh's threatened destruction,
> Which upset Jonah when it didn't occur. Anyway, you
> Can forget about it.[27]

Yes, But Is It Real?—The Substance of Hell

But of course you cannot forget about it. Even if one were inclined to accept everything McLaren says about the rhetorical purpose of hell, the question still remains: But is it real? To his credit, McLaren acknowledges the urgency of that question, and he puts it into the mouth of one of his most likeable characters: "Markus chuck-

23. Ibid., 64.
24. Ibid., 121.
25. Ibid., 71.
26. Another denial of the idea of hell having been revealed by God.
27. McLaren, *Last Word*, 26.

led, 'Of course, even if you buy all that, you're still left with the question of what hell is. Is it real, or is it just a rhetorical device?'"[28]

Before answering that question, McLaren lays some theological groundwork that will allow him to understand the substance of hell in a way that does not correspond to Jesus' words about it. He has Neil propose that perhaps Jesus did not intend for his words about fire, worms, and torment in hell to be understood literally, but rather that he used the language of hell as a "truth-depicting model," similar to what scientists do when they portray the atom as a group of balls with other balls swirling around them. "We use those models," Neil says, "even though we know they aren't literally true."[29] Even so, such models are not considered untrue, much less a lie, McLaren argues, because they are the best humans can do in their attempts to explain the concept lying behind them. They are "truth-depicting" and "truth-conveying." Perhaps this is what Jesus was doing with the language of hell: using a truth-depicting model, but without necessarily endorsing that model as the literal truth.[30]

With that established, McLaren floats a number of trial balloons in answer to the question of hell's substance, but it is never clear exactly what he believes on the matter. At times, he seems to be flirting with universalism and annihilationism, but then he usually backs away at the last moment. In *A New Kind of Christian*, for example, the reader is treated to a sermon on death and judgment by Neil in which he reads a portion of C. S. Lewis's *The Last Battle*. In the story a soldier who had spent his entire life serving the evil god Tash meets the great Lion Aslan, a representation of Christ. The soldier is fearful that Aslan will punish him for his service to Tash, but to his surprise, the Lion says to him that any good service he has done for Tash, he will account as service done for him.[31] The reader could be forgiven for thinking that Neo (and McLaren through him) was hinting toward a universalist understanding of the judgment. Not so. When Dan questions him about the sermon, Neo explains that the whole thing had been a head-fake, a metaphor, evocative language. "I know that moderns don't have much capacity for poetry," he says, "having been enslaved to modern technical correctness for so long. But Jesus—Jesus was allowed to be evocative in his language. Shouldn't we—or should I say, shouldn't you, as a pastor?"[32]

McLaren also seems at times almost to embrace an annihilationist understanding. In a note at the end of *The Last Word*, for example, he articulates the view of C. S. Lewis in *The Great Divorce* that hell is the process by which God causes wicked souls to shrink and decay into something less and less human and thus less and less capable of experiencing suffering. He then comments that such a thought might bring some

---

28. Ibid., 137.
29. Ibid., 72.
30. Ibid., 73.
31. McLaren, *New Kind of Christian*, 92.
32. Ibid., 95.

relief in the face of eternal conscious torment.[33] In the same note, McLaren also offers for consideration the position of author Jonathan Kvanvig, who proposes a modified annihilationism in which hell is understood as a continuing descent of the wicked soul toward utter nonbeing, but with the possibility that the final choice actually to finish the disintegration is left to the wicked soul itself.[34] Finally, however, McLaren demurs without commenting either positively or negatively on this position, reiterating his position that such questions about hell's substance are the wrong ones to ask.[35]

Beyond all this, there is one other conception of hell's substance that shows up repeatedly in McLaren's works. It finds its way into the mouths of several different characters, and is stated in several different ways. Because of its ubiquity, it seems reasonable to assume that this understanding of what hell might actually be is the one McLaren would most readily claim as his own. Put simply, hell is judgment. It is standing naked before the Creator and finding out that one's life has been wasted, that all one's years have been used not in the service of God's love and compassion, but rather for causing others pain and sorrow, for oppressing and ostracizing, and for working against God's good plan for his world. The character Markus puts it perhaps most clearly:

> Here's what I'd say. Judgment is real. Accountability is real. A good, just, reconciling, loving, living God is in everybody's future. The danger of wasting your life and ruining other people's lives is real. Whatever road you take, you'll end up facing God, and that means you'll face the truth about your life—what you've done, who you have become, who you truly are. That's good news—unless you're a bad dude, you know, unjust, hateful, unmerciful, ungenerous, selfish, lustful, greedy, hard-hearted toward God and your neighbor. You know, if God judges, forgives, and eliminates all the bad stuff, there might not be much left of you—maybe not enough to enjoy heaven, maybe not enough to feel too much in hell either.[36]

Put another way, people should not think of their eternal destiny as location in heaven or hell, but rather as relation to God. For those who lived in accordance with Jesus' teachings of love and compassion, to be in the presence of the all-merciful and all-compassionate God will be exquisite joy. For those who lived in opposition to God's plan, to be in his presence will mean agony, if not outright nonbeing.[37]

A Critique of McLaren's Treatment of the Doctrine of Hell

A comprehensive critique of McLaren's understanding of hell would begin with a restatement of the Bible's teaching on the subject and a refutation of the annihila-

33. McLaren, *Last Word*, 186–87.
34. Jonathan Kvanvig, *The Problem of Hell* (New York: Oxford University Press, 1993), 146, 168.
35. McLaren, *Last Word*, 188–89.
36. Ibid., 137.
37. Ibid., 164. See also McLaren, *New Kind of Christian*, 130.

tionist and universalist positions with which McLaren seems sometimes to flirt. Such an extensive project need not detain us here, since there are resources readily available that already have taken up and accomplished both those objectives.[38] Our unique interest is in McLaren's project of trying to turn the church's conversation away from the ontology of hell and toward its rhetorical use. Has McLaren's historical deconstruction of hell succeeded? Is he right to say that Christians have been distracted from the real meaning and purpose of the Bible's hell language? It seems to me that McLaren's reconception of the traditional doctrine of hell as primarily a rhetorical tool falters on at least two counts. First, his historical deconstruction of the doctrine is simply false. Second, in his description of Jesus' purpose in using the language of hell, he draws a false dichotomy between *warning* and *assertion of what is true*. Moreover, it seems to me that his proposal for how to understand hell's substance is woefully subbiblical, and confusing to the extreme. But it is to his case that hell's primary meaning is rhetorical that we first turn.

McLaren's Historical Deconstruction of the Doctrine of Hell

We have already seen that McLaren begins his deconstruction of hell by examining its history. He concludes that since the Old Testament contains no hint of the subject, the Jews must have picked up the idea from the cultures in which they were immersed during the intertestamental period: the Babylonians, Egyptians, Zoroastrians, and Greeks. Neither of those two assertions, however, comports with the facts of history.

First, it is simply not the case that the Old Testament contains no hint of the idea of hell. True, the word itself is not used, and we must acknowledge that what teaching there is about the eternal judgment of the wicked is not extensive. But there can be no doubt that when the ancient Jews looked forward to the great and awesome Day of the Lord, part of their hope was that God's enemies—and theirs—would be judged.[39] It is true that the hope of Israel seems to have been mainly an earthly one, tied to matters of land, throne, and power. But there are a few passages in the Old Testament that quite clearly reach beyond this life to an afterlife, a part of which will be the eternal punishment of the wicked. Take Daniel 12:2, for example, which speaks of the resurrection of the wicked "to shame and everlasting contempt." N. T. Wright and others have shown convincingly that while its immediate context is the return of the nation from exile, this passage undoubtedly looks forward to a bodily

---

38. For a statement of the Bible's teaching on the subject of hell, see the essays by Daniel Block, Robert Yarbrough, Douglas Moss, and Gregory Beale in Christopher W. Morgan and Robert A. Peterson, eds., *Hell Under Fire* (Grand Rapids: Zondervan, 2004). See also the systematic theologies of Wayne Grudem, Millard Erickson, Louis Berkhof, and Robert Reymond, just to name a few. For refutations of the annihilationist and universalist positions, see the essays by J. I. Packer and Christopher Morgan in *Hell Under Fire*, as well as the treatments of hell in Reymond's and Grudem's systematic theologies.

39. See, for example, Wright's comments on Psalm 73 and 49 in N. T. Wright, *The Resurrection of the Son of God* (Minneapolis: Fortress, 2003), 106–7.

resurrection in which some people will be sentenced to everlasting shame and contempt.[40] Even more to the point is Isaiah 66:24, the verse Jesus himself quoted in Mark 9:48 as a description of hell: "And they shall go out and look on the dead bodies of the men who have rebelled against me. For their worm shall not die, their fire shall not be quenched, and they shall be an abhorrence to all flesh." The fact that Jesus quotes this passage, rather than a Babylonian or Zoroastrian one, as the source of his teaching about hell is quite possibly enough all by itself to refute decisively McLaren's theory about hell's origins. For Jesus understood his teaching about hell to be rooted in the Old Testament's teaching of the punishment of the wicked at the end of the age, not in Zoroastrianism.[41]

Moreover, McLaren's assertion that the Jews had to have learned about the afterlife, and consequently about hell, from the Babylonians, Egyptians, Zoroastrians, and Greeks is simply not borne out by the evidence. Wright has shown decisively in his magisterial work *The Resurrection of the Son of God* that the idea of afterlife and resurrection is a natural outgrowth of Israelite hope and theology. "It would be easy, and wrong," Wright says, "to see the hope for the resurrection as a new and extraneous element, something which has come into ancient Israelite thinking by a backdoor or roundabout route."[42] On the contrary, belief in the afterlife and resurrection developed from Israel's faith that their covenant God would restore them from exile, including those who had been martyred for the faith of Yahweh.[43] In fact, Wright specifically refutes the idea that Israel learned of afterlife and resurrection from the Zoroastrians, pointing out that the idea finds its roots well before any likely influence from Persia, and that anyhow it would be exceeding strange if the Israelite idea of resurrection—which they took as the crowning emblem of their special status before God—turns out to have been borrowed from the very people who had the chosen people under foot![44] Now it is true that in all this, Wright's primary focus is not the judgment of the wicked. Nevertheless, if the hope of the afterlife and resurrection arose from within Israelite theology, it is entirely reasonable to imagine a doctrine of eternal punishment for God's and Israel's enemies similarly taking shape as a part of that hope, particularly given passages such as Daniel 12:2 and Isaiah 66:24.

McLaren's assertion that the idea of hell had to have arisen from Babylonian, Egyptian, Zoroastrian, and Greek myths is simply false. There is ample material in

40. See Wright, *Resurrection of the Son of God*, 109–15, and Daniel Block, "The Old Testament on Hell," in Morgan and Peterson, *Hell Under Fire*, 61–64.
41. Remarkably, McLaren mentions the crucial passage of Isaiah 66:24 only once in *Last Word*. It appears in a chart on pages 118–19, and his only comment is that it refers to "dead bodies, not disembodied souls." That is true of the passage in its Old Testament context, but Jesus clearly claimed the text as a source of his teaching about an eternal hell. How likely is it, really, that he was infusing that Old Testament text with an old Zoroastrian idea for mere rhetorical effect?
42. Wright, *Resurrection*, 121.
43. Ibid., 121–28.
44. Ibid., 124–25.

both the Old Testament and the literature of the intertestamental period to establish hell firmly as an extension of the Jewish hope for the resurrection of the righteous and the judgment of the wicked.

McLaren's Use of Speech-Act Theory

At one point in *The Last Word*, McLaren has Neo explain to Dan that his understanding of hell as primarily a rhetorical tool is an example of "rhetorical hermeneutics," also known as speech-act theory:

> "That reminds me—have you ever heard of rhetorical hermeneutics?" Neil asked.
> "Can't say that I have. What's that?"
> "It's an approach to Scripture that among other things tells us that we normally pay too much attention to what the writers are *saying* and not enough to what they're *doing*. Rhetorical interpretation would ask, 'What is Jesus trying to do by using the language of hell, plus all these other negative outcomes—missing the party, having to repay a debt, being cut to pieces, being sent into the darkness outside, whatever?"[45]

From there, McLaren makes his argument that Jesus' point was not to endorse the idea of hell or to suggest anything about its reality, but rather to warn and prod his listeners to do certain things with their lives. I believe McLaren makes two serious errors in his use of speech-act theory, the first of which blunts the force of his argument and the second of which actually turns back on him, jujitsu style, to firmly establish what McLaren is trying to deny.

First of all, in asserting that speech-act theory tells us that we should focus on what Jesus is *doing* with his words rather than on what he is *saying* is only a half-truth at best. He is right that speech-act theory is concerned with what words accomplish when they are spoken, but that does not in any way mean those words can only perform one job at a time. McLaren's major thrust seems to be that when Jesus talks about hell, what really matters is that he is warning his listeners, *not whether he is asserting anything about hell's reality.*[46] But speech-act theory does not say at all that a person can only do one thing at a time with a speech-act, nor is it legitimate to say that the act of warning is more important than the act of asserting. John Searle, one of the pioneers of speech-act theory, said that we do five basic things with our words: "we tell people how things are, we try to get them to do things, we commit ourselves to doing things, we express our feelings and attitudes, and we bring about changes through our utterances. Often, we do more than one of these at once in the same

---

45. McLaren, *Last Word*, 81.
46. It might be objected here that McLaren does allow that Jesus is saying *something* about hell's reality, since he allows that he might be using the language of hell as a "truth-depicting model." Fair enough, but McLaren could hardly be clearer, and he could hardly say more frequently, that the reality of hell is not the point and that compared to its rhetorical use, its reality and nature are unimportant.

utterance."[47] If that is so, then McLaren is guilty of oversimplification and a false dichotomy. It simply is not the case that what words are *doing* is more important than what they are *asserting*. In fact, asserting *is* doing. Thus it is entirely possible that when Jesus spoke of hell, he was actually doing two things of equal importance with his words: warning his hearers to live in a certain way, and asserting something about reality, namely the existence of a real hell.

Not only that, but speech-act theory would suggest that precisely because Jesus was using the language of hell as a warning, he actually *had* to have been asserting its reality at the same time. Kevin Vanhoozer, in his article "The Semantics of Biblical Literature," identifies a number of conditions that must be met in order for a speech-act to be legitimate. One of those is that the speaker must be sincere. So in the case of a warning like Jesus' about hell, "the speaker must really believe that a certain event is not in the best interest of the hearer."[48] Another condition is that the speaker must have good evidence for believing that what he is saying is actually the case. A warning, for instance, is illegitimate if the speaker knows that the event of which he is warning is not actually about to happen. In order for his speech-act to be legitimate, the speaker must have good evidence to believe that the event of which he is warning actually obtains.

Now the upshot of all this is that if Jesus' warnings about hell were legitimate and not frivolous—and we must assume that to be the case—then he cannot simply have been using the language of hell for its rhetorical punch. He must have had some reason to believe that his hearers were actually in some danger. Put another way, if Jesus was warning people about hell, and he did not believe (and have good reason to believe) that there was a real hell, then his warnings were illegitimate, frivolous, and even deceitful, not to mention insincere. For a legitimate warning requires that the speaker truly believe that his listeners are in danger; otherwise the warning is illegitimate and insincere. At the very least, all this would seem to undermine entirely McLaren's rhetoric about the reality of hell "not being the point." In fact the reality of hell *has to be* the point, for Jesus' warnings about it only make sense if he believes it to be real.

This argument is only strengthened when we consider that Jesus was the Son of God—which McLaren happily acknowledges—because then his beliefs about hell would have been based not on merely *good* evidence but on *certain* evidence. As the second person of the Trinity incarnate, Jesus was not simply giving his best guess as to the nature of the afterlife. He had perfect knowledge about it, and thus he knew perfectly and infallibly whether or not hell existed. It follows from this that when

47. John Searle, *Expression and Meaning: Studies in the Theory of Speech Acts* (London and New York: Cambridge University Press, 1979), 29. Quoted in Kevin J. Vanhoozer, "The Semantics of Biblical Literature: Truth and Scripture's Diverse Literary Forms," in D. A. Carson and John D. Woodbridge, eds., *Hermeneutics, Authority, and Canon* (Grand Rapids: Baker, 2005).
48. Vanhoozer, "Semantics," 96.

Jesus warned about hell, he was doing so with the certain knowledge that hell is real.[49] For if Jesus gave such warnings while knowing certainly that hell does *not* exist, then his warnings were beyond insincere and illegitimate; they were lies. Perhaps McLaren would object here that he does in fact acknowledge that Jesus thought his hearers were in real danger; He allows that Jesus' hell language is in some way a "truth-depicting model," though without specifying what reality lies behind that model. Indeed, it is true that Jesus could have been using metaphor to describe the danger of hell. We do not have to take his images of hell literally for his warnings to be legitimate and true. What is simply not allowable, however, is to say—as McLaren so often does—that it does not matter whether Jesus thought there was a hell or not. On the contrary, our very faith in him as the Son of God means that when we encounter his warnings about hell, we understand that behind those warnings is certain knowledge of a real danger. In other words, McLaren is simply wrong to say that Jesus was not asserting anything about hell's reality; for unless we are willing to make Jesus insincere or ignorant or worse, we must understand that implicit in and inherent to his warnings about hell is also an assertion of hell's reality.

McLaren's Proposal about Hell's Substance

What are we to make of McLaren's proposal that hell—if it is anything real at all— might be the experience of standing exposed before God and finding out that your life has been worthless? For one thing, we should note that there seems to be some unreconciled tension in McLaren's own mind about just how unpleasant such an experience would be. On the one hand, he is terribly uncomfortable with the Bible's imagery of hell as a place of everlasting fire and torment. For God to inflict something so horrible on mere human beings would make him cruel, capricious, merciless, and tyrannical.[50] Further, as we have already seen, he finds comfort in C. S. Lewis's suggestion that perhaps one effect of hell is to cause a person to become less and less human and thus less and less capable of suffering. On the other hand, McLaren also wants to say that thinking of hell in his terms is actually *worse* than the traditional doctrine. In fact, it is as serious and horrible a thing as one can imagine. "Nothing can be more serious than that," Neil says. "Compared to that, fire and brimstone are...."[51] At this point, it would not be unreasonable to ask McLaren to decide please whether he'd like to have his cake or eat it. Why is it that the traditional doctrine of hell earns such impassioned prose from him, if his own vision of hell so utterly outstrips it in terms of horror? Does he want hell to be unpleasant or not?

49. Vanhoozer writes on this point: "Divine warnings, since they infallibly fulfill the preparatory condition, will always be true, for God is all-knowing and will not only be justified in thinking that something is not in my best interest; He will be certain of it. When God asserts, His speech act implies that he has *certain* evidence for the truth of His assertion; when God warns, He has infallible reason to believe that something is not in the hearer's best interest." ("Semantics," 98.)

50. McLaren, *Last Word*, dedication page.

51. Ibid., 80 (ellipsis in original). The sentence dramatically trails off.

Even more importantly, the idea that hell consists merely of standing before God and becoming aware of one's own worthlessness does not even begin to do justice to Scripture's language and imagery about the final judgment of God's enemies. From beginning to end, the Bible portrays judgment as God's active retribution against sinners. That is the thrust of the passage Jesus quotes with reference to hell, Isaiah 66:24. The men who lie dead in the valley of Gehenna were those "who have rebelled against me." Similarly, those who are sent away to "eternal punishment" in Jesus' parable of the sheep and the goats (Matt. 25:31–46) are those who did not serve the Son of Man. The people thrown into the lake of fire at the final judgment were those who had served the beast instead of Christ, and who names were thus not found in the book of life (Rev. 20:15). All these are images of retribution, of action God takes in order to punish those who have set themselves against him. McLaren's proposal, which he evidently takes largely from C. S. Lewis's ideas in *The Great Divorce*, ignores all this. In his vision of hell, God is entirely passive. He does not punish his enemies, much less "cast them into hell," as Jesus seems to think he might (Luke 12:5). Perhaps it is most accurate—if we are allowed to take McLaren's metaphor on this point seriously—to say that God simply stares sternly at his enemies, the way a father might stare at a wayward child until the child realizes what an awful thing he has done. For "that," says Neil, "[is] judgment par excellence."[52] McLaren's hell is not one of just retribution; it is one of natural consequences. It does not involve a God who is active in the judgment of his enemies; it involves one who passively allows his creatures to become what they insist on becoming. Neither of these ideas is new, but they both still fall far short of what the Bible says about how God intends to deal with sin.

Finally, McLaren's proposal raises a number of theological questions. Is this annihilationism, or something close to it, like Kvanvig's proposal? Is it a modified universalism where everyone ends up in heaven after all evil is judged, forgiven, and forgotten? Or is it a sort of attenuated exclusivism in the mold of Lewis, where the torments of hell are lessened so as to make the thought more bearable? Moreover, even if we could finally untangle the theological and philosophical confusion here, where exactly would an idea like this—that perhaps God forgives people into oblivion—find any positive support in Scripture? McLaren would surely answer me by saying once again something like, "It doesn't matter. Don't you see you're missing the point? What hell *is* doesn't finally matter. What matters is what the language of hell spurs you to *do*." Furthermore, he could not be clearer (ironically) that the lack of clarity in his understanding of hell's substance does not bother him in the least. "Clarity is good," he says in the introduction to *The Last Word*, "but sometimes intrigue may be even more precious; clarity tends to put an end to further thinking,

52. Ibid., 80.

whereas intrigue makes one think more intensely, broadly, and deeply."[53] In the end, McLaren is willing to trade a clear doctrine he cannot abet for an ambiguity with which he can be comfortable.

The conclusion of all this must be that not one major point of McLaren's proposal for reimagining hell is able to stand up under scrutiny. For one thing, the idea that Jesus used it primarily as a rhetorical tool rests on the premise that the traditional doctrine of hell was not revealed by God—either in the Old Testament or by Jesus himself—but was rather an extraneous appendix to the Jewish faith taken from Babylonian, Egyptian, Zoroastrian, and Greek cultures. As we have seen, that is a position built on numerous historical blunders, as well as a sorely deficient understanding of Israel's faith. Furthermore, the rhetorical hermeneutics McLaren invokes to make his case actually end up working against him. Not only is it perfectly reasonable to think that Jesus could have been doing two things at once with his words (admonishing his hearers with the language of hell *and* making an assertion about its reality), the very fact that he was warning his hearers about it means that he must have had good evidence—indeed certain evidence, given his divinity—that hell really exists and that it is horrible. Finally, when McLaren is at last forced to address hell's substance, what he proposes must be judged to be severely subbiblical, refusing as it does to take seriously the Bible's teaching that God's response to his enemies will be active retribution. Moreover, it actually ends up creating more theological and philosophical confusion than it dispels. In the end, McLaren has offered no good reason to think that Jesus and the apostles intended to convey with their teaching about hell anything other than that it is a real experience of eternal conscious torment of God's enemies.

Whence McLaren's Discomfort with Hell?

One final question remains to be answered about McLaren's handling of the doctrine of hell. Why is he so uncomfortable with the traditional idea of hell as an experience of eternal, conscious torment for the enemies of God? We have already seen some of the reasons he states for his discomfort with the idea, but it seems to me there is another explanation as well, one having to do with his understanding of the gospel of the kingdom. I believe that McLaren's deficient reinterpretation of hell finds its best explanation in his deficient reinterpretation of the kingdom. Essentially, the kingdom he envisions is so present-focused, so socially and politically oriented that it has no obvious place for a doctrine like hell.

Guy Waters has offered in this volume a detailed summary of McLaren's view of the kingdom of God, so we need not remain long on the subject. Suffice it to say that McLaren believes that the church has traded Jesus's "gospel of the kingdom" for a gospel of "getting into heaven after you die." Instead of being concerned with matters of justice and injustice, good and evil on a global scale, the church has been sidetracked

---

53. Ibid., xv.

and hamstrung by the idea of (as Neil puts it delicately) "getting your butt into heaven." What McLaren envisions instead is a gospel that calls Christians to join Christ's mission of working for "God's dream" for the world, that is, what God intends the world to be. Practically, that means Christians will give their lives in compassionate and loving work for the good of humankind, especially for the poor, the outcast, and the oppressed.

Of course there is much in McLaren's telling of this story that is commendable and exciting. Surely he is right that Jesus' message is not merely about the future, and that it ought to have social, political, cultural, artistic, economic, and intellectual ramifications in our own lives. On top of that, what Christian's heart does not long to invade a world of darkness and hopelessness with Jesus' message of love and compassion and salvation? For all its commendable features, however, McLaren's view of the kingdom of God is not sufficient. He has sold the kingdom short, and in doing so he has missed out on a good part of what makes the gospel of the kingdom so glorious. I believe McLaren has made two fundamental errors in his understanding of the kingdom, errors that are strikingly reflective of those made by classic theological liberals: First, McLaren's emphasis is overwhelmingly on the kingdom as present, to the relative neglect of the kingdom as eschatological. And second, his emphasis is overwhelmingly on the kingdom as social and political, to the relative neglect of the kingdom as spiritual.

Concerning the first error—that McLaren's emphasis is overwhelmingly on the kingdom as present, to the relative neglect of the kingdom as eschatological—the first thing we must acknowledge is that McLaren is not wrong to point out that the kingdom of God has a present, here-and-now dimension. He is right that part of the shock of Jesus' message was that the kingdom of God was *at hand*. This was not something that the Jews expected. Based on their reading of the prophets, they expected that the kingdom of God would come in one explosive cataclysm at the end of time, when God himself would descend from heaven, establish his rule in the person of a restored Davidic king in Jerusalem, and subdue all the nations of the world under his dominion. Yet Jesus came preaching that all those prophecies and expectations of the coming kingdom had been fulfilled in him (Luke 4:16–21; Matt. 11:2–6). There was no cataclysm, no explosive descent from heaven, and no end of the world. Yet the kingdom was here—now! McLaren is right to emphasize all that, but there is another dimension of the kingdom that he seldom engages and never truly integrates into his program.

Even after Jesus' declaration that the "Age to Come" had broken into the present age, the expectation of an eschatological consummation of the kingdom remained. Both Jesus and the apostles preached this constantly. Even if we leave aside the prediction of future judgment in Matthew 24–25, given the debate over whether Jesus' words there refer to the eschaton or to the destruction of the temple in AD 70, the fact remains that Jesus frequently told of a final, consummative judgment that would take place sometime in the future. In John 5:28–29, for example, he says, "for an hour is coming when all who are in the tombs will hear his voice and come out, those who have done good to the resurrection of life, and those who have done evil to the resurrection of judgment." In Matthew 25 he tells of the separation of the sheep and the goats—based on their works in this life to be sure, but this is still a picture of a final, eschatological judgment. And how else but eschatologically can his words to the Pharisees be understood? "But I tell you, from now on you will see the Son of Man seated at the right hand of Power and coming on the clouds of heaven" (Matt. 26:64).

The apostles also look forward to a future resurrection and judgment. When Paul reminds the Corinthians of "the gospel I preached to you," he talks about the death and resurrection of Christ and then turns immediately to the resurrection of the dead in eternity (1 Corinthians 15). When he sings a hymn of praise to God for the gospel, he tells the Ephesians they have been sealed by the Holy Spirit "who is the guarantee of our inheritance *until we acquire possession of it . . .*" (Eph. 1:14). A chapter later, he says God has saved us "so that *in the coming ages* he might show the immeasurable riches of his grace in kindness toward us in Christ Jesus" (Eph. 2:7). Peter speaks of a "salvation ready to be revealed *in the last time*" and hopes that the genuineness of his readers' faith will be "found to result in praise and glory and honor at the revelation of Jesus Christ" (1 Pet. 1: 7). The author of Hebrews tells his readers that they are "strangers and exiles on the earth" and that they should look forward to "the city that has foundations" (Heb. 11:10). Finally, despite McLaren's efforts to pull it into the present, the Revelation of John remains a testimony to the eschatological expectation of the kingdom.[54]

Now I must admit here that I do not think McLaren would deny anything in those last two paragraphs. He does look forward to a final judgment, to a resurrection, and to a final consummation. But this eschatological dimension of the kingdom is vastly underemphasized in his books. He says at one point that the present, here-and-now dimension of the kingdom is "more significant" than the eschatological, and he even goes so far as to say that as good as Jesus' work of atonement and redemption is, it is "not terribly important" in terms of this present world and the status quo.[55] McLaren's attention, energy, and focus is all but exclusively on the kingdom as present, and the result is that he ends up with a gospel of the kingdom that is at least as emaciated as he would charge other Christians' eschaton-focused gospel of being.

With regard to the second error—that McLaren's emphasis is overwhelmingly on the kingdom as social and political, to the relative neglect of the kingdom as spiritual—any fair reading of his books will come to the conclusion that he sees the

54. See his treatment of Revelation in Brian McLaren, *The Secret Message of Jesus* (Nashville: W Pub., 2006), 171–72.
55. McLaren, *Story We Find Ourselves In*, 116; McLaren, *Secret Message of Jesus*, 33.

gospel of the kingdom primarily in political and social terms. Neo puts it like this, over and over again: "I think what Jesus was about, and really, what all the apostles were about at their best moments . . . was a global, *public* movement or *revolution* to bring holistic reconciliation, a reconnection with God, with others, with ourselves, with our environment. *True* religion, *revolutionary* religion. That's what got them in such trouble."[56] In other words, McLaren's gospel is a "historically rooted, politically engaged approach" in contrast to the "timeless truths approach" that dominates most of evangelicalism today.[57]

Again recognizing the good in what McLaren says—that there is a social, political, economic, intellectual, cultural, and artistic dimension to the gospel of the kingdom—I believe he has actually downplayed what is truly astonishing and revolutionary about the kingdom. What the Jews *expected* was a social and political kingdom. Had they gotten that, there would have been nothing much astonishing about it at all. What they got instead was a Messiah who went out of his way to make it clear that his kingdom was *not* of this world (John 8:23; 18:36)! He avoided language that would reinforce this-worldly thinking among the Jews, seldom, for instance, using the term "Messiah" because it held so many this-worldly connotations. If the people started thinking in terms of Messiah, they would try to make him king by force (John 6:15). So he used a term with less political baggage—"Son of Man." Whatever else it might be, Jesus' kingdom was a spiritual one.

This is even clearer when we consider that both the Old Testament prophets and Jesus himself preached that the kingdom confers certain benefits on its members. I appreciate McLaren's emphasis (learned apparently from Lesslie Newbigin), that Christians are elected to service, not privilege.[58] But the fact remains that both the prophets and Jesus taught about several benefits that are given to the people of the kingdom. The gift of eschatological salvation is one (see Ezek. 34:16, 22; Matt. 5:8; 25:21, 23, for example). Forgiveness of sin is another (see Isa. 33:24, Jer. 31:31–34; Ezek. 18:31; 36:22–28; Mark 1:4; 2:10; Luke 7:48, for example) and righteousness another (see Matt. 5:6; Luke 18:14, for example).[59]

Even beyond all this, McLaren misses what is perhaps the most astonishing surprise of the New Testament story: that Jesus simultaneously filled the roles of the Davidic Messiah, the Suffering Servant of Isaiah, and Daniel's Son of Man. That McLaren does not see this, or at least does not hint at it in his books, is all the more surprising because he is so careful otherwise to situate the story of Jesus in the narrative of the nation of Israel. The Suffering Servant of Isaiah and the Son of Man of Daniel 12 are not insignificant themes in the Old Testament, and they were not in-

---

56. McLaren, *New Kind of Christian*, 73.
57. McLaren, *Secret Message of Jesus*, 236.
58. McLaren, *Last Word*, 103.
59. Information in this paragraph learned from George Eldon Ladd, *A Theology of the New Testament*, rev. ed. (Grand Rapids: Eerdmans, 1993), 68–78.

significant ideas in the Jewish mind during the time of Jesus, either. How McLaren could ignore them so completely, not to mention the startling role they play in Jesus' own self-understanding, is nothing short of a mystery.

At least twice, McLaren accuses the church of imposing on Jesus a message of eternal, spiritual salvation. In his telling, Christians have misinterpreted Paul and John and then used those misreadings to silence the true message of the kingdom found in Matthew, Mark, and Luke. "Basically, it's a conspiracy theory about Paul and John ganging up against Matthew, Mark, and Luke—well, not really them, but people who interpret them."[60] But McLaren is wrong. It was no misinterpretation of Paul and John that injected eternal and soteriological meaning into the story of the kingdom. It was Jesus who did so. He declared himself to be the fulfillment of Israel's messianic hopes (that is, the head of the kingdom), and at the same time constantly referred to himself as the divine "Son of Man" from Daniel 12. Further, Jesus said of the Son of Man that he "came not to be served but to serve, and to give his life as a ransom for many"—an allusion to the Servant's being made an offering for sin in Isaiah 53:10. By making that allusion, Jesus "took over a term that appears in Daniel but that was not widely used in contemporary Jewish hopes, but radically reinterpreted it. . . . Jesus poured the content of the Suffering Servant into the Son of Man concept."[61]

The Jews had hopes for a kingly Messiah and also for a Servant of the Lord; they even had a vague expectation of a divine "son of man" who would appear at the end of the age. But no one ever pulled the three concepts together, at least not until Jesus. Jesus, however, took the divine nature of the Son of Man, joined to it the substitutionary and vicarious suffering of the Servant, and finally incorporated it all with his Messianic role. By the time Jesus finished gathering together all the threads of Jewish hope, the Head of the kingdom was infinitely more than an earthly revolutionary; he was a divine Messiah-King who would suffer and die for his people to win them spiritual salvation, not least so that they would be *able* to live the life of the kingdom on earth. That is why Jesus made one's response to his person and message the single determining factor in whether one would be included in the kingdom.[62] The only way into the kingdom was through the blood of the King.

When one begins to grasp that part of the New Testament narrative, one also begins to realize that McLaren is simply missing a huge part of the plot. His gospel of the kingdom is so focused on the kingdom's political and social ramifications that he seems blind to this entire astounding storyline. It is a grievous blindness, for it leaves McLaren with a gospel that, next to the real thing, seems truncated, unexciting, and rather pedestrian.

60. McLaren, *Last Word*, 149; see also McLaren, *Secret Message of Jesus*, 91.
61. George Eldon Ladd, *Theology of the New Testament*, 155.
62. Ibid., 62. See Matt. 8:11–12; 13:37–38; Mark 10:15.

This diminishing of the biblical teaching about the kingdom helps to explain McLaren's halting confusion about hell. He simply cannot, it seems, see how an eternal conscious judgment would have a place in a kingdom of God like the one he envisions. To be sure, if the kingdom is primarily about the here-and-now, the social, and the political, then the idea of God inflicting eternal punishment on people makes little sense. If the kingdom is all about including outsiders and empowering the oppressed, the idea of God creating a permanent "outsider" class in hell and then eternally disempowering them does not sit easily. But if the kingdom is understood in its full-orbed reality as Scripture presents it—not only present but also eschatological, not only social and political but also spiritual—then the judgment of God's enemies and the enemies of his people is not so alien a concept. It certainly was not so for the Jews. As we have already seen, when they looked forward to the establishing of God's kingdom at the end of the age, a crucial part of their hope was that God would judge his (and their) enemies. To be sure, Jesus took the idea, clarified it, and filled it with vivid content, but that new revelation was all still a part of the story that Scripture tells from start to finish, the story that ends with God's enemies punished and all evil subdued.[63] In the final analysis, an understanding of the kingdom that roots itself in the present, the political, and the social simply has no place for eternal judgment; but a kingdom that takes seriously the spiritual and eschatological purpose of God to save his people and vindicate his name cannot do without it.

Concluding Thoughts

A person who has read only *The Last Word*—or only this essay, for that matter—could easily make the mistake of thinking that the problem of hell is McLaren's primary concern. It is not. Nor is a critique of his handling of hell the most important critique that can be made about his works. Placed within its context, McLaren's subbiblical and ultimately untenable proposal for reimagining hell is only one symptom of the much larger malady that afflicts his entire theological project. There are other symptoms as well.

Consider his handling of Christ's work of atonement, for example. One of the most consistently puzzling things about McLaren's books is how little space or time he seems to have for the cross. McLaren asks for the benefit of the doubt here, saying in one of his books, "I know you will find weaknesses to point out. For example, you may wish I had said more on particular dimensions of Jesus' message or life that are of special importance to you."[64] He gets more specific in an endnote: "For example,

---

63. Robert Reymond follows Meredith Kline and Geerhardus Vos in arguing that hell is the fulfillment and consummation of the Old Testament principle of *herem*, the irrevocable giving over of persons and things to the Lord, often by destroying them. See Reymond, *A New Systematic Theology of the Christian Faith* (Nashville: Thomas Nelson, 1998), 1071; Meredith Kline, *Treaty of the Great King* (Grand Rapids: Eerdmans, 1963), 68; Geerhardus Vos, *Biblical Theology* (Banner of Truth, 1996), 141, 143.
64. McLaren, *Secret Message of Jesus*, xiii.

the theological meaning of Jesus' death is central to all streams of Christian thought and life, but since this is a book about Jesus' message, I limit my reflections on his death here to how it relates to his primary teaching theme. Emphasizing one theme is not meant to minimize the other."[65] But even if the benefit of the doubt is granted, the lack of attention McLaren gives to the cross across the whole of his theological project is not easily explained. The most extended treatment of the atonement takes place in *The Story We Find Ourselves In*. But even there, the conversation between the characters spans no more than six pages, and it amounts to the characters describing six different theories of the atonement and then pointing out what they see as the flaws of each. When Dan describes penal substitution, for example, one likeable character named Kerry wonders why God did not simply forgive us, if that is what he wanted to do. To punish an innocent person, she says, "sounds like divine child abuse."[66] This objection, commonly wielded by feminist theologians, is never answered. McLaren allows it to hang in the air of the story as if it were unanswerable.

Having rejected all the historic understandings of the atonement, McLaren offers up two theories of Christ's death on the cross that, so far as I can tell, are wholly his own. The first he calls the "powerful weakness" theory of the atonement, the idea of which is that by becoming vulnerable on the cross and dying at the hands of the Romans, Jesus shows the world that violence is not the answer, that what God wants is not retaliation and revenge, but rather kindness and forgiveness.[67] The second is based in Neo's experience of being betrayed by his wife and forgiving her. "When I think of the cross," Neo says, "I think it's all about God's agony being made visible— you know, the pain of forgiving, the pain of absorbing the betrayal. . . . It's not just words; it has to be embodied, and nails and thorns and sweat and tears and blood strike me as the only true language of betrayal and forgiveness."[68] But it must be objected against both these understandings of the atonement that neither of them makes of the cross anything more than a dramatic spectacle, something to be seen. In the first case, the cross is made a picture of power through weakness, and in the second, it is made a picture of God's pain. But however poignant such images may be, in neither case can the cross be understood actually to *accomplish* or *do* anything. How does a mere display of weakness or of God's pain do justice to Paul's statement that we are "justified by his blood" and "reconciled to God by the death of his Son" (Rom. 5:9–10)? The cross was not just a means for God to show the world something, whether weakness or pain or love. It was a saving act. It accomplished something. As the apostle John puts it, "The blood of Jesus his Son cleanses us from all sin" (1 John 1:7).

65. Ibid., 226.
66. McLaren, *Story We Find Ourselves In*, 102.
67. Ibid., 105.
68. Ibid., 107. See also McLaren, *Secret Message of Jesus*, 69–71, where the essence of these theories is restated.

Ultimately, I believe the explanation for this weakness in McLaren's thought with regard to atonement must lie in his deficient view of the gospel of the kingdom. McLaren's gospel is so socially and politically oriented, so focused on the present, and so unwilling to address the reality of eternity that it has no obvious place for concepts like substitution, justification, atonement, sacrifice, or propitiation. Yet those are the concepts and themes that come together in the Bible's narrative to give meaning to the cross. The fact is that the kind of kingdom McLaren wants Jesus to have preached—one where each person simply decides to live a life of compassion and love in an effort to redeem the world in the here-and-now and bring about "God's dream" for it—does not have any obvious use for a cross. Indeed it is difficult to see how McLaren's own two original theories of the atonement, the only ones not riddled with objections by his characters, are at all integral to his story. At best, they both make the cross a superfluous illustration of the kind of life the kingdom would call us to live.

Consider also how McLaren approaches non-Christian religions. Again, some of what he says on the subject is quite good. It is certainly true that Christians should love people of other religions, not seek to destroy their cultures, treat them with compassion and respect, and engage them in meaningful, respectful, and genuine dialogue.[69] None of that should be minimized, and if that were McLaren's only point, there would be no cause for concern. But McLaren seems to be doing more than calling for compassionate engagement and loving evangelism. At one point, for example, he has Neil assert that, "Dan, when it comes to other religions, . . . the question isn't so much whether we're right but whether we're good. And it strikes me that goodness, not just rightness, is what Jesus said the real issue was—you know, good trees produce good fruit, that sort of thing."[70] McLaren frequently objects to the idea that salvation depends upon, as he puts it, "being right" or "believing the right things." It is inconceivable to him that "all God will care about on judgment day is opening up our skulls and checking in our brains."[71] Of course, all evangelicals would happily join McLaren in hacking down that straw man. But even if the point were put less tendentiously, the argument that it does not matter what one believes about Jesus the King only makes sense if the gospel of the kingdom is reduced to living a life of compassion, love, and kindness. But if the kingdom is more than that, if one's place in the kingdom depends on one's response to the Messiah-King himself, then McLaren is far off the mark here. The question is not at all "whether we're good." It is whether we respond in faith to Jesus the King.

At another place, McLaren (or rather Neil) goes perhaps even further, saying, "In the long run, I'd have to say that the world is better off for having these religions than having no religions at all, or just one, even if it were ours."[72] Compassion is

69. McLaren, *Generous Orthodoxy*, 278–91.
70. McLaren, *New Kind of Christian*, 61.
71. McLaren, *Last Word*, 136.
72. McLaren, *New Kind of Christian*, 63.

certainly to be desired, as is respectful engagement of other religions, but surely McLaren has gone beyond appropriate compassion and respect here. Perhaps that is not so surprising, though, given his theological project. Again, if the kingdom is primarily about compassion, love, mercy, kindness, and the redemption and valuing of culture, then it makes perfect sense for McLaren to believe that non-Christian religions have given their adherents many wonderful things, and therefore that the world is better off for having them. But if the kingdom involves more than that, then non-Christian religions are not beautiful at all, cultural treasures notwithstanding. They are lies that keep people from knowing and responding to the King, and therefore from enjoying the benefits, and the life, of the kingdom.

In light of all this, the question cannot be merely whether or not McLaren has misfired on the doctrine of hell particularly. Rather, it has to be whether he has misunderstood the gospel as a whole. That is an important question because McLaren's audience is only growing, and the influence of his emergent network is only expanding. Besides, Brian McLaren himself seems to be gifted with exactly the kind of affable and disarming spirit that would make him uniquely suited to engage deeply and trenchantly with this postmodern generation about what God has done in Christ. Indeed it is precisely that irenic spirit which evidently has launched him on this project to make the gospel attractive to postmodern ears. Unfortunately, it is hard to avoid the conclusion—at least from his published writings—that the substance of that project has been to empty the gospel of anything that might be considered offensive to postmodern sensibilities. For in the process of articulating this new, more attractive gospel, McLaren has argued that religions which deny Jesus Christ are good for the world, he has lost sight of the meaning and centrality of the cross, he has all but ignored the eschatological and spiritual character of the kingdom of God, and he has done everything in his hermeneutical power to read the traditional doctrine of hell out of the Bible. All in all, there does not really seem to be much of the gospel there left to deny.

We live today in a difficult and demanding generation, one that does not hear spiritual truth with willing ears. Because of that, none of us has any choice but to think hard about how to communicate the gospel of Christ to a world that has little interest in hearing it, and that finds much of what we have to say repugnant. But has it not always been that way, even from the very beginning? Yet even then, when the apostle Paul said the gospel was to most everyone in his generation either a stumbling block or foolishness, faithfulness to the task was not a matter of reimagining the gospel, rethinking every doctrine, and removing every offense. Nor is that what faithfulness requires now. What it requires is that we engage people with a simple, profound, and very old truth: that Jesus Christ came, died, rose, and now rules so that we might "be saved by him from the wrath of God" (Rom. 5:9).

12

The Emergent Church

GARY GILLEY

~~~~~~~~

I n a recent article from *Christianity Today* Scot McKnight, quoting from Eddie Gibbs and Ryan Bolger's book *Emerging Churches: Creating Christian Community in Postmodern Cultures*, defined emerging churches this way:

> Emerging churches are communities that practice the way of Jesus within postmodern cultures. This definition encompasses nine practices. Emerging churches (1) identify with the life of Jesus, (2) transform the secular realm, and (3) live highly communal lives. Because of these three activities, they (4) welcome the stranger, (5) serve with generosity, (6) participate as producers, (7) create as created beings, (8) lead as a body, and (9) take part in spiritual activities.[1]

If we are willing to give the emerging church "conversation" the most positive of spins, we would affirm that its leaders are highly desirous of reaching a postmodern culture with the claims of Jesus Christ. The emerging church adherents do not believe the modern church, whether in its traditional or seeker-sensitive form, is capable of communicating with a generation enveloped in postmodern thinking. Thus the emergent church has developed methods, techniques, forums, philosophical systems, and even theologies to connect with a subculture that the more traditional expressions of the church will never reach. On the surface this is commendable, but all is not as it seems.

Our first order of business is to give a brief overview of postmodernity.

---

1. Scot McKnight, "Five Streams of the Emerging Church," *Christianity Today*, February 2007, 35–36.

Postmodernity

It is easier to define postmodernism by describing what it is not than by describing what it is. Wikipedia says that postmodernism

> is a term used in a variety of contexts to describe social conditions, movements in the arts, economic and social conditions and scholarship from the perspective that there is a definable and differentiable period after the modern, or that the 20th century can be divided into two broad periods. It is an idea that has been extremely controversial and difficult to define among scholars, intellectuals, and historians, largely because the term implies to many of these commentators that the modern historical period has ceased.... Scholars and historians most commonly hold postmodernism to be a movement of ideas arising from, but also critical of elements of modernism.... individuals who use the term are arguing that either there is something fundamentally different about the transmission of meaning, or that modernism has fundamental flaws in its system of knowledge.[2]

Postmodernism is therefore born out of the ashes of the failure of modernity. It is the reaction of the disillusioned. If the optimistic projections of the last two hundred years' efforts of reason, science, and technology have failed, and if the tenets of premodernism with its foundation of revelatory truth are preposterous, then all that is left is the pessimism of nothingness, emptiness, and uncertainty. The champions of postmodernity have stepped into this void. What have these thinkers brought to the table?

A Rejection of Universal Truth

Postmodernity is relatively complicated, so it is necessary to probe carefully both its worldview and its effect on cultures, as well as the church. At this point we simply want to recognize that at the hub of this philosophy, as well as all philosophies, is the issue of truth. To the premodernist, truth was found in revelation. To the modernist, truth can be found in reason and science. To the postmodernist, truth is not found (indeed it is not capable of being found); it is created. Absolute truth is a fable. It is possible for me to create my own truth and for cultures and subcultures to create their truth, but it is not possible to find universal truth that is applicable to all people. Such truth does not exist and should not be sought. Those who claim to possess absolute truth only do so in order to assert power over others.

Michael Kruger explains:

> Postmodernity, in contrast to modernity, rejects any notion of objective truth and insists that the only absolute in the universe is that there are no absolutes. Tolerance

---

2. See "Postmodernism," *Wikipedia, The Free Encyclopedia,* http://en.wikipedia.org/wiki/Postmodern (accessed May 23, 2008).

is the supreme virtue and exclusivity the supreme vice. Truth is not grounded in reality or in any sort of authoritative "text," but is simply constructed by the mind of the individual [or socially constructed].[3]

Douglas Groothuis elaborates, "For these postmodernist thinkers, the very idea of truth has decayed and disintegrated. It is no longer something knowable. . . . At the end of the day, truth is simply what we, as individuals and as communities, make it to be—and nothing more."[4]

That the rejection of absolute, universal truth lies at the center of postmodernity must be grasped to have any kind of handle on what is being taught. As with existentialism, there is a rejection of absolute truth. As in existentialism, truth is not found, it is created. But unlike existentialism, truth is constructed not individually but socially. That is, individual societies, cultures, and subcultures develop *their truth* to which members of that community must adhere. However, this socially-constructed truth is subject to change and is highly subjective.

Postmodernism rejects modernism's belief that absolute truth can be found through objective means. Still, choices must be made as one navigates throughout life. How does a postmodernist discern the best course of action? Kruger answers:

> What are the postmodernists' criteria for "truth"? Simply what works. Postmodernists are not concerned about absolute truth like the modernist; they define their "truth" by more pragmatic concerns: What makes me feel good? What solves my problems? What is attractive to me?[5]

Os Guinness is therefore right when he observes that, due to postmodernism's assault on truth and reason, "objective, experimental, scientific data [has been replaced] with personal, anecdotal experience [as the source of truth in society]."[6] In the Christian world, as we will see, things are not much better.

Relativism

Postmodern societies seem workable as long as communities, with their individualized brands of truth, stay isolated. But what happens when societies, each packing their own understanding of truth, collide? How are countries like America, with its melting pot of religions, ethnic backgrounds, and the like, to exist? They do so by adopting a relativism mindset, which recognizes everyone's truth as equal. Since, in the mind of a postmodernist, there is no absolute truth anyway, no one's beliefs are

3. Michael J. Kruger, "The Sufficiency of Scripture in Apologetics," *The Master's Seminary Journal* 12, no. 1 (2001): 72.
4. Douglas Groothuis, *Truth Decay* (Downers Grove: IL: InterVarsity, 2000), 20.
5. Kruger, "Sufficiency of Scripture," 73.
6. Os Guinness, *Time for Truth* (Grand Rapids, MI: Baker, 2000), 78.

superior to any other. We should all live and let live and by no means ever impose our understanding of right, wrongs, morals, and ethics on those of another philosophical community. This is the ultimate sin, perhaps the only sin, in a postmodern world.

To a postmodernist, society should not concern itself with truth claims; it should tell stories. The reason stories are important to these thinkers goes back to their understanding of truth. Since absolute, universal truth does not exist, all that remains is "our story" (or narrative). We cannot make truth claims; the best we can do is share our story. Since no one's story is superior to anyone else's, we must accept everyone's story as equally valid.

In other words, a true universal worldview is impossible because absolute truth is impossible. We may have values, morals, and concepts that work for us or our subculture, but we cannot expect other subcultures to adopt our understandings, which may not work for them. Truth is simply that which works for a particular community and nothing more.

Deconstructionism

Nothing is more important in the comprehension of postmodernism than its convoluted, incredible view of language. Gene Veith says it well:

> Postmodernists base this new relativism and the view that all meaning is socially constructed on a particular view of language. This set of theories, along with the analytical method that they make possible, can be referred to as "deconstruction." . . . Postmodernist theories begin with the assumption that language cannot render truths about the world in an objective way. Language, by its very nature, shapes what we think. Since language is a cultural creation, meaning is ultimately (again) a social construction.[7]

Kruger adds, "Deconstructionism has relegated all texts to simply societal constructions—i.e., the reader's own experience and perspective so conditions interpretations that there can be no one 'right' interpretation."[8]

Pluralism

We are told regularly by the media that we live in a pluralistic society, therefore we must never insinuate that we have the truth, for not only are such pronouncements offensive to others, they are downright arrogant. D. A. Carson writes:

> Philosophical pluralism has generated many approaches in support of one stance: namely, that any notion that a particular ideological or religious claim is intrinsically

7. Gene Edward Veith Jr., *Postmodern Times* (Wheaton, IL: Crossway, 1994), 51.
8. Kruger, "Sufficiency of Scripture," 73.

superior to another is *necessarily* wrong. The only absolute creed is the creed of plural-ism. No religion has the right to pronounce itself right or true, and the others false, or even (in the majority view) relatively inferior.[9]

Once again this reduces life to the telling of stories, which leads to a new understand-ing of tolerance. Tolerance of people, even while rejecting their ideas, was one of the linchpins of early democracy. Tolerance, under postmodernity, means we must accept everyone's ideas as equally valid. To be critical of anyone's ideas is a sign of intoler-ance—which cannot be tolerated (the irony is obvious).

Contradictory Thinking
The ability to believe contradictory things simultaneously is a hallmark of postmod-ern thinking. A few years ago Barna Research Group documented that two thirds of Americans do not believe in absolute truth (this number has recently risen to 78 percent).[10] To believe absolute truth does not exist is a self-contradiction, for that opinion must be based on a belief in something that is true—in this case that truth does not exist. So the one absolute allowed in postmodern thought is that absolutes do not exist. But it gets worse: the same Barna poll showed that 53 percent of evan-gelical Christians believe there are no absolutes.[11] Veith makes this comment about these statistics:

> This means the majority of those who say that they believe in the authority of the Bible and know Christ as their Savior nevertheless agree that "there is no such thing as absolute truth." Not Christ? No, although He presumably "works for them." Not the Bible? Apparently not, although 88 percent of evangelicals believe that "The Bible is the written Word of God and is totally accurate in all it teaches." Bizarrely, 70 percent of all Americans claim to accept this high view of Scripture, which is practically the same number of those who say "there are no absolutes."[12]

This kind of contradictory thinking would be unacceptable in any other age but is commonplace today, even among Christians. Only in such an intellectual environ-ment could the very same people embrace scores of competing ideologies.

Power Plays
Since the one absolute accepted by postmodernists is that there exists absolutely no absolutes, how do postmodernists view those who claim to possess some form of absolute truth? They view them with suspicion. Whether in the realm of history,

9. D. A. Carson, *The Gagging of God* (Grand Rapids: Zondervan, 1996,) 19.
10. Gerald L. Zelizer, "Quick Dose of 9–11 Religion Soothes, Doesn't Transform," *USA Today*, January 8, 2002, 13A; see the Barna Group, "The Barna Update, November 26, 2001, http://www.barna.org/FlexPage. aspx?Page=BarnaUpdate&BarnaUpdateID=102.
11. George Barna, *The Barna Report: What Americans Believe* (Ventura, CA: Regal, 1991), 83–85, 120.
12. Veith, *Postmodern Times*, 16.

religion, science, or even medicine, the postmodern thinker believes that all truth claims are attempts to manipulate others. In other words, truth claims are nothing more than cover-ups for power plays. The only reason anyone would claim to know anything with certainty, since such a thing is impossible, is because he wants to empower himself and enslave others.

Douglas Groothuis laments:

> Some Christians are hailing postmodernism as the trend that will make the church interesting and exciting to postmoderns. We are told that Christians must shift their emphasis from objective truth to communal experience, from rational argument to subjective appeal, from doctrinal orthodoxy to "relevant" practices. I have reasoned throughout this book that this move is nothing less than fatal to Christian integrity and biblical witness. It is also illogical philosophically. We have something far better to offer.[13]

A Church for the Postmodern Culture

A very appropriate question at this point is how does the church of Christ reach a generation steeped in a postmodern mindset? One approach, which has demanded much attention and is increasingly being accepted by evangelicals, is called the emerging church. The name "emerging church" speaks of a church that is, as we might expect, emerging from something. This means it is coming out of the more traditional expressions of the church and emerging into a postmodern expression. What it will actually become is still a matter of speculation, but its adherents see it as a postmodern church for a postmodern culture.

As we begin to discuss this "conversation" (as the emergent leaders like to call it), we must recognize that the emerging/emergent movement is not monolithic.[14] Some of the more conservative adherents, such as Mark Driscoll and, to some degree, Dan Kimball, would distinguish between emerging churches that would retain and promote many orthodox theological truths while adopting practices and methodologies they believe reach the postmodern generation, and emergent figures such as Brian McLaren, Spencer Burke, Rob Bell, and Steve Chalke, who call into question or simply deny cardinal doctrines.[15]

Others, such as Southern Baptist missiologist Ed Stetzer, divide the movement into three categories: (1) the relevant, who accept the historic gospel but seek to communicate it relevantly to the postmodern culture, (2) the reconstructionists, who retain the same gospel but are creating more radical forms of church expres-

---

13. Groothuis, *Truth Decay*, 265.
14. Some of the best-known leaders include Tony Jones, the national coordinator of Emergent; Spencer Burke, founder of TheOOZE.com; Mark Driscoll, pastor of Mars Hill Church, Seattle, and founder of the Acts 29; Karen Ward, pastor of the Church of the Apostles, Fremont, WA; Erwin McManus, pastor of Mosaic in Southern California; Dan Kimball, Brian McLaren, Rob Bell, Donald Miller, Leonard Sweet, and numerous others.
15. See "Emerging church," *Wikipedia, The Free Encyclopedia,* http://en.wikipedia.org/wiki/Emerging_Church (accessed April 15, 2008).

sion—such as house churches, and (3) the revisionists, who deconstruct and recon-struct both the church and the gospel.[16]

Emergent church leaders do not all agree on where the church goes from here, but they all believe that it must go somewhere, for they are convinced the modern church cannot connect with the postmodern mind. The reason this is true, as Dan Kimball writes in his book *The Emerging Church*, is because "the basis of learning has shifted from logic and rational, systematic thought to the realm of experience. People increasingly long for the mystical and the spiritual rather than the evidential and facts-based faith of the modern soil."[17]

Kimball suggests that the seeker-sensitive church, the church that chased the last generation's culture, is already out of date: "The things that seeker-sensitive churches removed from their churches are the very things [postmodern] nonbelievers want to experience if they attend a worship service."[18] Postmoderns want to reconnect to the past. They want traditions and religious symbols rather than the slick excellence, polished performance, and state-of-the-art structures found in modernity. That translates into a very different look and feel.

For example, it is not likely that you will find a sign along the highway pointing to the First Baptist Emergent Church. Names like *Baptist* and denominational ties are too modern. Popular emergent church names are Solomon's Porch, House of Mercy, The Rock, Jacob's Ladder, Circle of Hope, Ikon, Vintage Faith, New Begin-nings, and Mosaic. They sponsor Web sites like vintagefaith.com, emergentvillage.org, and TheOOZE.com. The emerging church appears to be the latest flavor of the day in a church age that allows itself to be defined by its culture rather than by Scripture. D. A. Carson reminds us:

> What drove the Reformation was the conviction, among all its leaders, that the Roman Catholic Church had departed from Scripture and had introduced theology and practices that were inimical to genuine Christian faith. In other words, they wanted things to change, not because they perceived that new developments had taken place in the culture so that the church was called to adapt its approach to the new cultural profile, but because they perceived that new theology and practices had developed in the church that contravened Scripture, and therefore that things needed to be reformed by the Word of God. By contrast, although the emerging church movement challenges, on biblical grounds, some of the beliefs and practices of evangelicalism, by and large it insists it is preserving traditional confessionalism by changing the emphases because the culture has changed, and so inevitably those who are culturally sensitive see things

16. Justin Taylor, "An Emerging Church Primer," *9marks,* http://www.9marks.org/CC/article/0,,PTID314526%7CCHID598014%7CCIID2249226,00.html.
17. Dan Kimball, *The Emerging Church* (Grand Rapids: Zondervan, 2003), 60.
18. Ibid., 115.

in a fresh perspective. In other words, at the heart of the emerging reformation lies a perception of a major change in culture.[19]

How does the Christian community go about chasing down the culture? It can do so either through methods or message. The emergent/emerging church does both. Those who identify themselves as emerging claim to focus on methodology, while retaining at least basic doctrinal beliefs. Those in the emergent camp see the importance of new methodologies but also are willing to challenge even the most cherished doctrinal beliefs.

Emerging Methodology

Turning first to methodology we find that emergents and emergent leaders are in agreement that the under-thirty generations are profoundly spiritual. They are interested in religious experiences and feelings. They want a sense of the supernatural. They are not interested in systematic theology, tightly woven apologetic arguments, or logical reasoning. But they are attracted to spiritual mystery. The Baby Busters and Mosaics are tired of "church-lite," consumer spirituality, church buildings that look like warehouses or malls, CEO pastors, educational programs structured like community colleges, and church services that are reminiscent of a Broadway musical. They want the transcendent.

So the emergent/emerging church loads up on such things. There is a return to what Kimball calls the "vintage church," which combines some excellent things such as singing hymns and reading Scripture with (questionable, at best) medieval rituals, prayer stations, labyrinths, candles, incense, icons, stained glass, contemplative prayer, mantras, Benedictine chants, and darkness. Kimball makes the point that postmoderns want to experience God with all five senses—as the vintage church did. It should be pointed out, however, that the vintage church to which Kimball refers is not a return to the New Testament church. The vintage church has been waylaid by medieval Catholicism, which we must remember may have experienced the spiritual through the senses, but nevertheless was an apostate religion. Simply providing unbelievers with a religious experience, which they might interpret as an encounter with God, may do them more harm than good. Just as the seeker-sensitive church saw felt-needs as the means of connecting with unbelievers, so the emerging church sees spiritual experience. The philosophy is basically the same, just the methods have changed.

Emergent Theology

If this were the end of the story we might even find comfort in what is basically a reaction to the stripped-down model of Christianity that the seeker-sensitive church

19. D. A. Carson, *Becoming Conversant with the Emerging Church* (Grand Rapids: Zondervan, 2005), 42.

has offered for the last few decades. But as Rob Bell is quick to inform us, "This is not just the same old message with new methods. We're rediscovering Christianity as an Eastern religion, as a way of life."[20]

This is something new in the cultural-identifying churches. The seeker-sensitive church loudly proclaimed that it was fine-tuning the methodology but not tampering with the message of the evangelical church (even though it often was). The emergent church is concerned about methods, but many within the movement are even more concerned about the message. They believe that theologically evangelical Christianity has it all wrong. From the Scriptures to essential doctrines to the gospel itself, the church so far just doesn't get it. And the emergent people include themselves in the same camp. As Brian McLaren, at this time the foremost emergent statesman writes, "I don't think we've got the gospel right yet. What does it mean to be saved? . . . None of us have arrived at orthodoxy."[21]

Before we jump into the specific doctrinal distinctive of the emergent church we must first detail the philosophy that undergirds the movement. What we see, read, and perceive is filtered, at least to some degree, through our presuppositions and worldview. The worldview of the emergent church is decidedly postmodern. Attempting to combine postmodern philosophy with biblical theology is a tricky business, as one might imagine; we should not be surprised that unanimity in the understanding of this attempted merger will not be found. Nevertheless, some common threads are evident throughout the movement.

Truth Claims. As we have seen, truth claims are held with suspicion within postmodernism, and we find a precarious juggling act in emergent circles as they try to reach a wary culture with the claims of Christ. The emerging church is concerned about presenting genuine Christianity in a way the postmodern culture understands. Since the very heart of postmodernity is rejection of absolute authoritative truth, yet Christianity claims to be the proclamation of absolute authoritative truth, a head-on collision is almost unavoidable. What is to be done? Something has to give, and that something is often the certainty of truth. McLaren is representative of many:

> Ask me if Christianity (my version of it, yours, the Pope's, whoever's) is orthodox, meaning true, and here's my honest answer: a little, but not yet. Assuming by Christianity you mean the Christian understanding of the world and God, Christian opinions on soul, text, and culture . . . I'd have to say that we probably have a couple of things right, but a lot of things wrong, and even more spreads before us unseen and unimagined. But at least our eyes are open! To be a Christian in a generously orthodox way is not to claim to have the truth captured, stuffed, and mounted on the wall.[22]

20. Andy Crouch, "The Emergent Mystique," *Christianity Today*, November 2004, 38.
21. Ibid., 40.
22. Brian McLaren, *A Generous Orthodoxy* (Grand Rapids: Zondervan, 2004), 293.

This is almost a complete capitulation to postmodernity's concept of truth. After two thousand years of study of the completed Canon, we Christians find ourselves in a position of having maybe a "couple" of things right—and I am sure that those couple of things would be up for grabs. This uncertainty about the truth carries over to the Scriptures themselves, of course. Rob Bell and his wife Kristen, in an interview with *Christianity Today*, reflect this view. They started questioning their assumptions about the Bible itself—"discovering the Bible as a human product."[23] "I grew up thinking that we've figured out the Bible," Kristen says, "that we knew what it means. Now I have no idea what most of it means, and yet I feel like life is big again—like life used to be black and white, and now it's in color."[24] To the postmodern mind it is more important, as Rob Bell says, to "embrace mystery, rather than conquer it."[25]

Emergent church leaders are asking us to embrace a faith without certainty, a Bible that has value due to its mystery, and a reality that is individual, subjective, and changeable. One has to wonder what Jude had in mind when he wrote, "I found it necessary to write appealing to you to contend for the faith that was once for all delivered to the saints" (v. 3).

Deconstruction. In everyday language deconstruction means that we can never be certain we have the right interpretation of words. What matters then is not what the author or speaker meant, because that doubtfully can be discerned; rather the important thing is what the reader/listener experienced. Deconstruction guts words of their meaning and redefines them according to one's own preference. This is obviously convoluted, but it is a central piece in postmodern thought.

How does this work out in the postmodern church? In order to be consistent with absolute truth (or, better, lack of truth) the emergent thinkers must dispose of dogmatic truth claims (i.e., doctrines). They must purge the church of an exclusive gospel,[26] an authoritative Bible, and irritating doctrines such as hell.[27] Also on the cutting floor is the doctrine of original sin. McLaren writes, "The church latched on to that old doctrine of original sin like a dog to a stick, and before you knew it, the whole gospel got twisted around it. Instead of being God's big message of saving love for the whole world, the gospel became a little bit of secret information on how to solve the pesky legal problem of original sin."[28]

Before the emergent church leaders have even finished, all the essential teachings of the Bible have been deconstructed, redefined, or dismissed. And what has been put in their place? Oddly, but consistent with postmodern thinking, mostly mystery

23. Crouch, "Emergent Mystique," 38.
24. Ibid.
25. Ibid.
26. Kimball, *Emerging Church*, 175.
27. McLaren's book *The Last Word and the Word After That* (San Francisco: Jossey-Bass, 2005) is primarily a deconstruction of the doctrine of hell.
28. McLaren, *Last Word*, 134.

and questions. Even McLaren admits, "What will appear beyond the deconstruction remains to be seen. Perhaps something better will emerge—that is my hope and prayer, but the outcome is by no means certain even now that I have finished writing this book."[29]

Pluralistic Relativism. If nobody is right, then everybody is right. This is the logical conclusion of the postmodern worldview. The emergent church thinkers are reluctantly willing to accept this concept, at least for a time. McLaren states:

> Because I and others, while we aren't "for" pluralistic relativism, do see it as a kind of needed chemotherapy. We see modernity with its absolutisms and colonialisms and totalitarianisms as a kind of static dream. . . . In Christian theology, this anti-emergent thinking is expressed in systematic theologies that claim . . . to have final orthodoxy nailed down. . . . Emergent Christians see pluralistic relativism as a dangerous treatment for stage 4 absolutist/colonial/totalitarian modernity (to use language from cancer diagnosis), something that saves a life by nearly killing it.[30]

Since truth and Scripture have been deconstructed, all that is left is relativism. Until we figure out where to go from here we will have to be content with that. We may or may not arrive at a better place some day, but at least objective truth claims are being eradicated—and that is a good thing. So say the emergent church leaders.

Emergent Doctrine in General

It is time to examine where emergent church philosophy leads us theologically. Al Mohler, theologian and president of Southern Baptist Seminary in Louisville, Kentucky, provides this scathing critique:

> The worldview of postmodernism—complete with an epistemology that denies the possibility of or need for propositional truth—affords the movement an opportunity to hop, skip and jump throughout the Bible and the history of Christian thought in order to take whatever pieces they want from one theology and attach them, like doctrinal post-it notes, to whatever picture they would want to draw.[31]

Most emergent church leaders claim fidelity to the Scriptures as well as the historic doctrines and even creeds of the church. Sounds good on the surface—but then they force these things through the filter of postmodern deconstruction, and what comes out are distorted and unrecognizable understandings of theology. Dan Kimball says

29. Ibid., xviii.
30. McLaren, *Generous Orthodoxy*, 286–87.
31. Quoted by David Roach, "Leaders Call 'Emerging Church Movement' a Threat to Gospel," *BP News*, March 23, 2005, http://www.bpnews.net/bpnews.asp?ID=20420.

that the church must "deconstruct, reconstruct, and redefine biblical terms."[32] What that means and how it is done will vary.

Kimball, who is on the conservative side of the emerging spectrum, believes there exists a core of doctrines (those found in the Apostles' and Nicene Creeds and a few others), which we can proclaim with certainty. In his contribution to a book entitled *Listening to Beliefs of Emerging Churches*[33] Kimball frequently identifies himself as a Nicene Creed Christian, yet he goes far beyond this ancient creed in his affirmation of salvation by faith alone, and even the substitutionary atonement. Kimball also believes in the doctrine of hell and the inspiration of Scripture. Concerning Scripture, Kimball is correct when he states, "The Scriptures are intended for transformation, not just information." But he goes too far, I believe, when he likens Scripture to a compass. "A compass," he writes, "gives direction but doesn't go into specifics. I see the Bible as a spiritually-inspired compass, where it gives us strong direction but leaves many specifics a mystery. It gives direction rather than acting as a how-to-answer book."[34]

I believe this is a false dichotomy. The Bible serves as both a compass and the final word from God on how to live our lives to his glory. It provides authoritative answers on hundreds of subjects, everything from morals to finances to marriage to work ethics. This does not discount the true mysteries that are found in Scripture, but neither does it minimize the abundance of certainty that the Word provides.

Kimball, nevertheless, sees the value and importance of maintaining sound doctrine, at least in the essentials.

Others on the opposite end of the spectrum, such as Spencer Burke and Brian McLaren, would disagree, saying that our old theological systems are flawed and something new is needed. "I meet people along the way who model for me, each in a different way, what a new kind of Christian might look like. They differ in many ways, but they generally agree that the old show is over," writes McLaren, "the modern jig is up, and it's time for something radically new. . . . Either Christianity itself is flawed, failing, untrue, or our modern, Western, commercialized, industrial strength version is in need of a fresh look, a serious revision."[35]

Rob Bell chips in to make certain we understand that he and others are talking about more than methodology:

> By this I do not mean cosmetic, superficial changes like better lights and music, sharper graphics, and new methods with easy-to-follow steps. I mean theology: the beliefs

---

32. Kimball, *Emergent Church*, 178.
33. This book was in pre-publication form when I read it. I was able to read Kimball's chapter by the gracious consent of both Dan Kimball and Zondervan.
34. Kimball, *Emergent Church*, 178.
35. Brian McLaren, *A New Kind of Christian* (San Francisco: Jossey-Bass, 2001), xiv–xv.

about God, Jesus, the Bible, salvation, the future. We must keep reforming the way
the Christian faith is defined, lived and explained.[36]

How far is Bell willing to take all of this? Which doctrines can be changed, altered,
or even eliminated before we no longer have the Christian faith? Apparently nothing
is off limits. While personally claiming to affirm historic Christian theology, Bell
writes that it would not bother him to discover that we have been wrong all along
concerning the basic elements of the faith. For example, if it could be proven "that
Jesus had a real, earthly, biological father named Larry . . . and that the virgin birth
was just a bit of mythologizing the Gospel writers threw in. . . . Could you still be a
Christian?"[37] Bell doesn't see a problem. As a matter of fact, if our faith depends on
such doctrines "then it wasn't that strong in the first place, was it?"[38]

What doctrines does Bell regard as dispensable? In this brief statement alone he
sees as superfluous the virgin birth, the incarnation, the hypostatic union of Christ,
and the inspiration of Scripture (since the Gospel writers lied about the person of
Christ). Of course, as these doctrines fall, like dominos, they take others with them,
not least of which would be the substitutionary atonement, since a mere man could
not die for our sins. In one stroke of the pen Bell has undermined the whole Christian faith, but he sees it as a nonissue.

To Bell, and many other emergent leaders, Jesus is not the way and the truth, if
by that we mean he is the embodiment of truth and the only way to God. No, to
these men the "way of Jesus is the best possible way to live."[39] We could continue to
live the "Christian life" without the truth of Scripture. We could still love God and
be a Christian, because what we believe is not important. The only question is, "Is
the way of Jesus still the best possible way to live?"[40] It is not about what we believe,
Bell would insist. "Perhaps a better question than who's right, is who's living
rightly?"[41]

McLaren reinforces this major tenant of emergent "theology": "We place less
emphasis on whose lineage, rites, doctrines, structures, and terminology are right
and more emphasis on whose actions, service, outreach, kindness, and effectiveness
are good."[42] "A turn from doctrines to practices"[43] is one of the four major legs that
the emerging church stands on, according to McLaren. Being, rather than believing,
is a major component in the emergent philosophy. The New Testament, on the other
hand, does not sacrifice one for the other. We are called in Scripture to live godly

36. Rob Bell, *Velvet Elvis* (Grand Rapids, Zondervan, 2005), 12.
37. Ibid., 26.
38. Ibid., 27.
39. Ibid., 20 (cf. 21).
40. Ibid., 27.
41. Ibid., 21.
42. McLaren, *Generous Orthodoxy,* 223.
43. Ibid., 197.

lives, but first we must believe (John 1:12; Rom. 10:9–10; Eph. 2:8–9). Christlike living is a fruit of salvation, not the cause. We can "be" moral and decent people and not be Christians, but we cannot deny or ignore the true historic, biblical person and work of Jesus Christ and be saved. The emergent church has turned this truth on its head.

Mark Oestreicher, president of Youth Specialties, makes these comments in *The Emerging Church* which are not only dangerously close to a denial of the gospel itself but actually cross the line:

> Does a little dose of Buddhism thrown into a belief system somehow kill off the Christian part? My Buddhist cousin, except for her unfortunate inability to embrace Jesus, is a better "Christian" (based on Jesus' descriptions of what a Christian does) than almost every Christian I know. If we are using Matthew 26 [*sic*] as a guide, she'd be a sheep; and almost every Christian I know personally would be a goat.[44]

Emergent Doctrine Specifics

How far are emergent leaders willing to go in their deconstruction of biblical theology? What doctrines are they willing to jettison, or at least seriously draw into question?

The doctrine of God. Even though Jesus has come to reveal and explain the Father (John 1:14, 18), "God," McLaren insists, "can't ever really be an object to be studied."[45] To emergent leaders, theology is not a matter of knowing God but a quest for beauty and truth.

The doctrine of original sin. McLaren writes, "Many of us have grown uneasy with this understanding of 'the fall' (and with it an exaggerated understanding of the doctrine of 'original sin'). We are suspicious that it has become a kind of Western Neo-Platonic invasive species that ravages the harmonious balance inherent in the enduring Jewish concepts of creation as God's world."[46]

The substitutionary atonement. Steve Chalke, the most recognizable leader of the emergent movement in the United Kingdom, accuses those who believe in penal substitution as promoting divine child abuse. The evangelical church, Chalke claims, has misunderstood the cross:

> The fact is that the cross isn't a form of cosmic child abuse—a vengeful father, punishing his son for an offence he has not even committed [as penal substitution

---

44. Kimball, *Emergent Church*, 53.
45. McLaren, *New Kind of Christian,* 161.
46. McLaren, *Generous Orthodoxy,* 235.

teaches]. . . . Understandably, both people inside and outside of the church have found this twisted version of events morally dubious and a huge barrier to faith. Deeper than that, however, is that such a concept stands in total contradiction to the statement "God is Love."[47]

The doctrine of hell. So odious is the doctrine of hell to many in the emergent community that McLaren devoted his book *The Last Word and the Word After That* to the issue. McLaren introduces his subject with an exaggerated distortion of the evangelical position:

> *God loves you and has a wonderful plan for your life, and if you don't love God back and cooperate with God's plans in exactly the prescribed way, God will torture you with unimaginable abuse, forever*—that sort of thing. Human parents who "love" their children with these kinds of implied ultimatums tend to produce the most dysfunctional families. . . .[48]

If the idea of hell is so ridiculous, then why did Jesus teach it? McLaren concocts a fanciful view that the Jews during the intertestamental period wove together the mythological views of the Mesopotamian, Egyptian, Zoroastrian, and Persian religions and created the doctrine of hell. When Jesus came on the scene, the Pharisees were using hell as a club to keep the people in line. Through the threat of hell the Pharisees could motivate sinners to stop sinning, and then perhaps God would send the Messiah along with his kingdom. Jesus takes the Pharisees' club and turns it on them. Jesus didn't really believe in or endorse hell, as we understand it; he just used it as a "truth-depicting model."[49] Jesus used hell "to threaten those who excluded sinners and other undesirables, showing that God's righteousness was compassionate and merciful, that God's kingdom welcomed the undeserving, that for God there was no out-group."[50]

This convoluted argumentation leads to there being "no out-group." If there is no out-group, does that mean McLaren is a universalist? While he flirts with this possibility stating, "Universalism is not as bankrupt of biblical support as some suggest,"[51] he never firmly lights on it.[52] But without question McLaren, and most of the emergent leaders, does hold to the doctrine of inclusivism, which teaches that while salvation has been made possible by Jesus Christ, it is not necessary to know who Jesus is or the precise nature of what he has done in order to be "in."[53]

47. Steve Chalke and Alan Mann, *The Lost Message of Jesus* (Grand Rapids: Zondervan, 2003), 182–83.
48. McLaren, *Last Word*, xii.
49. Ibid., 61–64, 71–79.
50. Ibid., 74.
51. Ibid., 103 (cf. 182–83).
52. McLaren, *Generous Orthodoxy*, 37.
53. Ibid., *Last Word,* 182.

Emergent church leaders follow the reasoning of missionary theologian Lesslie Newbigin concerning Christ and salvation, which runs along these lines: Exclusive in the sense of affirming the unique truth of the revelation of Jesus Christ, but not in the sense of denying the possibility of salvation to those outside the Christian faith. Inclusive in the sense of refusing to limit the saving grace of God to Christians, but not in the sense of viewing other religions as salvific.[54] In other words, salvation is not exclusively found in the gospel, therefore there are saved Hindus, Muslims, Buddhists, and so forth. Soon hell becomes a moot issue because no one seems to be going there anyway.

Spencer Burke, founder of TheOOZE.com, echoes these remarks in his recently published book, *The Heretic's Guide to Eternity*. In an interview concerning this book with his friend Charlie Wear, Burke states, "For me, I think that grace says we are in. We are all beloved children of God . . . you are in. . . . [Jesus] comes and brings life, and everyone gets life . . . [but] God's love gives us the choice to choose, to opt-out."[55]

The doctrine of salvation. The doctrine of hell is determined to a large degree by the all-important understanding of the gospel. The emergent leaders see a wide gate opening to eternal life. "It bothers me to use *exclusive* and *Jesus* in the same sentence. Everything about Jesus' life and message seemed to be about inclusion, not exclusion,"[56] writes McLaren. He adds later in his discussion, "Maybe God's plan is an opt-out plan, not an opt-in one. If you want to stay out of the party, you can. But it's hard for me to imagine somebody being more stubbornly ornery than God is gracious."[57]

Burke states,

> I actually think you can become a Christian and never even know who Jesus is. . . . Many of my friends are now out in Muslim countries ministering. In the past we would have said we want people to convert to Christianity. We don't do that anymore. We invite people to follow Jesus. They are not even asking them to leave their Muslim faith, they are asking them to simply follow Jesus.[58]

The clear implication is that we are all "in" unless we want "out." But the next question is (and this is where it gets tricky), in or out of what? The short answer is "the kingdom of God." But the short answer leads to a long explanation that leaves us scratching our heads (which is appropriate since the emergent people prize mystery over clarity).

54. Ibid., 183.
55. Charlie Wear, "An Interview with Spencer Burke: Author of *A Heretic's Guide to Eternity*," Next-Wave, August 2006, http://www.the-next-wave-ezine.info/issue92/index.cfm?id=158ref=coverstory.
56. McLaren, *Last Word,* 35.
57. Ibid., 138.
58. Wear, "Interview with Spencer Burke."

The gospel, according to the emergent thinkers, is not about individual conversion. It is not about how to get people "in." It is about "how the world will be saved from human sin and all that goes with it. . . ."[59] This sounds close to the mark until we examine more thoroughly what is meant by the terminology. Their concept of "world" does not simply involve humans who don't believe in Christ. The emergent gospel is not just bringing unbelievers to the Savior for the forgiveness of sin and the imputation of God's righteousness. There is more, as Rob Bell informs us:

> Salvation is the entire universe being brought back into harmony with its maker. This has huge implications for how people present the message of Jesus. Yes, Jesus can come into our hearts. But we can join a movement that is as wide and as big as the universe itself. Rocks and trees and birds and swamps and ecosystems. God's desire is to restore all of it.[60]

McLaren continues the thought: "Is getting individual souls into heaven the focal point of the gospel? I'd have to say no, for any number of reasons. Don't you think that God is concerned about saving the whole world? . . . It is the redemption of the world, the stars, the animals, the planets, the whole show."[61] According to McLaren, "The church exists for the world—to be God's catalyst so that the world can receive and enter God's kingdom more and more."[62]

When asked to define the gospel, Neo (the main philosophical character in McLaren's novels) replies that it could not be reduced to a little formula, other than "the Kingdom of God is at hand."[63] Narrowing this definition is not easy, but McLaren gives some insight when he writes,

> I am a Christian because I believe that, in all these ways, Jesus is saving the world. By the "world" I mean planet Earth and all life on it, because left to ourselves, un-judged, un-forgiven, and un-taught, we will certainly destroy this planet and its residents.[64]

As we are discovering, the emerging church is very concerned with the planet, with the ecosystems, pollution, and the environment; so much so that apparently in some sense Christ died for the physical planet, and it is the job of the follower of Christ to help restore and protect this world. He is also concerned with injustice. McLaren asks, "And could our preoccupation with individual salvation from hell after death distract us from speaking prophetically about injustice in our world today?"[65]

59. Mclaren, *Last Word*, 69.
60. Bell, *Velvet Elvis*, 109–10.
61. McLaren, *New Kind of Christian,* 129.
62. Ibid., 84.
63. Ibid., 106.
64. McLaren, *Generous Orthodoxy*, 97.
65. McLaren, *Last Word*, 84.

Emergent leaders have a deep concern that if we are preoccupied with who is "in" and who is "out," who is going to heaven and who is not, we will ignore present physical needs of the planet and social issues such as injustice, poverty, and AIDS. McLaren argues, "When Matthew, Mark, and Luke talk about the Kingdom of God, it's always closely related to social justice. . . . The gospel of the kingdom is about God's will being done on earth for everybody, but we're interested in getting away from earth entirely as individuals, and into heaven instead."[66] While McLaren elevates men such as Martin Luther King Jr. as examples of those who had the right gospel emphasis,[67] he faults the evangelical church for being too wrapped up in eternity to care about what is happening right now on planet earth and being too anxious over who is saved from sin to notice who is suffering from man's inhumanity to man.

It does not seem to be an option to the emergent church thinkers that eternal salvation and present concerns of our planet can both be, and have been, attended to by God's people. But, despite opinions to the contrary, the priority of Scripture is on man's relationship to God. It is because men are alienated from God that they mistreat one another. The spiritually redeemed and transformed person should and will care about social sins. But, again, the gospel is about man's alienation from God and what God has done through Christ to reconcile us to himself (Rom. 5:6–11), not about the ozone layer and elimination of poverty. Neither Jesus nor the apostles made these latter things the focus of their ministries; it was the reconciliation of souls to God that was at the heart of their message. Once we begin to draw our gospel from the culture, no matter what culture that might be, we have altered the true gospel. Emergent leaders are not wrong to be concerned about the environment and social justice; they are wrong to confuse it with the gospel of Jesus Christ.

How those professing to be believers understand the message of the gospel will determine how they view their mission in this life. Since the emergent church sees the gospel not merely as the redemption of lost souls but also as the restoration of the planet and salvation from man's inhumanity to man, they comprehend their task as Christians differently from that of most evangelicals. They call it "missional."

The Missional Emergent Church

"Missional" is a term that seems to be have been popularized by missiologist Lesslie Newbigin, who pops up all over emergent literature. It is difficult to pin down a good definition of "missional," but it seems to mean that as Christians we exist to

---

66. Ibid., 149. McLaren has adopted N. T. Wright's understanding of the gospel, which is termed the New Perspective. The New Perspective says that we have misunderstood the New Testament and that the real focus of such books as Romans is not to explain the gospel but how to bring Jews and Gentiles together in the kingdom of God (see 149–53).
67. Ibid., 153.

serve. We serve by loving and living in such a way that we bless those around us. But more than that, we are to be engaged in changing and even creating culture as we bring the kingdom of God to earth. Rather than calling people out of this world system and into "the kingdom of His beloved Son" (Col. 1:13, NASB), we are to bring the kingdom to them. It would appear that the goal of the missional Christian is to transform the "domain of darkness" (Col. 1:13, NASB) into the kingdom of God. McLaren tells us that his missional calling is summed up in these words: "Blessed in this life to be a blessing to everyone on earth."[68] He adds, "My mission isn't to figure out who is already blessed, or not blessed, or unblessable. My calling is to be blessed so I can bless everyone."[69]

We get a better understanding of where McLaren is headed when he writes, "I hope that both they [people everywhere] and I will become better people, transformed by God's Spirit, more pleasing to God, more of a blessing to the world, so that God's kingdom . . . comes on earth as in heaven."[70] And what kind of people will populate this kingdom? Apparently people from all faiths and religions:

> Although I don't hope all Buddhists will become (cultural) Christians, I do hope all who feel so called will become Buddhist followers of Jesus; I believe they should be given that opportunity and invitation. I don't hope all Jews or Hindus will become members of the Christian religion. But I do hope all who feel so called will become Jewish or Hindu followers of Jesus.[71]

It doesn't take long to realize that the kingdom of the emergent community is not the kingdom of God, or the church, as described in Scripture—unless the missional mandate is to fill the kingdom with tares (Matt. 13:24–30, 36–43). But once this unbiblical view of God's kingdom is accepted, what is our mission—that is, how do we live missionally?

Rob Bell writes, "For Jesus, the question wasn't how do I get into Heaven? but how do I bring heaven here? . . . The goal isn't escaping this world but making this world the kind of place God can come to. And God is remaking us into the kind of people who can do this kind of work."[72] This quote is a good example of half truths twisted into distorted vision. Did Jesus show compassion and minister to the poor? Certainly. Did Jesus, or the apostles after him, fight for social justice on behalf of the poor and needy? Not at all. While Jesus, through the transformation of lives, began a process that would revolutionize much of the world in regard to injustice, he never made these things a central platform of his ministry or that of the church. Jesus said virtually

68. McLaren, *Generous Orthodoxy*, 113.
69. Ibid.
70. Ibid., 263.
71. Ibid., 264.
72. Bell, *Velvet Elvis,* 147, 150.

nothing about the environment, political tyranny, eradication of poverty and illiteracy, elimination of deadly disease, or other social ills. This does not mean that these things are not important, but they were obviously not the heart of his ministry, which was to save us from our sins and enable us to "become the righteousness of God" (2 Cor. 5:21). Jesus could have started a social revolution without going to the cross, but without the cross we could not be redeemed from sin. Our mission is to call people "out of darkness into His marvelous light" (1 Pet. 2:9, NASB).

But the missional agenda is different. Here we are to bless people, for that is why God has chosen us—to be a blessing to others.[73] What does it mean to be a blessing? Apparently it does not mean introducing people to saving faith in Christ, because Bell tells us that "God blesses everybody. People who don't believe in God. People who are opposed to God. People who do violent, evil things. God's intention is to bless everybody."[74] And how does this blessing happen? It happens as the church gives up its efforts to convert people to Christ and simply serves them: "The most powerful things happen when the church surrenders its desire to convert people and convince them to join. It is when the church gives itself away in radical acts of service and compassion, expecting nothing in return, that the way of Jesus is most vividly put on display."[75] In this way (Bell tells us) the "gospel is good news, especially for those who don't believe it. . . . [As a matter of fact] if the gospel isn't good news for everybody, then it isn't good news for anybody."[76]

Is the gospel good news for everybody? It may very well be a blessing to have Christian people treat everyone with the love of Christ, but Jesus and the Scriptures could not be more clear that those who do not know Christ are under the wrath of God (Rom. 1:18ff), will perish (2 Thess. 1:9), are eternally doomed (Luke 12:46–48), and will spend eternity in the lake of fire (Rev. 20:11–15)—hardly good news to those who reject him.

Emergent Scripture

Many of the unusual positions held by the emergent leaders stem directly from their theology of the Scriptures as well as their hermeneutical approach. First, insiders of the emerging church "conversation" are fond of expressing their excitement and fidelity to the Word of God, even as they undermine it. McLaren says, "I want to affirm that my regard for Scripture is higher than ever."[77] Bell tells us that for more than ten years he has oriented his life around studying, reading, and trying to understand the Bible.[78] One would have to wonder why Bell devotes so much time to the under-

73. Ibid., 165.
74. Ibid.
75. Ibid., 167.
76. Ibid., 166–67.
77. McLaren, *Last Word*, 111.
78. Bell, *Velvet Elvis*, 41.

standing of the Bible since he apparently agrees with his wife, as mentioned earlier, that she has "no idea what most of it means. And yet life is big again."[79]

In order to press home their views, the emergent leaders must perform some interesting gymnastics with the Scriptures. How can someone express high regard for Scripture yet come up with such fanciful interpretations? First, they question inspiration. Wondering out loud about Paul's epistles, Bell writes, "A man named Paul is writing this, so is it his word or God's Word?"[80] McLaren pulls out the old Jesus versus Paul card: "We retained Jesus as Savior but promoted the apostle Paul (or someone else) to Lord and Teacher. . . . And/or decided that Jesus' life and teachings were completely interpreted by Paul."[81]

Bell, in complete ignorance of history and the doctrine of biblical preservation, informs his readers that the canon came about as a result of a vote of the church fathers: "In reaction to abuses by the church, a group of believers during a time called the Reformation claimed that we only need the authority of the Bible. But the problem is that we got the Bible from the church voting on what the Bible even is."[82]

Anyone still clinging tenaciously to the Word, after inspiration is denied, will further loosen his grip when he discovers that the Scriptures are not inerrant, infallible, or authoritative. McLaren said these are words related to a philosophical belief system that he used to hold. But he no longer believes the "Bible is absolutely equivalent to the phrase 'the Word of God' as used in the Bible. Although I do find the term inerrancy useful . . . I would prefer to use the term inherency to describe my view of Scripture."[83] By the use of *inherency* he is dusting off the neo-orthodox view of the Scriptures, which taught that the Bible contains the "word of God" but is not the completed Word of God, for God's Word can be found in anything he "inspires."

If you have any confidence left in Scripture at this point, McLaren and his friends can take care of that by telling you that you have been misreading the Bible all along. "There is more than one way to 'kill' the Bible," he says. "You can dissect it, analyze it, abstract it. You can read its ragged stories and ragamuffin poetry, and from them you can derive neat abstractions, sterile propositions, and sharp-edged principles."[84]

To the emergent people the Bible was never intended to be studied and analyzed; it was meant to be embraced as art, to be read as a story. The proof is that it is written as narrative and poetry and story. Granted, much of it is in this genre but, as D. A. Carson points out, much of it is also "law, lament, instruction, wisdom, ethical injunction, warning, apocalyptic imagery, letters, promises, reports, propositions, ritual, and more. The easy appeal to the overarching narrative proves immensely

79. Crouch, "Emergent Mystique," 38.
80. Bell, *Velvet Elvis*, 42.
81. McLaren, *Generous Orthodoxy*, 86.
82. Bell, *Velvet Elvis*, 68.
83. McLaren, *Last Word*, 111.
84. McLaren, *New Kind of Christian*, 158.

distortive."[85] Regarding Scripture, Carson leaves us with a powerful warning: "At some juncture churches have to decide whether they will, by God's grace, try to live in submission to Scripture, or try to domesticate Scripture."[86]

With this approach to the Bible we see a deliberate movement away from the words and message of Scripture to a new message beyond the pages of the Word. In the process, the Bible becomes nothing more than a shell or perhaps a museum piece to be admired but ignored. Scripture as handed down by God has been replaced with the imaginations of man in order to fit better with our culture. But, if we have no authoritative word from God, with what is the church left? We are left with little more than mystery and mysticism.

Mystery

As we have seen, the emerging church is not excited about truth (as a matter of fact, staying true to their postmodern roots, they are suspicious of truth claims and are more comfortable with uncertainty), but it is enamored with mystery. Donald Miller wrote his book *Blue Like Jazz* to develop this very theme. He summarizes his thoughts:

> At the end of the day, when I am lying in bed and I know the chances of any of our theology being exactly right are a million to one, I need to know that God has things figured out, that if my math is wrong we are still going to be okay. And wonder is that feeling we get when we let go of our silly answers, our mapped out rules that we want God to follow. I don't think there is any better worship than wonder.[87]

Faced with giving answers to the pertinent issues of life such as heaven, hell, suicide, the devil, God, love, or rape, Rob Bell has no answers—just hugs. During question-and-answer/dialogue sessions at his church Bell details his approach: "Most of my responses were about how we need others to carry our burdens and how our real needs in life are not for more information but for loving community with other people on the journey."[88]

Perhaps the emergent position is best summarized by McLaren, who virtually closes his book *A Generous Orthodoxy* with this statement:

> Consider for a minute what it would mean to get the glory of God finally and fully right in your thinking or to get a fully formed opinion of God's goodness or holiness. Then I think you'll feel the irony: *all these years of pursuing orthodoxy ended up like this—in front of all this glory understanding nothing.*[89]

85. Carson, *Becoming Conversant*, 164.
86. Ibid., 172.
87. Donald Miller, *Blue Like Jazz* (Nashville: Thomas Nelson, 2003), 206.
88. Bell, *Velvet Elvis*, 30.
89. McLaren, *Generous Orthodoxy*, 294.

There we have it. Ultimately, we know nothing. Even though Jesus was clear that we worship God in spirit and in truth (John 4:23), in the emergent church there is little truth, a minimal theology, and virtually no clear understanding of God. However, this does not stop the adherents from embracing the presence of God, or so we are told. How does such a "faith" survive? It survives on the basis of mysticism.

Mysticism

Peter Rollins, emergent leader with Ikon in Northern Ireland, says, "We at Ikon are developing a theology which derives from the mystics, a theology without theology to complement our religion without religion."[90] Emergent leaders can say such things because of their overbearing emphasis on experience. Dan Kimball (quoting Leith Anderson) has it backwards when he asserts, "The old paradigm taught that if you had the right teaching, you will experience God. The new paradigm says that if you experience God, you will have the right teaching."[91]

Carson is correct: "For almost everyone within the movement, this works out in an emphasis on feeling and affections over against linear thought and rationality, on experience over against truth."[92] The emerging church is a movement in search of an experience, not the truth. It seems to have little realization that an experience based on anything but truth is a mirage. The Scriptures never deny the proper place of experience, but our Lord says, "You will know the truth, and the truth will make you free" (John 8:32, NASB). The emergent church is a movement that is in bondage to its own imagination, not one held captive to the truth of God.

90. "Iconic, Apocalyptic, Heretical, Emerging, Failing / Pete Rollins Pops In for a Drop of the Black Stuff," interview with Peter Rollins, Stories from the Virtual Cafe, *Emergingchurch.info*, September 2003, http://www.emergingchurch.info/stories/cafe/peterollins.
91. Kimball, *Emergent Church,* 188.
92. Carson, *Becoming Conversant,* 29.

Index

Abraham, W. J., 31n21
absolute idealism, 96
absolute truth, 270–72, 273, 277–78
absolutism, 123, 127
accommodation, 37–38, 60, 221
Adam, in garden, 121
affluence, 9–10, 12
afterlife, 249, 254
ambiguity, 217
Anabaptism, 124
analogia entis, 160
analogy, 158n25, 159–60, 162, 163
Ancient Near East, myths of, 52
Anderson, Leith, 291
Anglicanism, 124
annihilationism, 245, 248, 252, 253–54
Anselm, 78, 241
anthropology, 30
antifoundationalism, 64–65n11
apostasy, 221
Apostles' Creed, 75, 125, 280
Archer, Gleason, 23n21
archetype/ectype distinction, 96, 113, 137,
        159–60, 161, 162, 163, 164
Aristotle, 147n88
Arminianism, 20n11
arrogance, 132–33
Athanasian Creed, 126–27
atonement, 22, 195–96, 209, 238, 241, 265–67.
        See also substitutionary atonement
Auburn Affirmation, 25–26
Augustine, 62, 82–84, 89, 148–49n92, 239–40
Augustinian voluntarism, 149–50, 152n109
"authentic," 21, 182

autonomy, 113, 120, 123, 143, 153, 163, 165,
        184
Awakening (film), 228

baby boomers, 12, 117
Babylonians, 149, 254–55
Baker, Herschel, 145
Baker, Mark, 22
Barker, William, 139
Barna, George, 10, 11, 273
Barr, James, 28, 32, 36, 42, 54
Barth, Karl, 19, 30, 86, 172, 180
        influence on Berkouwer, 41
        influence on Bloesch, 43–44
        on Jesus Christ as foundation, 99–100
        Pinnock on, 46
        and postmodernism, 16–17
        on Scripture, 32, 33, 39
Barthians, 61
basic beliefs, 79n74, 156, 158, 164
Baumann, Zygmunt, 114–15, 117
Bavinck, Herman, 23n21, 62, 64n8, 160, 240
        on accommodation, 38
        critique of Ritschl, 180–81
        on inspiration, 29n10, 31
        metaphysics of, 79–82
        methodology of, 65n13, 67, 170–71, 173,
                176, 177–85, 187
        realism of, 89
        on revelation, 60
        on Scripture, 40–42, 57, 78
        on systematic theology, 76–77
beauty, 57
Becker, Carl L., 114

Beegle, Dewey, 50n105
beliefs, 95, 97
Bell, Kristen, 182, 278
Bell, Rob, 172, 182, 274, 277, 278, 280–81, 285,
    287–88, 289, 290
Berkhof, Hendrikus, 71, 73–74
Berkhof, Louis, 65, 81–82
Berkouwer, G. C., 29, 39n68, 40, 41–42, 44, 46,
    57, 86
Bible
    authority of, 102, 187, 244
    and christological analogy, 38–40, 49–50, 59
    and church tradition, 66
    clarity of, 38, 218
    and dogmatics, 178
    ECM on, 186, 279–80, 281, 288–90
    humanity of, 28–61
    inerrancy of, 20, 21–26, 28–29, 219n17, 225
    infallibility of, 109
    inspiration of, 28, 29
    narrative approach to, 33
    objectivity of, 111, 183
    as provisional, 50–51, 54–55
    self-attestation of, 37, 102n24, 109, 163
    in servant form, 40–42
    "spectacles of," 151–52
    as witness, 37, 43, 107n38
"biblical evangelicalism" (Bloesch), 42–44
biblical narrative structures, 71–74
biblical theology, 66–69
biblicism, 62, 78
blessing, 288
Blocher, Henri, 40n69
Bloesch, Donald, 29nn6–7, 32, 37, 42–45
Bloom, Harold, 125
body, 208
Böhme, Jacob, 179
Bolger, Roger, 228–29, 230, 231
Boston, Thomas, 57
boundaries, 112, 118, 121–25, 126–27, 121
    ECM on, 213, 220, 223
Braaten, Carl, 66
Bradley, James E., 22
Briggs, Charles A., 23–26
Brow, Robert, 219n18
Brueggemann, Walter, 189
Brunner, Emil, 16, 17, 32
Buddhism, 282
Bultmann, Rudolf, 113
Burke, John, 232
Burke, Spencer, 172, 214n10, 274, 280, 284

Calvin, John, 37–38, 75, 113, 148n92, 160, 180
Caneday, A. B., 141
canon, 289
Canons of Dort, 88
Carson, D. A., 21, 23n21, 50n106, 53, 223n26,
    227, 272–73, 275–76, 289–90, 291
Cartesian foundationalism, 23n21
catholicity, and boundaries, 125–28
certainty, 94, 107–8, 109, 110–11, 115, 158
    Bavinck on, 184–85
    as modern, 215
    Van Til on, 163
Chalcedon, 123, 125
Chalke, Stephen, 172, 181, 219n18, 274, 282–83
Chesterton, G. K., 244
Chicago Statement on Biblical Inerrancy, 28
choices, 118
Christian antiquity, 112, 114, 120, 126
Christian consciousness, 178, 179, 183–84, 185
Christian philosophy, 72–73
Christianity Today, 211, 278
christological analogy (Scripture), 38–40, 49–50,
    59
church. See ecclesiology
Clark, Gordon, 25–26
classic evangelicalism, pietism as, 23
Clifford, W. K., 157
communication, 59
communism, 216
community, 70, 169–70, 176, 177, 178, 186
compassion, 242, 267–68
concursus, 29n10
conditional immortality, 245
confessional, church as, 235
confessional boundaries, weakening of, 118
confessional subscription, at Old Princeton,
    139–40
consumerism, 11, 186
consummation, 262
contemplative prayer, 169
context, 95, 96–97, 103, 105–6
contextualization, 16, 35, 95, 238
conversation, as dynamic and unpredictable,
    98–99
core, 101, 110
correspondence theory of truth, 34n37
covenant, as witness, 37
covenantal nomism, 171
creation, 120–21, 208
creation-fall-redemption-consummation, 71,
    72, 209
Creator-creature distinction, 120n40, 136, 160

creeds, 125–27, 239
Creegan, Nicola Hoggard, 16
cross, McLaren on, 265–66
culture, 13, 76, 103–7
    captivity to, 12
    ECM on, 275–76
    and gospel, 103–7, 224–44
    and interpretation, 97
    and religion, 19
    and tradition, 99
cynicism, 115, 215

Darwin, Charles, 216
Day of the Lord, 254
de Bres, Guido, 124
deconstruction, 30, 272
    in ECM, 278–79
    of hell, 248–51, 254
    of theology, 135
defense of the faith, 218–19, 221
deism, 31, 221
de la Saussaye, Daniel Chantepie, 177, 179–80,
    182, 187
denominational ties, 275
deontology, 156, 157, 159
depravity, 210
Derrida, Jacques, 180
Descartes, René, 65n11, 94, 115, 120, 155, 157,
    216
de Zengotita, Thomas, 117–18
Disney World, 11
diversity, 212–14, 217, 222, 223
Docetism, 39, 41, 42, 46, 49, 54, 58, 107, 110
doctrinal indifference, 213–14, 218–22
doctrine
    as drama, 119
    ECM on, 213
dogmatics, and ethics, 177–78
dogmatism, 131, 140, 215
"doing theology," 172
Dooyeweerd, Herman, 72
Douglas, Ann, 130
Douma, Jochem, 177
"Down Grade" controversy, 222n24
Driscoll, Mark, 212, 213, 223, 232–33, 274
Dunn, James D. G., 23n22, 171, 175
Duns Scotus, John, 160

Ebionitism, 39, 46
ecclesiology
    of ECM, 176, 182, 269, 274
    paradigm shift in, 174–76, 186

eclecticism, 118
ecology, 241, 285
Edwards, Jonathan, 151, 208–9
Egyptians, 249, 254–55
embodiment, of gospel, 228–29, 233
emerging church movement (ECM)
    Carson on, 20–21
    on community, 169–70, 176, 178, 186
    as "conversation," 171, 186, 274
    desire for "tangible" religion, 169, 186
    disdain for tradition, 168, 186
    diversity of, 212–14, 222, 223
    doctrinal indifference in, 218–22
    ecclesiology of, 182
    feminism in, 187
    influences upon, 172
    and liberalism, 181, 226–27, 231–32
    liquidity of, 116
    orthopraxis of, 90
    as postmodern, 212, 213, 214–18
    and Schleiermacher, 16
    on Scripture, 186
    superficiality of, 217n12
emerging vs. emergent, 188n1, 233, 274
emotions, 147n88, 150
empiricism, 79, 113, 115, 120
enculturation, 54
Enlightenment, 10–11, 15, 20, 31, 44, 113, 119,
    184–85, 229, 233
    on accommodation, 38
    on knowledge, 107–8
    Wright on, 190
Enns, Peter, 29n6, 38n61, 40, 42, 49–55, 56
enthusiasm, 125
epistemology, 78, 107n38, 156, 158, 215
Erickson, Millard J., 19, 69–70, 71, 76
eschatology, 58, 59n134
eternal life, 197, 199
eternal punishment, 199, 209, 259, 265
ethical relativism, 181, 216
Ethical Theologians, 170, 179, 182–83, 187
evangelical rationalism, 42–45, 92
Evangelical Theological Society, 219n17
evangelicalism, 15, 116, 120
    critique by ECM, 216n12
    decline of, 166–67, 221–22
    desire for "tangible" religion, 167, 169
    disdain for tradition, 167, 168–69
    doctrinal indifference of, 213–14
    McLaren and Wright on, 208
    paradigm shift in, 20, 21, 117, 174–76, 186,
        219n18
    shallowness of, 220

evidentialism, 156, 157, 159
evolutionism, 33
exclusivism, 123, 127, 284
exegetical theology, 67–68
exile, 191, 193
existentialism, 187, 271
experience, 116, 125, 155, 158, 185, 276, 291

Fackre, Gabriel, 71–72
faculty psychology, 147
fads, in theology, 172, 178
fall, 150, 199
false teachers, 218
fascism, 216
Federal Vision, 171, 174, 175, 176
feelings, 21, 276
feminism, 187
Ferguson, Sinclair, 15
Fesko, J. V., 137
fideism, 86
Fiering, Norman, 149
final judgment, 259, 262
finitum non capax infiniti, 120
Fisher, G. P., 233
forgiveness of sins, 193, 195, 205, 242
Foucault, Michel, 180
foundationalism, 12, 64–65n9, 99, 127, 154–59,
    216
    in Bloesch, 45
    and Franke, 93, 94, 97, 101
    in Van Til, 163
Fox, R. L., 33n31
Frame, John, 48
framework, 101, 110
Franke, John R., 93–107, 130n4, 132n10, 133–
    34n14, 154n2
freedom, 33
Frei, Hans, 19, 172, 180
Fuller Theological Seminary, 22
fundamentalism, 44, 91, 116, 157–58, 167

Gaffin, Richard, 174–75
general revelation, 76, 86
generous orthodoxy, 118
Gen Xers, 12
Gerrish, B. A., 16
Gibbs, Eddie, 228–29, 230, 231
gnosticism, 89, 91, 125, 143, 191
God
    and creation, 160
    doctrine of, 282
    holiness of, 210

immanence of, 31, 158
justice of, 251
as *principium essendi*, 80, 162
transcendence of, 31
Goldingay, J., 29n6
gospel, 288
    and culture, 98, 101, 103–7, 224–44
    McLaren on, 206–7, 209, 241–43
    Wright on, 209
Graham, Billy, 219–20n19e
Greco-Roman culture, 238, 239–40, 249,
    254–55
Greek philosophy, 235
Green, Joel, 22
Grenz, Stanley, 16, 20, 23, 48, 70–71, 154n2,
    172, 180
Groothuis, Douglas, 271, 274
Grudem, Wayne, 38n61, 41, 45n85, 69, 76
guilt, 199, 210
Guinness, Os, 21, 271
Gunton, Colin, 35–36

Hall, G. Stanley, 77n68
Harnack, Adolf von, 92n136
Harris, H., 35n38
Harrison, Carol, 148–49n92
Harrison, R. K., 23n21
Hart, D. G., 166
heart, 149n94, 150, 153
heaven, 197, 198, 241, 242, 260, 287
Hegel, G. W. F., 179, 183, 187
hell, 225, 241, 245–68, 280, 283
Helm, Paul, 51n108, 148n92
Henry, Carl F. H., 23n21, 133n11
Herder, John Gottfried, 38
heresy, 90, 214, 233–35, 240, 244
hermeneutics, 65
Herrmann, Wilhelm, 172
Hick, John, 98
Hicks, Peter, 136n27
Hippolytus of Rome, 234–35
historia revelationis, 68, 76
historic Christianity, 13, 18
historicism, 33
historiography, 53, 59
Hodge, A. A., 29n10, 38n59, 67–68, 153
Hodge, Charles, 20n11, 67, 139, 141, 150, 151
Hofstadter, Richard, 130
holism, 157n20, 158, 164
Holy Spirit
    internal witness of, 43, 102, 162–63, 164–65
    and revelation, 60–61

Hoopes, Robert, 144, 146, 152
Horton, Michael, 229
house churches, 275
Howard, Thomas, 169
human fallibility, 32, 109
human finitude, 136
human nature, 30
humility, 215, 217–18
Huxley, Aldous, 117
Hybels, Bill, 11, 12

idealism, 79
image of God, 30n13, 56–57, 59, 90, 92
immorality, 244
imputation, of righteousness of Christ, 207
incarnation, 281
incarnational model (Bible), 38–40, 49–50, 107
inclusivity, 201, 204, 205, 207, 283–84
individualism, 21
inductive method, 67
injustice, 247, 285–86
"inside-out" epistemology, 158, 159, 164
integrative themes, in theology, 70–71
integrity, 13
intellect, 79–81
intellectualism, 148n92, 149
interactive model (Franke), 105
International Council on Biblical Inerrancy, 219
interpretation, 120
intertestamental period, 249, 255–56
Irenaeus, 234

Jenkins, Philip, 9
Jerome, 240
Jesus
    death, 192–93, 194–95, 201–4
    on hell, 250–52, 256–60, 283
    Jewish context, 191–92
    temple action, 192, 200–201
judgment, 202, 205–6, 209, 253, 259, 262
Junius, Franciscus, 159–60
justice, 242
justification, 174–75, 176, 205, 267
justified true belief, 163

Kant, Immanuel, 15, 31, 114, 179, 183, 187
Kierkegaard, Søren, 31, 92n136
Kim, Seyoon, 22
Kimball, Dan, 172, 229n14, 232, 239, 275,
    279–80, 291
Kinball, Dan, 274
King, Martin Luther, Jr., 286

kingdom of God, 260–61, 284–86, 287
    as eschatological, 58, 261–62, 264–65
    McLaren on, 197–98, 199–200
    N. T. Wright on, 191–92, 194
    Paul on, 203–4, 209
    as social and political, 262–65, 267
Kline, Meredith G., 52, 59, 265n63
knowledge
    as power, 96
    and revelation, 160–62
    as universal, 94
knowledge of God, 137–38
Kruger, Michael, 270, 272
Küng, Hans, 56
Kuyper, Abraham, 23n21, 68n24, 160, 163n44
Kvanvig, Jonathan, 253, 259

Lamott, Anne, 172
language, 90, 126, 158, 187
late modernism, 115, 118. *See also* liquid
    modernity
latitudinarianism, 217
legalism, 213
Leith, John, 173–74
Leithart, Peter, 235
Lessing, G. E., 113
Levie, Jacques, 55
Lewis, C. S., 252, 258–59
liberalism, 91, 129, 130, 155, 174, 238
    and ECM, 226–27, 229–33
    foundationalism of, 157–58
liberation theology, 241
Lindbeck, George, 19, 176
Lindsell, Harold, 35
liquid foundationalism, 119
liquid modernity, 114–15, 123, 126, 127
Locke, John, 155, 157
Logos, 80, 89
Lonergan, Bernard, 63
Lord's Supper, 192
lordship of Christ, 204, 205, 206, 209
Luther, Martin, 114, 160
Lyotard, Jean-François, 180

MacArthur, John, 218
Machen, J. Gresham, 153, 229–30
mainline denominations, 222
marketing, 11–12, 13, 226
Marxism, 187, 216
Mathews, Shailer, 231
Matthewes-Green, Frederica, 229n14
McGrath, Alister, 195

McKim, D. K., 23n23, 29n6, 38n59
McKnight, Scot, 90, 212, 213, 269
McLaren, Brian, 21–22, 172, 173, 181, 188,
    274, 290
  on changing the gospel message, 240–43
  criticisms of evangelicalism, 225–26
  on doctrine, 280–84
  on hell, 245–68, 283
  influence of, 211
  influences upon, 180
  on Jesus and the gospels, 189–90, 196–208
  on judgment, 202, 205–6
  on kingdom of God, 197–98, 199–200
  on missional calling, 287
  on original sin, 278, 282
  on orthodoxy, 277
  on pluralistic relativism, 279
  as provocative, 217
  on signification, 124–25
  on Scripture, 288
  sympathy to Roman Catholicism, 169
  theological method, 116–28
  on tradition, 168
  on world religions, 178n62, 182, 267–68,
    287
  on wrath of God, 219n18
mechanical inspiration, 42
megachurch, 11, 166, 168, 169, 186, 187
Meijers, S., 178
Messiah, 263–64, 267
metaphors, 157
metaphysics, 76n62, 78, 79–82, 88–92
metapolis, 58
method, 63–66, 67, 89
method of correlation (Tillich), 24n25, 65n12
methodology, of ECM, 276
militancy, 219, 220
Miller, Donald, 172, 181, 290
Miller, Perry, 149n94
mind, 79–81
missional, 186, 235, 286–88
modernism, 230–31
  and accommodation, 38
  epistemologies of, 36
modernity, 18, 113–15, 123, 126
  failure of, 270
  postmoderns on, 215–16
modernization, 10, 13
Mohler, Al, 279
Moltmann, Jürgen, 172, 180
monophysitism, 39
Moo, Douglas, 23n21

Muller, Richard, 23n21, 75n56, 148n92,
    152n109
multiculturalism, 227
Murphy, Nancey, 45, 154n2, 155, 157–59, 163
Murray, Iain, 167
Murray, John, 68, 76
Myers, David, 9
mystery, 217, 276, 278, 290–91
mysticism, 183, 185, 290
myth, 52

naive theological realists, 136
narcissism, 118, 123
narrative, 33, 208, 209
naturalism, 33
natural reason, 85
natural revelation, 86, 162
natural theology, 16–17, 161
natures, 123, 124
neo-evangelicalism, 117, 167
neoorthodoxy, 31, 35, 39, 43, 44, 46, 289
Nestorianism, 39
neutrality, 143
new creation, 58, 203
New Perspective on Paul, 171, 174, 175, 176
Newbigin, Lesslie, 248, 263, 284, 286
Nicene Creed, 125, 239, 240, 280
Nicene-Constantinopolitan Creed, 126, 239
Nietzsche, Friedrich, 115, 118
Noll, Mark, 167
nonbasic beliefs, 156, 158, 159, 164
nonfoundationalism, 94–101, 132
noumenal, 114
novelties, 234
nuda Scriptura, 63

objective knowledge, 94, 107–8, 130n4, 136, 141
objective truth, 12, 144, 214, 270–71
  as arrogant, 12
obsolescence, 229, 243
occasionalism, 37, 43
Oestreicher, Mark, 282
Old Princeton, 20, 21, 22–25, 42, 129–53
Oliphint, K. Scott, 154n2
Olson, Roger, 19, 20n11, 21, 23, 136, 154n2,
    172, 180
onto-theology, 91
Open Theism, 20, 21, 47–48, 219
organic inspiration, 29n10, 40–42, 57
Origen, 104, 105
original sin, 150, 278, 282
Orr, James, 40

orthodoxy, 90, 222, 244
orthopraxy, 90, 222, 244
Orwell, George, 117
"outside-in" theology, 158, 159
Owen, John, 209

Packer, J. I., 39n68, 46, 49, 172–73
pagan philosophy, 235
Pagitt, Doug, 172, 181, 212, 222n25, 230, 232,
    236–40
Pannenberg, Wolfhart, 78, 172, 180
pantheism, 31
Parker, Dorothy, 127
particularism, of Christian faith, 104, 108
passion, 147
Patterson, Mark, 17
Paul
    on boundaries in creation, 121
    on foundation of Christ, 106
Pelagianism, 240
Pelagius, 239–40, 244
Pelikan, Jaroslav, 125–26
penal substitution, 12, 20, 21–22, 181, 219, 222,
    266. *See also* substitutionary atonement
Pentecostal worship, 92n136
performance, 34
Perkins, William, 173
perspectivalism, 136n26, 152n109
Pharisees, 250–51, 283
phenomenal, 114
philosophy, 235
pietism, 23, 117
Pinnock, Clark, 28n5, 29n6, 30–31, 35, 39, 42,
    46–48, 52, 172
pistology, 73
Plantinga, Alvin, 79n74, 94, 155–57, 159,
    163–64
pluralism, 272–73, 279
pneumatology, 70–71
Polanus, 38
post-conservatism, 16, 17–18, 19, 131
postfoundationalism, 114, 119
postliberalism, 19
postmodernism, 11, 13, 15, 33, 112, 114, 117,
    187, 227, 229, 269–74
    and accommodation, 38
    and Barth, 16–17
    of ECM, 212, 213, 277
    epistemology, 64n7
    McLaren on, 189
    as nonfoundational, 94
    and offense of the gospel, 268

in Pinnock, 48
    relativism of, 55
    and right reason, 144
    and Scripture, 27
    on truth, 144
    uncertainty of, 33, 154, 217
    worldview of, 279
poststructuralism, 119
power, 115–16, 273–74
Poythress, Vern S., 30n11, 136n26
pragmatism, 11, 21, 187, 271
prayer labyrinths, 169
predicamentalism, 248
Presbyterian Church in America, 173
principium cognoscendi, 162
principium cognoscendi externum, 80, 162
principium cognoscendi internum, 80, 162, 164
principium essendi, 80, 162
progress, in theology, 131, 134–35, 135–39, 140,
    141–42
progressive revelation, Pinnock on, 47
proper basicality, 94
propitiation, 210, 267
propositional truth, 23, 90, 220, 279
Providence, 117
provisionality, 133n14
psychoanalysis, 187

Ramsey, Boniface, 83
Raschke, Carl, 15, 91–92, 143
rationalism, 21, 79, 113, 115, 120, 185
reader response, 127
realist epistemology, 64n7, 67, 79–81, 89
reason, 78, 270. *See also* right reason
    and faith, 87
    instrumental use of, 163
    and revelation, 63
reconciliation, 203–5, 209
    divine-human, 206–7, 210
    as horizontal, 203–4, 206–7, 209–10
reconstructionists (ECM), 212n2, 274–75
redemptive history, 73
Reformation, antihumanistic heritage, 152–53
Reformed epistemology, 94
Reformed scholasticism, 20, 24, 38n59,
    152n109, 161, 235n38
Reformed theology, Olson on, 20n11
regeneration, 151–52, 153
Rehnman, Sebastian, 62–63
Reid, J. K. S., 34, 56
"Reidian" foundationalism, 155n4
relationality, 91

relativism, 33, 35, 55, 78, 123, 181, 182, 216, 271–72, 279
relevance, 21
relevants (ECM), 212n2, 274
religion, and culture, 19
repentance, 242
resurrection, 197–98, 234, 255, 262
retribution, 225, 260
retrogressive heterodoxy, 141–42
revelation, 63, 80, 90, 160–62, 270
revisionists (ECM), 212n2, 275
Reymond, Robert, 68–69, 265n63
Ridderbos, Herman, 73
right reason, 143–50
righteousness of God, 207
rigidity, 131, 132
Ritschl, Albrecht, 76n62, 172, 179, 180–81, 182, 183, 187
Robinson, John, 134
Rogers, Jack, 23n23, 29n6, 38n59, 146
Rollins, Peter, 90, 291
Rorty, Richard, 180
Ruether, Rosemary, 187
Runia, Klaas, 39, 44

sacrifice, 267
salvation
    ECM on, 284–86
    soteriology, paradigm shift in, 174–76
Sanders, E. P., 171, 172, 175
Sanders, John, 219n17
Sayers, Dorothy, 119
scapegoat factor, 249–50
Schaeffer, Francis, 238
Schleiermacher, Friedrich, 15–16, 17–18, 23, 26, 65n12, 74, 116, 172, 179, 180, 182, 183, 185, 187
Scholasticism. See Reformed scholasticism
Schopenhaur, Arthur, 116n14
Schweitzer, Albert, 172, 175
science, 80, 187, 270
Scripture. See Bible
Second Great Awakening, 185
Second Temple Judaism, 171
secularism, 11, 170
seeker-sensitive church, 15, 275, 276
self-consciousness, 118
self-defense, of ECM, 214, 223
Semler, Johann S., 38
senses, 276
sensus plenior, 45
Shepherd, Norman, 171–72, 174

Shindler, Robert, 221–22
Shuts, LeRon, 90
signification, 124–25
sin, noetic effects of, 148n92
situatedness, 95, 97, 103, 106–7
skepticism, 109, 115, 119, 126, 215
slippery slope argument, 225
Social Gospel, 181
social justice, 247, 285–86, 287–88
Socinianism, 221
Socinus, Faustus, 244
sociology, 103, 107
Sokal, Alan D., 64n7
sola Scriptura, 62, 76, 78
Son of Man, 263–64
soul, 149
space, 115
Sparks, Kenton L., 22–23n21
speech-act theory, 256–57
spirituality, vs. religion, 12, 17–18
Spurgeon, 221–22
Spykman, Gordon J., 71, 72–73, 74
Stackhouse, John, 167
Stendahl, Krister, 172
Stetzer, Ed, 212, 213, 274
story, 71, 208, 236, 273
Stuhlmacher, Peter, 175
subject/object relation, 164–65
subjectivism, 33, 115, 127, 183, 184, 186
substitutionary atonement, 202–3, 205, 209, 210, 225, 241, 282–83
Suffering Servant, 263–64
superintendence (inerrancy), 29n10
Sweet, Leonard, 172
Synod of Dort, 116
systematic theology, 65, 66–76, 138–39

Taylor, Barry, 18–19
Taylor, Justin, 188n1
technology, 9
teleology, 33
Tertullian, 233, 234–35
theological principia, 158n25, 159–60, 162–63, 164
theology, 64
    as contextual, 105–6
    of ECM, 276–86
    as local, 104
    professionalization of, 173
    purpose of, 78
    as second-order discourse, 100–103, 141
    as sociology, 103

as story, 236
as transcultural, 104
theology of the cross, 114
theology of glory, 114
Thirty-Nine Articles, 124
Thomas Aquinas, 62, 80, 82, 84–86, 89, 147n88,
    148n92, 160
Thompson, Mark D., 35n38, 36n45, 60
Tillich, Paul, 24n25, 65n12
time, 115
tolerance, 21, 213, 217, 222, 270–71, 273
Tomlinson, Dave, 23n22
tradition
    disdain for, 18, 168, 186
    and interpretation of Scripture, 66
    postmoderns on, 275
    and systematic theology, 76–77
transcendence, 276
translation model, 104–5
transubstantiation, 45
Trinity, 235, 239, 240
triumphalism, 96
Troeltsch, Ernst, 45
Trueman, Carl R., 133n11, 152n109
truth, 13, 43, 89, 109–10
    as action, 34
    Augustine on, 83–84
    Barth on, 17
    ECM on, 90
    as foundational, 95, 96
    Franke on, 107
    postmodernism, 92
    as socially-constructed, 271
    as subjective, 214–15
    Thomas Aquinas on, 84–85
    Turretin on, 86–88
Turretin, Francis, 62, 63, 76, 82, 86–88, 89
twofold knowledge of God, 75–76
Tyndale, William, 220n20
Tyrell, George, 230

uncertainty, of postmodernism, 33, 217
ungodliness, 244
unitarianism, 221
unity, vs. diversity, 222–23
universalism, 245, 248, 252, 254, 283
universality, of knowledge, 94, 107–8, 270–72
universals, 119, 126, 128

Vanhoozer, Kevin, 34n36, 40, 158n49, 257
Van Huysteen, J. Wetzel, 158–59n28
Van Mastricht, Peter, 23n21
Van Til, Cornelius, 23n21, 155, 159–65
Veith, Gene, 272, 273

"vintage church" (Kimball), 276
virgin birth, 281
Vollenhoven, Th., 72
voluntarism, 148n92
Vos, Geerhardus, 68n24, 73, 265n63
votive candles, 169

Walton, Brad, 147n88
Ward, Karen, 232
Warfield, B. B., 20n11, 23, 25, 36, 39n68, 46,
    134–39
    on the dogmatic spirit, 131–33
    on inerrancy, 38n59
    on inspiration, 29, 43
    on Scripture, 44, 57
Waters, Guy, 175, 260
weak foundationalism, 94
Webber, Robert, 20, 21, 154n2, 172, 212, 213,
    217, 232
Webster, John, 31, 37, 60
Wells, David, 90, 167, 170, 172, 173, 174, 176,
    182, 184, 187, 230, 231, 238
Western Christianity, decline of, 9–10, 13
Westminster Confession of Faith, 132, 209
Westphal, Merold, 96, 110
Wilbur, Ken, 123
will to power, 115, 119
Willard, Dallas, 189
Williams, D. A., 34n36
Williams, D. H., 168
Wink, Walter, 189
Wolterstorff, Nicholas, 79n74
Woodbridge, John, 23n23, 35
Word of God, 60–61, 289
world religions
    Billy Graham on, 220n19
    ECM on, 182
    McLaren on, 178n62, 182, 267–68, 287
worldview, 72–73, 240
    of ECM, 184, 277
Wrede, William, 172
Wright, Christopher J. H., 170n23
Wright, N. T., 22, 58, 171, 175, 254–55, 286n66
    on the gospels, 190–96
    influence on McLaren, 189, 196–97, 198,
        199, 210

Yale School, 19, 172, 176
Yoder, John Howard, 172, 180, 189
Young, E. J., 23n21

Zaher, Holly Rankin, 231n21
Zoroastrians, 249, 254–55